Britain In The Early Nineteenth Century

Britain In The Early Nineteenth Century

A D Harvey
Faculty of History
University of Cambridge

St. Martin's Press
New York

All rights reserved. For information, write:
St. Martin's Press, Inc., 175 Fifth Avenue, New York, N.Y. 10010
Printed in Great Britain
Library of Congress Catalog Card Number 77-15016
ISBN 0-312-09747-6
First published in the United States of America in 1978

Library of Congress Cataloging in Publication Data

Harvey, A D
   Britain in the early nineteenth century.

   Bibliography, p.
   Includes index.
   1. Great Britain—History—1800-1937. I. Title.
DA535.H37 941.07'3 77-15016
ISBN 0-312-09747-6

Contents

NOTES TO CHAPTERS
INTRODUCTION

ACKNOWLEDGMENTS

MANUSCRIPT sources have been quoted with the kind permission of the Duke of Abercorn and the Deputy Keeper of Records, Public Record Office of Northern Ireland, Earl Fitzwilliam and his Trustees and the Director of Sheffield Public Libraries, the Earl of Harewood, Viscount Sidmouth, Viscount Ridley, Lord Kenyon, Mr Robert Close-Smith, Mr Charles Wyvill (through the North Yorkshire Record Office), the Warden and Fellows of All Souls College, Oxford, the Controller of HM Stationery Office (for material in the Public Record Office), the British Library Board, the Trustees of the National Library of Scotland, the Director of the National Library of Ireland, the Keeper of Manuscripts and Records, the National Library of Wales, the Syndics of Cambridge University Library, the Keeper of Western Manuscripts in the Bodleian Library, Oxford, the Department of Palaeography and Diplomatic, Durham University, the Victoria and Albert Museum, the Buckinghamshire Record Office (with regard to material owned by Lord Cottesloe), the Devon Record Office (with regard to material owned by Lady Margaret Fortescue and her Trustees), and the Record Offices of Berkshire, Durham, Lancashire and Northumberland.

Research on these manuscript sources was financed by grants of £450 from the Political Science Fund of Cambridge University and £150 from the Arnold Fund of Oxford University. I was also assisted by the hospitality of Ann and David Booy, Judy and Terrell Carver, Bess Clues, Jennifer and Nicholas Collings, Iris and Philip McConnellogue, Helen Mayer, Richard Roberts, Sara and John Turner, and Jane and Andrew Whetnall.

Finally, I wish to thank Dr I. S. Asquith, Dr J. R. Dinwiddy, Dr I. P. H. Duffy, Dr J. O. Foster, Dr M. G. Hinton, Dr P. K. O'Brien, Dr W. E. Saxton, Dr J. Stevenson and Dr W. A. L. Seaman for permission to use material embodied in their doctoral dissertations, Mr P. A. Bezodis for permission to quote his Trinity College Cambridge fellowship dissertation, and Dr J. D. Walsh of Jesus College, Oxford, and Mr P. N. Virgin for their advice on religious denominations.

Introduction

FROM the viewpoint of the second half of the twentieth century the first years of the nineteenth century seem a period of inconsistencies and paradoxes. Most men still wore knee-breeches and three-cornered hats, and tied their hair in queues, at a time when gas lighting was being introduced into the streets of London. Edmund Cartwright, the inventor of power weaving, who was working on an internal combustion engine at the time of his death, was not merely a writer of sentimental poetry, but also a private chaplain to a duke: a form of relationship which seems more characteristic of the Middle Ages than of the Industrial Revolution. Moreover, Lord Chief Justice Ellenborough, who established the legal doctrine that an aeronaut was not guilty of trespass when flying over other people's property, was also the last judge to order an appeal for murder to be decided in a trial by combat.[1]

There were paradoxes at a more fundamental level, too. The upper-class régime, at the very apex of its power, went through a phase of almost unparalleled political ineffectuality, yet at the same time, almost by virtue of its ineffectuality, presided over the achievement of long-term gains which crucially affected society as a whole.

The global war in which Britain was engaged till 1815 led to a major redistribution of wealth within Britain, in which the manufacturing classes benefited at the expense of nearly everyone else; contributed to the pauperization of the poorer classes; and, by dealing the death-blow to Dutch, Danish and Spanish commerce, and by hampering that of the Americans and French, established the pattern of the British economy that subsisted for nearly half a century, in which dominance of international trade was associated with a relative neglect of the home market. At the same time the reactionariness of the Tories and the feebleness of the Whigs—major factors till well after the passing of the 1832 Reform Act—both stemmed from war-time conditions, as did indeed the very alignment of political parties.

There were, however, many other issues of this period which cannot easily be understood by reference to what came after. Historians tend to seek for the earlier manifestation of those themes which have some kind of relevance to their own age. Since we live in an age when the working classes have unprecedented political power, it is fashionable to look back to the earlier mani-festations of working class political consciousness. Since we live in an age when political debate takes place at a fairly refined level of ideological abstraction, it is fashionable to look back to a long tradition of ideological partisanship. This selectivity can lead to a bias of interpretation that seriously misrepresents the past. The period of the French Wars, for example, saw the gradual emergence of the two-party system which is with us today. Consequently we might expect to find in the rival platforms of the two parties of the 1800s elements of ideological conflict analogous to the conflicts of our own times, or at least, a crude polarity of progress and reaction. But such is not the case.

It is certainly true that there were issues, such as Catholic relief and parliamentary reform which appear connected with the perennial conflict of progress and reaction, but the attempts that have been made to analyze the party conflict of the period in those terms have all broken down in confusion on points of detail. The Portland Whigs, for example, had a fuller understanding than Pitt and Dundas of the extent to which the French Revolution introduced a new political era. Consequently they joined Pitt and Dundas in order to fight it. Did that make them more or less reactionary than Pitt or Dundas? Later there was widespread opposition to Pitt's project to replace laws against Catholicism in Ireland by laws against political reformers. Which was reactionary, the proposal or the opposition? The paradox that the men who campaigned for the abolition of the slave trade—presumably a progressive cause if ever there was one—were also in favour of political repression at home has long been familiar to historians: if, as has been recently argued, the abolitionists were concerned to re-establish traditional sanctions which the relatively recent institution of colonial slavery transgressed, were they really on the side of the future or of the past?[2]

The real key to political conflict at this time was in fact not the issue of reform or reaction, but the issue of royal prerogative. George III's authority, over central government at least, was much more than nominal. Ministers felt they were the King's servants in fact as well as in name, and the limits of the duty they owed to the sovereign were a question of real importance. Since royal prerogative is an issue which dropped out of sight after 1832, historians, more anxious to concentrate on apparent continuities rather than discontinuities, have virtually overlooked it, or else discussed it in terms of its being merely one of a number of issues, of no more importance than, for example, Catholic relief or parliamentary reform. There were indeed numerous questions in dispute during this period, often causing conflict amongst members of the same party, but only the question of prerogative involved divisions *between* parties. At the same time views on prerogative give no clue to the views of politicians on the other, inferior issues. Prerogative split the pro-Catholic and pro-reform lobbies virtually down the middle, creating a confusing continuum of political groups which each agreed with some other group on one point but not on others: the Foxites who opposed prerogative and favoured Catholic relief and parliamentary reform, the Grenvilles who opposed prerogative *and* reform but favoured relief, Pitt's friends who opposed reform but favoured relief *and* prerogative, the Addingtonians and their country gentlemen sympathizers who opposed reform and relief and favoured prerogative, Wilberforce and his group of Evangelicals known as 'The Saints', who to some extent stood aloof from party, and who opposed relief and favoured prerogative and reform, and the Prince of Wales's following amongst the Whigs (often called the Carlton House Group) who included the heirs of the old eighteenth-century Country Party, and who opposed prerogative and relief but favoured reform. The situation may be best represented diagrammatically:

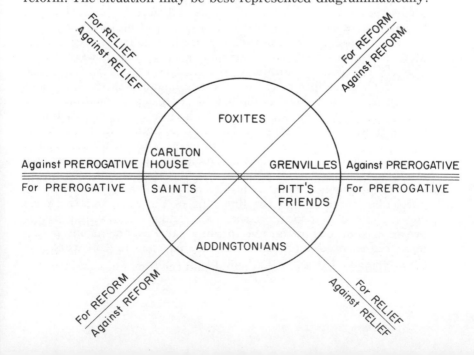

A significant feature of these years was the extent to which party leaders, trapped in their own rhetoric of opposition to or exaltation of prerogative, were unable to relate adequately to other issues which seemed crucial to supporters or to others existing in the less rarefied politic al atmosphere outside London's West End and the country seats of the great magnates, and this caused an alienation between parliamentary politics and many voters. Yet prerogative was the issue that brought about the establishment of the two-party system (a fact which is commemorated in the revival of the term 'Tory', which has been in continuous use as a party label only since this period). The party system did not, of course, emerge fully fledged overnight. Still less did it have the full equipage of ideology which has been imposed on it in retrospect. It is for this reason that the author prefers the contemporary usage of the period and employs the denominations 'government' and 'opposition' rather than the party labels 'Tory' and 'Whig' which, if used too facilely, confuse our understanding of the way in which the two-party system evolved.

Another respect in which this period differs at close view from the appearance it has in retrospect is the power of the upper classes. Modern research is progressively undermining the old view that the aristocratic political system of the pre-reform era was replaced, as it were overnight, by a bourgeois-dominated system as a result of the 1832 Reform Act. Nevertheless it is undeniable that the reform of Parliament did open a breach in the defences of the *ancien régime* which eventually led to its dissolution, and so it is tempting to look for indications that the aristocracy was already on the defensive before 1832. Such is not however the case: the upper classes were, right up to the very eve of the 1832 Reform Act, in the process of actually increasing their hold on the institutions of British society—the boroughs, the Church, the county administrations. The century which ended with the near eclipse of the aristocracy began with three decades during which they were at the height of their political and economic power. Yet the system over which they presided was undergoing fundamental changes. There was increasing poverty for some, and increasing commercial prosperity for others, and both processes led to a developing challenge to the long-accepted aristocratic monopoly of political activity. Parliament, dominated by the upper class, dealt with only a limited range of issues—in particular, the war, and the financing of the war—but the lower classes looked to it for more than that, and the following chapters are an account of how far and in what way Parliament and goverment represented the needs of the ruling class and in what way they responded to pressure from other sectors.

Part One of this book, describing the context of politics, and Part Three, which discusses how far the political system of the 1800s made any positive contribution to social and economic change in this period, deal by and large with the whole 22 years of the Revolutionary and Napoleonic Wars, but Part Two, the core of this book, confines itself to a mere 12 years. It was felt that to have attempted to discuss an even longer span of political events would have involved the risk of sacrificing analysis to narrative. The 12 years discussed were anyway the crucial ones, which not only saw the emergence of the two-party system and the failure of the Whigs to establish themselves as a genuine popular party, but saw also a major political crisis. Sir Herbert Butterfield once claimed that Britain's French Revolution was in 1780.[3] In fact Britain was much nearer to revolution in 1809-12. It is true the ideological disputes of those years seem less interesting to modern ears than the arguments of 30 years earlier, but the upper classes were more generally discredited, the reformers less moderate, and there was more working-class disturbance and more risk of economic collapse.

It is only by examining the political, social and economic developments of these years in their full interrelation that any real understanding of this period can be achieved. It is hoped that the political narrative in Part Two of this book and the analysis of policies in Part Three will contribute to an appreciation of the social relationships outlined in Part One, and that at the same time both the politics and the policies will be recognized as a product of those relationships and only to be understood in terms of them. It is, of course, a familiar complaint that political history, social history and economic history are too often studied in isolation, and the author is conscious that he has not succeeded in integrating them in this book as fully as he had wished. A history book is inevitably more structured than the events it describes. But the opening years of the nineteenth century have hitherto suffered more than any other period of British history from the custom of studying events in *genres*, and the author hopes he has at least brought previously isolated issues sufficiently close together to prepare the way for more comprehensive investigations in the future.

PART ONE: The Social And Ideological Context Of Politics

1
Oligarchy

Caste

DESPITE the influence the King still exerted on the central government, Britain in 1800 was effectively ruled by an oligarchy. There were reckoned to be 9,458 armigerous families in England in 1798, and 4,000 in Scotland, and though some of these families had sunk into poverty and obscurity, these figures roughly define the size of the oligarchic caste.[1] Neither wealth, political power, nor even titles were equally distributed throughout this caste, some of whose members possessed estates and local patronage extending through several counties, and were established at court and in Whitehall, while others were merely squires in isolated rural parishes. Yet a caste it was nonetheless, in that it was a hereditary social group, difficult if not impossible for non-members to join, and distinguished from the rest of society for reasons not purely economic, and in that its members had a sense of equality amongst themselves.

In 1800 there were 257 English and British* peers (a fifth of whom also had Irish or Scots peerages) and 159 Irish and 72 Scots peers, with the various titles of duke, marquess, earl, viscount and baron. These titles brought with them social precedence, membership in person or by representation in the House of Lords, minor privileges such as exemption from jury service, and were so highly regarded that, for example, titled military officers were normally referred to by their title rather than by their rank. Nevertheless, a virtual equality was recognized even between a duke and an ordinary country gentleman. Hereditary titles did not always mean hereditary wealth. Some peers were very poor,

---

*English peers were those created before the Union with Scotland in 1707; British peers those created between 1707 and 1800.

such as Lords Strangford, Kingsale, Falkland and Bellenden: the last was even reduced in middle-age to writing begging letters to affluent relatives of his old school friends, describing himself as 'one of those exigent mortals, who having but a slender income of two or three hundred a year to live upon, am often liable to be thrown into embarrassment'.[2] At the same time many gentlemen, of no title at all, owned vast Palladian mansions and extensive country estates. Title and wealth had their importance, but to be a gentleman was the chief thing, and so long as one was a gentleman, wealth counted more than title. Even members of the royal family spoke of themselves as 'gentlemen'. The pattern of marriage extended across the class, for example, only 27.5 per cent of all sons of peers born between 1760 and 1779 married daughters of peers: most of the others married daughters of gentlemen.[3]

The practice of duelling, which seems to have been increasing during this period, also demonstrated this social equality. The duel was essentially a method of settling points of honour between equals. It will be remembered that in the more hierarchical Tudor period, Queen Elizabeth had forbidden Philip Sidney's quarrel with the Earl of Oxford because of:

'the difference in degree between Earls and Gentlemen; the respect inferiors ought to their superiors; and the necessity in Princes to maintain their own creatures, as degrees descending between the peoples licentiousness, and the anoynted Soveraignty of Crowns'[4]

By Georgian times however this hierarchical view of society had disappeared. Duels between peers and commoners were quite frequent: both Lord Camelford and Lord Falkland were killed in duels with commoners. Even the King's second son, HRH the Duke of York, once fought a duel against a man who, though he later inherited a dukedom, was at the time merely an untitled commoner. The wearing of swords in public, and consequently their use in duels, had gone out of fashion by the 1780s, and the use of pistols for duelling meant that relatively unsophisticated squireens no longer suffered their former disadvantage when quarrelling with fashionable patricians trained to fence by experts.

While distinctions of rank between members of the upper class were increasingly minimized, the separation between them and the rest of society remained of crucial importance. This exclusiveness was never total, except in such distinctions as between barristers, who were all assumed to be gentlemen, and attorneys who were assumed to be not, and there was a largish area of semi-shadow between the poorer squires and the richer yeomen, but the separation between the upper classes and the rest of the population was probably at its height in 1800. Sir Lewis Namier's exposition of the English upper class in the eighteenth century as open to all-comers, with younger sons of peers going into trade, and trades-men founding noble dynasties, is a serious misrepresentation.[5] The story he quotes of the first Lord Craven boasting, 'I am William Lord Craven, my father was Lord Mayor of London, and my grand-father was the Lord knows who . . .' is neither very plausible nor, since it relates to the early Stuart period, very relevant.

In fact, mobility either upward or downward, in or out of the gentlemen caste, was becoming increasingly unusual. As early as 1711 Addison was regretting that so many well-born younger sons passed a life of idle dependency on the heads of their families rather than demean themselves by seeking a career in trade.[6] At the same time there was a decreasing tendency for the larger commercial fortunes to be invested in land, so as to enable businessmen to establish themselves in county society. Peter Thellusson, created Baron Rendlesham in 1806, the first Sir Robert Peel, and Sir Richard Arkwright with his lavish attempts to break into Derbyshire society, were not exceptional, but they represented a declining trend. The obsession with gentility of descent, which had been sufficiently ridiculed in the Tudor period, continued to be a standard topic of satire, as in the characters of Sir Walter Elliot in Jane Austen's novel *Persuasion*, of Lady Lofty and Sir Matthew Maukish in John Moore's novel *Edward*, and as a major theme in Holcroft's *Anna St. Ives*. The widespread belief that Pitt as Prime Minister favoured *pervenus* 'to the almost total exclusion of the old nobility and gentry' occasioned much complaint. Corbbett wrote:

'The people, we mean the better sort of people, resent the neglect and ill-treatment of those whom they have been, from their infancy, in the habit of respecting, more especially when the honours and favours due to them are conferred on persons of mean birth.'[7]

Lady Holland thought 'there is not a man of the Corresponding Society more bitter against the aristocracy than Pitt and Canning are'.[8] Earl Grosvenor even went so far as to protest personally to Pitt at his excessive creation of peers,[9] and the Marquess of Abercorn described the Scots peerage, in which there had been no new creations since 1707, as 'the only Peerage which a Gentleman can any longer feel a pride in belonging to'.[10] In fact Pitt ennobled no one not of genteel birth, with the exception of some of his judges, and the tradition of his 'plebeian aristocracy' derives from the jealousy of the Whig patricians whom he excluded from power. Nonetheless, it indicates how sensitive people were to the possi-bility of social upstarts being promoted.

It is true that this period of exclusiveness was on the very eve of the retreat of the gentleman caste before the industrial bourgeoisie. Indeed, one or two of the individuals of bourgeois origin who did establish themselves within the oligarchy made an impact greater than any of their sort had achieved before. William Wilberforce, of a Hull merchant dynasty, became leader of the great philanthropic movement of the age and representative of Yorkshire, the largest constituency in the country, though he himself wrote:

'All circumstances considered . . . my mercantile origin, my want of connexion or acquaintance with any of the nobility or gentry of Yorkshire . . . my being elected for that great county seems to me upon the retrospect to have been so utterly improbable that I cannot but wonder—and in truth I ascribe it to a providential intimation—that the idea of my obtaining that high honour suggested itself to my imagination.'[11]

Henry Addington, son of a royal physician, became Prime Minister. Samuel Whitbread, the brewer, and George Tierney, of a family of international merchants, became prominent in the Whig party. But it is surely significant that when Wilberforce retired he was succeeded as MP for Yorkshire by a large landowner chiefly interested in extending the laws protecting game against proletarian hunters; that Addington was jeered at as 'The Doctor' and eventually laughed out of office by 'the fashionable part of London society; or as old Lord Liverpool described and pronounced it, the *biumond*';[12] and that political opponents sneered at Whitbread as a 'brewer of bad porter';[13] even one of Addington's friends wrote of Whitbread, 'He has not one spark, it seems to me, of gentlemanly feeling or British spirit about him—but I recollect, he does not deal in spirit but beer.'[14]

This antipathy was mutual. John Nicholls, like Addington, the son of a royal physician, told Tierney:

'These great families, this oligarchy, destroy us, Sir. Yes, Sir, they oppress us. Why look at them individually? Have they any single merit? Why, there is Ld. Fitzwilliam, a flat retailer in dull prose of Burke's poetical, mad flights: has he not plunged us in this war? There's Ld. Spencer recovering from epilepsy merely to squander thousands upon an early edition. As to the house of Russell, Sir, Mr. Burke has handled them properly. The Cavendishes, Sir, are so notoriously stupid that they blunt satire; but see the head of them, Sir, the D. of Devonshire, Sir, why, I assure you I am credibly informed, I have it from the best authority, Sir, that he is a *mere sensualist*.'[15]

There was a similar animosity in the stinging rebuke which Lord Chancellor Thurlow delivered to the Duke of Grafton when the latter sneered at Thurlow's humble origins in a speech in the Lords,[16] and Lord Chief Justice Kenyon, also from the border-

lands between gentility and non-gentility, used to denounce 'titled
adulterers' and other aristocratic evil-doers, from the bench, even
during trials on quite different matters.

The participation of noblemen like Earl Stanhope and, to a
lesser extent, the Dukes of Bedford and Norfolk, in the reform
controversies of the 1790s was a further cause of bourgeois dislike
for the peerage. Several of the anti-reform novels of the period
have a reform-minded nobleman as their villain, such as the peer's
brother Fitzosborne in Jane West's *A Tale of the Times* (1799) and
the Duke's nephew, Marauder, in Charles Lucas's *The Infernal
Quixote* (1801); and the hypocrisy of reform-minded peers was
lampooned in Chapter 27 of Henry James Pye's *The Democrat*
(1795). It is curious that duelling, as a characteristic practice of
the upper class, was denounced both by novelists favouring reform,
such as Holcroft and Godwin, and by writers opposed to reform,
such as Lucas.[17]

Internal Groupings
Within the ruling caste, the most important groupings were of
family and clientage. It was not true, as is sometimes assumed,
that the upper classes were all interrelated—there were far too
many of them for that, and cousinhood links were further limited
by the popularity of first-cousin marriages, which reinforced
existing relationships instead of creating new ones. Nevertheless,
the extent and influence of some of the cousinages were impressive.
In 1800 the first cousins of the Grenville brothers (the Marquess of
Buckingham, Thomas Grenville, and William, Lord Grenville, the
Foreign Secretary) included the Prime Minister, William Pitt, his
brother the Earl of Chatham (Lord President of the Council),
Lord Glastonbury and *his* brother General Richard Grenville (a
favourite equerry of the King), the Earl of Egremont, the wife of
Lord Romney, and both the deceased first wife and the living second
wife of the prominent reformer, Earl Stanhope. Their brothers-in-
law were Lord Camelford (first cousin once removed of their own
Pitt cousins), Earl Fortescue, Lord Braybrooke, and the Earl of
Carysfort. A nephew, Sir Watkin Williams Wynn, was head of
the richest family in North Wales. In the same year Lord Granville
Leveson, younger son of the first Marquess of Stafford by a
second marriage, was the nephew of the Earl of Galloway, brother-
in-law to the Countess *suo jure* of Sutherland, to the Earl of Carlisle,
the Hon. William Eliot, the Marquess of Worcester and the future
Lord Harrowby, first cousin of the Earl of Upper Ossory and his
brother, General the Hon. Richard Fitzpatrick MP, of Viscount
Fincastle, the Marquis of Douglas and the Earl of Aboyne, and
first cousin once removed of the third Lord Holland and of the

Duke of Bedford.

It is a familiar notion that in the relatively stable pre-industrial and early industrial era there existed a phenomenon now known as the 'extended family', where two or three generations of the same family lived together in a mutually supportive community. It is not sufficiently realized how far such 'extended families' were kept together, not by tradition or sentiment, but because the members could not afford to break away and establish separate households. Amongst the upper classes there was no real extended family — once sons married they set up their own independent homes and, if they married well, they might in their own neighbourhood rival the local influence of their own fathers. Of course sons would still defer to their fathers in accordance with Biblical precept. Thus the son of the Duke of Beccleuch could tell a friend 'I have allways [sic] made it a rule to think what my father does, is right; & at all times to adopt his views, & his sentiments.'[18] Relatives would still visit one another, often for protracted stays, but the upper classes anyway used each other's homes when they travelled about in preference to staying at inns. And there were exceptions. Pitt and William Grenville did not become friends until they were both in Parliament in the 1780s, and Thomas Grenville, originally a political opponent of his cousin, later claimed he had never been in his company till 1793.[19]

Neither of the cousinhoods described above acted together in public life. The Grenvilles and the Pitts were great bastions of government, yet they were closely related to the two most *outré* Jacobinical peers of the day, Stanhope and Camelford (though it had been originally assumed that Camelford would support his family and 'the first time he divided in the minority, it was so little expected that the Chancellor sent to him to assure him that he had made a mistake.'[20] But other families had a tradition of mutual support. The Hon. Edward Harbord told his father:

'I think that whatever our several opinions may be, my brother and I should act together; we should do so for our own credit, and for (most of all) the family importance. While acting together, the family interest is of consequence, which is entirely destroyed by our dividing in the House (of Commons), by that we annihilate each other's weight and influence.'[21]

Where political sympathy and kinship coincided they might form a bond of double strength, which might be acknowledged by others. Lord Holland, the nephew of Charles James Fox, was seen by many as the *political* heir of the Whig leader when the latter died in September 1806. Much play was also made with the kinship of Pitt and Lord Grenville.

At the same time, men like Pitt drew about them many who

looked up to them as leaders and patrons, who had no blood connection to recommend them. Though most young men born into the ruling class had some uncle or cousin already established, whose influence they could look to, a few were totally dependent on their powers of ingratiation, men like Canning, the son of a disinherited father, who owed his career to Pitt. In some ways family connection seems to have counted for less than clientage. Where two powerful families intermarried, the sense of kinship might well disappear within a couple of generations, for as neither family needed any help from the other, so there was no scope for either favours or gratitude on either side. It was unusual for members of the greatest families to refer to their blood ties except in the case of first cousins, yet much more distant relatives were acknowledged, providing they were in a dependent situation. Thus James Talbot, a very distant cousin of the Marchioness of Buckingham, was recommended to the Ambassador at St Petersburg by the Marchioness's brother-in-law, with the explanation, 'his connection with a part of my family makes me desirous that you should show him such attention and kindness as I am willing to believe his character will fairly justify'.[22]

Clientage, the informal process whereby men with national or local power fostered the careers of less powerful individuals who, in return, could be expected to uphold their patron's influence, was a natural development in the pre-meritocratic era. It was also the natural expression of a society where relationships even within the administrative machine were personal rather than official. It invaded every sphere of life. When the Receiver for the Property Tax in Hertfordshire transferred the meeting at which the tax collectors paid over their receipts from 'The Bull' at Ware to 'The Saracen's Head', because the landlord of 'The Bull' had voted for the wrong candidate at the last election, he was invoking one of the sanctions of the clientage system.[23]

Voters at parliamentary elections frequently claimed the status of deserving dependents:

'Tho' I am a perfect Stranger to your Lordship, I hope your Goodness will induce you to excuse the great liberty I am about to take in soliciting a favour, on the Grounds of my having, at the late Election for the County, given Lord Milton a Plumper* & also exercised every interest in my power to be of use to him...'[24]

and:

I take leave to inform your Grace that being a Freeman of the

---

*In most constituencies, two members were returned, and all voters had *two* votes. By using only one of these votes (which was known as 'plumping') voters avoided giving their second vote to a candidate who might beat their own favourite into third place.

City of Oxford I have always been in your Interest, I am now in Years and humbly solicit your Grace to honor me so as that I may get into some situation in the Customs or India House, which at my Time of Life will make me very Comfortable, in return for which both my self *and relations* will at all Times be happy to show our Gratitude.'[25]

Out of 49 letters received by Earl Fitzwilliam in three months of 1809, and now preserved at Northampton, 26 were requests for money, jobs, or other help.[26] These were attempts to board an already over-crowded vehicle; Fitzwilliam, like all great lords, already supported an army of grateful tenants, bailiffs, tradesmen and so forth, who administered his estates and formed the basis of his local power.

But clientage did not operate merely at the local level, and in the relations between rich and poor. It was equally in evidence amongst members of the upper class. Thus when Lord Grenville resigned office in February 1801 he received numerous letters from eminent persons, pledging lifelong loyalty and obedience. Lord Whitworth wrote, 'It is to you and your friends that I owe everything, and it is to you and your friends that I am and ever shall be proud to think that I belong'.[27] William Wickham of the Home Department was more fervent still[28]—at Grenville's request he took office under Addington, but after Addington's own resignation three years later he insisted on his desire 'to attach my political fortunes to those of your Lordship so as that they may never be severed'.[29]

Even the relationship between the King and favoured ministers partook of the character of the relationship between patron and protégé. Charles Yorke, for example, boasted, 'I have no Protector but His Majesty, to whom I have ever accustomed myself to look up, on Earth; and I never can expect nor do I desire to meet with any other.'[30] Lord Chancellor Eldon said, weeping, during the regency debates, 'Of his Majesty I can never speak without gratitude for the favours, the obligations, the King has heaped upon me.'[31] Of course the King differed from other patrons in kind as well as in the quantity of the patronage he had (at least theoretically) at his disposal. It was the fashion for all but the Foxites to speak of him with reverence, and some pretended to prize public office chiefly as a means of demonstrating to the world the possession of royal favours. For example, John Reeves asked to be made Judge Advocate in 1806 so that he would be 'relieved from the mortification, which I may otherwise carry to my grave, of being rejected by the King, in the face of the Public'.[32] The professed personal element was present, whatever the status of patron or protégé.

For persons promoted into the ruling class from outside, such as some of the bishops, clientage seems to have been felt to be obligatory, as if their obscure origins disqualified them from the true independence wielded by the great families. Samuel Goodenough, Bishop of Carlisle, had formerly been headmaster of a school in Ealing to which both Viscount Sidmouth and his son had gone; the late Duke of Portland had also sent his son there. In April 1812 Goodenough told Sidmouth:

> 'henceforth I should consider myself as yours . . . you would have nothing to do but signify your wishes & to rely upon my fulfilling them. You know well my attachment to the late Duke of Portland, & the reasons on which it was founded. As the present Duke of Portland disclaims all political interference, I consider myself as in Duty bound to turn to you as my next Friend, & to bind myself to you, as I did to him (the late Duke).'[33]

The system of clientage was so useful both to client and patron that it was rarely found necessary to insist on the obligations involved. A letter from Sir Charles Malet to Lord Grenville in 1795 complaining of having been passed over in a desirable appointment, is an unusual instance, and it is perhaps significant that Malet seems to have had difficulty in expressing himself clearly:

> 'It is true, my Lord, that, by this dereliction of your powerful patronage in pursuit of the above objects, great inconvenience and prejudice to my interest may ensure. . . . I apprehend that, with chilled affection and frozen zeal, my services would in future rather be measured by the treatment they have experienced, than by that energy with which hitherto I have, and should in future wish to exert myself. A certain reciprocity of attention is due even in the relation of servant and served; and, though obedience at all events is incumbent, as long as the relation subsists, yet the more delicate energies of zealous attachment are generated only by the genial warmth of liberal confidence and generous protection. These withdrawn, mutual estrangement will, I apprehend, ensue.'[34]

With respect to one kind of political obligation, however, kinship and clientage seem to have been regarded in an identical light. It was expected that a man's good name and character would be defended by all those connected with him in whatever way, regardless of political or even personal differences. Thus Canning thought the Foxite Charles Grey owed it to Viscount Melville not to attack him on the subject of the Navy Pay Office funds, because Melville had once defended Grey's own father (who was not a Foxite) against parliamentary censure.[35] Ingratitude was also the burden of Wellesley-Pole's outburst in 1810 when so many of Pitt's former followers joined the attack on his unfortunate brother the Earl of Chatham on the Walcheren issue:

> 'I was . . . not prepared for many things that happen'd — such as

Wynn & Temple feeling the necessity of performing their *duty*
so very much at variance with their inclination, by speaking
violently as well as voting against the brother of the great
aggrandizer and benefactor of their family — such as Mr Canning
being impell'd also to speak against the brother of his creator, &
becoming at last the mover of the question that sets his sun for
ever, forgetting, I suppose, for the moment in his zeal for the
good of the country — the seat in Parliament — the sinecure
place — the pensions for the Miss Hunns — the office of the
Secretary of State &c &c &c which he had attained through the
protection and partiality of Mr Pitt — such as Lord Castlereagh
finding it indispensable *distinctly* to take the very worst view
of Ld Chatham's case that was put to the House in the course
of the debate — notwithstanding all his enthusiasm for Mr Pitt's
memory, and all the favors and honors conferr'd upon him, and
his family through his kindness — these things certainly in some
degree surprised me, and gave rise to many melancholy reflections upon human nature.'[36]
But this was perhaps a case of the pot calling the kettle black, as
Wynn, one of the people denounced by Wellesley-Pole, had
himself once complained of Wellesley Pole's own brother's 'dirty &
ungrateful conduct to the person who since they were both
children has protected raised & served him'[37] — that is, to Lord
Grenville, who was himself accused of ingratitude to Pitt.

Party politics represented a third mode of sub-division within
the ruling caste. In some ways party had a smaller scope than
family and clientage. Everyone had relatives. Everyone, even
country gentlemen leading retired lives, had dependents and
obligations. Not everyone had party politics. In 1800 party strife
had yet to be established in the public mind as a legitimate enterprise. There was only one party, the Foxite Whigs, and they were
unpopular and discredited.

The government and the parliamentary opposition were not
regarded as interchangeable and complementary, as in a true two-
party system. The government was regarded as a permanent
fixture, consisting of the chosen servants of the King, and there
was no distinction made between the politics of the ministers who
sat in Parliament and the politics of subordinates who did not. The
opposition, on the other hand, was not seen as fulfilling any useful
constitutional rôle. It was regarded as harmful, factious and
involving personal disloyalty to the King. Even after 1804, when
the government of the day was increasingly seen as a party
comparable to the opposition, objections continued. Wilberforce
thought party was 'achieving the ruin of our country . . . half the
people are employed in the very service which the worst enemies of

the country would be glad to hire agents to affect—in fermenting discontent, in damping ardour, in checking public spirit'.[38] It was perhaps to be expected that a ministerialist pamphleteer should claim:

> PARTY and CABAL are more injurious to this country than the sword of Buonaparte. Were we firmly united, we might proudly bid defiance to the world; but, instead of promoting that union, and strengthening the hands of the government we naturally look up to for support, we perceive a set of men, by every subtle means, weakening the administration, and, as far as in them lies, rendering its measures ineffectual'.[39]

But it was a reformer who wrote, 'By internal dissensions, the independence of a country is imminently endangered, for domestic feuds unnerve the body politic...England in particular has endured much injury from the strife of her parties'.[40] Pamphleteers who were not actually in Foxite pay and who thought party rivalry was 'legitimate warfare' that benefited the country were an exception.[41]

Many MPs regarded it as their duty to support the government whatever its political complexion. Charles Abbot, on entering Parliament in 1795 decided:

> 'upon all general occasions to vote in support of the minister of the day, be he Pitt or Fox; for to me they are as indifferent as Pompey or Caesar, and I hate, because I disapprove, a teasing, barking, cavilling, unprincipled opposition. In the next place, upon particular and important questions, open by their nature to the discussion of all men, I should give my vote upon the balance of the question, either silently, or with reasons, if I could contribute information, or should think it necessary to avow principles or assign reasons.'[42]

Others were more independently minded: Sir Richard Hill, addressing the Shropshire electors on his retirement in 1806, wrote:

> 'I humbly trust the long test you have had of my Parliamentary conduct, has cast no blot, either through the power of corrupt influence, or by an undue bias to this or that set of men; never leaning to opposition or ministry, but as I was persuaded in my conscience that opposition or ministry leaned to the public good; sometimes voting with one side, sometimes with the other, though I have always supported government so far as I thought government measures were for the good of the nation.'[43]

Some favoured neutrality on private rather than public grounds: Charles Yorke, who professed to regard himself as the King's servant rather than a party man, advised his brother, an officer in the Navy, '*you are a Professional man, & have a Family* (likely to be an *encreasing* one) to provide for. Consequently, you should only meddle with *party* or *House of Commons Politics, incidentally, moderately,* & as a *secondary* object'.[44]

Membership of Parliament was commonly regarded, not as a means of promoting party objectives, but as one of the duties of rank; and the higher the rank, the more pressing the duty. Thus Earl Fitzwilliam was told that his son:

'has from his birth & rank in society a weighty obligation of publick duties upon him. These he ought not in any degree to sacrifice to his own domestick comforts. On the contrary, in proportion as he is now, I trust, more likely to leave a long posterity behind him to inherit his honours, & be influenced by his example, he should so much the more feel an incentive to aim at transmitting to them with his & your titles & estate, a constitution & system of polity, which may give lustre to the one, & security to the other.'[45]

At the same time, government was not a thing apart from the rest of upper-class life. Just as, within it, relationships remained personal rather than bureaucratic, so in its corporate *persona* it was able to enter into the normal processes of expectation and obligation. Attitudes to government were often phrased in personal rather than political terms. One back-bencher wrote:

'At the repeated Insults I have received from Government I express no surprise. I owe them no obligation. I have been absurdly partial to them in times when others thought it more prudent to desert them, & they, in return, perhaps wisely, seem to fancy it correct to buy their former enemies at the price of their former friends.'[46]

Having received a government circular asking for a contribution to a charity, Earl Grosvenor replied:

'Lord Grosvenor presents his Compliments to Mr. Dundas, having had the Honor of receiving his Letter yesterday; he takes the liberty of acquainting him, that when he perceives the least inclination in the *Leading Members* of Government to take notice, of *any* Application he has, or may make to them, he shall be ever ready to give theirs a reciprocal attention.'[48]

In 1806 Sir William Grant, Master of the Rolls, explained his boycott of sittings of the Lords Commissioners of Appeals in Prize Causes by claiming he had been 'deemed a fit object of measures of personal hostility by some of the Members of administration'.[48] In a similar way, political parties were seen, by their adherents if not by their critics, as extensions of the ties and obligations of friendship. 'The Friends of Mr. Fox' were not always friends in the literal sense. According to Philip Francis, who himself evidently disliked Fox, the only person apart from Horne

Tooke 'whom Fox positively could not endure' was his own political associate Sheridan, 'with some antipathy rather than enmity to George Tierney'—Tierney of course being another of the party.[49] But the idiom of friendship was preserved throughout.

Political Control

Not merely was it the case that party was the preoccupation only of a minority—admittedly a growing minority—of parliamentarians, but its ramifications extended only a little way into the structure of society as a whole. In a few towns like Bristol and Preston, national party labels were adopted as a weapon in the rivalry of municipal factions, but this did not involve members of the upper class (except for the Earl of Derby in his character as a borough patron on one side of the Preston struggle), and far from there being any instances of county families adopting party as a mean to prosecute local rivalries, there seems to have been a tendency to paper over disputes outside Parliament and to present a united front to social inferiors, lest partisan politics suffered discredit from the involvement of the lower classes. Consequently party politics were rarely an issue at elections, and in some cases, such as in the Essex county constituency, there was an informal compromise between Foxites and ministerialists to prevent contests.

Though it would be incorrect to make a distinction between peers and commoners, or between men with incomes of over £5,000 a year and men without, it was richer individuals, usually with titles, who had more prominence in public life than the poorer members of their caste. Connections and wealth gave the *entrée* to the centres of power, and local influence gave leverage where it was desirable to exert pressure. As well as being, for the most part, entitled to sit in the House of Lords, the greater magnates were able, through their local power, to dominate the House of Commons. Their control was not slackening in the decades just before the great Reform Act, it was being extended. In England and Wales in 1793, 71 peers nominated 88 MPs, and influenced the election of 72. In 1816 87 peers nominated 115 MPs, and influenced the election of 103.[50] This increase was only partly due to formerly non-noble borough-mongers such as Sir Francis Basset being raised to the peerage. Of the nine greatest patrons in 1816, who between them controlled or influenced the return of 67 MPs, three (the Duke of Norfolk, the Earl of Darlington, and Lord Carrington) had achieved their position within the previous 15 years, and two others, the Duke of Rutland and the Marquess of Buckingham, had gained most of their power since 1780.

A number of country gentlemen were also borough patrons.

With a few exceptions, such as James Buller and Sir Christopher Hawkins in Cornwall, it was the case that individuals controlled only the one seat needed for their own membership of Parliament. In 1793, 91 commoners nominated 82 MPs, and influenced the elections of 57. In 1816, 90 commoners nominated 84 MPs, and influenced the elections of 53.

Some patrons exerted a jealous control of their nominees' conduct in Parliament. In 1806, for example, the Duke of North-humberland, in resentment at not being consulted at the formation of the Fox-Grenville ministry, circularized his members:

'Not having received any intimation as to the principles of the new administration, or any assurance that Lord Grenville and his colleagues had consented to abandon those principles of government which, when they were last in power, led to the annual suspension of the Habeas Corpus act, as well as the passing of certain acts highly inimical to Magna Carta and the Bill of Rights, I must desire that you and my other friends will *refrain from taking any part in the debates, as well as giving your vote upon such propositions as may be offered to the House by the new administration, until I am able to judge of the principles upon which this new Coalition intend to govern the country.*'[51]

But other patrons were less interfering and often elected friends or relatives with established political reputations, for whom such admonitions would have been neither appropriate nor diplomatic.

The proportion of blue blood in the Commons was also rising. In 1734 there were 75 sons of peers and Irish peers sitting in a House of 558 members (13.4 per cent); in both 1802 and 1812, in a House enlarged by the Act of Union with Ireland to 658 members there were 143 (21.7 per cent); in 1826 there were 165 (25 per cent).[52] Very few of the others, it might be added in passing, were not armigerous. Of course the number of peers had increased in this period, but so had the numbers of all other classes of society. Manifestly, the titled nobility were extending their corporate power. Some of these lordlings in the Commons rarely attended debates and never spoke, but others provided the core of parliament-ary leadership. Pitt, Fox, Perceval, Petty, Erskine, were the younger sons of peers; Castlereagh, and after 1801, Grey, were eldest sons; the unsuccessful Addington was unique amongst parlia-mentary leaders in having no near titled connections. There was of course a natural backwardness in all new MPs when it came to addressing the House, but with most MPs personal modesty was reinforced both by their particular notion of why they were there —most of them seem to have thought they were there to listen and judge, not to talk and persuade—and by the deference which even

wealthy landed gentlemen felt towards the brilliant scions of
the greater magnate families. Some of this sort of MP—and the
commercial MPs such as Baring and Peel—only took it upon
themselves to speak on issues on which their particular expertise
was well known.

In the government, as distinct from Parliament, the domination
of the titled nobility was even more evident. The Cabinet ministers
who sat in the Commons—themselves usually the sons of peers—
were invariably outnumbered in the Cabinet by members of the
House of Lords. Pitt's second Cabinet in 1804, and Perceval's Cabinet in 1809 were entirely composed of peers or the sons of peers. Even
the plebeian Addington had a Cabinet which, with the exception
of himself, was noble. Of course not all these peers had old titles,
but they nearly all had long pedigrees; Lord Grenville, for example,
belonged to a family whose head claimed 719 heraldic quarterings.
Nor were these ministers ruled by their civil service machines as
is the case nowadays. The Secretaries of State transacted a great
deal of their own departmental business, and regularly gave at
least one of the Under-Secretaryships to personal clients who
could assist them. The rest of the departmental staffs were tiny.
In 1800 there were only 29 clerks at the Treasury, 13 at the Home
Department, 11 at the Foreign Department, six at the War
Department and seven at the Board of Trade, all transacting
merely routine business.

Control of Professions
The preponderating influence of the great noble families in politics
was mirrored by the domination of the Army and the Church
(though not of the more meritocratic naval and legal professions,
which were, on the contrary, the principal means whereby a few
obscure gentry families were able to elevate themselves to prominence and title). For heads of the greater families, the management
or at least the enjoyment of one's estates and local influence was
often sufficient employment. Younger brothers, if not adequately
provided for by inheritance, often lived as parasites on their
relatives and in the peerage at least were more than twice as likely
as their older brothers not to marry and establish separate households.[53] Relatively few peers or their sons pursued professions,
but in the church and army at least these few enjoyed a success
which illuminates the facts of life of the period.

The movement of the nobility into the church was a comparatively recent development. Following the death in 1721 of
Nathaniel, Lord Crew, Bishop of Durham, two years passed
without a single nobleman on the bench, though the Archbishop
of York, Sir William Dawes, was a baronet. Then, in 1723, the

Hon. Henry Egerton was created Bishop of Hereford. Though two more baronets were appointed to the bench in the 1730s, Egerton was the only nobly born bishop for over 20 years. Then, between 1744 and 1749 four more sons of peers were made bishops. By December 1800 six out of 26 English bishops were sons of peers — seven including Charles Manners Sutton, whose father had a courtesy title as a duke's son. By 1817 both archbishops and six bishops were of noble birth.

The involvement of the nobility in the Army was of much longer standing, being one of the original traditions of European aristocracy, yet in 1800 at a time when Britain was involved in a desperate war, out of about 1,500 adult peers and sons of peers, probably less than 250 were commissioned in an Army of 12,000 officers. Yet all four non-royal field marshals were noblemen. The 56 full generals included seven hereditary peers, seven younger sons, plus HRH the Duke of Kent and three new creations, and the 67 lieutenant-generals included six peers and four younger sons. By 1812, when the number of noblemen in the Army as a whole had increased by perhaps a quarter, the 83 full generals included (beside three royal princes) 17 peers and six younger sons; the 178 lieutenant-generals included nine hereditary peers, two eldest sons yet to inherit their titles, eight younger sons, two new peers who were also younger sons, and the deaf and dumb Lord Seaforth, the heir to an attainted Scots earldom who had been created an Irish baron.

This relative prominence of noblemen in the upper ranks of the army was largely due to the system of promotion by purchase, taken with the low pay of all officers below the rank of colonel. Promotions by seniority in the regiment, in the case of vacancies caused by death in action, did occur, but few officers benefited more than once from such accidents, and most vacancies were filled by selling them to qualified candidates. Though described by one critic as 'ruinous and disgraceful',[54] this system gave worn-out officers an incentive to retire by selling out, without the necessity of establishing a comprehensive pension scheme; and the inability of the Commander-in-Chief to dismiss officers from their 'property' was still regarded as a constitutional safeguard.[55] But the tariff for commissions was high—from £400 for an ensigncy up to £3,500 for a lieutenant-colonelcy in the line, or £5,350 for a lieutenant-colonelcy of horse[56]—and the annexed pay was low—£73 5s 10d a year for an ensign in the line, £114 for a lieutenant-colonel,[57] which was much less than was needed for messing and other expenses. Consequently all but the most junior commissioned ranks were closed to all but the affluent. This was generally recognised: None could enter the army as officers who had not something else besides their mere pay', said the Secretary of State for War in 1806; 'This was important, in a constitutional view, since it prevented them from becoming mercenaries, and gave them an interest in the country they defended.'[58] But it also meant that the richer one was, the faster one's promotion. This was especially true before HRH the Duke of York became Commander-in-Chief in 1795 and enforced regulations requiring officers to have been subalterns two years before becoming captains, and officers six years before becoming majors. Under the previous Commander-in-Chief, Lord Amherst, the future Duke of Wellington rose to lieutenant-colonel in seven years, selling in and out of five infantry and two cavalry regiments in the process; Lord Charles Stewart, commissioned at 12, was a lieutenant-colonel at 18; Lord Paget, who had the temporary rank of lieutenant-colonel but was anxious to have permanent rank also, sold from lieutenant to lieutenant-colonel in four months.

Above the rank of lieutenant-colonel promotion was by 'brevet', that is, by seniority. When there was a promotion, all officers of a certain seniority would go up a grade, the size of the batch depending merely on how far it was decided to go down the list of seniority. A lieutenant-colonel, providing he was not first retired on half-pay, could expect to be a colonel in perhaps three years. Previous to the war with France breaking out in 1793, the step from colonel to major-general took up to 11 years, but some of those promoted colonel in 1794 became major-generals in 1796. The colonels of the 1802-3 brevet waited seven years for their next step, but those of 1808-9 only three years. The wait for promotion from major-general to lieutenant-general and from lieutenant-general to general was up to 14 years in peace time, and five or six years in war time.

This system of promotion by batch led to overcrowding of the upper ranks: in 1812 there were 564 generals of all grades, as compared to only 226 colonels, and the proportion of general officers to regular soldiers had risen from 1,615 in 1800 to 1,425 by 1812. Many of these generals never held commands and therefore, till new regulations were established in 1814, received no pay other than as colonels of regiments. In 1800 there were only seven generals or lieutenant-generals out of 133 with recent experience of independent command in Europe. The others included the Marquess of Lansdowne, formerly Prime Minister, who had last seen active service as an aide-de-camp to George II, and the Duke of Northumberland who though comparatively young (58) was crippled with arthritis. In 1812 there were only 23 generals and lieutenant-generals out of 261 with recent European command experience; others of course had held commands within Britain. The fact that merit or experience did not enter into the system favoured those rich enough to attain the rank of lieutenant-colonel while still young, and noblemen, being usually the richest of the upper class, tended to reach senior ranks at relatively low ages.

Contrary to what is generally supposed, the Navy contained a higher proportion of noble officers than the regular Army. Authorities such as Halévy, Namier and G. P. Judd agree in asserting that the Navy was the less aristocratic service when trying to explain how it was that there were far more Army officers than Navy officers in Parliament. In fact this numerical difference is explained by there being four times more officers in the Army, which was not only twice the size of the Navy, but had a far higher proportion of officers to other ranks. Perhaps one naval officer in 27 was of noble birth during the Revolutionary and Napoleonic Wars,[59] as compared to perhaps one in 50 in the Army. Nor were all these noble officers necessarily younger sons. The eldest sons of the first Lord Mulgrave, of the first Earl of Carysfort and of General the Earl of Cathcart were all naval officers: in all three cases they predeceased their fathers (in two cases on active service) so that the family titles were eventually inherited by younger brothers who were in the Army.

Where the Navy *was* less aristocratic was in the upper ranks. Whereas more than one officer in five of lieutenant-general's rank, or upwards in the Army was of noble birth, compared to one in 50 for all officers, in the Navy the proportion of noble admirals was much the same as it was for all ranks. In 1801, of 144 flag officers, only six were sons of peers (all of them younger sons) and they were outnumbered by men who had been ennobled for meritorious service—the reverse of the situation in the Army where inherited titles were commoner than titles that had been earned. There was some justification for the objection of one of Jane Austen's characters that the Navy was 'the means of bringing persons of obscure birth into undue distinction, and raising men to honours their fathers and grandfathers never dreamt of'.[60]

The reason for the relatively greater popularity of the Navy was that it provided an active and varied career for a young man, whereas the Army was not only expensive but held out few immediate prospects beyond that of incurring ruinous gambling debts in some provincial garrison town. The reason for the relative failure of noblemen to pack the upper ranks of the Navy was the system of promotion. Promotion up to the rank of captain depended on vacancies, and in a navy operating in widely dispersed squadrons, and frequently engaged in sanguinary conflict, every officer had a more equal chance in the scramble. Nor were private means necessary for maintaining one's status: lieutenants, paid

108 guineas a year, had mess bills of only £60 a year. A captain of a first-rate ship (a three-decker) earned £418 12s 0d a year; a captain of a sixth-rate (small frigate) only £228 8s 0d—which was still twice a lieutenant-colonel's pay. Of course, influence still operated to some extent—the promotion of 19-year-old the Hon. Charles Paget from midshipman to captain in four months, or the appointment of Thomas John Cochrane to a captaincy of a ship at the age of 17, by his own father while commanding in the West Indies, are instances of this. But the favour of senior officers on the spot counted for more than patronage at home, and on active service senior officers were more likely to be impressed by talent than by consanguinity with dukes. Promotion to flag-rank from post-captain (i.e. captain of a ship of the sixth-rate or larger) was a question of seniority. In St Vincent's day the wait from post-captain to rear-admiral was no less than 27 years. Nelson, who had been exceptionally fortunate to achieve post-rank at 20, waited for 18 years, for some of which he was on the beach drawing half-pay, and some officers junior to him waited 20 or 22 years.

The least aristocratically dominated of the genteel professions was the law. As was the case with the Church, it was unusual for the heirs to peerages to go into the law: Henry Bathurst did, and became Lord Chancellor as Lord Apsley before inheriting his father's earldom; William Schaw Cathcart was admitted advocate in Scotland before inheriting his father's barony and beginning a new career in the Army; Lord Maitland, too, became a Scots advocate while heir to his father the Earl of Lauderdale. Younger sons were more frequently called to the Bar, but often they went on circuit only for a few years, merely to gain experience of men and affairs. Even Pitt practised as a barrister in the early 1780s. But of these noble lawyers, perhaps only the brothers of the Earl of Buchan, the Hon. Henry and Hon. Thomas Erskine, who dominated the Scots and English Bars respectively in the 1790s (the latter making £10,000 a year at the height of his practice), and the Hon. Spencer Perceval can be said to have made successful full-time legal careers. John Campbell, later Lord Chancellor, explained:

'Practice at the English bar depends by no means so much upon family interests as at the Scotch, and whoever distinguishes himself is sure of employment. Those who have powerful connections no doubt have a much better opportunity for displaying their talents, but if they are dull and dissipated no interest however great can push them on. They must yield to those who, joining attention to talent, have shone into notice notwithstanding the seemingly impenetrable fog in which fate has enveloped them.'[61]

There were few short cuts. While on circuit relatives of local magnates might find cases in individual county towns merely on the strength of the family name, but few families' influence extended over even two county towns. In London, the favouritisms of political and social life cut no ice in the law courts, where the ability to cajole juries was of more value than connections. The most important thing was to be well-known to the attorneys who were the source of briefs, but systematically buttering up to attorneys, which was known as *huggery,* was altogether disapproved of, probably as much out of snobbishness as on grounds of professional ethics.

The recognized route to becoming Lord Chief Justice was via the office of Solicitor-General, then Attorney-General, or possibly Master of the Rolls, posts that were given only to active politicians. But the puisne judges were appointed out of the ranks of the profession, and were often the scions of the minor gentry who would have had much less chance of flourishing in the Church or in the Army. The names of the puisne judges of the 1800s—Sir Soulden Laurence, Sir Nash Grose, Sir Simon le Blanc, Sir Alan Chambré, Sir Beaumont Hotham—have a Plantagenet flavour, as if their eponymous forebears had been knights at Crécy or Agincourt. Such romantic notions are actually confirmed by closer investigation: Sir Soulden Laurence was descended from a knight whose gallantry at the Siege of Acre had been regarded by Richard Coeur de Lion with a grant of a coat of arms; Sir Alan Chambré, son of the Recorder of Kendal, traced his ancestry back to the Norman Conquest; an ancestor of Sir Beaumont Hotham had been Sheriff of York in 1218. As representatives of the King and of the majesty of the law, girded about by the complex theatre of their already anachronistic costumes, their stately progress from assize town to assize town, and the drama of the trial process itself, they were able to exert an authority which their private means would not have entitled them to assume, and in doing so they asserted, not so much the vicarious authority of the King but the substantial equality which existed between the poorest gentleman and the most magnificent noble.

Local Control
But essentially the basis of upper class power was local, and it was at the local level that clientage systems were most evident, and the influence of aristocratic individuals was most deferred to. In Scotland individual noblemen owned a great part of the land surface of several counties—the Countess of Sutherland over 90 per cent of Sutherland, the Duke of Buccleuch over 40 per cent of Dumfries, the Duke of Richmond 40 per cent of Banff—and

thereby added to the surviving sanctions of the clan system the advantages of a landlord's power over his tenantry. This was not the case in England. Fourteen per cent of the land surface of Derbyshire, including much of the Peak District, was owned by the Duke of Devonshire; 14 per cent of Northumberland by the Duke of Northumberland; 11 per cent of Bedfordshire by the Duke of Bedford. These were exceptions, and the three dukes in question were exceptionally powerful within those counties. In general, however, the local power of magnates derived less from the direct control of large estates and numerous tenants than from a complex system of clientage, especially the manipulation of local institutions. Even in Derbyshire, Northumberland and Bedfordshire over 85 per cent of the land, and perhaps more than 85 per cent of the wealth, was owned by persons not directly under the influence of the individuals who nevertheless contrived to dominate the life of these three counties.

Calculations showing the percentage of each country that was included in estates over 10,000 acres give no useful indication of the realities of institutional organization.[62] Cambridgeshire, one of the counties with the smallest proportion of great estates—only 11 per cent of total acreage—was in fact dominated by the Earl of Hardwicke, whose own possessions comprised less than four per cent of the county's territory. Buckinghamshire and Cumberland, also low on the list—only 19 per cent in great estates—were controlled to an even greater extent by the Marquess of Buckingham and the Earl of Lonsdale respectively. On the other hand, Dorset and Wiltshire, with 36 per cent of total acreage in great estates, managed to elude the control of individual magnates, because instead of having one dominant family they had numerous great families whose power cancelled out one another's at the county level, while at the same time the gentry were sufficiently numerous and independently minded to combine informally to resist an aristocratic take-over.

The overwhelming power of a few great magnates in certain counties may seem to imply a fallacy in the idea that noblemen and gentlemen belonged to a virtually unified social caste. In fact the most powerful magnates often had inferior rank in the peerage, and smaller incomes, than other noblemen who for local reasons had not been able to accumulate a similiar extent of power, and even the most firmly controlled local 'empire' depended on the co-operation and active friendship of the local gentry. The Dukes of Devonshire, Northumberland and Bedford did not so much rule their counties, as preside over local patronage networks of which the upper ranks, at least, consisted of men sufficiently well born to assume a social equality in their conduct to the dukes.

Foremost amongst the institutions which a great magnate might seek to control was the county administration. The senior official functionary in each county was the Lord Lieutenant, who was responsible for the defence of the county, and the administration of the militia and volunteers, and who was normally also *Custos Rotulorum,* or principal magistrate. (In County Durham, the Bishop of Durham was always *custos rotulorum;* in 1800 the Earl of Darlington was Lord Lieutenant, without civil authority.) The Lord Lieutenant was usually the leading peer in each country; when a Lord Lieutenancy became vacant (usually by death, for resignation was unusual and the dismissal of the Duke of Norfolk from the Lieutenancy of the West Riding in 1798, and of his successor Earl Fitzwilliam in 1819 were both exceptional) the government would hope to appoint a peer friendly to itself, but its choice was limited in that the Lord Lieutenant could hardly succeed in his post unless he already had great local prestige. For this reason, on the deaths of the Duke of Devonshire in 1811 and of the Marquess of Buckingham in 1813, their sons were appointed in succession even though they were in opposition; no other appointee would have been influential enough. Similarly, when the Duke of Northumberland resigned the Lieutenancy of Northumberland in May 1798 the Home Secretary was unable to find a successor; a letter from the Duke reminding the government of his resignation was impatiently endorsed 'There is no doing any thing with this *pettish* Duke but to find Persons to take the Lieut:cy in commission for there is no *individual* to take it'.[63] When there was no one commanding influence, the government had more scope as to choice: Lord Rodney was appointed Lord Lieutenant of Radnorshire in 1805 even though he had no property in that county. Four men were Lords Lieutenant of pairs of adjacent counties: the Earl of Powis of Shropshire and Montgomeryshire, the Duke of Beaufort of Brecknockshire and Monmouthshire, the Earl of Lonsdale of Cumberland and Westmorland, and Sir Watkin Williams Wynn of Denbighshire and Merionethshire; the Earl of Uxbridge was Lord-Lieutenant of two counties not adjacent, Anglesey and Staffordshire.

Though the Lord Lieutenant had little to do with the routine county administration, his responsibility for nominating deputy lieutenants and (as *Custos*) JPs and for corresponding with the Home Department, gave him much real power, which was customarily wielded in favour of his own family interest. 'I have no further concern', wrote the Earl of Powis, '. . . than to take care that the situation I have the honour to hold is not degraded and as Guardian and Trustee of the Powis family to maintain its influence intact'.[64]

Yet it is not always clear how much room for manoeuvre the Lord Lieutenant had. The Duke of Norfolk's standing orders for the nomination of JPs in the West Riding were probably standard: a list was drawn up of all persons possessing over £300 per annum, and adult heirs of 'principal persons', adding all the county's barristers, and striking out all the practising attorneys and manufacturers. The list was then submitted to the Sessions at Pontefract for more striking out, and to the county MPs who could add extra names.[65] In 1795 the list submitted under this system by the Lord Lieutenant of Devon to his assembled JPs was returned unopened; not that the JPs had no wish to recommend insertions or omissions, but because they 'did not choose to be the persons who were *finally* to determine it'.[66]

Areas lacking JPs sometimes petitioned for local residents to be appointed to the bench.[67] Objections were noted from a variety of sources: of five clergymen successfully objected to in Devon in 1795, one was denounced to the Lord Lieutenant by an anonymous letter beginning, 'The groans of thousands oppressed by the Reverend Thomas Pearce Hockin in his justiciary Capacity can reach y[r] Lordship's ear thro no other channel than that of an anonymous correspondence'; two others were 'objected to by the Justices of the Barnstaple Division as an obnoxious person', another was 'a bad man in every respect', and the fifth was 'objected to by the Bishop'.[68]

Some Lord Lieutenant had evidently more control of nominations than others: in Derbyshire and Sussex clergymen, who were commonly JPs in other counties, were excluded from the bench; in Norfolk, political factors influenced nominations, as is shown by a curious letter from the Earl of Orford, the Lord Lieutenant, to Coke of Holkham in February 1807:

'I am truly sorry to trouble you once more but in my list of Justices of the peace I omitted the name of a Gentleman in this neighbourhood who I perceive voted for you. I have therefore inserted the list as Corrected by the insertion of the Name of Mr Dennis Gunton of Matlask.'

This was endorsed by Windham, one of the county MPs and a Cabinet minister, 'Did not Mr G. vote against me & is not he supposed to be very much [illegible] over to [Blackling?] Ask Mr. Lukin.' And Lukin, Windham's nephew, added a further note, 'Yes he certainly is not entitled to any favour from you'.[69]

The second county institution which a magnate might wish to control was the county representation in Parliament. In some counties the gentry considered it a point of honour that noblemen's sons should *not* be elected as knights of the shire, for the pretensions of the son of a peer still living derived mainly from his

status as his father's representative, and in the more independent
counties it was considered desirable to elect people on their own
personal claims. Wiltshire, Somersetshire, Cornwall, Devon, Essex
and Cheshire never returned peers' sons in this period, and
Northamptonshire only in the brief 1806-7 Parliament. Viscount
Althorp's success in Northamptonshire in 1806 was in spite of
considerable opposition to him on the grounds of his being a
peer's son:

> 'the Lords have already purchased most of the Boroughs in
> the Kingdom, and so send pretty nigh Half the Members of
> Parliament already; and if we are Fools enough to let them send
> the *other* Half, by electing their Sons for the *Counties*—why,
> their Business is done, and then good bye to our Liberty!'[70]

Propaganda in Althorp's favour argued:

> 'Exclude the Aristocracy from all Connexion with the soundest
> Part of our Constitution—cut them off from all confidential
> Intercourse with the People—teach them to think and feel of
> and for themselves, and themselves alone—and you extinguish
> that Spirit which animates them to guard your Rights and
> Privileges with the same Zeal and Attention with which they
> guard their own.'[71]

Elsewhere however the county representation was accepted as a
proper ambition for the son of the leading magnate, and the two
seats of a county would either be shared between the candidate of
the gentry and the candidate of the prevailing noble interest, as in
Lancashire, Derbyshire and Lincolnshire, or else shared between
two noble interests as in Buckinghamshire, Huntingdonshire,
Cambridgeshire and Sussex. In Westmorland, uniquely, both
county seats were controlled by one interest, that of the Earl of
Lonsdale, who also controlled one of the Cumberland seats. The
counties were not contested as often as boroughs, and when they
were it was not the custom for landlords to force their tenants to
vote for the candidate of the landlord's choice, as was the practice
in Ireland. The election of county MPs in fact was normally less a
display of the power of influence than an affirmation of the spirit
of compromise on which influence depended. The contest in Norfolk
in 1806 which cost £70,000, and in Yorkshire in 1807, in which
nearly a quarter of a million pounds were spent, were object
lesson in what might ensue if local compromise broke down.

As well as proclaiming a family's local prestige, and excluding
possible rivals from the *éclat* of being the county representative,
the control of county seats was a means of power in itself. County
MPs regularly sat on parliamentary select committees investigating problems relating to their localities, and had great weight in
their deliberations, and it was also the custom of the county MPs

to be consulted on the disposal of government patronage—tax receiverships, posts in the excise and so forth—within their county. Thus while the Lord Lieutenant handled the routine communication between Whitehall and his county, the county MPs had a more active role in directing patronage and government policy initiatives with regard to the provinces. Edward Harbord—MP for a borough rather than a county, though it was a borough large enough to involve a network of influence almost as widespread as that of a county—was able to answer his father's protests at his intention of giving up Parliament:

'As to my being justifiable in thus abandoning the interests of my family after the money that has been spent in bringing me into Parliament for Yarmouth, I have only to answer that the money so spent has, I think, been well spent. Your Lord Lieutenancy and Petre's [his brother-in-law] Receiver Generalship have been the consequence. In point of pecuniary advantage to the family, the Receiver Generalship pays more than the interest of the capital sunk.'72

Few families were quite as unsentimental in their calculations as the Harbords, but in this instance Harbord was merely saying what was usually taken for granted.

A third way in which a magnate could exert influence was through the Militia, the Yeomanry, the Volunteers, and the Local Militia set up in 1808 to replace the Volunteers. In the Militia proper the soldiers were chosen by ballot and since being an officer was, in war time, a full-time job, the officers below the rank of colonel were not usually drawn from the best local families: they included a number of regular soldiers commissioned from the ranks who found in the Militia employment for their declining years. The colonels however were frequently local peers, and in the Berkshire, Buckinghamshire, Cambridgeshire, Cumberland, Durham, Gloucestershire, Huntingdonshire, Leicestershire, Monmouthshire, Shropshire, Somerset, Sussex and the 1st West Riding regiments, the colonel was the Lord Lieutenant; in Buckinghamshire, moreover, the second-in-command was the Lord Lieutenant's son, and in Cambridgeshire, the Lord Lieutenant's brother.

In the Yoemanry and Volunteers, the units were formed on the initiative of local gentlemen, and the troops had to volunteer, and so these institutions were effectively an agency for strengthening already existing bonds of local influence. Consequently they were more aristocratic than the Militia. Thus, for example, while the Northamptonshire Militia had no titled officers at all, the Northamptonshire Yeomanry had Earl Spencer as colonel, Earl Fitzwilliam as lieutenant-colonel, and the Hon. George Watson, the

Earl of Carysfort, and the Earl of Pomfret amongst the captains. The extra prestige of the Yeomanry was also evident from the fact that some men were officers in both, with more junior rank in the Yeomanry, even though it was Militia officers who had seniority over Yoemanry officers of equivalent rank rather than the other way round; thus Richard Calcraft was a captain in the Dorset Militia and a lieutenant in the Yeomanry, and the Hon. William Grimston a captain-lieutenant in the Hertfordshire Militia and a lieutenant in the Yeomanry.

Participation in such units took up a great deal of time and energy, and local magnates often took a leading part not so much in a deliberate attempt to extend their influence but in response to the expectations of neighbours and clients. Earl Fitzwilliam, who was colonel of the 1st Regiment of West Riding militia, colonel of the West Riding Yeomanry, and lieutenant-colonel of the Northamptonshire Yeomanry probably gained little additional leverage in county affairs from his investment of time, but he at least had the satisfaction of doing what was expected of him.

At the same time, it was evident that in some counties magnates made a deliberate attempt to monopolize commands: whereas there were 27 different Volunteer and Yeomanry units in Berkshire in 1804, and 50 in Derbyshire, all with different commanding officers, in Buckinghamshire there were only six, of much larger average size of course, all commanded by the same man, the Marquess of Buckingham, who was also Lord-Lieutenant and colonel of the Militia: his lieutenant-colonels in the three Yeomanry regiments (which, being cavalry, were more prestigious than the volunteer units, which were infantry) were his two brothers and a family friend. Not that the Volunteer system altogether succeeded as an agency of aristocratic influence. In the 1801 Devon food riots, so many Volunteers refused to act or even joined the rioters, that the two corps had to be disbanded, and others were purged: 33 out of 51 privates in the Kingsbridge Volunteers, for example, were dismissed. Some Volunteer units in towns adopted unmilitary regulations, such as a system of blackball with regard to prospective recruits, or the settling of disputes not by the CO but by a committee. In some respects they resembled working men's loyalist clubs rather than anything else, but in the country the Volunteers were merely a department, however imperfect, of landlord control.

Impact of the Industrial Revolution
There were few signs of any challenge to the hegemony of the upper class in this period. One MP thought that the failure of the Foxite Whigs after 1807 was due in part to the support given to

the government by the great increase of the number of mercantile men in the H. of C. above all former precedent, & their having become from the circumstances of the war & the new commercial system more entirely in the power of Government than ever'.[74] In reality the extension of aristocratic control meant that despite the growth of the commercial sector the number of genuinely mercantile MPs increased only fractionally. There had always been a number of them, of course, but they had never established themselves as a pressure group, and did not do so during the Industrial Revolution. For many of them, like the first Sir Robert Peel, a seat in Parliament was a means, like his baronetcy and his carefully acquired landed estate, of buying himself into the upper class. Commercial wealth, despite the increase of class exclusiveness, was generally respected, and Peel even set himself up as a parliamentary expert on commercial issues, but it can hardly be said that he cultivated a distinction between himself and the old landed families. At the same time the leaders thrown up by the aristocratic system, Pitt, Grenville, Perceval, though they had their roots in landed estates in southern England, showed themselves sympathetic to the new commercial developments.

Perhaps the only instance of the emergent industrial society coming into head-on collision with the old order was at Preston, a town which had long been dominated by the gentry and by the great landed magnate of the area, the Earl of Derby. In 1791 John Horrocks, a 23-year-old ex-quarryman from near Bolton, who had established himself in a small way as a trader in cotton yarn, quarrelled with John Watson, one of his customers in Preston, and decided to establish himself in Preston in direct competition with his ex-customer. Watson was the protégé of the Earl of Derby but Horrocks found favour with the corporation which resented Derby's influence, and his business flourished. He was made a bailiff (deputy mayor) in 1794, and in the 1796 General Election was run unsuccessfully by the corporation against the Derby interest. By 1802 he had built at least five spinning factories and had erected handloom sheds and cottages in New Preston. In that year the Derby interest was obliged to concede him one of the Preston seats, but he was only an MP for two years, dying in 1804, worth £150,000, being then the second largest cotton master after Sir Robert Peel.[75] Contrary to what is usually assumed about the political impact of industrialization on party fortunes, Derby, the representative of the old order, was a Whig: Horrocks, like Peel, was a ministerialist.

The widely accepted notion that the 1832 Reform Act resulted from a confrontation between the industrial *nouveaux riches* and the old landed aristocracy, and that it must have been adumbrated

by a number of local conflicts such as the one just described at
Preston, derives from the belief that the Industrial Revolution
caused an alteration in the relative wealth of the landed and of the
commercial-industrial classes. That there was such a shift in the
long run is obvious, though it was almost certainly much greater
after 1832 than before, but it was not as large as might be assumed,
and by no means all the profits of industrialization went to bourgeois
entrepreneurs.

Noblemen were sometimes themselves entrepreneurs, though not
always very successfully. The Earl of Derby, who built a mill known
as 'Lord's Factory' in Preston in 1794 with a view to combating
Horrocks's growing influence,[76] seems to have been unfortunate in
his business associates. One, Thomas Leeming was nearly arrested
for debt, probably because of Derby's own tardiness in paying
£1,500 he owed Leeming.[77] Another, Horrocks's rival John Watson,
failed in 1807 for nearly £500,000.[78] Then there was the most
remarkable noble industrialist of them all, the ninth Earl of
Dundonald. To a much greater extent than any other industrialist
of the period, whether nobleman or commoner, Dundonald
possessed all the necessary technological know-how, but his credit
was bad, his luck was worse, and he was too unbending, too high
minded, too much the *ancien régime* gentleman to be successful in
his dealings with men much craftier and greedier than himself. He
was not only frequently cheated, even by members of his own
family, but he showed a lack of elementary judgement, for example,
a coaltar factory he established in Shropshire failed because Dundonald was quite unable to find a market for all the tar pitch and
and ammonia, which it produced.[79] Dundonald began his entre-
preneurial career supervising the coal mines on his family estate
at Culross Abbey, but as his schemes and projects multiplied, so
his debts increased, and he was finally reduced to pawning his
clothes,[80] lodging with a poor tinplate worker in Marylebone,[81]
and writing to Lady Liverpool for fifteen pounds, 'to enable me to
procure proper Cloaths to wait on Lord Liverpool and on a few
friends whom my situation precluded me from calling on During
these Ten Months past'.[82] As late as 1814, after more than ten
years of destitution and neglect by his family, Dundonald was still
sufficiently confident to be able to tell the Earl of Liverpool, 'My
late Discoveries were I possessed of the Money necessary to take
out the patents would be an ample Fortune to me But I have it *not*,
and am willing to lay all my late Discoveries and Improvements
open, on receiving a *Moderate Support* from Government.'[83] All
he received from government at this time, however, was £50 from
the Royal Bounty, which he spent on redeeming his clothes from
pawn and on buying some desperately needed shirts, stockings

and shoes.[84] Subsequently, he received small grants from the Literary Fund, but he remained in poverty till the end of his life.

Other noblemen were almost as active. Lord Delaval took a close interest, not only in his coal mines, but in his glassworks at Hartley, even taking pains personally to recruit skilled workmen for specialized processes.[85] Admiral John Elliot, uncle to the first Earl of Minto, was a partner in a lead and copper mining company. As a teenager he had toured Cornish and Yorkshire mines taking notes on practical geology and smelting techniques.[86] The Earl of Balcarres's coal mines in Lancashire went far beyond the prudent diversification of the large landowner. He actually warned his family against purchasing farmland 'as destructive to our system as colliers; it would 'keep our family in increasing poverty and distress'. His ironworks were not especially profitable, but as a coal-owner he was extremely successful; and he was active in devising new sales outlets, and even experimented with calorific values on his bedroom grate. 'Colliers we are,' he told his grandson, 'and colliers we must ever remain'.[87]

Many noblemen were inactive participants in other industrial projects: the Marquess of Stafford owned his own ironworks, the Earl of Dartmouth provided the finance for most of the textile mills on his Yorkshire estates, the Duke of Atholl was involved in the scheme to light London by gas, and so on. But perhaps in such cases their direct intervention was scarcely sufficient to justify their being called entrepreneurs. In fact the most important part played by the upper class in the Industrial Revolution was not in entrepreneurship as such, but in their control of mineral resources. As landowners the nobility dominated the mining industry, but the extent of their dominance is not normally appreciated. The current interest in the phenomenon of factory organization has tended to divert attention from the fact that mining was still the most important industry in this period, even though expanding less rapidly than textiles. And it was not only a major contributor to Britain's position in world trade—for example Britain was the world's major copper producer in this period—but it was also the one industry which by producing the fuel for power and the metal for machinery made all the others possible. Furthermore it was the major area of large-scale capital investment.

All the largest coal owners were members of the House of Lords. The Bishop of Durham was possibly the largest single coal owner in the country, being the principal owner in Co. Durham, with six and a half mines producing for export and another ten producing for local sale, with an aggregate output of nearly a million tons annually.[88] North of the Tyne, the exploitation of the Duke of Northumberland's mines increased the Alnwick rent roll from

£8,607 in 1749 to £50,000 in 1770.[89] The Earl of Carlisle and Lord Delaval were the other largest mine owners in Northumberland. In Yorkshire, Earl Fitzwilliam, the Duke of Norfolk and the earls of Pomfret and Effingham were the principal coal owners. In Nottinghamshire, the Duke of Newcastle and Lord Middleton were the largest owners. In Cumberland the Earl of Lonsdale was the greatest of the country's three great coal owning families and one of his workings at Whitehaven was the largest in Britain in the 1790s, being two and a half miles wide by one and a half miles long, and with one shaft 340 yards deep.[90] In Staffordshire, Lord Dudley owned and worked most of the coal in the south of the county, deriving from his mines more than half his income of £30,000 per annum,[91] and the Marquess of Stafford was the largest owner in the north of the country. The Duke of Bridgewater's Worsley mines were probably the largest in Lancashire, and when he died in 1803 they were added to the second Marquess of Stafford's estate. In Leicestershire the Earl of Moira was the largest coal owner; in Glamorganshire, the Marquess of Bute; in Monmouthshire the Earl of Abergavenny. Even as romantic a figure as Lord Byron was a coal owner, and married a coal heiress; after many attempts he finally sold off his family mines at Rochdale in 1823 in time to help pay for his fatal Greek venture.

The nobility's domination of the coal industry was however less total than it was in other branches of mining. Out of a total of 86 lead mines on the great lead fields of Co. Durham, the Bishop owned 23 and the Earl of Darlington 47.[92] The Duke of Devonshire owned most of the lead in Derbyshire, and Earl Grosvenor most of it in Flintshire. The principal lead mines in Scotland were those of the Earl of Hopetoun at Leadhills in Lanarkshire, and the Duke of Queensberry at Wanlockhead. One of the largest lead mines in Wales was at Rhandir-mywn, in the parish of Llanfair-ar-y-bryn, Carmarthenshire, owned by Lord Cawdor, which was said to have yielded £300,000 profit in the eighteenth century.[93] The Duke of Devonshire owned a once flourishing copper mine at Ecton-Hill, Staffordshire, but the ore was giving out by 1800. The great Parys Mountain, a hill consisting entirely of copper ore, three quarters of which was owned by the Earl of Uxbridge, had also been nearly dug out by 1800. This left the chief share of copper production to Cornwall, where Lords de Dunstanville and Falmouth were the principal owners. The Cornish mines in 1800 yielded 2,522 tons of smelted tin worth £255,000, and 5,200 tons of smelted copper.[94]

Of course, not all mine owners were themselves responsible for the exploitation of their property. All the Bishop of Durham's coal and lead mines were leased out, and all but one of the Earl of Darlington's lead mines. Lord Byron never even set eyes on his coal mines at Rochdale. The Duke of Northumberland had leased out all his mines by 1799. According to F. M. L. Thompson, there was a tendency for the great landlords to give up direct exploitation of their mineral possessions in the period after 1800 and to assume the safer role of *rentiers*.[95] This is not altogether true, and anyway not much to the point. There were, first of all, numerous instances of continued direct exploitation, as in the case of the Earl of Lonsdale's and the Earl of Balcarres's collieries. There were also several instances of landlords commencing direct exploitation only after 1800. For example, it was not till the end of the Napoleonic Wars that the Marquess of Anglesey (formely Earl of Uxbridge) took over the working of the Parys Mountain mines, and the Dudley Estate in Staffordshire only began to process its own iron after 1839; it had earlier led the way in Staffordshire in attempting to employ miners direct, instead of depending on the 'butty' system of labour sub-contracting.[96] In Co. Durham there was actually a general movement away from leases after 1800, the system 'having been found one of the most troublesome, expensive, and to the Coal Owners unproductive ever resorted to'.[97] Furthermore, the switch from direct exploitation to leasing, where it did occur, often meant little substantial difference. It certainly did not mean that the great landlords were transformed from active participants into uninvolved bystanders.

Even when a mineral owner exploited his mines directly, he did not normally run the business himself, but employed an agent to do so. On the other hand, even when a mine was leased the owner might still be actively concerned. The terms of leases varied. In Co. Durham some lessees were responsible for paying taxes and compensation for damaged ground, but more frequently it was the landlord who was responsible for these things and also for making new sinkings and for the repair and running of the pumping and winding engines.[98] It was because landlords usually had to cover the expense of new workings, new machines, new wagonways, increases in the price of fodder for the horses and the cost of furnishing the workmen's houses, yet had to leave it to the lessees' discretion to decide how far to increase or decrease production in good or bad years, and so bore the brunt themselves of market fluctuations while at the same time being at the mercy of the lessees' good will, that leasing went out of favour in Co. Durham.[99] A similar situation existed north of the Tyne, where the Duke of Northumberland continued to own part of the working stock of his leased-out collieries till the 1860s.[100]

There is no reason to suppose that men who leased mines were generally any the less jealously observed than men who leased farms. In some cases it is evident that they were more so. In South

Wales, for example, some mining leases enabled the landlord to nominate part of his tenant's workforce 'in order to render . . . an Account of the Quantity of Coal or Culm that shall be worked raised and landed . . . (but) performing the like work as other Workman in a similar situation'.[101] (The record for ignorance concerning one's own business affairs was almost certainly in the farming sector. In agricultural East Anglia, one land steward made £100,000 out of working for the Earl of Leicester,[102] and another led his master, Lord Chedworth, to believe that his estates were worth only £1,600 a year, till Pitt's income tax obliged Chedworth to learn the precise amount of his property: within a few years Chedworth had £150,000 to leave in his will.[103])

In the mining counties there were even instances of great land-owners being lessees of mines. The partnership of the Marquess of Bute, the Marquess of Hertford and Miss Simpson leased two coal mines in Co. Durham, though it is probable that the partner's superintendance was confined to inspecting the annual balance sheets. The Earl of Strathmore, Sir Thomas Liddell (created Lord Ravensworth in 1821) and James Stuart Wortley (nephew of the Marquess of Bute, and created Lord Wharncliffe in 1826) operated on an even grander scale, owning and leasing mines in North-humberland, Durham and the West Riding, and being known as 'The Grand Allies'.

Thus in terms neither of profits nor of personal involvement, was it the case that the upper class were by-passed by the Industrial Revolution. The real shift of economic power came later in the nineteenth century. In 1800, they were still firmly entrenched in all the commanding sectors of British society.

2
Voters And Public Opinion

Voters

BELOW the ruling class there was a much larger (though still relatively small) class whose co-operation was necessary to the ruling class—the voters. Many of the ruling class were themselves voters, of course; but most voters had no pretence to gentility, and not the least prospect of entering Parliament, and recognized themselves as very much junior partners in the system of government.

In 1800 there were about 300,000 parliamentary electors in Britain, nearly all male, though a small handful of women were entitled to vote by right of burgage or freehold tenures. Perhaps five-ninths of the voters were freeholders in the county constituencies, but in every county the freeholders included many inhabitants of towns which came within the county boundaries. In Middlesex 63 per cent of the county electorate was urban, in Hampshire, Durham, and Surrey 34 per cent.[1] Consequently, taking county and borough electors together, less than half of all voters were countrymen, squires, parsons, tenant farmers, yeomen, graziers, village tradesmen, who came within the standard pattern of paternalist dependence and deference: the urban voters, who stood slightly to one side of the aristocratic-dominated society, were not only more numerous but proportionately returned more members to Parliament, because of the much smaller average size of borough constituencies: the 40 English counties had only two MPs each while there were 203 English boroughs, two returning four MPs, five returning one, and the rest two each.

The urban voters had no uniform socio-economic status. This was because there were five major types of franchise amongst the 203 English boroughs. There were 12 boroughs where the vote was enjoyed by the resident householders, the largest being Northampton with 1,000 voters, the smallest St. Germans with 20. There were 92 boroughs where the vote was enjoyed by freemen; included in this group were boroughs where both freemen and householders had the vote, as at Bedford, and boroughs where both freemen and freeholders within the town boundary had the vote, as at Nottingham, Exeter and Bristol. London, where the voters were not freemen as such but members of the livery companies, was the largest such constituency with 7,000 voters, and Camelford was the smallest with 20. Ten of the 12 Welsh borough constituencies also had a freeman franchise. Then there were 37 English boroughs where the voting qualification depended on the payment of local rates known in this instance as Scot and Lot. The largest of these were Westminster with over 12,000 voters and Southwark with 2,000, and the smallest was Gatton, with one voter who owned all six houses in the borough, occupied one and rented out the other five by the week.[2] The Flintshire boroughs of Flint, Caergwrle, Caerwys, Overton and Rhuddlan, which returned one member between them, also had a Scot and Lot franchise. In 27 English boroughs the vote was restricted to members of the corporation who recruited themselves by co-option. Beaumaris in Wales also had a corporation franchise, and in Scotland all 15 burgh constituencies were effectively corporation boroughs — 14 of the constituencies were groups of four or five burghs from which the corporations appointed representatives to elect the MP, and in Edinburgh the corporation elected one MP direct. Finally, in 35 English boroughs, ranging from Malton with 300 voters to Old Sarum, an uninhabited field with seven voters chosen on election day by the prioprietor, the with seven voters chosen on election day by the proprietor, Lord Camelford, the vote depended on the ownership of certain

Except in the burgage boroughs which were all small, and in the corporation boroughs, of which only Bath was a large urban centre, the franchise was broad enough to include most of those who had been successful in their trades or professions, but in some boroughs the franchise was no broader than that, in some places much broader. Many freemen, for example, were relatively poor, some were not even householders, and in some boroughs it was not even necessary for them to reside locally in order to retain their voting rights. A prosperous tradesman living in his native town where there was a freeman franchise would probably be a freeman voter; it did not follow that all his brother freemen would be prosperous, or even as well off as many who were not freemen. Also the average income of freemen varied from place to place, depending on the vagaries of local political as well as local economic conditions. For some freemen their votes were virtually their sole possession: a businessman conversing in a Sheffield public house with poor men from whom he was collecting rent on behalf of 'a decayed old lady' was surprised to find that one of them, who had been involved in the recent Sheffield food riots, was a freeman of Lincoln and that he had 'sold his vote, though he talked so loudly of Reform.'[3] At the same time the Westminster Scot and Lot franchise, though it excluded half the adult males of the city, was evidently much wider than any freeholder franchise. Voters, in fact, ranged from near paupers (though if they were actually paupers they might lose their vote) to fabulously wealthy London merchant princes, country gentlemen and peers' sons voting by right of the title deeds of town houses.

Yet only a fraction of people within this income range actually had the vote, such were the local anomalies. In 1803, 1,059,314 persons were assessed as having annual incomes over £60;[4] some voters were probably below this income level; most would have been above, but they numbered less than a third of the total of people with incomes over £60. There is no breakdown by income levels for tax assessments after 1801, but in 1801, when only 320,759 persons were assessed, the breakdown was as follows:

£60 — 95 per annum	140,429 worth	£9,555,854
£95 — 130 per annum	59,457 worth	£6,133,636
£130 — 165 per annum	33,407 worth	£4,626,541
£165 — 200 per annum	18,406 worth	£3,209,074
£200 — 500 per annum	42,694 worth	£12,239,081
£500 — 1,000 per annum	14,762 worth	£9,498,471
£1,000 — 2,000 per annum	6,927 worth	£9,041,154
£2,000 — 5,000 per annum	3,657 worth	£10,402,749
£5,000 upwards per annum	1,020 worth	£9,970,394

As these figures omit 70 per cent of those later assessed as having incomes over £60 they provide only a rough guide, but it may be presumed that it was mainly persons in the lower income groups, say under £200 per annum, who escaped assessment in 1801. Some of the richer persons who were disqualified from voting because they were peers. Probably everyone with an income over £200 per annum and not a peer, could vote; in which case, with only 300,000 voters altogether, fewer than a quarter of those in the £60-200 per annum bracket could have been voters. It was anomalies at the £200 and under income level that the 1832 Reform Act attempted to eliminate: it was certainly not aimed at enfranchizing industrial plutocrats, many of whom probably had simultaneous voting rights in several different constituencies long before 1832.

Probably the only thing that can be stated about the urban electorate as a whole is that it included a large proportion of Dissenters. Undoubtedly the majority of voters gave such religious allegiance as they had to the Established Church, but it is probable that as Dissent was a middle-class phenomenon most adult male Dissenters had the vote (though in corporation boroughs where formal notice was still taken of their legal disabilities they were of course excluded from the electorate). Consequently the political significance of Dissent was greater than its overall numbers might suggest. In Norwich and the county of Essex, Dissenters provided the core of the Whig vote; they were also a major force in boroughs such as Maldon, Sudbury, Lewes and Taunton. At Bridport it was even said one of the MPs 'maintained His parliamentary interest . . . by professing to be a *Dissenter*'.[5]

Essentially, however, the urban vote had no general characteristics as its mobilization depended on factors such as numbers and organization which were different in almost every borough. Most smaller boroughs were controlled by systems of clientage similar to those prevailing in the surrounding countryside. In some boroughs the obligations of dependence were enforced with a strictness such as would rarely be attempted in any other sphere. In the 1802 election, the electors of Ilchester, where the vote was exercised by all inhabitant householders not receiving poor relief, voted against the interest of the patron Sir William Manners, who revenged himself by pulling down 100 out of the 160 houses in the town, and building a workhouse to accommodate those who had defied him.[6] At Malton a revolt by Earl Fitzwilliam's tenants was followed by a wave of evictions, and other tenants were instructed to dismiss employees who had voted on the wrong side: a list drawn up at the time entitled, 'Names and Number of Persons to be turned out of their Houses in Malton in consequence of their Bad Conduct in 1807 and 1808', is still preserved in the family records.[7]

Other patrons strove to make their favour indispensable. The Duke of Leeds not only built lavish municipal buildings at Helston but paid the poor and church rates (about £1,000 p.a.) for the whole town.[8] The Duke of Marlborough maintained his influence with the freemen voters of Oxford by providing banners for the trade companies and game for freemen's club dinners.[9] Such gifts were not seen as bribery: the Earl of Radnor described his influence at Salisbury, a little ingenuously, as:

'an Interest neither begun, nor kept up by the gross Mode of Corruption, nor the common Mode of obtaining Favors from Government. It has . . . been preserved by individual Attentions, & general upright and fair Conduct—'

and then he added as an afterthought:
> '—I might add the very handsome Council House erected at my sole Expense of many Thousand Pounds must have some Hold upon honourable Minds.'[10]

In some boroughs, noblemen even accepted the position of Mayor in order to consolidate their influence. The personal element was emphasied by the custom of holding lavish celebrations of the patron's family festivals, such as twenty-first birthdays and weddings, so that the connection with a patron provided the excuse and the funds for the largest bean-feasts normally held in a small town. Sometimes the initiative for such celebrations came not from the patron himself, but from his supporters, as was the case with Lord Stanley's birthday feast at Preston in 1796.[11] At Higham Ferrers, one of Earl Fitzwilliam's proprietary boroughs, his son's coming of age was the occasion for the donation of a roasted ox to the townspeople; even more lavish entertainment was provided at Fitzwilliam's two country houses, Milton in Northamptonshire and Wentworth in the West Riding; at Wentworth three oxen, 26 sheep, two bullocks, three lambs, three calves, ten hams, 54 fowls, 72 hogsheads of ale, six of small beer, 473 bottles of wine and 79 bottles of spirit were provided.[12] Elections themselves were the occasion for feasting and drunkenness at the patron's expense, especially if there was a contest. The bill for the Liskeard by-election in 1804 included the cost of 563 bottles of port, 19 of madeira, 40 of sherry, 48 of Lisbon, £13-worth of punch, £16 17s 6d-worth of negus, and the cost of 18 dozen bottles 'broke & taken away'.[13]

In some small boroughs, however, an established patron-client system had broken down, and there was a free for all, votes being sold to the highest bidder, and the right to vote being regarded, not as a means to repay favours, but merely as an occasional source of income. These venal boroughs were often thought of as being degenerate, economically stagnant places, inhabited by mercenary wretches devoid of community spirit. In fact the physical seediness of such venal boroughs, as compared to the prosperous neatness of boroughs flourishing under the influence of a patron, was largely due to the fact that, having no patron, they had no one to pay for new public buildings. The townspeople themselves were not necessarily less politically self-conscious, merely because of the absence of a clientage system. It was at an election in the proprietary corporation borough of Malmesbury that the patron was told by his agent, 'You must take care, Sir, to make the burgesses remember the names before going to the town-hall on Tuesday', and, on answering, 'I will take care of that, I will write them down', was informed, 'That won't do, Sir, for the burgesses cannot read'.[14] In some small non-proprietary boroughs caucuses were formed to organize the selling of votes to the best bidders.

Arundel had such a society, known as the Malt-house Club, and New Shoreham had a similar organization known as the Christian Society, the improper activities of which had resulted in the electorate being altered by statute in 1770.

In the very largest boroughs, the patron was replaced by the faction. The pyramid of clientage was surmounted, not by some wealthy outsider, some *deus ex machina* prepared to invest his time and outside revenues in establishing his tutelage, but by rival cliques of political bosses whose social and financial interests were bound up much more integrally with the life of the town. In Ipswich the rival factions were known as the Blues and the Yellows; in Retford the Blues and the Pinks; in Bristol it was the Union Club *versus* the Steadfast Society, and later the Loyal and Constitutional Club *versus* the White Lion Club, and in Norwich the Blues and Whites *versus* the Oranges and Purples. In Nottingham, where the vote was held by both freemen and freeholders, the rivalry was between the poorer freemen, who identified themselves with the Whiggish corporation which granted them their freedoms, and the freeholders who were in general both more affluent and more conservative. In the 1806 election, the corporation not only called on all its tenants to vote for the reformer Joseph Birch, but also promised to find homes for all persons evicted by landlords for voting for him.[15] At Exeter, Leicester, Liverpool and Norwich, the corporations were Anglican, and the opposing factions had a core of Dissenters. Such constituencies often experienced extremely violent and expensive elections, in which the candidates (more accustomed to the amenities of Park Lane drawing rooms) found themselves caught up in local feuds for which they had neither comprehension nor sympathy.

Not all large constituencies were like that, of course. In others, the voters prided themselves on their sobriety and intelligence. A candidate canvassing the trade companies of Newcastle upon Tyne in 1807 reported:

'We met with the same attention as at the late time (hardly 4 months) without any apparent distinction between Mr Brandling & myself except from a Shoemaker (Callaway) who in the Cordwainers Company made an Attack upon me respecting the Bill, invidiously called the Catholick Bill, my Explanation I believe gave Satisfaction to everyone except the Accuser, and we concluded the Business about ¼ Past 4 o Clock.'[16]

Yet such instances of public interest in national issues seem to have been rare in elections. To a large extent, voting seemed one thing, public opinion another.

Public Opinion

What was public opinion? 'When I talk of the Sense of the People', said one coadjutor of the elder Pitt,' I mean the Middling People of England—the Manufacturer, the Yeoman, the Merchant, the Country Gentn, they who bear all the heat of the day, and pay all the Taxes to supply the Expenses of Court and Government'.[17] Forty years later few people would have quarrelled with this definition. But though there is a certain analytic utility in thus excluding from consideration the non-tax-paying majority of the population, there still remains enormous difficulty in assessing precisely what 'the Middling People of England' as a group thought. Not all of them had the vote, and the electoral system was scarcely designed to reflect even the personal views of the voters. The difficulty was familiar to contemporaries too, and often enough they referred not to public opinion as such, but to the talk of the City of London, which was relatively easy to assess from the gossip of the coffee houses and of the Exchange, and from the fluctuations of government stock. But too much reliance on the opinion of London could be misleading, as one foreign observer noted:

> 'Notwithstanding their lamentations and complaints, and the avowed expectation of a dreadful crisis, the inhabitants of London live just as if they had nothing to fear; amuse themselves, and attend to their business in perfect security. It would seem as if all this clamour was only a habit, a sort of plaintive mania,—and yet they appear so much in earnest that I do not know what to think of it.'[18]

Yet for most of those involved in parliamentary politics, the remoteness of public opinion was due less to difficulties of analysis than to its irrelevance. Of course the upper class were not totally contemptuous of public feeling: MPs of counties and of the larger towns had to keep their voters contented, and the clientage system worked both ways, requiring the solicitude of the patron as well as the deference of the client. Though the British government devoted much less energy to internal propaganda than the Napoleonic régime in contemporary France,[10] considerable importance was attached to public impressions. This for example was the basis of Lord Grenville's objections to systematic opposition, that it would discredit all politicians in the public mind. In 1794 Burke wrote, 'Opinion (never without its effect) has obtained a greater dominion over human affairs than ever it possessed; and...must grow just in proportion as the implicit reverence for old institutions is found to decline.'[20] Nevertheless there was a sense in which public opinion could not affect the politicians. For the most part it could not affect their parliamentary seats, for only in the city of Westminster did public alienation find effective electoral expression.

The indifference of politicians was bolstered by the constitu-

tional theories of the day which did not favour the participation of
the general population in the parliamentary process. Indeed one
minister, William Windham, while acknowledging the right of
Foxite MPs to denounce the war with France as unjust and unnecessary, asked, 'was it a desirable thing that the public at
large, that the lower classes of the community from one end of the
kingdom to the other, should, from day to day, be told so?'[21]
Eight years later an anonymous writer claimed,
   'supposing a ministry even ever so depraved at heart, (and how
   dare any person pretend to judge of the heart of man,) no one
   in England, (out of parliament,) is warranted by law, justice,
   honesty, or any other principle, in publishing observations
   upon the existing government of this country, tending to make
   one individual regard that government with contempt, distrust, or hatred.'[22]
Four years later again, Charles Yorke caused a furore by demanding that the newspaper reporters should be cleared out of
the gallery of the Commons during the discussion of the Walcheren
expedition: but most of his fellow MPs admitted the propriety of
his proposal. Once elected MPs regarded themselves as independent of the electors. Much of the contemporary disapproval of
systematic opposition politics derived from fears of its effect in
arousing public controversy. On the whole politicians regarded
public curiosity about government affairs with suspicion. Thus
the real significance of public opinion at this time was not its
impact on Parliament, so much as the fact that there developed
a political consciousness separate from, and largely hostile to,
parliamentary politics.

The Press
The public interest in current events is evident from the circulation of newspapers. During periods of peace, 1802-3 and after
1815, when there was less chance of extraordinary developments,
the circulation of newspapers fell. Until 1855 each newspaper had
to be stamped, this being a means both of government control
and of raising revenue, and the fluctuations of circulation can be
gauged from the fluctuations in the sales of newspaper stamps.

	Number of stamps sold (England only)	Value of stamps
1800	—	£176,425
1801	15,090,805	£173,857
1802	14,264,289	£160,055
1803	15,885,921	£192,041
1804	16,921,768	£205,638

	Number of stamps sold (England only)	Value of stamps
1814	24,931,910	£304,962
1815	23,075,985	£301,218
1816	21,053,627	£285,064[23]

Though often assumed to be a vehicle of public opinion, newspapers at this time were largely the adjuncts of the increasingly discredited parliamentary politics. Only William Cobbett's *The Political Register*, Henry White's *The Independent Whig* and Benjamin Flower's *The Cambridge Advertiser* took a determinedly independent anti-Establishment line; other independently minded newspapers like *The Sheffield Register*, *The Manchester Herald*, *The Edinburgh Gazetteer*, *The Argus* and *The Newark Herald* which had made some impact in the 1790s had been driven out of business by prosecution or difficulties of circulation. *The Times* which with 5,000 copies sold each day had one of the widest circulations of any paper, transformed itself from an organ of Addington's government (1801-1804) into a respectable independent daily, but the views it expressed were generally moderate and unadventurous, and it contained a much smaller proportion of editorial opinion than, say, *The Political Register*. It was described as having 'great influence on the public mind, especially on the mercantile world', and one of the ministers was told in 1808:

> 'Till of late it was much more with you than against you, and at the same time, from the independent spirit which it breathed, and the broad British ground which it took, it did you more good than any other newspaper.'[24]

The Courier, selling 5,800 copies a day, was the government mouthpiece; *The Morning Chronicle*, selling 3,400 a day, was the Foxite organ, though one Foxite leader thought it 'but little conducive to the political interests of our friends, it seemed to be wholy (sic) devoted to Advertisements.'[25]

The Times, *The Courier*, *The Morning Chronicle*, and the other London dailies consisted only of four closely printed sides. During the parliamentary session reports of important debates might take up nearly the entire paper, but the usual format was advertisements all over the front page and on part of the second, and news, public announcements, stock market and law reports filling the rest. Because of difficulties of transportation and printing (even the press invented by Earl Stanhope could print only 250 sheets an hour), London papers had little circulation outside the metropolis. Provincial papers contained more advertising, less news (and that largely copied from the London papers) and almost no comment. They made dull enough reading, and their real importance was not as propaganda, for they contained very little such, but as means of keeping readers informed of what was going on. In many ways the bald paragraphs of news, the lengthy transcripts of debates, gave the public a very meagre notion of what the men and issues of the day really stood for. Even London editors were often badly informed; more than one had difficulty distinguishing between the Marquess of Buckingham, Lord Grenville's brother, and the Earl of Buckinghamshire, the ally of Lord Sidmouth. Nevertheless such information as the public had to form its opinions on, did derive from the papers. They did not lead opinion, they fed it.

This was not in fact the belief of politicians. Sir Arthur Wellesley thought 'newspapers . . . rule every thing in this country'.[26] Large sums of money were paid out by the government in subsidizing friendly papers. *The Courier* received perhaps as much as £2,000 for supporting the Perceval ministry late in 1809.[27] Lewis Goldsmith was paid £1,200 a year for two years running, 1811 and 1812, for his *The Anti-Gallican Monitor*.[28] Friendly editors were also helped with advance notice of official news and by concealed subsidies in the form of advertisements by various government departments: the discrimination of Pitt's second ministry against the Whig *The Morning Chronicle* and the patronage of the Talents ministry 1806-7 can be seen in the following figures for departmental advertisements in that paper between 1804 and 1810:

1804	419
1805	112
1806	609
1807	666
1808	535
1809	370
1810	361

The Ordnance Office under the Earl of Moira, 1806-7, placed 180 advertisements in *The Morning Chronicle*. Under the Earl of Chatham, who was Master-General of the Ordnance both before and after the Talents ministry, the Office placed none at all. The Victualling Office's boycott was largely responsible for the drop in 1805 and 1809-10.[29] Yet the ministers were not always wise in their choice of which papers to subsidize—two papers owned by F. W. Blagdon which were subsidized by Perceval's ministry (1809-12) were such failures that even their names have not survived to posterity.[30] And since, in their own calculations, more daily papers were favourable to ministers than otherwise at the period of their greatest unpopularity,[31] it may well be wondered if politicians did not totally misconceive the power of the press to mould public opinion. Only a few individuals, like Windham and Charles Yorke, seem to have realized that what mattered was less the editorial slanting of news, than the straightforward, unedited statement of what was actually said and done in Parliament.

Public Meetings

The most important measure of public opinion was not the newspaper, but the public meeting. Of course, there were what were in effect public meetings at contested elections, but during elections all discussion was naturally dominated by the rival candidates, and for this reason was generally kept within the confines of personalities and local rivalries. In 1807 the General Election was indeed fought on a national issue, 'No Popery', but both government and opposition were firmly aligned, for and against this and therefore led the debate. By the time of the next dissolution in 1812, the reform agitation had temporarily died away. Both parliamentary parties were fortunate in that no General Election had to be fought in the years between 1807 and 1812, when their public standing was at its lowest point, and when the reform issue had introduced a new element in politics which neither party knew how to control. Only one large constituency was contested between 1808 and 1810: Essex, and there a coalition of Whigs and Tories combined to defeat the reform candidate, Montagu Burgoyne. But there was, during these crisis years, a very large number of public meetings in large towns and county centres, specifically called in order to put pressure on the government: meetings to vote thanks for Wardle, to petition for reform, or to petition against the Orders in Council forbidding trade with enemy countries. Except in politically backward areas like Cornwall and Montgomeryshire, the local establishment found it impossible to control these meetings, and for this reason they were resented even by relatively progressive MPs, like Viscount Althorp, who wrote:

> 'I am no friend to County meetings, which must always be composed of the most ignorant and prejudiced of men viz. country gentlemen to lead them & a positive mob to follow such leaders; it is impossible to know where they will stop when they have begun however well you may set them off. . . .'[32]

Even the backwoods gentlemen had their fears, according to the veteran reformer Wyvill:

> 'Their dread of plunder & outrage from the Mob is so great, that They consider every Meeting even of the Freeholders to be attended with Danger, as holding out encouragement to the Lower Classes, & likely to end in disturbance. The support of Government in all its measures appears to Them the only security against a Revolution.'[33]

In fact though the last-minute cancellation of a town meeting at the Manchester Exchange in 1812 led to a full-scale riot, none of

these meetings, once actually convened, led to any serious rowdi-
ness. Cobbett described the Hampshire country meeting on 1809
which he attended as 'an assembly of sober, intelligent men of property—a fair representation of the sense and integrity of the
country',[34] and it was possibly the seriousness and sensibleness of
such meetings, rather than any opposite qualities, which aroused the
suspicion of the upper class. Large public meetings threatened a
transformation of the political system which few of the protagonists
of parliamentary politics were ready for, and threatened too, the
mobilization of the lower classes whose insurrectionary disposition
was a constant fear to the generation living in the aftermath of the
French Revolution. It is to these lower classes that we shall
now turn.

3
The Political Consciousness
Of The Working Classes

The Different Working Classes

ACCORDING to the 1801 census, there were 2,260,802 families in Britain. Of these more than half had incomes under £60 a year, and a further third had incomes not much over £60. In 1803, 1,059,314 persons were charged with the property tax, that is, found to have incomes of over £60, and in 1801, with a less efficient assessment, only 320,759 persons were charged with the tax, so it may be presumed that nearly all the 700,000 or so people not taxed in 1801 and taxed in 1803 were border-line cases.[1] Of those below the tax threshold, perhaps a fifth were paupers. In 1803, 734,817 persons, including those too young or too old to work— perhaps 250,000 families—were permanently on relief, and 305,899 occasionally on relief.[2] Thus two million or so families, ranging from paupers to lower bracket property tax payers, were the working classes. Whether they were also the classes that possessed a working-class political consciousness is another question.

Class consciousness largely depends on the local situation of the particular class. In Britain, at the beginning of the nineteenth century, the situation of the workers was in no way standard all over the country. Two types of worker had indeed already been socially isolated, the farm labourer and the factory operative. As the peasant small-holding had virtually disappeared in rural England, the farm labourers formed a distinct class, with no intermediary group between them and the next rural class above, the tenant farmers and village tradesmen. Equally, in the new cotton towns of Lancashire, where self-employed artisans had disappeared, if they had ever existed, and service industries had not yet grown up, there was an unfilled social gulf between the operatives and the factory managers. As late as 1851, the proportion of persons employed in administration, the armed forces, and the professional, domestic, commercial, transport and food sectors in the mill town of Oldham was less than half that so employed in the older industrial centre of Northampton.[3] But the mill towns were exceptional

In most of the great centres of population, in London, Birmingham, Sheffield, Bristol, Norwich, and in the smaller towns of southern England, the big employer was a rarity and the service sectors were comparatively large, comprising the household servants of the rich and middling sort, shopkeepers and their employees, and the variety of people involved with local markets. The small-scale manufacturer of these cities and towns, if he did not depend chiefly on the assistance of his own family, would employ journeymen and labourers, but he would also employ apprentices who would expect to become, one day, small-scale manufacturers in their own right. Between the manufacturer, his apprentice, his journeyman, and his unskilled labourer, there might be only a small social gap. Yet sometimes these 'small' manufacturers might be extremely wealthy, only assuming the appearance of modesty out of habit or in order to gratify customers. Francis Place, whose net profits as a tailor in 1816 were £3,000, remarked of his customers:

'Had these persons been told that I had never read a book, that I was ignorant of everything but my business, that I sotted in a public-house, they would not have made the least objection to me. I should have been a "fellow" beneath them, and they would have patronised me; but ... to accumulate books and to be supposed to know something of their contents, to seek for friends, too, among literary and scientific men, was putting myself on an equality with themselves, if not, indeed, assuming a superiority; it was an abominable offence in a tailor, if not a crime, which deserved punishment.'[4]

It was out of urban communities of this 'mixed' type that the lower-class movements emerged which had the greatest impact in the ruling class of Britain. It is true that more than a quarter of the 70 or so provincial reform societies which were in touch with the London Corresponding Society in the 1790s were in the eight northern counties which contained, equally, more than a quarter of England's population, but the largest of these northern reform societies was at Sheffield, a community of the small artisan type, and if we exclude London from our computations, we find that the northern societies were in towns of much larger average size than those that harboured reform societies in the south. We find something similar in the metropolitan area itself. The City of Westminster, with a population of 153,272 in 1801, was a community of 'mixed' type—artisans, apprentices, servants, shop-

keepers, professional men—as was the adjacent City of London.
East of the City of London were the parishes of St Mary Stratford
at Bow, St Mary Whitechapel, St Anne's Limehouse, St John's
Wapping, St Paul's Shadwell, St George in the East, Christ
Church Spitalfields, St Matthew's Bethnal Green and the four
hamlets of Mile End Old and New Town, Ratcliff and Poplar. The
population of this area was 138,993 in 1801, and had grown to
exceed that of Westminster by 1811.[5] These parishes were poor,
containing few employers. The population was partly supported
by the docks, partly by large-scale organized sweated industries,
and had more in common with the mill-hands of Oldham or Bolton
than had the inhabitants of any other urban community outside
the North-West.

The inhabitants of this part were as politically passive as their
neighbours in Westminster were active, in spite of the emergence
of labour organizations prior to the 1790s. When, in December
1795, the London Corresponding Society was divided into four
districts, the eastern district was given a boundary running from
Blackfriars Bridge, through Ludgate Hill, and effectively consisted of the City of London, minus the Temple: no district further
east was required. (The other districts were the southern, consisting of Southwark, the northern or central, consisting of the
Holborn, Tottenham Court Road area, and the western, consisting
of Westminster.)[6] With the exception of Colonel Despard, who was
arrested in Lambeth, even the most extreme reformers operated in
Westminster or the western part of the City of London. Spence
had a shop at 8 Little Turnstile, Holborn, but later moved to
Oxford Street. After his death his disciples met at 'The Cock',
Grafton Street, Soho, and later at Greystoke Place, Fetter Lane.
The Cato Street conspiracy originated at 4 Fox's Court, Gray's
Inn Lane, before moving to Cato Street, off the Edgware Road.
There were a few riots in the East End involving foreign seamen or
Irish navvies quarrelling over such important topics as whether
Connaught or Munster produced the best men,[7] and at least one
of the riotous assemblies of 'low Irish' at Blackwall and Poplar
had to be dispersed by the Volunteers,[8] but the authorities had no
other occasion to pay attention to the teeming tens of thousands
of the East End, till in December 1811 the sensational Ratcliffe
Highway murders—the massacre of two separate households by
an unknown assailant—provoked a nationwide panic, parliamentary discussion and almost as much correspondence addressed to
the Home Department as was inspired by months of machine-
breaking in the North.

In Westminster the ostensible working-class movement had
many components of dubious working-class origin. The view of

the authorities concerning the main lower class reform group, the London Corresponding Society (LCS), was that:

'from the character, habits, and condition of those who compose it, compared with the style and language, as well as the method and contrivance discovered in their proceedings, it is most probable that it must have been guided by persons of superior education and more cultivated talents.'[9]

Modern historians, anxious to vindicate the working class's capacity for self-determination, have written off this judgment as a typical instance of ruling-class prejudice. And it is certainly true that the majority of LCS members were of plebeian background. Of the 145 members whose trade is recorded out of the 187 members of four divisions analyzed by Dr Seaman, the largest occupational groups were shoemakers (16), tailors (11), watchmakers (9) and weavers (8).[10] But the reformers of the 1790s were less class conscious than later historians. They accepted amongst their leaders such people as Joseph Gerrald, the barrister, John Frost, the solicitor, John Gale Jones, the surgeon, John Thelwall, the professional lecturer and teacher of elocution, Robert Watson, the physician, and Jeremiah Joyce, the nobleman's tutor. Up until the wave of arrests in 1794, the LCS worked closely with the distinctly bourgeois Society For Constitutional Information, through a Committee of Correspondence and Co-operation, consisting of six members from each society.

Nor were the handcraftsmen members of the LCS hopelessly poor, merely because they worked with their hands. Most of them seem to have been young men in their 20s, with their best years still ahead of them. They seemed to have joined the LCS, not out of frustration, still less out of desperation, but rather as part of a process of self-betterment. At a commemorative dinner held in 1822, Francis Place met 24 former members of the General Committee, of whom 20 had been journeymen or shopmen in the 1790s, and who were now all flourishing, some of them even rich.[11] These men had no reason to be shy of middle-class radicals like Thelwall or Gerrald. Men like Place, Hardy, or John Binns, who are often taken to exemplify the plebian core of the LCS, were, if anything, lower middle-class, with access to capital and respectable family backgrounds.

Of course they did not grow up in the lower middle-class suburban ghettos as their counterparts of a later generation might have done, but in the promiscuously overcrowded cities of the late eighteenth century where the poor and the not so poor lived in close proximity. In his autobiographical writings, Francis Place, the son of a publican, recounted many details of the proletarian urban culture of the day, such as the brutal baiting of animals, wholesale pilfering, and sexual licence.[12] Though not typically working class himself, Place grew up amongst them. Others of far more genteel backgrounds found no difficulty in mixing in the bustling, democratic world of the London artisan. Even men as exotic as the Geneva-educated wine-importer's son, Maurice Margarot, or the failed colonial governor, Colonel Despard, could be accepted, perhaps even on their own terms. Actors, journalists, young lawyers, lived alongside craftsmen and shopkeepers, lounged in the same coffee houses, fed at the same chop-houses. Many taverns had a *table d'hôte* where a meal costs 2s 6d and an evening's wine 6d (within the income of men earning £100 a year) and men not otherwise acquainted could come together to talk over the problems of the time. 'The faculties of mutual approach, the communication of particular intelligence, the discussion of diurnal topics, and the enforcement of political opinions, were upon a scale quite different from that which the reserve of modern days allows', it was later recalled.[13] At 'The Finish' in Covent Garden, for example — 'the highest and lowest, the most whimsical and the most extraordinary of all these places of resort'— market people and curious onlookers could rub shoulders with late revellers from the West End.[14] The distinction between genteel and ungenteel, so crucially important in the country at large, was here in abeyance:

> 'the finest gentlmen to be seen in the streets of London are the men who serve at the linen-drapers' and mercers'. Early in the morning they are drest cap-a-pied, the hair feathered and frosted with a delicacy which no hat is to derange through the day: and as this is a leisure time with them, they are to be seen at their respective shop-doors, paring their nails and adjusting their cravats.'[15]

The foppishness of some was matched by the intellectual pretensions of others. Such was the ambience of the LCS: a community whose personal contacts extended from beggars and street-walkers on the one hand to Members of Parliament on the other; literate, largely exposed to newspapers and pamphlets; neither working class nor middle class in any generally accepted meaning of the terms. Such communities were also found, on a much smaller scale, in the old provincial centres. In the new towns of the north, however, they had no counterpart.

It was because it was from such communities that the reform movement emerged, that the reform ideology evinced the rationalism and materialism which distinguished it from many earlier manifestations of urban discontent. As Norman Cohn has argued, millenarian fantasies are characteristic of societies in the grip of crisis, whereas flourishing, upwardly mobile classes tend to be more realistic, less eschatological.[16] The Westminster reformers were upwardly mobile, confident, resilient; they had no need to seek consolation in millenarian fantasies. In Lancashire and the North Midlands, by contrast, where less sophisticated workers were more seriously affected by the economic crisis of the war years, religious enthusiasm and half-baked conspiracy seems to have taken a rather firmer hold.

Information

We know much less about the life of the new industrial towns than we do about lower-class Westminster. The chief difference seems to have been a much greater degree of social uniformity, a much smaller degree of interpenetration of social classes. There was a lower degree of literacy too, but perhaps not significantly so: anyway it varied from locality to locality, depending on the voluntary educational provisions of each area. At Deane on the outskirts of Bolton, only 46.6 per cent of the men and 14.5 per cent of the women were literate; at Eccleston, near St Helen's, 70.5 per cent of the men and 32.4 per cent of the women were literate.[17] More could read than could write properly, because for most working-class children the only time for lessons was on Sunday, and the teaching of writing (as distinct from reading the Bible) was regarded as a desecration of the sabbath.[18] Of 7,000 prisoners who passed through Norwich Castle between 1826 and 1843, (who should, however, be taken as representative of working-class literacy amongst the rural and older urban communities of the *South* rather than in the North) 2,391 were totally illiterate, 1,986 could read and write, 1,158 could read, 951 could read only a little and 574 knew only their alphabets; many of the illiterate learnt to read quickly in prison, being provided with teachers for the first time in their lives.[19]

For most workers outside London the problem was not literacy, however, but want of material to read. In London there was a choice of several newspapers, numerous pamphlets, cheap second-hand books. In the provinces there was often nothing but one local paper, usually of a sternly conservative complexion, and like all newspapers of the day, not very informative. If often the working class of the North seemed uninterested in the vagaries of parliamentary politics and more concerned with bread and butter issues nearer home, it was not altogether that in times of hardship they had no energy for the refinements of politics in the distant capital. Often they were not so much preoccupied with issues nearer at home, as lacking the necessary minimum of information concerning wider matters.

E. P. Thompson has written of the opaque society, the society of the lower classes impenetrable to the observing eyes of their social superios,[20] but it is perhaps not unfair to suggest that this opacity may have worked in both directions, concealing from the lower classes the political world of the rich, just as it concealed from the rich the political world of the lower classes. There were exceptions, of course. Alexander Richmond, the Scots union leader, published in 1825 a pamphlet entitled *Narrative of the Conditions of the Manufacturing Population,* written in the densest, most orotund style of the upper classes, beginning with a reference to Adam Smith, ending with a quotation from Goldsmith, and citing Beccaria in the preface. But perhaps there were plenty of others who resembled a convict of a generation later, one T.H., a labourer, married with six children, serving one month in the House of Correction at Preston for selling ale without a licence, early in the 1840s. He had been at school for two or three years but could not read. He did not know the Lord's Prayer but had heard of 'the Scriptures' as being 'about another world'. He had heard of Wellington and also of Nelson who 'was a great soldier'. 'Had heard of Jack Sheppard and Dick Turpin. . . . Heard books read about 'em; they were thieves — clever chaps.' He had heard of the battle of Waterloo but did not know who fought there. He did not know the name of the Queen (this examination took place during Victoria's reign) or of the last King. Asked about the Chartists, he described them as 'Men as stands up for their rights, and for sending who they like for parliament-men.' Asked about the Tories, he answered, 'They are gentlemen; they are against the poor.' The Whigs: 'Same way as Tories.' 'Where does iron come from?' I've heard 'em say they get it out of the ground, but I never believ'd them.' He did not even know the names of the months of the year, or the date of Christmas or the New Year.[21]

Organization

Though the northern communities lacked the broader perspectives brought by a greater degree of social intermixture, they did not reap much benefit in terms of class solidarity from their comparatively uniform social structure. This development was only to come later, in the 1820s and 1830s.

The early stages of industrialization had created a flourishing class of artisans, not actually independent of the entrepreneurs, but able to command a high price for their labour; men like shearmen in the wool-cloth trade, or muslin weavers whose trade 'was that of a gentleman: they brought home their work in top boots and ruffled shirts; they had a cane, and took a coach in some instances, and appeared as well as military officers of the first degree when they appeared alone'.[22] It was later recalled:

'Many weavers at that time used to walk about the streets with a five pound Bank of England note spread out under their hat-bands; they would smoke none but long "church-warden" pipes, and objected to the instrusion of any other handicrafts-men into the particular rooms in the public houses which they frequented.'[23]

These independent types were already in decline in the 1790s, with the price of a 24-yard piece of muslin plummeting from four guineas in 1793 to 29s. in 1797, but they still maintained a separate identity, a separate code of aspirations and despairs from the factory operatives. In the factories, the encouragement for the formation of a group consciousness, which might have seemed inseparable from the employment of large numbers of persons on single premises, was mitigated by the fact that a large proportion of the mill labour force was composed of children or women. In 1816, three-fifths of the labour in Manchester spinning factories was under 18[24] and probably a majority of the rest were women who even — perhaps especially — in the working classes had not been admitted to social or organizational equality with their menfolk. Even in a traditional male preserve like weaving, where the coming of the war had coincided with an increase in the demand for labour, the numbers of women employed were increasing. At the beginning of the war 'the Journeymen in such numbers enlisted and went off, that the householders took the girls and learnt them, rather than let their looms stand'.[25] In some parts of Lancashire there were as many female weavers as men.[26] It was more than once claimed that a particularly large proportion of men in the textile manufacturing areas joined the Army during these war years, those of them who had been factory apprentices joining up as soon as their engagements had ended.[27] Registers of recruitment at this period no longer exist to confirm this, though of about 3,000 deserters from line regiments whose place of enlistment is recorded, only 33 were from Manchester, eight from Salford, three from Preston, three from Warrington and one from Bolton, which suggests, if anything, that Lancashire was under-represented in the Army.[28] Even if this was so, and most Lancashire men found employment locally, it does appear that adult males were a minority of the labour force in the textile areas, and the intermixture of such a large proportion of women and children seems to have inhibited the growth of labour consciousness.

In spite of these conditions, and in spite of the fact that trade unions were illegal by the terms of the Combination Acts of 1799 and 1800, the deteriorating economic situation of textile workers did lead to some far-flung, though short-lived, organization. In 1802 there were a series of disturbances in the Wiltshire woollen townships, and a Yorkshire shearman's club ticket, without which it was impossible to find work in the West Riding, was found in Bradford on Avon.[29] It was suspected that the Wiltshire shearmen first thought of combining only as a result of a communication from Leeds.[30] At the end of September, 1802, just as the Wiltshire disturbances had died away, 80 shearmen employed by the West Riding firm of Wormald, Gott & Wormald staged a walk out because the firm had apprenticed two boys over the legal age.[31] They had a strike fund sufficient, at least initially, for strike pay of 18s. a week.[32] The strike soon spread throughout the Leeds area: Wormald, Gott & Wormald actually had to advertise in the recently pacified Wiltshire and Somerset wool towns in an attempt to recruit black-leg labour.[33] Eventually they had to accept their employees' demands.

In 1810 a General Union of cotton spinners, directed by 40 or 50 delegates from Stockport, Macclesfield and the other cotton towns as far north as Preston, planned a strike to bring the country wages up to the level of those paid in Manchester. Meetings were held under the guise of legally enrolled sick clubs.[34] This scheme led to between 8,000 and 10,000 workers in the Stalybridge area east of Manchester being locked out for over three months. They were financed at the rate of over £1,000 a week by the other areas, but when the funds ran out they were starved into submission.[35] Several of those involved were convicted under the Combination Acts but the sentences were mostly quashed on technical grounds at the next Quarter Sessions.[36]

In 1812 an organization of cotton workers in Scotland and Cumberland brought nearly 40,000 men out on strike. After three weeks, the five man co-ordinating committee was arrested and the strike collapsed.

Because these labour organizations grew up in areas of insurrectionary conspiracy, and because certain outbreaks of violence, such as machine-breaking, were specific to industries with more advanced labour organization, there is a tendency to conflate secret workers' combinations with a proletarian revolutionary underground. Thus E. P. Thompson argues, 'the whole atmosphere was one which will have encouraged revolutionary talk, even when the immediate objective was industrial'.[37] This conflation was actually made at the time, and the general committee of weavers which met at Bolton in 1799, with delegates from Manchester, Stockport, Wigan, Warrington, Blackburn, Bury and elesewhere, complained of 'the mean artifice of stigmatizing us with the name of Jacobins'.[38]

Though there must have been some overlap of personnel between the trade combinations and the abortive secret conspiracies, it does seem the case that the union leaders, though technically in breach of the law, were loyal, well-disposed men. One of their achievements, long recalled as an epoch in labour history, was their joining with the bosses to petition Parliament for minimum wage legislation in 1808. The fact that the rejection of the minimum wage bill led to extensive riots in Lancashire, with at least one fatality and the sacking of a cotton mill, can hardly be blamed on the seditious disposition of the labour leaders, especially as it was one of the employers, a lieutenant-colonel of Volunteers, who was convicted for inciting the mob.

Both strikes and petitions were the results of the crystallization of popular opinion on issues with which every textile worker was intimately concerned. The minimum-wage petition and, to a greater extent, agitation for peace or for the cancellation of the Orders in Council, was mainly organized by the middle classes, with the initiative coming from Manchester or from the old established merchant caucuses of Liverpool.* The strikes on the other hand, were entirely working-class affairs, but though the leaders thrown up by the ferment seem, from the evidence they gave before subsequent parliamentary committees, to have been remarkably sensible and, considering their educations and normal avocations, very well informed persons, yet their concentration on specific issues, as compared to the rather woolly-minded speculativeness encouraged by, for example, the London Corresponding Society, is very striking; and, at the same time, it does suggest that many of the national issues of the day may well have passed them by.

Riots

There were, of course, other ways in which the working classes expressed their views, apart from organizing themselves to strike or petition. Between 1790 and 1810 there were 740 full-scale riots in England, 26 of which involved loss of life.[39] Besides 16 rescues or instances of resisting police officers, 13 attacks on individuals, eight theatre riots and six battles between smugglers and excisemen, there were:—

335.5 food riots†	45.3 per cent of total
148 riots against impressment, militia balloting, crimps	20.0 per cent of total

*See pp. 292

† Half a riot is calculated by attributing the riot of two distinct causes.

58.5 political riots†   7.9 per cent of total
43.5 labour riots†   5.9 per cent of total
38   brawls   5.1 per cent of total
10   enclosure riots   1.4 per cent of total[40]

As the greatest single cause of riot was food shortage, the years in which riots were most numerous were naturally the years of famine, 1795 with 178 riots, and 1800 with 132.[41]

It is no longer possible to regard riots merely as outbreaks of sheer brutality or blind frustration on the part of the dregs of the populace. It has indeed been pointed out that the view of the riot as essentially ineffective and pointless derives from an unhistorical prejudice in favour of long-term peaceful organization, and the rejection of tactics that aim only at temporary solutions.[42] Riots, especially food riots, did in fact frequently achieve their object, in forcing the lowering of prices for example, or in drawing the attention of the authorities to local grievances.

Often riots aimed at the preservation of social norms: the liberation of unfairly impounded livestock, or of prisoners unfairly arrested, or the breaking down of fences on land that had been regarded as common, or the expulsion of undesirable neighbours such as adulterers or strike-breakers.[43] The attempted lynching of a prostitute suspected of murdering a customer in 1799, several assaults on homosexuals in 1810, and an incident in which some Marylebone mechanics ducked, stripped and pelted a man who had indecently exposed himself, were all instances of popular enforcement of social norms.[44]

One of the most celebrated riots of the period, the Old Prices riots in 1809 were occasioned by the increase in price of tickets at Covent Garden Theatre going up from 3s.6d. to 4s., and involved not a working-class mob but otherwise respectable persons, led by the barrister, Henry Clifford. An earlier theatre riot, at the Haymarket Theatre on 15 August 1805, was a protest against Foote's burlesque *The Devil among the Tailors*. The military had to be called in, and 16 tailors were arrested. They had been protesting against what they regarded as a gratuitous insult to their trade.[45]

Even in food riots, in which urban mobs went to local markets to force tradesmen to lower the price of grain or flour, and occasionally butter, as at Sheerness and Southampton in 1800, or of potatoes, as at Birmingham in 1810, or else sallied forth into the country to force local farmers to promise to bring their produce to market at reasonable prices, the over-priced commodities were not stolen, but had their prices fixed at a level regarded as just by the rioters. Often the local authorities, while not actually turning a

†Half a riot is calculated by attributing the riot to two distinct causes.

blind eye, were sufficiently impressed by the equity of such proceedings not to act very firmly, and were sometimes even rebuked
by the Home Department for their negligence.[46] Following food
riots at Totnes, only one merchant was anxious to press charges,
and this was contrary to the wishes both of the local magistrates
and of the other corn merchants involved. The mob was acknowledged to have had justice on its side.[47]

Nevertheless it is a mistake to see riots in a political void, as
part of the normal mechanism of a somewhat violent society, only
technically illegal in the same way as duelling was. Riots did not
take place in a political void. Some of the most serious riots of the
period were specifically political, such as the Burdett riots of
1810* and, even where the cause of riot was not originally
political, the consciousness of confronting the system of government frequently brought to the surface underlying political discontents. Forcible price fixing was often announced, or threatened,
in advance, and was frequently preceded by a spate of slogan
writing. At Chelmsford in 1800, anonymous threats of price-fixing
were accompanied by chalked slogans on walls such as 'No
Quakers', 'No White Jews', and a paper was fixed to the door of a
Volunteer officer saying:

> 'you a Captain of the
> Volunteers Damn you
> we will play hell, with
> you & your house on
> Friday next.'[48]

And as the riots themselves often continued sporadically over a
period of days, there was plenty of opportunity for the posting up
and distribution of seditious papers.

Most riots, taking place in small communities, involved people
who would be known by sight, if not by name, to the victims,
though in at least one Scots food riot the perpetrators were
disguised.[49] This was in keeping with their function of reaffirming communal standards; they were public acts. But under a
government increasingly hostile to popular demonstrations, and
in circumstances where the rioters were frequently of lower social
status than their intended victims, the riot gave way to the secret
outrage, such as machine breaking in Wiltshire in 1802, and in
Nottinghamshire in 1811-12, and outbreaks of rick burning and
sheep mutilation in rural areas. That the secret outrage was seen
as a more effective alternative to the public riot is indicated by a
letter found in the courtyard of the Post Office at Bath following
the destruction of a local brewery by fire:

---

*See pp. 269

'Peace
and Large Bread
or
A King without a Head
. . . .
As we can't make a Riot
We'll do things more quiet
As provisions get higher:
The greater the Fire!
Beware
A stitch in time saves Nine.'

These secret outrages seem to have filled the perpetrators with glee at their own cleverness, and gave them a sense of achievement in a world which gave little opportunity to the poor to feel much satisfaction: 'We once wear poor men but now we are Gentlemen', announced the writer of an anonymous threatening letter at Pontefract. This sense of new-found status is evident in the rhetorical flourishes of many threatening letters. Often the writers adopted military titles, such as General Ludd or, amongst the writers of letters sent out during industrial disputes in the 1820s, 'Capt. Bloodthersty', 'Captain of the Vitriol Forces' (this one illustrated by a drawing of a jug labelled 'Vitriol') and 'Captain of the Blood-red Knights' (this one illustrated by a skull and cross-bones, a coffin, crossed pistols and a heart impaled on a dagger).[51] Even in riots the leaders often adopted military titles; the leader of a food riot at Modbury in 1801 used the soubriquet 'General Bonaparte',[52] and the leader of the Totnes food riots of the same year wore a cocked hat and powdered wig to represent an officer, and called himself the 'Provost Marshall'.[53] (Compare the much earlier 'Captains Poverty, Pity, Faith and Charity' amongst the Cumberland peasant rebels of 1536, and the later 'Captain Swing'.) Signing seditious announcement 'God Save The King' after the fashion of official proclamations was another form such self-indulging fantasies took. The classic heroes of revolution also provided soubriquets. A handbill denouncing Robert Laing who had organized a loyal address to the King in North Shields said, 'O Laing thou art damnd so Low for this Conspiracy there is not a Sin in Hells Catalogue can Sink the Deeper — Sydney'.[54] Someone else chalked up at Banbury market in September 1801 'No 45 Liberty or Death. A Second Oliver Cromwell.'[55] But sometimes the writers of anonymous notes could be brutally to the point, as in the case of a letter sent to William Hetley of Adwalton, Huntingdonshire: 'If you Dont fall your flower to 3s 6d @ Stone next Saturday we will pull yours mills over your heads &

take your flower away we will pull you about the Markett Place on Saturday next. You Jacknipps.'[56]

Riots and secret terrorism resembled strikes in that however much they were coloured by general discontents, they concerned specific aspects of lower-class life. They were indicative of a fragmentized, partial consciousness, very different from the all-embracing self-awareness which the London Corresponding Society and its associated societies tried, however unsuccessfully, to develop in the 1790s. But these societies, the most highly developed organs of lower-class consciousness of the period, were not really working class at all. They were in fact the organ of the labour aristocracy, the small employers, the young men at the outset of respectable careers. Lower-class opinion as such was the opinion of the topmost echelons of the lower class, the bottommost haves rather than the genuine have-nots. Even the perpetrators of riot and outrage seem not to have been the poorest of their neighbourhoods, but the not-quite poorest. The most desperate, least protected members of society seem by comparison to have been acquiescent, and it was in the areas where unmitigated hardship was most commonly found, in London's East End, or in the coalmining areas, that there were the fewest indications of disaffection.

4
Church And Religion

New Trends
SO far we have discussed British society as a secular organization. But it was also a religious organization, or rather a set of inter-locking religious organizations. Ecclesiastical affairs were intimately bound up at all sorts of levels with the ramifications of secular society; they affected everyone to some extent and were for many the area of their greatest communal involvement, but they did not faithfully mirror and extend the relationships of secular society, rather they introduced distinct and peculiar features.

The early nineteenth century was an era of religious as well as political upheaval, and this fact has led to attempts to combine the two phenomena, as for example in the theory first elaborated by Halévy and developed by E. P. Thompson that the growth of Methodism prevented a political revolution in Britain. Historians' concentration on Methodism has diverted attention from major alterations in the structure of Old Dissent in the period, from certain crucial developments within the Church of England, and from the steady progress of free-thinking.

Owing to the laws against blasphemy, little concrete evidence has survived concerning free-thinking. Holland House, the home of Lord Holland, was spoken of as the resort of free-thinkers, including Dr John Allen, (who was known as 'Lady Holland's Atheist'), Sir William Drummond, and the Hon. John William Ward.[1] There were also free-thinkers amongst the lower classes. When the question, 'Whether the Doctrines of Deism or Christianity were Better Calculated to Ensure the Happiness of Mankind', was discussed in a proletarian debating club at Royton, near Oldham, hundreds had to be turned away for lack of space, and nobody spoke for Christianity.[2]

At the same time there was a revival of chiliasm. The fashion of

millenarian prophesying had not died out during the Enlightenment and was in fact, as a topic of speculative enquiry, much
favoured by the Unitarians, themselves the most rationalist of
Christians. Benjamin Vaughan, MP for Calne, who fled to France
because he was suspected of complicity with British exiles in
Paris, wrote a treatise showing that the French Revolution was a
fulfilment of the Book of Daniel.[3]

John Hammond and William Frend, who both gave up promising
careers in the Church of England by becoming Unitarians — it
was Hammond who was the villain in a famous incident in
Evangelical history, being the lecturer at Holy Trinity,
Cambridge, in whose favour the parishioners rioted when the
Evangelical Charles Simeon was appointed to the living over his
head — both thought the French Revolution was foretold by
Revelations.[4]

For others the imminent Millenium was not a question of
abstract theory, but of conviction and commitment. Richard
Brothers, a half-pay naval lieutenant, became convinced that he
was the Nephew of God. His exhortations to George III to deliver
up his crown led to his arrest in March 1795 on suspicion of
treasonable practices, and to subsequent confinement as a
criminal lunatic till 1806. Nevertheless he managed to persuade
Nathaniel Brassey Halhed, MP for Lymington, that the Millenium
would begin on 19 November 1795 'at or about sun-rise, in the
latitude of Jerusalem'.[5] Halhed addressed the Commons three
times on the subject of Brothers, and distributed 1,000 copies of
his pamphlet vindicating Brothers to MPs and to other persons in
public positions, including his electors, the mayor and corporation
of Lymington.[6] The latter were apparently unimpressed, and when
Parliament was dissolved in 1796, Halhed did not seek re-election.

After seven years most of Brothers' disciples were seduced by
Joanna Southcott, a middle-aged west country spinster, formerly
a domestic servant, who enjoyed a much greater vogue as a pro-
phetess up until her death on 27 December 1814. For 14 months
prior to her death, though in her sixty-fifth year, she believed
herself pregnant with Shiloh, 'the Second Christ'. Most of her
disciples seem to have survived their disappointment at her
pregnancy turning out to be imaginary, and the sect she founded
still exists today. During her lifetime there was a flourishing
Southcottian chapel in Southwark, where services were conducted
by a minister in a white surplice, who read most of the Church of
England prayers and preached an unexceptionable sermon: there
were however paintings of prophetic scenes on the walls.[7] There
was another congregation in the Leeds area, led by the prophet
George Turner, a former disciple of Brothers. Compared to

the metropolitan group, the Leeds congregation may have been more exclusively working class, more specifically rooted in the credulity and fantasies of poor, uprooted workers not otherwise provided with spiritual guidance. A prominent member of the Leeds congregation was Mary Bateman, the daughter of small farming folk at Aisenby near Thirsk, who achieved local celebrity as a 'wise women', i.e., a witch, before being hanged at York for poisoning in 1809.[8] Neither the Leeds nor the Southwark congregation seems to have been particularly large and the attempts of another of Joanna's converts, the Rev. Thomas Philip Foley, to proselytize in the rural Worcestershire village of Old Swinford met with little success, despite his position as a parish priest there. It would appear that, despite the social and economic upheavals of the day, millenarianism had only a marginal appeal.

The Church of England
The vast majority of Englishmen were members of the Church of England, the Established Church. It was a rich man's church, increasingly seen as an integral part of civil society. Its priesthood has been largely drawn into the net of ruling-class patronage, and provided openings both for younger sons and for dependents like ex-tutors and secretaries. Ecclesiastical benefices were mostly in the gift of laymen or church dignitaries. The Earl of Lonsdale, with 24 livings in his gift, was the largest single patron in Cumberland, the Duke of Devonshire with 18⅓, the largest in Derbyshire, the Duke of Bedford the largest in Bedfordshire. Normally, however, individual laymen had fewer livings than bishops of deans and chapters, though there were more lay patrons than clerical ones.

Some great noblemen collected livings as a means of extending their local influence. The Earl of Egremont, who inherited only two livings collected 15 more at the cost of £45,000, all in the neighbourhood of his stately home at Petworth, save one in Lincolnshire subsequently swapped for a Crown living.[9] The Earl of Lonsdale seems to have usurped the patronage of several Cumberland livings formerly in the gift of parishioners. Other lay patrons, country squires with only one or perhaps two livings in their gift, regarded their livings as legacies for their younger sons.

Bishops, deans and canons, patrons by virtue of their ecclesiastical positions, also had relatives and friends who had the first claim on their patronage. A memorandum written by Walker King, Bishop of Rochester, one of the executors of Edmund Burke, is worth quoting at length for its unusually direct statement of his intentions:

'M.' *Venables* my nephew, has a small Vicarage in Somersetshire; and I must take the first opportunity for procuring for
him by exchange, or otherwise, some additional Preferment.
M.' *Davies* my Curate at Burnham. He is soon to marry a near
Relation of mine, and I have long promised him the first Living
of moderate value that I may have in my Gift.
M.' *Buckland* formerly my College Tutor, now my Chaplain; In
addition to a valuable Sinecure The Chancellor has just given
him a good Living in my Neighbourhood. They are worth
together 12 or 1300 a year. I am therefore no longer anxious
about him, but he will expect to have the disposal of something
as opportunities may offer.
M.' *Etherington.* About Twenty five years ago came out of
Yorkshire, a poor self taught Scholar, and found his way to
M.' Burke. I received him from M.' Burke; We got him into
orders and he has ever since been a Fag of mine at Grays Inn
and on other occasions .....
D.' *Winstanley* the Principal of S.' Albans Hall Oxford. He was
unsuccessful in a Competition with me, for a Fellowship, soon
after we entered at College .... I was engaged with him in the
early part of my life in several literary projects, and pursuits ....
These, I believe are all the personal claims there are upon me.'[10]
Patronage indeed was everything. Coleridge was indulging in
pious self-deception when he wrote:
'the revenues of the Church are in some sort the reversionary
property of every family, that may have a member educated
for the Church, or a daughter that may marry a clergyman.
Instead of being foreclosed and unmovable, it is in fact the
only species of landed property, that is essentially moving
and circulative.'[11]
In reality all circulation had become totally clogged in the
desperate scramble for preferment. Patrons were bombarded with
requests whenever a living supposedly in their gift seemed about
to fall vacant. Replying to one such application from the Marquess
Wellesley, the Lord Chancellor, who had the disposal of Crown
livings, wrote:
'The Living of Stansfield has been expected to be daily vacant
ever since I first became Chancellor in 1801: and I can venture to
assure your Lordship that no Week has passed since that period,
which has not loaded me with Applications for it, save in the
fourteen Months in which I was not Chancellor.'[12]
Yet once beneficed a clergyman was well off. It was true that in
Wales, and in parts of Cumberland and Westmorland, clergymen
were as poor as their parishioners and lived in the same style of
rusticity and ignorance,[13] but such was not the case in less

remote areas. The life might be boring as most people (and an even greater proportion of parishes) were still to be found in country districts. One prospective cleric complained:

'I can not bear the conversation and Company of the rustics. Nothing but having a family of my own, which I hope I shall one day have, or a very good neighbourhood, could make the country tolerable to me for a continuance. I almost wish I had gone to the Law, in spite of my laziness.'[14]

Sydney Smith regarded the enforcement of his residence at Foston-le-Clay as hideous exile. But the obligation to hold services twice on one day a week was hardly onerous. Absenteeism, with or without episcopal licence, was always possible (only 60 per cent of beneficed clergy resided in any one of their livings), and the priest might well find himself a leading figure in local society.

Except in London, the inflation of land values was causing a rise in clerical incomes. In addition, most Enclosure Acts provided for tithes to be commuted for anything up to a fifth of the land enclosed, resulting in glebes — the land attached to each benefice — increasing enormously in size.[15] In Rutland and Cardiganshire, clerical incomes actually doubled in the first decade of the nineteenth century. Donnington, a large parish of 60 square miles in the fens near Ely, worth only £22 4s 11d at the Reformation, had its annual income increased by the drainage and cultivation of the fens to a stupendous £7,306 by 1831. (As the climate was unhealthily damp there, the rectors did not normally reside, but employed a curate at £150.). But there were 3,528 other parishes worth less than £150, and 297 worth less than £50.[16] The majority of incumbents were nonpluralistic, but there were still over 2,000 pluralists, and it was still possible to amass a profitable string of livings — 50 priests had four livings each, and six had five each. Increasingly, clergymen also tended to have private means, and so, on the whole, parish priests had never been more prosperous. This was reflected in the fact that a quarter of all magistrates were clergymen. Owing to the policy of the Lords-Lieutenant, the Dukes of Devonshire and Richmond, neither Derbyshire nor Sussex had any clerical magistrates, even though in the latter county, in 1800, the parish priest was the largest landowner in 22 out of 265 parishes.[17] But in Lincolnshire and the Isle of Ely clergymen comprised nearly half the bench, and in Caernarvonshire, more than half.

Moreover, as well as being powerful within their own communities, members of the clergy had a strong notion of their independence. The proposal to enforce residence was objected to on the grounds that it would increase episcopal power over parish priests. Sydney Smith wrote:

'We ought to recollect....that the clergy constitute a body of 12 or 15,000 educated persons; that the whole concern of education devolves upon them; that some share of the talents and information which exist in the country must naturally fall to their lot and that the complete subjugation of such a body of men cannot, in any point of view, be a matter of indifference to a free country.... Since we have enjoyed practically a free constitution, the bishops have, in point of fact, possessed little or no power of oppression over their clergy.'[18]

Once beneficed indeed, parish clergy were virtually irremovable. The Rev. Dr. Edward Drax Free, rector of Sutton in Bedfordshire from 1809, fathered at least five children by three different members of his household staff, ill-treated another servant pregnant by him so severely that she miscarried, held no services for over a year, grazed horses, swine and cattle in the churchyard even though the horses sometimes broke through into the graves, foddered cattle in the church porch, locked up the vestry to prevent vestry meetings, sold the lead off the church roof, demanded excessive fees, drank, swore and pilfered from shops, yet managed to escape deprivation for years. At one time his case was before five different courts — the Court of Arches, the King's Bench, the House of Lords, the Court of Delegates and even, by writ of error owing to a procedural mistake, the Court of Exchequer. When he was finally deprived he held out in his rectory for a month, using his pistols to keep his victorious churchwardens at bay.[19]

Perhaps even more remarkable was the career of the Rev. Thomas Philip Foley, third cousin of the Earl of Uxbridge and third cousin of Lord Foley, who had placed him in the family living of Old Swinford, near Stourbridge. He was also appointed to the living of Wombourne with Trysull in Staffordshire in 1801. Foley became a disciple of Joanna Southcott in December 1801. Amongst the first persons he told of his conversion was his kinsman, the Hon. Edward Foley, MP for Worcestershire:

'His eye widened; & he seemed in perfect astonishment at what he heard — and concluded *I had lost my senses* — This report flew like lightening thro' the neighbourhood, & I had a Gentleman of the Faculty [i.e. a physician] to visit me several days to see whether I was *really mad;* but finding *"a method"* in my supposed derangement, he ceased coming any more to my house — However, as I have given up mostly all dining from home, and having circulated as far as I possibly could *my full*

and decided belief in Joanna Southcott & Richard Brothers, &
what is fast hastening on this nation for their wickedness &
unbelief — I am put down *as mad* and very fortunately I am
left to myself — to pursue my own road.'[20]

Though he hastened to inform his ecclesiastical superiors of his
belief in the imminence of the Second Coming and in Joanna's
prophetic mission, Foley did not resign his church preferment.[21]
When, in 1806, a group of his parishioners, including his own
curate, formally complained to the Bishop of Worcester, Foley
successfully vindicated himself in an interview with his superior.[22]
He remained rector of Old Swinford and vicar of Wombourne till
his death in 1835.

Above the grade of parish priest the social and financial
prospects of the clergy were even better. The Archbishop of
Canterbury and the Bishop of Durham had gross incomes of
£20,000 a year. The poorest bishopric was Llandaff, at £1,008 a
year, with Carlisle, St David's and Gloucester coming next at a
comfortable £2,500. Residence was not regarded as necessary;
while Bishop of Llandaff, Richard Watson, lived in the Lake
District; and Lort Mansel, Bishop of Bristol and also Master of
Trinity, contrived to be an assiduous chairman of the Cambridgeshire Quarter Session.

Deaneries ranged from £4,422 at Durham to £69 at Hereford.
There were a few canonries, at Durham or St Paul's, for example,
worth over £1,000, though many grossed less than £100, but even
that was generous, as the most arduous duty of canons was
sharing out the ecclesiastical patronage belonging to their
chapter.

Even without the higher notions of the priestly office that were
being established in the public mind by the Evangelicals, the
inadequacy and in some areas the actual unpopularity of the clergy
was increasingly recognized as a problem, but the clerical profession was so generally regarded in worldly terms that there was
great reluctance to see beyond the various immediate but purely
materialistic reasons for postponing reformation. Thus, for
example, Sir William Scott wrote in 1797 on the subject of the
equalization of parishes:

'parity in the provision for the clergy . . . has been deemed by
no means desirable for the interests either of Church or State.
Large livings are family provisions for the sons of the nobility
and gentry of the country, who are invited by them into the
church, and, by holding preferments in it, connect the safety of
its interests with those of the other great establishments of our
ancient Constitution. They are likewise provisions for men of
superior ability and attainments.'[23]

It was not surprising therefore that many Church of England clergy were alienated from the lower classes. The Church and King mobs of the 1790s testified to the reality of popular Anglicanism in some areas, but often priest and parishioner had no personal contact outside the formalities of the liturgy. For every humble, devoted parson as described by George Eliot in *Scenes from Clerical Life,* or by Goldsmith in *The Deserted Village,*

'...in his duty prompt at every call,
He watch'd and wept, he pray'd and felt, for all,'

there were two or three others who, as younger sons of the gentry, or themselves heirs to broad acres, magistrates, landlords, large scale farmers, represented less the values of another world, than the oppressive authority structure of this one. Sometimes they even acted as the agents of Whitehall, as in 1801 when they collected details of the state of agriculture, and in 1814 when they were circularized with instructions to tell their parishioners how to secure any prize money due to them.[24] Yet much of the parishioners' communal life passed them by. The festivals of the village year had become separated from the ecclesiastical calendar, and *a fortiori,* from parsonical supervision.[25] A 'cunning man' or 'cunning woman' — that is, a white witch — was to be found near every town, even in the London area.[26] There was an instance of 'scoring' a witch at Great Paxton, Huntingdonshire, in 1808,[27] and another near Taunton in 1811.[28] Evidently traditions of belief still flourished over which the clergy had little control.

More serious, perhaps, was the failure of the Church of England to keep abreast of the redistribution of population. Clergymen with no spiritual authority in rural parishes were bad enough; extensive urban slums with no clerical presence at all, represented an even more serious failure. The situation was at its worst in the dioceses of Chester (which included industrial Lancashire) and London. In Chester diocese, in the parishes which had over 2,000 people and which were unable to seat half, there were 950,788 parishioners and seating for only 188,076. And the larger the community, the proportionately worse was the situation:

	Population	Seating
Manchester	79,459	10,950
Stockport	33,973	2,500
Bolton	26,121	3,500

The situation was almost as bad in the West Riding:

	Population	Seating
Leeds	[78,000]	10,400
Sheffield	55,000	6,280
Bradford	33,000	6,700

Huddersfield	18,357	3,960
Halifax	11,159	4,200[29]

Evangelicalism — the informal movement which sought to bring the Church of England back to its primitive missionary zeal and devotional commitment — was relatively strong in the West Riding, and the clergy of the West Riding wool towns enjoyed an unusual degree of popularity. At St Peter's, Leeds, there were sometimes as many as 1,400 communicants, and the officiating clergy had to take the sacrament round to the pews in order to prevent too large a crowd forming in front of the altar.[30] Leeds was also one of the first places where a serious attempt was made to increase church space. As well as the parish church of St Peter's, there were two smaller churches consecrated in 1664 and 1727 respectively, and two new churches were consecrated in this period, St Paul's, seating 1,500, in 1793, and St James's, apparently a former Dissenting chapel seating 1,600, in 1801.[31] But that still left four-fifths of the population with no facilities for Anglican worship.

Wesleyan Methodism

The growth of Wesleyan Methodism, the best known aspect of religious life in this period, scarcely made up for the Church of England's failure in the new urban areas. The real growth of Methodism came after 1815. In some places Methodist membership actually declined between the time of Wesley's death and the end of the French Wars. Only a fraction — anything from a half to a fifth — of people who attended Methodist worship were members, the ratio of members to attenders varying with time and place according to the onerousness or lightness of the duties demanded from full members, but the following figures indicate at least stagnation, if not actual decline, in certain strategic areas:

Numbers of Methodists

	1791	1815
Bradford on Avon	952	440
Wolverhampton	612	460
Macclesfield	1,140	1,030
Keighley	900	850
Colne	1,020	580
Blackburn	955	650

Elsewhere membership did not keep abreast of population increases.

Numbers of Methodists

	1791	1815
Manchester	2,090	2,800
Bradford, Yorks.	1,095	1,800

| Wakefield | 730 | 1,045 |
| Huddersfield | 780 | 1,012[32] |

Methodism moreover, though it often did well in areas of Church of England weakness, such as out-towns and scattered parishes with absentee parsons, did not flourish in areas where the Church of England was virtually eclipsed, such as parts of industrial Lancashire. In the West Riding, where Methodism was relatively successful, it seems to have been complementary to Church of England Evangelicalism. It was said of the Yorkshire Methodists in 1799, 'most of them attend the Gospel preached here in the Churches having no meetings open, in the time of the services in the establishment.[33]

Methodism's greatest success was not in industrial areas however, but in those rural areas where the Church of England clergy had rendered themselves particularly obnoxious, especially Lincolnshire and Caernarvonshire, the two counties where the clergy had the most dominant role in rural society and where clerical magistrates were proportionately most numerous. In Lincolnshire, between 1791 and 1800, 144 temporary and 15 permanent Wesleyan chapels were opened. Between 1801 and 1810, the numbers were 161, and 53 respectively, and between 1811 and 1820, 103 and 31 respectively. In addition, 352 temporary and 57 permanent chapels of no specified sect were opened in the decade 1811 to 1820. In Caernarvonshire, between 1801 and 1810, 36 permanent Wesleyan chapels were opened, and during the years 1811 to 1820 one temporary and two permanent Wesleyan chapels were opened. Moreover, in the latter decade two temporary and 43 permanent chapels of no specified sect were opened — most of them probably Calvinistic Methodist.[34]

It is difficult to take seriously E. P. Thompson's contention that Methodism played a major part in preventing revolution by providing a kind of psychic safety valve which diverted revolutionary tensions into the religious sector. The Methodists were neither numerous enough nor sufficiently strategically placed to have any such effect, and as the peaks of agitation and of Methodist recruitment coincided it would appear that disaffection and Methodism flourished together, rather than waxing and waning alternately as E. P. Thompson suggests.[35] Nor was Methodism as unambiguously conservative as E. P. Thompson pretends. Wesley himself and many of the ministers who followed him preached submission and obedience, but their doctrine was not universally embraced. It was claimed:

'The late Mr Wesley was a high Tory, but since his death Preachers in general (a few excepted) have become Whigs, and the younger Methodists are generally inclining to the same

Side, whilst the older Methodists are Tories, but with them the prejudice is declining.[36]

It was surely not mere obliviousness and ingratitude that caused the authorities to equate Methodism with subversion. In areas like Lincolnshire it was all too obvious that Methodism was a form of direct protest against the clerical — and it was also the political — establishment. Southey thought, 'they are literally & precisely speaking, an Ecclesiastical Corresponding Society — a set of United Methodists,'[37] and many people would have agreed

Old Dissent — Presbyterians, Independents and Baptists

Probably the most important political consequence of the rise of Methodism was that it inadvertently encouraged a revival of Old Dissent, especially the Particular Baptists and the Independents. At the beginning of the eighteenth century, two thirds of the Old Dissenting body had been Presbyterians, but by the 1800s the proportion had declined to one twentieth.[38] This rapid decline of English Presbyterianism had been partly due to some Presbyterians adopting views which placed more stress on practical religion than on correct doctrine, which had caused an active confessional faith to be replaced by a blandly intellectual, almost Deist form of religion that had little attraction for the average worshipper. Other Presbyterian clergy adhered to a rigid orthodoxy which was equally unappealing.[39] This self-conscious but arid religion had little to offer flourishing commercial men who, as they grew richer, saw more and more the social advantages of embracing the Church of England, the denomination of the rich: 'tens of thousands', it was said, 'were restored to the Church of England by indifference and social emulation.'[40] Others, like the Rev. David Bogue, the dissenting historian, who was originally a Presbyterian minister at Camberwell, became Independents.

By the beginning of the nineteenth century there were not 12 Presbyterian congregations in England with a membership of over 500, and only their old endowments kept most Presbyterian churches solvent.[41] In 1715-16 there had been 903 Presbyterian and Independent congregations in England and Wales; by 1772 there were only 803.[42] From the 1740s onwards, however, the Methodists not only set the Old Dissenters an example of missionary zeal which they were quick to profit from, but also supplied Old Dissenting congregations with converts. By professing their membership of the Church of England, itinerant Methodist preachers reached audiences who would normally never have dreamt of entering a Dissenting chapel, so firmly was Old Dissent established as an alien entity within the community. These itinerant Methodists made many members of the Church of

England dissatisfied with the uninspired and negligent demeanour of their parish clergy, and once the itinerant preacher had passed on his way they would look about for some other source of evangelical comfort, and often enough found it in the Independent chapel.[43]

Wesley sought to prevent this, by urging on his hearers loyalty to the Church of England, but his precept was not always followed, and there was also the Calvinistic section of the Methodist movement over which Wesley had no influence, and of which whole congregations became Independents,[44] though frequently, despite their doctrinal resemblance, the Independents regarded the Calvinistic Methodists with suspicion.[45] The Baptists too, in Yorkshire at least, benefited from the accession of recruits converted by Methodists and Church of England Evangelicals.[46]

The revival of Old Dissent, especially Independency, became evident in the final quarter of the eighteenth century, though decline continued in the Somerset, Gloucestershire and Worcestershire area, and in the Leicestershire, Rutland, Northamptonshire area. It is true that Old Dissent neither equalled the growth rate of Methodism (which probably overtook it in numerical strength by 1815) nor even kept abreast of increases of population. Yet Old Dissent was not the less significant for all that. Methodism generally attracted the lower middle classes. Old Dissent, though also the religion of the artisan and the petit bourgeois, seems to have attracted a somewhat more affluent and socially self-confident element, though admittedly many congregations emerged in this period which lacked the exclusiveness and morale of the old established inward-looking communities of the earlier eighteenth century. Very few Methodists were actually rich, but a number of mercantile Old Dissenters were.

Old Dissent was also more intellectually self-confident. Dissenting academics like those at Warrington and Hackney had made a major contribution to secular education in the eighteenth century: the former especially produced a number of reformers and publicists such as John Aikin and Thomas Percival. Moreover the political import of Methodism was ambiguous, whereas Old Dissent was staunchly and confirmedly hostile to the Establishment. Its adherents were no longer generally Republicans, and they had on the whole accepted the legal disqualifications which, often only theoretically, gave them the status of second-class citizens, but Whiggism was one of the strongest of their traditions, they were grateful for the Whig leaders' part in the unsuccessful attempt to repeal the Test Act,[47] and without being notably aggressive, they could not but favour reform.

Old Dissent was also important in that it had much in common with a key element within the Church of England. In this it had common ground with the Calvinistic, as opposed to the Wesleyan Methodists. The Wesleyans' belief that man could save his eternal soul by his spiritual endeavours during life was derived from High Church doctrine, though most High Churchmen were too socially reactionary to have sympathy with Methodist enthusiasm. The Independents, the Particular Baptists, and the Calvinistic section of the Methodist movement believed that each man's salvation was predetermined, a doctrine favoured by most, though not all, of the Evangelicals in the Church of England. Thus, though the Evangelicals admired Wesley's missionary success, doctrinally they felt closer to the Independents and to the Calvinistic Methodists. There was indeed a considerable degree of free movement of ideas, and even of personnel, between the groups. The most prominent Evangelical layman, Wilberforce, a couple of times actually took communion in Dissenting chapels, as did Hannah More.[48] There were even, in the southern Midlands in the 1790s, non-denominational itinerancies established, such as the Bedfordshire Union, supported by both Old Dissent and the Church of England.

The Bible Society
The Church of England Evangelicals were mostly supporters of Pitt and his successors, whereas the Old Dissenters favoured the Foxite opposition. But the Evangelicals were moderate government men; whatever their hostility to the atheistical French Revolution, they were not apostles of reaction. Co-operation between the two groups had long seemed possible and had been attempted in The London Missionary Society of 1795 and The Religious Tract Society of 1799. It was finally established on a nation-wide institutional base in 1804 when the British and Foreign Bible Society was set up. The president was Lord Teignmouth, formerly Governor-General of Bengal. The original vice-presidents included four bishops, and the two most prominent Evangelical MPs, Wilberforce and Henry Thornton. The aim of the society was quite simply to distribute Bibles. The revenue raised in the year 1806-7 was £5,363, plus £889 from the sale of Bibles; in 1809-10 £14,284 plus £6,428 from the sale of Bibles; in 1812-3 no less than £65,748 plus £9,525 from the sale of Bibles. This large increase in revenue was due to the establishment from 1809 onwards of Auxiliary Societies to collect smaller contributions from those unable to afford the full subscription. By 1812 there were 115 Auxiliary Societies up and down the country. The Auxiliary Societies not only provided a great deal of money, but also involved large numbers of people in provincial towns in the

Bible Society and its aims.

Significantly enough, these Auxiliary Societies were established not so much in the traditional centres of religious observance but in the areas most in need of a missionary initiative. The first Auxiliary Society was established in Birmingham, and Nottingham, Leeds, Manchester, Sheffield, Rotherham and Huddersfield all had Auxiliary Societies by the end of 1810, costing from 2s to 7s to join, and thereafter 6d or 1s per month.[49] Many of these local societies were set up under the auspices of local magnates such as Lord Harewood at Leeds, Earl Fitzwilliam at Sheffield, and his son Lord Milton at Rotherham.

Criticism of the Bible Society began within months of its inauguration and became more bitter once the Auxiliary Societies began to be set up. Though theoretically organized by members of the Church of England, the Bible Society did not exclude Dissenters from participation, and especially in the Auxiliary Societies it was the Dissenters who bore the burden of administration. For this reason more conservative members of the Church of England saw the Bible Society as a scheme to introduce Dissenters into the bosom of the Church under the specious guise of co-operation in pursuit of common interests. The Bible Society was also accused of competing with the exclusively Church of England Society for the Propagation of Christian Knowledge, which had been set up in 1698 and which, with an income of £23,547 in 1811-12, had been quickly outstripped by the Bible Society as a fund-raising organization. A further objection, introduced by Herbert Marsh's *An Inquiry into the Consequences of Neglecting to give the Prayer Book with the Bible,* published in 1810, was that it was potentially dangerous to give Bibles to the uninstructed, without also giving them prayer books to show them the true doctrinal interpretation. During the following decade over 100 pamphlets were published on the subject, with stimulating titles like *A Review of Mr Norris's Attack upon the British and Foreign Bible Society* and *A Churchman's Reasons for Declining a Connexion with the Bible Society.*

Many of the Bible Society's leaders had joined the SPCK in the days before the Bible Society had been set up: Wilberforce in 1786, Thornton in 1787. But Evangelicals who came later on the scene were treated with suspicion: Simeon for example was black-balled and only admitted after pressure from the Bishop of London.[50] The SPCK extended its activity in competition with the Bible Society, its numbers growing from 2,000 members in 1800 and 3,560 in 1810 to 14,530 in 1820, this increase being partly due to the initial subscriptions being waived for curates and the poorer incumbents, and to the recruitment of country members by setting up local committees from 1810 onwards, in imitation of the Auxiliary Bible Societies.[51]

It has been argued that the rivalry between the SPCK and the Bible Society was part of what was nothing less than a full-scale struggle between the High Churchmen and the Evangelicals for control of the Church of England.[52] The controversy over the setting up of an Auxiliary Bible Society in Cambridge, for example, and the election of HH the Duke of Gloucester as Chancellor of Cambridge University have been interpreted as fully orchestrated tactical projects.[53] In fact, the cohesion of the Evangelical and of the High Church parties, can be exaggerated. Many great noblemen who patronized the Bible Societies and other Evangelical-organized charities were not themselves Evangelicals. Earl Grosvenor, who subscribed to 24 charitable societies organized by Evangelicals, and was president of four of the 24, was principally interested in horse racing. The Marquess of Cholmondeley, who subscribed to 23 and presided over four, was a gambler and libertine, and boon companion of the Prince of Wales. It is really not possible to represent the Church of England in this period as a battleground between Evangelicalism and the High Church. There were disagreements and tensions, but there were not two armed camps. If anything, these disagreements and tensions were symptoms of health, indications of the somewhat fitful and inadequate attempts the Church of England was making to adjust to social change.

5
Lower Class Unrest Before 1803

The Early 1790s
During the earlier part of the 1790s over 100 different British towns and cities had reform societies, the earliest being the Sheffield Constitutional Society, formed in the late autumn of 1791, and the largest being the London Corresponding Society, membership of which, however, never exceeded 4,000. Only a small proportion of the lower classes joined these societies: the strongest local movements, relative to the potential support, were in the two great provincial centres of skilled artisan labour, Norwich and Sheffield, with up to 2,000 members of reform societies. In Norwich indeed, where there was not one but three separate societies, the strength of reform was such that Army officers, who were naturally identified with the unpopular war with France, risked being assaulted if they appeared in the streets after dark.[1] Elsewhere reform societies made less impact on the people, and were little more than self-conscious talking shops.

But the ruling class, horrified by the excesses of the French Revolution, and genuinely believing that the reformers aimed at the subversion of civilized society, saw in the reform societies a threat against which they had to defend themselves by all the means at their disposal. The reformers were given the opprobrious name of Jacobins, as if they were colleagues of Robespierre or Danton — one Norwich reformer proudly adopted the title, though the use of the term Jacobin does not seem to have been common amongst reformers.[2] There was a general movement towards reaction amongst the ruling class, and even a section of the Whig opposition rallied to the government, leaving the rest of the opposition, led by Fox, an increasingly discredited rump.

During the earlier 1790s, the repressive task of the authorities was relatively easy as the reformers, not even suspecting how far they were feared by the ruling class, conducted their activities in a blaze of publicity. The last year of peace, 1792, the year in which the reform societies began to flourish, saw the royal proclamation against seditious writings, the dismissal from their military commissions of Lord Sempill, John Gawler, and Lord Edward Fitzgerald, the future United Irish conspirator, and the trial in his absence for sedition of Thomas Paine, who had already fled abroad. In February 1793 John Frost, a solicitor, a member of the London Corresponding Society, and veteran of the reform movement of the 1780s, was jailed for six months for defining equality as meaning 'No King'. In May, William Frend was expelled from Cambridge University for his attack on the liturgy. In July, William Winterbotham was jailed for four years for seditious libel. In November, Daniel Holt, a Newark printer, was jailed for republishing John Cartwright's *An Address to the Tradesmen, Mechanics, Labourers, and other Inhabitants of the Town of Newark, on a Parliamentary Reform*, a tract which had not been considered actionable on its original appearance in 1782. In Scotland, Thomas Muir was sentenced to 14 years' transportation in August, and the Rev. Thomas Fysshe Palmer (a former fellow of Queens', Cambridge and one time friend of Samuel Johnson) to seven years' transportation in September. An attempt to hold a National Convention at Edinburgh led to more arrests in December, and William Skirving, the organizer, and two English delegates, Maurice Margarot and Joseph Gerrald, were transported. Of these five transportees, only Margarot ever saw Britain again.

After the breaking up of the Edinburgh Convention the reformers in England knew their days were numbered, though English juries were less easily influenced than those in Scotland, and English judges were more impartial than Robert McQueen, Lord Braxfield, the Lord Justice Clerk, who presided at the Scots trials and who, when it was pointed out that even Christ was a reformer, responded, 'Muckle he made o' that, he was hanget'. Eight Manchester reformers were tried for conspiracy at Lancaster in April 1794, and acquitted, even though a local loyalist group, the Manchester Association For Preserving Liberty, Order And Property, had been engaged since the previous July in concocting a case against them. Early in May, Benjamin Vaughan, MP for Calne in the Marquess of Lansdowne's interest, was summoned before the Privy Council to be questioned about his connections with English *emigrés* resident in France, but fearing prosecution he fled across the Channel. During the following week most of the leaders of the London Corresponding Society and of the middle-class Society for Constitutional Information were rounded up in a series of raids. Those arrested included Thomas Hardy, secretary of the London Corresponding Society, John Thelwall, the society's principal propagandist, Horne Tooke of the Society for Constitutional Information, and Jeremiah Joyce, a member of both societies, and tutor to the children of the reforming peer Earl Stanhope. Joyce had actually been teaching Stanhope's sons when the Under-Secretary of State for the Home Department arrived with a warrant for his arrest.

Twelve of those arrested were indicted for treason, the rest released. The trials of Hardy, Thelwall and Horne Tooke led to their triumphant acquittal: no evidence was offered against Baxter and Richter, and the others were discharged. The trials were a personal triumph for the defence counsel, the Hon. Thomas Erskine, and Hardy received such an increase of custom in his shoemaking business that his journeymen struck for more pay. But the Corresponding Society never recovered from these trials. Though Horne Tooke stood for Westminster as a reform candidate in the 1796 election, and Thelwall continued his lecturing, others of those indicted, like Hardy, avoided further implication. Consequently, a more prominent role was assumed by extremists like John Binns and Dr Robert Watson, the former secretary of Lord George Gordon, who had been earlier rejected by the central committee as a divisional delegate, but now became chairman.[5] The prominence of the more moderate Francis Place also dates from this period, but he was unable either to step up membership nor control the growing extremism of the other leaders.

On 27 September 1794 Paul Lemaitre, a young watchmaker and Corresponding Society member was arrested at pistol-point, accused of conspiring to assassinate the King with an air-gun. (This scheme soon became notorious as the 'Pop-gun Plot'.) Two associates, John Smith and George Higgins were also arrested. Lemaitre was released pending trial in May 1795, and eventually acquitted a year later. The London Corresponding Society experienced a revival in 1795, partly because of the food shortages of that year, but the passing of the so-called Pitt and Grenville Acts at the end of the year virtually brought the society to an end as a popular movement. These two Acts, passed in response to the mobbing of the King's coach on 29 October 1795, extended the law of treason to cover writing about the death or deposition of the King (as distinct from an actual overt act) and extended the law of sedition to cover criticism of the established government. They also limited public meetings to 50 persons, and virtually brought all public gatherings, however orderly, within the terms of the Riot Act.

As a last effort before these acts came into force, the Corresponding Society organized two public meetings in Copenhagen Fields (a tract of open land that is now the area of seedy dwellings between Kentish Town and Islington, bisected by Camden Road). Although the Corresponding Society claimed that 'upwards of Two Hundred Thousand Citizens' attended the first of these rallies,[6] they were not a success politically. One witness recorded: 'The meeting I saw looked like a fair, — Men, women, & children — The Declaimers are the Mountebanks.— There are stalls selling gin and gingerbread; & men moving abt the field (with placards on poles, containing the title of some favourite publication) selling sedition by wholesail. At the stalls you are saluted 'Gin! Citizens, Gin! Fine patriotic gin! take a glass of my best democratic! &c. &c.— I addressed a placardist "Come give me sixpenny worth of sedition."— This I said jeeringly, & loud, yet I did not observe a single fierce countenance reprove me for jesting with what they might think serious.— The man himself, cooly supplied me with songs addresses &c &c as if he was selling so much gingerbread. . . . There were three tribunes; & the audience (excepting the bodyguard) fluctuated from one to the other, as the speakers happened to grow dull or entertaining. — You may have seen in the Papers of prodigious numbers being at the meeting.— This is not true in the sense such accounts wd be understood.— In the course of the day many thousands were doubtless in the field; but never at one time.— I was there between 2 & 3 & I don't believe there were 500 in the field, & I saw it at the fullest time as far as I can understand.'[7]

In Norwich a petition against the Pitt and Grenville Acts received 5,284 signatures.[8] Yet on the whole the Acts received widespread support. 'Infamous as these laws were', Francis Place wrote afterwards, 'they were popular measures. The people, ay, the mass of the shoopkeepers and working people, may be said to have approved them without understanding them.'[9]

The more moderate members of the London Corresponding Society fell away. Place himself resigned from the General Committee in 1796, and gave up his membership of the society altogether in June 1797.[10] All over the country propaganda against the reformers gained ground in the popular mind. Under pressure from licensing JPs, publicans in Manchester, Birmingham and elsewhere adorned their public houses with notices saying 'No Jacobins Admitted Here'. There were loyalist riots. At Derby, in March 1797, a mob collected with horns and drums outside a Baptist chapel where Thelwall was lecturing, and broke the windows. Thelwall, normally the timidest of men, passed through the mob with a pistol in his hand, declaring he would shoot any person who molested him. Meanwhile the authorities did not relax their efforts. In April 1797 John Gale Jones, who since 1794 had nearly rivalled Thelwall as a leading reform spokesman, was convicted of sedition at Warwick. On 31 July of that year an illegal open-air meeting at St Pancras was dispersed by the magistrates, and six leaders were arrested.

Sources of Information

From this point on the activities of the reformers are wrapped in increasing mystery. Reform was at last going underground. Henceforth the problem of assessing inadequate information would be one of the chief preoccupations of the Home Department. Much of the information the Home Department had to rely on was mere gossip:

'A Gentleman, who travelled with me in a Postchaise yesterday afternoon, informed me that a Gentleman from the West Riding of Yorkshire, had been mentioning to him, that in the Town of *Huddersfield* in that Riding and its vicinity, there were Persons who were active in administering oaths to the People; and that the Persons who were supposed to be thus sworn, were called *Ezekielites*. This name, which coincides with the account I received in Manchester of the nature of the oath and the manner of administering it, inclines me to believe it, as a very worthy Magistrate of the Corporation of Macclesfield, at whose house I at present am, says that he has no doubt but the conspiracy has gained ground in Yorkshire from the general reports he has received, though there is nothing which he can particularly substantiate.'[11]*

The Oddfellows, a charitable and social institution still flourishing today, was more than once denounced, and on one occasion 42 members were arrested at Portsmouth.[12] Some informants seem to have been motivated by vanity or the hope of reward. Men such as T. H. Hirst, a discharged soldier who, though he had the astuteness to name Despard as a principal conspirator two months before Despard's arrest, nevertheless thought fit to claim he was involved with plotters intending 'to Ristore the throne Back from this present Royal Family, which Rob'd the Stuard Family of it',[13] or Sergeant James Lawson who first introduced himself to the notice of the authorities by reporting a plot to poison the troops at Chelmsford,[14] and later revealed a conspiracy extending throughout England, Scotland and Ireland, led by one 'Lord Lovat' who received letters from Talleyrand beginning 'My Beloved Couzin'.[15] Upton, who invented the 'Pop-gun Plot' was probably motivated by revenge or the fear of being himself denounced to the London Corresponding Society by his principal victim, Lemaitre.[16]

---

* These Ezekielites were followers of Richard Brothers. They may have been the same as a group at Bradford, led by one Zachary Robinson, a former Methodist preacher, known as Jerusalemites.

Other information, purporting to come from actual conspirators, was hardly more reliable. A man at Tynemouth who boasted that he 'was a Member of the London Corresponding Society, and was one of 500 who were Tried for Treason & acquitted. He said likewise that Bonaparte was a particular Friend of his but he had not seen him for some time', was evidently drunk.[17] An anonymous letter claiming 'we have a hundred and fifty thousand men in essex and suffock and a multitude from norfock now rady to come to London at a days worning and if we come wo Be unto gorg the 4 and to that great city of London', caused the man who forwarded it to the Home Department to remark with surprise, 'I always understood heretofore, the people of this country were well affected & contented'.[18] Probably it was an example of that tendency to fantasize which had earlier produced reports that the affluent Maurice Margarot, chairman of the London Corresponding Society, lodged in a garret and presided over 'an infernal club of chimney Sweepers' and that Fysshe Palmer, a Bedfordshire man farming in Scotland and a former fellow of Queens', Cambridge, was 'a bankrupt butcher from Birmingham'.[19]

For the bulk of its local information the Home Department relied on the Lords-Lieutenant. Some of the Lords-Lieutenant, like Earl Fitzwilliam in the West Riding or Earl Fortescue in Devon, were active, conscientious and eminently sane, but others were less effectual, and the Duke of Devonshire, responsible for the frequently disturbed county of Derbyshire, never once sent in a report of any unrest. The Home Department also heard occasionally from generals commanding military districts, and later, during the Luddite troubles, Major-General Maitland became a frequent and valued correspondent.

But the major part of the Home Department's information came from a tiny handful of JPs who, year in and year out, impelled by a sense of duty or by a passion for interference, anxiously collected information from any number of random sources, interrogated suspects, and organized spies. Lancashire and Cheshire were blessed by an outstanding quartet of this sort: Ralph Fletcher and the Rev. Thomas Bancroft, respectively lieutenant-colonel and chaplain of the Bolton Volunteers, J. Lloyd of Stockport and the Rev. W. R. Hay. It was these four men, and the spies they hired, who supplied most of what evidence there is for the existence of a widespread Jacobin underground.

The ultimate responsibility for evaluating reports from the localities rested with the Secretary of State for the Home Department, assisted by two Under-Secretaries of State. Isolated in Whitehall, it was easy to make mistakes. Viscount Sidmouth in particular, who took over the Home Department at the peak of the

Luddite troubles, seems to have succumbed altogether to the sense of unreality and lack of proportion that was perhaps inseparable from the task of directing a counter-revolution from a London office. Robert Plumer Ward recorded a conversation he had with Sidmouth on the subject of the radicals in 1819:

'I told him I had just been through their country, as well as all over the north; which for the most part I found very peacable, and even civil, and very *anti-Radical*. He shook his head, and pointing to volumes of papers, said, if I knew their contents I would not say so, for the pictures were frightful.'[20]

The only reliable and experienced persons available to investigate local reports were the 27 metropolitan stipendiary magistrates, belonging to the Bow Street Office, the River Police Office, and the seven Public Offices established in 1792. These men also had their routine duties to perform, and often there were other official calls on their time. Henry James Pye presumably needed to spare only a little energy for his additional post of Poet Laureate, but Aaron Graham spent a great deal of time on his duties as Inspector of Convict Hulks, and also lived for a period at Sheerness, following the Nore mutinies, because there was no local JP. James Read of the Shadwell Office, soon after passing some weeks in Wiltshire investigating the frame-breaking disturbances there, was sent to Germany to reorganize British espionage in that country. When these stipendiary magistrates were actually sent down to the provinces, they often needed only a few days to disperse the tangled web of interference and rumour spun by the local authorities.

The United Englishmen

Towards the end of January 1798 the authorities began to receive reports of a new lower-class organization more sinister than any hitherto suspected, apparently modelled on the United Irish movement, at that time active in Ireland. The first report seems to have been an anonymous information of 27 January 1798 claiming that there were five divisions of the Society of United Englishmen in Leeds, and many others in the Dewsbury neighbourhood, each consisting of ten men.[21] On 15 February, the Rev. John Waring claimed that an Irishman had called on him and said he was a free mason, a Knight Templar, and a United Englishman, and that there were 20,000 United Englishmen in Manchester.[22] At about this time, two United Irish leaders, Arthur O'Connor and Father James O'Coigly were arrested in Kent, attempting to leave the country. John Binns of the London Corresponding Society was arrested with them. O'Coigly was found to be in the possession of an address from 'the Secret Committee of England' to the French Directory. O'Coigly had been in London in January and had been in touch with some of the London reformers, and one of his Irish companions had given the details of the United Irish organization to John Binns' brother Benjamin, and to Thomas Evans, 'a sort of absurd fanatic, continually operated on by impulses'.[23]

After the arrest of O'Connor, O'Coigly and John Binns, Benjamin Binns and Thomas Evans seem to have set about organizing a group in London modelled on the United Irishmen. An anonymous informant deposed on 12 March 1798 that the United Englishmen had existed in the capital for 12 months, and the group was organized in seven sections, three of them in the St. Pancras area, two meeting in Virginia Street, and two in Compton Street, Clerkenwell. On the same day John Scotson, of Torrington Street,, Ratcliffe Highway, deposed that John Wheelwright, a lemon and orange seller, had asked him to join a United English cell in Rotherhithe.[24] In fact not a single division was formed, for the inaugural meeting on 18 April 1798 at 'The George', St John's: Street, Clerkenwell, was broken up by the authorities, and those present were arrested. A form for an oath of secrecy was found on the floor, and in Evans' pocket another oath was discovered, expressing willingness 'to join the society of True Britons, to learn the use of arms'.[25] Next day the Committee of the Corresponding Society, including the unfortunate Lemaitre, was also seized. The total apprehended at these two meetings was 27.[26]

The Home Department continued to receive information of flourishing United English societies in the north, and they finally concluded that the United Englishmen were established in Manchester 'before the year 1797' by Binns and O'Coigly, and that there were 40 divisions in London, half of which had regular meeting places and times.[27] This was of course sheer fantasy. It would appear that, in spite of numerous depositions under oath to the contrary, there had never been any substantial metropolitan organization as such, nor any movement connected with O'Coigly or either of the Binns brothers other than the abortive inaugural meeting of 18 April, and that in the northern counties of the United Englishmen were no more than a handful of men who had talked of armed insurrection and sworn oaths from late 1797 onwards, but who had no significant London contacts. In many areas reports and rumours of a revolutionary underground persisted for so many years that it seems rash to dismiss them thus lightly, but it is surely significant that one of the most alarming incidents of the early days of the alleged movement, when ten Cumberland land-owners received letters in the name of the Council or Committee of the United Englishmen at Workington, demanding money to pay for arms, turned out to be the sole and unique instance of reported United English activity in Cumberland.[28] Three of the landowners apparently paid over the money demanded. What became of it never transpired.

O'Coigly was hanged for treason in July 1798. During the following spring a secret committee of the House of Commons decided there was a nationwide conspiracy in existence. An Act (39 Geo. III c.79) was passed prohibiting all societies acting in branches or divisions, banning the London Corresponding Society and the United Englishmen by name, and requiring all debating societies and reading rooms to be licensed. This marked the final demise of the London Corresponding Society, which had not actually met, even in divisions, since the previous April, and had dwindled to 200 nominal members.[29] Habeas Corpus was suspended too, and various suspects were confined without trial, mostly in the Middlesex House of Correction at Cold Bath Fields, popularly known as 'The Bastile'.*

For some months after the secret committee's report, nothing more was heard of the United Englishmen. During the harsh winter of 1799-1800 however, when food riots and incendiarism became frequent, the rumours revived. An anonymous letter to Lord Eldon claimed there were 30,000 sworn United Englishmen in Saddleworth, 50,000 in Cheshire and Derbyshire, and at least as many in Lancashire.[30] Disturbances continued throughout 1800, increasing in the autumn when for the second year running, the harvest turned out to be below average. A paper posted up on the wall of the Bank of England in September announced 'the time is come For you to Revenge your Wrongs. Be no Longer Slaves or Dupes of a Despottic Tyrannical *Government* the Reagular soldiers are your Freands you have only a Few Feather Bed milk sops to oppose you'.[31] Another paper, pasted to the wall of the Cold Bath Fields prison said:

'Cold Bath fields
on Sunday Night
10 Thousand Men
will meet there!!!
Remember the Bastile.'[32]

A month later, a paper found at Birmingham headed 'Vive la Republic', urging people to join 'the army of Redress, at the Head of which, in a few Days you will find Earl Stanhope, Duke of Bedford, and others equally great and Noble who are determined to set you free or meet a glorious Death'.[33] These seditious papers were naturally supposed by the authorities to be connected with the outbreaks of food-rioting, and a handbill found at Wolverhampton appeared to demonstrate such a link:

---

*This prison stood in a corner of the open marsh south of Pentonville, on a site now occupied by Mount Pleasant Sorting Office.

'To the well wishers of themselves
Whereas the Lower Class of People are desired to be assembled
together on Monday the 24 of Nov! 1800 at the Iron Bridge
to take the readiest and speediest Method of bringing down the
high Price of Provisions that so long has been the cause of so
much Murmuring in England. J.A. hopes that none of you will
come empty handed that is not to come without a sufficient
Weapon to maintain so bold an Enterprize; I have won the
hearts of the Cavalry so you need not be afraid of them & I will
be in the midst of you & will do my best endeavours to maintain the Noble Cause of liberty as I have had a Letter from the
Chief Consul Buonaparte Who says he will be amongst us &
Death or Liberty must be our Souls desire
No King Buonaparte for Ever.'[34]
The Lord-Lieutenant of Worcestershire reported:
'The Miners, Colliers, &c, are ready to rise in a Mass are armed
& about Walsal & in Staffordshire I am informed that Irish
pikes are made & in the hands of a very desperate Set of Villains
who are ripe for any Mischief.'[35]
Aaron Graham was sent by the Home Secretary to investigate,
and troops were distributed throughout the Midlands in anticipation of trouble, but in the end Graham reported that both
Birmingham and Wolverhampton were quiet, and that in the latter
place, apart from the regulars of one ale-house, and 'two Inhabitants who are Methodists and politically mad', there was nothing
left of 'the old Corresponding-society-school'.[36]
In the West Riding, however, there were several reports of
night meetings. At one, it was stated, 'an orator in a Mask
harangues the people—reads letters from distant societies by the
light of a candle & immediately burns them'.[37] At another, there
was talk of manufacturing pikes: the informant, being recognized
as a spy, tried to placate the crowd of about 1,000 by suggesting
that the employers should buy wheat and sell it to their workmen
at a lower price. This was answered by cries of 'Wouldn't do, we
must strike at the Root of the Evil.'
'The Informant then asked them, what they conceived to be the
Root of the Evil — He was answered — "Government". That Mr
Pitt and all his measures were execrable to Human Nature —
That nothing could prosper in the present Hands, He would
starve them all to Death. That nothing would relieve them but a
change of Ministers exterminating Mr Pitt and putting
Charles Fox in his place'.[38]
There were meetings, too, in Lancashire. A spy employed by local
JPs spoke of Bolton as being 'in a State of Rebellion' and added
'I am perfectly satisfied for 20 miles round this Place 9/10 of the

People are sworn to overthrow the present Constitution.'[39] A new secret committee of the Commons, reporting on 13 April 1801, decided there was a serious increase of conspiracy, and again recommended the suspension of Habeas Corpus. Earl Fitzwilliam, responsible as Lord Lieutenant for the West Riding where allegedly the plotting was at its worst, was less convinced, telling the Home Secretary:

'Loose Conversation, taking its rise in the pressure of the Times, from scarcity & dearness of provisions, & from want of employment, has certainly been holden by the Lower Orders of the People, & They talk'd of revolution, as the remedy for famine. It is suppos'd that Oaths have been taken, but nothing certain seems to have come to the knowledge of any of the Magistrates, with whom I have convers'd, nor they do seem to give much importance to any suppos'd Conspiracies, or Combinations, or to be in alarm on account of the Temper of the People.'[40]

During the early summer of 1801 frequent meetings were held by night in the hills around the West Riding wool towns. It proved impossible for the JPs to learn of their location beforehand, even though this information seemed common knowledge amongst the poorer people. At a meeting on Staincliff Common, near Dewsbury, 'the numbers who went out of curiosity were so great as to disturb the proceedings of the disaffected who dispersed very early without doing any business', yet the authorities knew nothing of this till afterwards.[41] In April, copies of a paper were thrust under doors and into market stalls at Myrtlegrove, proposing a meeting 'in Order to take into consideration the exorbitant price of Provisions — To expose fraud and every Species of Heredtary Government. To lessen the oppression of Taxes, to propose plans for the Education of helpless Infancy, and the comfortable support of the Aged and destressed, to endeavour to conciliate Nations to each other, to exterpate the horrid practice of War. To promote universal Peace Civilisation and Commerce, to breake the Chains of Political Superstition, to raise degraded Man to his proper Rank....'

This eloquent conflation of Paine, Rousseau and Thelwall degenerated into a denunciation of the parliamentary majority of:

'mercenary Hirleings, Government Pimps — Corndealers — Placemen — Pentioners — Paracites &c. .... No let them exist not one Day longer, we are the Sovereignity; rise then from your lethergy and attend at the place apointed — drag the Constitution from its hidden place — and lay it open to publick inspection — Shake the Earth to its Center — And make the Authors of an unjust War, the Victims of its Fury.'[42]

This paper was sent to Fitzwilliam, but he maintained his opinion that the West Riding night meetings were relatively innocuous. He reported:

'No specified Object was profess'd, but generally a promise was held out, that great Publick benefit would be deriv'd from these Meetings, provided the Members stuck steadily together; That in pursuit of these good ends, no means, but the most innocent, would be used: Life & Property were to be held most sacred & inviolate: That such was the nature, & such the tendency of these Ends, that Dukes, Lords, & great Men of every description approv'd of the Meetings, & would take part in them, whenever occasion requir'd.'[43]

In June there were alleged to be over 30,000 United Englishmen in the Leeds area, though there were supposedly complaints within the movement of a falling off of support at Halifax, Bradford and Huddersfield.[44] This last report actually came from Lancashire, and one Lancashire JP, Ralph Fletcher, from the vantage point of Bolton, gained the impression that the West Riding was 'more infected with Jacobin Principles' even than Lancashire;[45] but in Yorkshire itself it was felt by the end of August that the movement was dying away.[46]

There were also meetings in Lancashire. A projected daytime rally at Tandle Hill was expected to attract 50,000.[47] In the event one tenth of that number met on Sunday 3 May 1801 at Buckton Castle, near the meeting place of the Lancashire, Yorkshire and Cheshire borders, and a squadron of dragoons chased the crowd from one hill top to another, from nine in the morning till four in the afternoon, before they eventually dispersed.[48] At another meeting, at Rivington Pike, three weeks later, only 200 were present, of whom 21 were arrested, including two spinners, a stonemason, three coal miners and 12 weavers.[49] In mid-May it was acknowledged that the disaffected had not yet acquired any arms, but five weeks later an informant claimed to have seen armed men drilling.[50] Printed cards and a printed constituion were also found.[51] It was not till January 1802 that the Lancashire JPs admitted that the conspiracy seemed at a standstill.[52]

It was not long before the spate of alarmist reports revived. On 3 April 1802 Ralph Fletcher informed the Home Department that one William Cheetham was being sent by the Manchester committee of the United Englishmen as a delegate to the national committee in London, with the help of a contribution of £5 19s 0d from the Leeds, Wakefield and Sheffield committees. A delegate from Stockport had already been in London, and returned with orders. The number of professed members in Lancashire, Yorkshire, Cheshire and Derbyshire, exclusive of the Congleton district for which no return had yet been made, was 17,120.[53] On 25 June 1802, an anonymous letter to the Secretary at War, Charles Yorke, claimed that there were many thousands of pikeheads ready at Sheffield and that there was a nationwide conspiracy in England, Scotland and Ireland.[54] On 7 July, Fletcher passed on a report of his favourite spy 'B' claiming that at a meeting of the London Directory of the United Englishmen at 'The Pewter Platter', Holborn, one of several soldiers present had made proposals concerning the seizure of the Tower, the Bank, Woolwich Arsenal and the Houses of Parliament. The others had thought it better to wait till Parliament was dissolved, and it was reaffirmed that 'no private property must be meddled with on any pretext whatsoever.' There were 15,000 Irish and nearly 57,000 English joined in the conspiracy in London; there were organizations in the south and west of the country, and 160,000 sworn men ready in Ireland. Another of Fletcher's spies, identified as 'D', stated that 574 men had joined the conspiracy at Stockport, 330 at Buxton and 241 at Newcastle under Lyme. As proof of the existence of Cheetham, the Manchester delegate, Fletcher forwarded a printed identity card used by collectors for a subscription for John Nicholls who had been jailed at Gloucester under the Habeas Corpus suspension: Cheetham's name was printed on the card as the organizing officer.[55] There were also night meetings in Yorkshire, but Fitzwilliam assured the Home Secretary that these were merely to further industrial wage claims.[56] A month later, he suggested that the 'vague reports of nocturnal meetings' sent to one Richard Walker were probably a joke, intended 'merely to play upon M.r W's alarms, for he seems to have rather a tendency that way, which his Neighbours may have discover'd'.[57] Fitzwilliam does not seem to have paid much attention to a letter sent to General George Bernard threatening that his house would be 'blown down' unless he provided arms. He duly passed on a request from his JPs meeting at Bradford that troops should be sent to Yorkshire,[58] but even after three months of reports he wrote on the subject of night meetings, 'that there are, or that there have been such, is still so much the belief of many respectable persons, that I know not how to withhold my own altogether, though nothing is made out to my satisfaction'.[59] In the end he concluded that there may have been meetings to promote illicit trade unionisms, but nothing worse than that.[60]

The worst trouble of the year was not in the north at all, but in the woollen towns of Wiltshire, Gloucestershire and Somerset, where there was an outbreak of machine breaking by shearmen, or croppers, many of them recently demobilized soldiers who were threatened with redundancy by the introduction of gig mills. At Bradford on Avon, a mill was shot at for half an hour.[61] At Steeple

Ashton a factory was burnt down by an armed mob.[62] The shear-men evidently had some organization, and several men were eventually prosecuted for administering unlawful oaths. James Read was sent down from London to assist the local magistrates and initially seemed anxious to prove the combinations were part of a wider conspiracy, though after a while the tone of his reports to the Home Department suggested that the scale of the disaffection was relatively trivial.[63]

On 16 November 1802 Colonel Edward Marcus Despard and 35 fellow conspirators were arrested at 'The Oakley Arms', Lambeth. Despard, a former Governor of Honduras, had been involved with the reform movement for some years, and had been detained under the Habeas Corpus suspension. His plot to assassinate the King and seize the Tower of London and the Bank rather confirmed Ralph Fletcher's reports from Bolton that there was a widespread revolutionary conspiracy, and, after Despard's arrest, Fletcher's spy 'B' reported that money was being collected in Manchester for Despard's legal expenses.[64] Yet even the assiduous Fletcher was unable to gather any real evidence that Despard's plot had any ramifications outside London. Two men, William and Edward Simmnet, confessed to having been sworn in as United Englishmen at Sheffield,[65] and a box was seized containing seven large pikeheads, a crooked cutting instrument and four pieces of steel,[66] but that was about all. After Despard was executed, a man was prosecuted at Leeds for saying he wished Despard's head was down George III's throat,[67] and at Wolverhampton another man was arrested for distributing copies of Despard's valedictory address,[68] but there was no evidence that either man had ever heard of Despard prior to the latter's arrest.

After the execution of Despard, the rumours of conspiracy and oath-taking, the night meetings, the reports of secret conferences in the backrooms of London taverns, all died away. In May 1803 the war with France resumed. 'What then are we to Fight for?' asked a poster printed in London for a Nottingham customer in July 1803. 'Not for our Country, but for the Oppressors of it—Not for Ourselves, but for those who injure us—Not for our Liberty and Property, for both are invaded.' Another printed poster, dated a month later, asserted, 'this war is like the last unjust and unnecessary but it is a war of the rich men against the most sober honest and industrious part of the people of this nation'.[69] But anti-war propaganda of this sort was much rarer after 1803 than it had been in the 1790s; for the first three or four years at least the war was not unpopular, and opposition to the war ceased to be a major ingredient of reform ideology. Food prices remained high, but did not return to the critical level of 1800. It was eight years before the reports of a nationwide conspiracy began to revive.

The Problem of Interpretation

The belief of men like Ralph Fletcher that there really was a nation-wide plot in these years, and the disbelief of men like Earl Fitzwilliam, is echoed by the conflicting opinion of modern historians. One group, led by E. P. Thompson, believe that there was widespread support for a revolutionary underground, arguing that the process of industrialization must have necessarily involved the workers in increasing hardship and degradation. This group assert that the workers must inevitably have responded by elaborating the vision of an alternative society which under the system of authority prevailing at the time could only have been achieved by violent revolution. A rival group, currently led by Malcolm Thomis, deny this.

It is true that the fragmentary nature of the evidence suggests that the revolutionary movement was equally fragmentary and in fact not what one would call a movement at all. Yet it was certainly the case that a great deal did occur in this period that the authorities could not keep track of. For example, out of the 1,105 French prisoners who absconded from parole depots up and down the country between 1803 and 1814, 674 got clean away, often with local help.[70] More to the point, in Ireland during the 1790s the authorities received reports of a rising being planned, just as the authorities did in Britain. The tone and circumstantial detail of these reports were very similar in quality, but in Ireland the rising really did take place, though perhaps significantly it occurred in an area where disaffection had been least suspected.

The confused and sometimes contradictory clues described in the preceding pages might well be merely the tip of an iceberg, all that has survived of a vigorous and determined organization which, somehow, never quite brought off the revolution it had been planning for so long. The question might be stated thus: were the rumours and disturbances in various areas a surfacing of some of the myriad tentacles of a far-flung secret conspiracy, or were they merely isolated, thoughtless outbreaks over which credulous, perhaps even paranoiac, persons attempted to throw a net of spurious connections?

In fact, both these hypotheses are defective, and for the same reason. It is implied in the far-flung conspiracy theory on the one hand that there must have been a genuine threat of revolution, because there was a conspiracy, and by the unco-ordinated outbreak theory on the other hand that there could not have been a real conspiracy because there was no evidence of a real threat. Both theories fail to take into account the possibility that scores of intelligent men could over a period of several years devote their lives to organizing the overthrow of society, without ever posing any real threat to it.

Today, by coincidence, we live in an era analogous to the early nineteenth century in that clandestine political organizations exist beyond the pale of parliamentary debate. These organizations are not today illegal (with the exception of the IRA), but they are no less the object of suspicion to the authorities. As in the early nineteenth century, these organizations operate in the context of discontents which they do not create, and it is surely as mistaken to regard them as irresponsible lunatic fringe as it is to see them as crucial and potent agencies of revolution. E. P. Thompson, who has cleverly exposed the reluctance of Fabian historians like the Hammonds to accept the intrusions of the 'Jacobin' tradition of violence into the historical process by which British constitutional democracy developed, has himself been guilty of an ultra-leftist tendency towards wish-fulfilment, and has projected today's dream of a powerful revolutionary party in Britain back 180 years to a period when it was as fondly desired, and as sadly non-existent.

We may reconstruct the situation in the following way: there must have been individuals, or small groups amongst the lower classes *circa* 1800 committed to violence. It is not necessary to read the numerous spies' reports to be convinced of this. The undeniable fact that Despard in 1802 and later Thistlewood in 1819 organized conspiracies to overthrow the government by violence shows that the idea was not alien to the times. Even the belief of some amongst the ruling class that the lower sort were plotting bloody insurrection may be taken as proof that this was the sort of scheme which might at least have occurred to a few early nineteenth century reformers. 'There doubtless may be some evil & disaffected spirits, enough to create alarms, where the disposition is inclined to receive the impression, & so there will be in all large communities to the end of time', wrote one of Fitz-william's fellow sceptics.[71]

How many of these violent revolutionaries were there? The answer must surely be, not very many. Not every person involved in a riot needed to be committed to the violent overthrow of government. In fact riots, though demonstrating frustration and discontent, do not need to involve a single individual of established revolutionary principles. Where there were sustained campaigns of violence, as in Wiltshire in 1802, and in the North in 1811-14 (which latter will be discussed in a later chapter) relatively small groups of people were active. Both in 1802 and in 1811-14 the disturbances had their origin in industrial disputes, so that it might well be that a majority of those involved, though actually

committed to industrial militancy, had no larger views of general
political revolution. Consequently it is probable that of the
relatively small groups of activists, only a small proportion were
genuine, long-term revolutionary conspirators. If there had been
more revolutionaries, the groups of which they formed only the
nuclei, must have been larger. Even the most extraordinary claims
of large-scale organization are not inconsistent with this model,
for it would be natural enough, in any period of food shortage,
wage reduction, or other widespread discontent, for the revolutionaries to resume their activity of propaganda, of preaching to men
already half converted by circumstances, of proferring oaths to
those tempted by any solution to a situation they could not master;
and soon enough their activity, their half-formed projects, their
armies of half-convinced but still confused listeners, would be
transformed by rumour or report into concrete schemes and well-
drilled battalions.

One of the most striking features of this shadow underground
was its geographical extent. Some of the reports of delegates and
correspondence have never been substantiated, but others have.
Yet after all, there were migrant workers, pedlars, drovers,
soldiers, sailors, all accustomed to move quite freely over large
parts of the country. By means of such persons it was possible to
send letters by hand. Other missives are known to have been
rashly entrusted to the Post Office where they came under the
eagle eye of the Secretary of the Post Office, Francis Freeling.
Nor was it necessary for each item of news to rely on one single
carrier. The news of food riots, or frame breakings, could be spread
from village to village, over long distances, merely by one person
from each village walking over to the next hamlet to repeat his
story there. And as the handful of revolutionaries were spread
widely though thinly, it would not be long before the news of a
disturbance reached the ears of individuals who had long been
awaiting the trumpet cry of insurrection, and whose hopes would
briefly revive and inspire a spate of anonymous threatening letters
or slogan scrawling.

To say that there was no connection between outbreaks in
different localities at the same time is nonsense. On any given day
in any given place there would probably be someone actually from
or acquainted with a locality where there had been a disturbance,,
and someone else (or possibly the same man) familiar with some
of the revolutionary doctrines which were perhaps, at that very
moment, being given yet another optimistic airing in the wake of
the rioting or sabotage. Consequently a disturbance in any one
place would, almost automatically, create sinister ripples over a
wide area: and yet those widespread responses reflected not an

actual revolutionary underground, but the illusion of one.[72] This does not mean that the revolutionaries were at all a negligible group. Revolutionaries and their organizations do not cause revolutions; nor, once revolutions begin, do they always exert very effective control of the course of events. Revolutionaries do, however, create and broadcast the new framework of ideas and aspirations which, in the process of revolution, necessarily replaces the ideology of the system which is being thrown off, and helps shape the new system that is coming into being. The British Jacobins seem to have been as well equipped for that task as any other revolutionary group.

6
The Ideas of the Jacobins

FOR an understanding of the ideas of the reformers it is necessary to go back to the days before they became a proscribed underground: back to the earlier 1790s when an enormous number of reformist pamphlets were published, some dealing with particular issues, others discussing politics generally.

These pamphlets, written by many different hands, from many different points of view, differed on more issues than they agreed on. There was no rigid system of reform ideology.

Perhaps the only notion held in common was hostility to the war with revolutionary France which began in 1793. This hostility was of course shared by the parliamentary opposition who were not otherwise in tune with reform doctrines. *A View of the Causes and Consequences of the Present War with France* by the Hon. Thomas Erskine, a leading oppositionist, went through 48 editions, testifying to public dissatisfaction with the war. Like Erskine, the reformers saw the war as an integral part of the ministerial régime. They believed, in Thelwall's words, that 'the System of War and the System of Corruption have gone hand in hand', and that

'the more miserable the condition of the people, the more easy it is for unprincipled and ambitious rulers to continue the system of War; as also, that, in proportion to the calamities of the people, this system becomes more and more profitable to the ministers and tools of Corruption.'[1]

John Cartwright called it 'The Rotten Borough War'.[2] Pitt, the Prime Minister, was 'that miserable Quixote, whose whole life has been one uniform series of projects wickedly planned and weakly executed, of assertions pompously made and ignominiously retracted, of reforms factiously proposed and treacherously abandoned'.[3]

There was already some suspicion that the opposition partook of this 'System of Corruption'. Gerrald claimed that 'Parties are only a succession of birds of prey, of which the people are the banquet',[4] and Horne Tooke opposed both parties in the Westminster elections of 1790 and 1796, arguing that 'throughout the history of the world, down to the present moment, all personal parties and factions have always been found dangerous to the liberties of every free people.'[5] Yet John Gale Jones of the London Corresponding Society published a defence of Fox, the opposition leader, in which he stated:

'To Mr Fox, Sir, do I look for the restoration of that peace and tranquillity, which is so essential to the liberty and happiness of mankind: in opposing the destructive measures of the present minister, he has consulted the welfare, and is therefore, I think, justly entitled to the confidence of the people of England.'[6]

Nor was there any consensus on the role of monarchy. The classic denunciation of kingship, Paine's *The Rights of Man* had an enormous circulation—how enormous it is not quite clear as the usual figure quoted of half a million is surely exaggerated. The London Corresponding Society actually published *The Rights of Man* and according to Francis Place all its leaders were republicans—'This they were taught by the writings of Thomas Paine, and confirmed in them by Mr Winterbottoms history of the United States of North America'[7]—yet for obvious reasons of prudence they did not draw attention to their republicanism. *The Happy Reign of George the Last* by 'A Republican', probably published in 1795, was violent against *'courtiers,* and their *cringing creatures'* but mentioned the King only in the title. Daniel Isaac Eaton's pamphlet *Hog Wash* denounced George III as 'a gamecock: a haughty sanguinary tyrant, nursed in blood and slaughter from his infancy'. For publishing this Eaton was prosecuted, but most reformers were too prudent to run such a risk. Paine associated monarchy with tyranny, though whether as cause or symptom he did not make altogether clear—monarchy, he wrote, 'is all a bubble, a mere court artifice to procure money.... It is the master fraud, which shelters all others.'[8]—but Horne Tooke on the other hand defended monarchy, warning that when the borough-mongers had established their power, 'the most loyal adherents of royalty will be destroyed as traitors against their new majesties: the king will have no means left to protect his most faithful subjects; and the crown may find itself without a defender.'[9] He told the mob at the Westminster hustings on 30 May 1796:

'I love the king *according to law,* but I love my country better. A king may employ his time in hunting the harmless stag or timorous hare, whilst his ministers may enjoy the more sanguinary chase of running down his people. At present, therefore, I say, I love my king according to law; and whenever a king shall protect me and my fellow subjects from the murderous plots and conspiracies of his ministers, I will love him beyond the law, beyond the letter of the bond.'[10]

of the bond.'[10]

Thelwall of the London Corresponding Society agreed with this view of the King as a potential fellow-victim: 'with pure genuine, whole-length aristocrats, princes and people are alike indifferent: alike obnoxious when they aspire to any share of power; and alike acceptable as the tools and instruments of their ambition.'[11]

Nevertheless there was a considerable amount of speaking against the King: James Douglas, a Bolton weaver, was jailed for saying in an alehouse, 'I don't care a Damn for anybody, no I don't care for old George, he might kiss my arse for an old Rascal.'[12] John Richards, a Holborn tailor, was committed for assault and for saying 'the King ought to have been sent to Greenland Dock [the whale fishery depot] twenty Years ago, to have the Blubber boiled out of his head.'[13] A ferocious letter of abuse addressed in 1800 to the 'Eternal Villain Generally called the Duke of Portland' contained the wish, 'May the Ribs of Portland & them of Pitt be Transfered into the bottomless Pitt of hell, there to make Grid Irons to broyle the Heart of your Master Georgy.'[14] this sentiment seems to have been quite popular, for it was a toast in an Andover pub, and was found chalked on walls in Birmingham several months later.[15] A certain William Bowen refused to drink an oath to the King on the grounds that, 'he was of no Service, that he went to Parliament, & signed any Paper that was given to him, without knowing the Contents, & that he (the King) did not know anything of the Business of the Nation',[16] but a paper to a quite contrary effect was circulated in Merthyr Tydvil during the food riots there in September 1800:

'There is a great many men that believes the King has no power, but what is given him by parliament, it tis true that it twas intended that it should be so in the beginning but the Case is altered very much for he and his Ministry has got all the power, and both houses of parliament are no more than a shadow or image for he has got such means to bribe and corrupt them, so that the major part of them will give their Votes with him, Let him propose what he will.'[17]

Partly because of this concentration on the role of the King, the reformers failed to see politics in class terms. Both those who believed that royal authority was being usurped by Parliament, and those who thought Parliament was the tool of the King, conceived the parliamentary leaders to be a clique rather than the representatives of a social class. They failed also therefore to perceive the material basis of political inequality. Though Paine recommended progressive taxation 'to extirpate the unjust and unnatural law of primogeniture, and the vicious influence of the aristocratic system',[18] few other reformers attacked the rich and the noble as such.

Equally, most reformers totally rejected 'an unjust and absurd violation of private property'.[19] The London Corresponding Society, in keeping with its character as a movement of artisans and tradesmen, regarded property as 'sacred and inviolable', and the voluminous writings of Thelwall, the Society's chief publicist, are virtually devoid of any statement on economics beyond a vague endorsement of the claim that monopoly 'frustrates the Beneficence of our Seasons, and forbids the industrious Poor the immediate Necessaries of Life'.[20] E. P. Thompson's evocation of Thelwall as a thinker whose 'emphasis . . . upon economic and social questions . . . took Jacobinism to the borders of Socialism'[21] is sheer fantasy, or perhaps a comment on E. P. Thompson's notion of Socialism. In the 1790s one man, and one man only, conducted a sustained campaign against private property. This man was Thomas Spence. The son of an Aberdonian, either a hardware dealer or a shoemaker, Spence was brought up as a member of a sect called the Glassites, who practised a measure of community of property with regard to the needs of the poor.[22] During the 1770s, while living as a schoolteacher in Newcastle, Spence developed his ideas on the common ownership of land; in spite of his north of England experience he never seemed aware of the newer forms of property brought into prominence by the Industrial Revolution. His lecture *The Real Rights of Man*, published in 1775, was immediately seen as a bold and subversive attack on landlords as a class, though such had not been Spence's apparent intention. The lecture did not even mention the political aspects of the landlord's dominant position in society. It was merely an example of the abstract theorizing which was so fashionbable during the Enlightenment. Spence was naturally shocked and disgusted by the rabid response to his theoretical specualtions, and by the 1790s abstraction had given way to polemic:

'When a People create Landlords, they create a numerous host of hereditary Tyrants and Oppressors, who not content with their Lordly Revenue of Rents, seize also upon the Government, and parcel it out among themselves, and take as enormous salaries for the Places they occupy therein, as if they were poor men.'[23]

He even attacked Paine. The Young Man in his dialogue *The End of Oppression* wonders 'that Paine and the other Democrats should level all their Artillery at Kings, without striking like Spence at this root of every abuse and every grievance'—i.e. landlords—and the Old Man replies, 'The reason is evident: They have no chance of being Kings; but many of them are already, and the rest foolishly and wickedly hope to be sometime or other Landlords, lesser or greater.' What Spence argued for was communal ownership: 'I would not have the Land national, nor provincial, but parochial property.'[24] He envisaged free trade between parishes, and claimed, 'Surely nothing can be wanting to encourage both Trade and Labour, but

open Ports, Liberty, and security of Property.'[25] He in no sense
advocated nationalization, and later rebuked Charles Hall for
  'sliding into the System of Sir Thomas More's Utopia wherein he
  makes every kind of Property the Property of the Nation and the
  People obliged to work under Gang Masters. . . . But I don't
  think you will find many desirous to go into such a State of
  Barbarism and Slavery.'[26]
Each man was still to be personally and intimately involved with
his property, but it would not belong to him as an individual, but as
a member of a small community of joint-proprietors. These notions
were regarded with horror by the majority of reformers. Francis
Place, who rather admired Spence, regarded him as a political innocent,
'unpractised in the ways of the world, to an extent few could imagine
in a man who had been pushed about in it as he had been'.[27] One
opposition MP thought Spence's ideas demonstrated that he was
mad, and asked the AttorneyGeneral, following Spence's trial for
seditious libel in 1801, 'Whether every individual of the numerous
audience upon that occasion did not feel a sort of indignation at a
man being put upon his trial who was a fitter object of confinement
in Bedlam?'[28] Spence had few followers in the 1790s, but the influence
of his ideas was spreading by 1800, and it was eventually to be seen
that, mad or not, he had provided an ideological framework for men
whose eagerness for reform went beyond the moderation of the
London Corresponding Society.

Refusing to countenance the invasion of private property, most
reformers also rejected direct action as a remedy to Pitt's
misgovernment. Joseph Gerrald and some of the Scots reformers
believed that a British Convention 'the interposition of the great
body of the people themselves, electing deputies in whom they can
confide, and imparting instructions which they must injoin to be
executed',[29] would abolish war, envy, crime, ignorance and poverty
and create a new society, in which
  'the temptation to commit crimes would be lessened; and every
  man would feel a pride in obeying those laws, which he had
  contributed to enact. . . . Ignorance, the parent of vice, would be
  soon destroyed; as all men being trained to public business,
  would have their understandings enlightened upon the duties
  which they were bound to perform.'[30]
After the Convention at Edinburgh was broken up in December
1793, the reformers were left with no master strategy. They indulged
a pious hope that the dissemination of ideas, what Thelwall glibly
called the 'energies of reason',[31] would eventually have some effect
on the government. The two leading advocates of this view were
close friends, Thomas Holcroft and William Godwin. Holcroft first
expounded his ideas in his novel of rivalry in love and attempted

rape, *Anna St Ives*, which came out in 1792. Godwin's more systematic *Enquiry Concerning Political Justice* came out some months later. This latter book, which argued that 'government is . . . an evil, an usurpation upon the private judgment and individual conscience of mankind',[32] was the classic exposition of the power of reason to transform society. Godwin looked forward to the extinction of all government. 'The true supporters of government', he claimed, 'are the weak and uninformed, and not the wise. In proportion as weakness and ignorance shall diminish, the basis of government will also decay.'[33] Even representative institutions, in which the decisions of the majority shackled the minority, would wither away when 'the empire of reason' established itself. There would be no need for a legislative body as one could not make law, what was not previously just.[34] With the spread of correct ideas, disparity of wealth 'will subside, by gradual and incessant progress, into its true level',[35] and eventually the very notion of property would disappear. Godwin, himself the Englishman of his generation most influenced by continental *philosophes* like Holbach and Condorcet, had a major impact on the thinking of Wordsworth and Coleridge as young men, and later on Shelley and on Thomas Hodgskin, a relatively unknown ideologue of the 1820s who was himself an influence on Marx. Marx's ideas about the withering away of the state possibly derived directly from Godwin. In the 1790s Godwin's utopianism was comforting to many who saw no practical alternative. Others, such as Francis Place and other London Corresponding Society leaders, though not in favour of direct action, believed, 'that no reform would ever be obtained, but that ministers would on some occasion drive the King to extremities and then the whole system of Government would break up'.[36] It was only a very small minority who favoured armed insurrection, and even hoped for a French invasion.

The essential conservatism of most of the reformers is shown by the way in which, in order to justify their campaign, they adopted legalistic arguments. The appeal to an abstract theory of the nature of society, though attempted by Paine, by Spence and by Godwin, and though underpinning much of Thelwall's vague bombast, had much less influence than the doctrine that there had been an ideal constitution in the Anglo-Saxon period (in abeyance since the Norman Conquest) to which the people had the legal right to return. Appeals to the past of this kind had been denounced by Paine in *Common Sense* in 1776. But like so much of Paine's teachings, his views on this point were admired but ignored. The idea of the perfect Anglo-Saxon constitution and its illegal replacement by the Norman Yoke had originated in the sixteenth century and had become popular parliamentarian doctrine in the seventeenth.[37] It had been revived in 1771 by an anonymous pamphlet entitled *An Historical Essay on the English Constitution.* In the 1790s Gerrald cited the Anglo-Saxon folkmoot as the precedent for his Convention.[38] Lord Sempill wrote of 'the political constitutions of the Anglo-Saxons, the wisest and most friendly to mankind'.[39] John Baxter in his *New and Impartial History of England* claimed that 'The Revolution of 1688 did no more than expel a tyrant, and confirm the Saxon laws' and that 'our constitution is no more derived from the Norman Conquest, than from the revolution, but from our Saxon ancestors'.[40] Even Cartwright, who spoke much of natural rights, looked back to King Alfred's reign, when England had been populated by a race of freemen, sturdy farmers, incorruptible voters, and ready warriors.[41] Horne Tooke did not go back in history quite so far as this, but he too in his denunciations of modern corruptions worked to extol a lost Golden Age that perhaps never was. The appeal was not to *what ought to be* but to *what once was,* to a lawful system even yet in the process of being unlawfully usurped.

As Christopher Hill has pointed out, the Norman Yoke theory represented a new departure in that it provided a secular rather than a religious critique of government.[42] Indeed most of the reformers were secular minded. In the London Corresponding Society, according to Place,

'Nearly all the leading members were either Deists or Atheists . . . Religious topics never were discussed scarcely ever mentioned. It was a standing rule in all the divisions and in the committee also that no discussions or disputes on any subject with religion should be permitted and none were permitted . . . . Thomas Hardy was a religious man. John Bone was a saint, and a busy man at times in attempting to make converts among the irreligious.'[43]

The London Corresponding Society published both *The Age of Reason* by Paine, and *The Ruins; Or a Survey of the Revolutions of Empires* by Constantin François de Volney. This latter work, which first appeared in France in 1791 and in translation in England in 1795, is a kind of fantasy. It begins with a splendid, almost Shelley-like evocation of the wanderings of a traveller in the desolate wastes of Arabia. Amongst the ruins of Palmyra an apparition appears to the traveller, and teaches him about the origins of society and the downfall of states. Then the traveller sees, in a kind of vision, a general congress of the entire peoples of the world, who gather anxious for 'but one law, that of nature; one code, that of reason; one throne, that of justice; one altar, that of union'. It is convincingly demonstrated, in 13 sections, that all religions are supersitisions, and the vision ends with the promulgation of several laws of nature. As a grafting together of some of the ideas of the *philosophes* with the style and mood of exotic romanticism, Volney's *The Ruins* is interesting. As a political tract, however, it is not impressive, and its respectful reception in England illustrates the reformers' commitment to the rationalistic interpretation of religion. Yet of direct attacks on organized religion, especially the Church of England, there were few. William Frend's *Peace And Union Recommended to the Associated Bodies of Republicans and Anti-Republicans* contained an attack on the Anglican liturgy, but though, like many Unitarians, Frend became a reformer, his attack must be seen in the particular tradition of Unitarian criticism of the Anglican church, which dates from the beginnings of Unitarianism, rather than as generally characteristic of the movement of the 1790s. Reformers were soon drinking toasts to 'Religion without Priests, and Government without Kings', and wishing, 'May the Age of Superstition be annihilated, and the Age of Reason be established in its stead',[44] but this was largely by way of drunken exuberance.

The reformers had in fact moved beyond religion. Thomas Preston, a member of the London Corresponding Society in the 1790s, later a Spencean conspirator and eventually a Chartist, quoted with approval the 'cunning woman' of Brentford who

'would insist upon it, that my enemies would make me a great man, and occasion me much celebrity; that I should be exposed to great perils; and that I was to make my mind very happy, notwithstanding, for that no prison would long contain me.'

but even Preston said of this prophecy, 'I have not the weakness to put implicit confidence in it, myself, yet if my enemies choose to take a lesson from it, they may.'[45] Even such equivocative credulousness was rare in reform circles. Yet the 1790s were a period of religious ferment, as is shown by the spread of Methodism and the rise of Richard Brothers the prophet. 'The Doctrine of an approaching Millenium has found many converts', claimed the secret committee of the Commons, though it had to admit, with regard to Brothers' followers at least, 'The views of the people seem totally unconnected with any political object.'[46] This separation of the political and religious enthusiasms of the day cannot be passed over without comment.

The ideology of the reformers of the 1790s showed its sophistication, it may be said, not so much by what it contained as by what it omitted. It was purely political and materialistic. There was no attack on out-groups such as had happened as recently as the Gordon Riots of 1780, and as was happening all over the country during the 1790s, with the reformers themselves as the outgroup, increasingly the focus of the fears and suspicions of growing sections of the community. The reformers did not for example, attempt to cash in on the popular hatred of the Quakers who were widely disliked as corn speculators.[47] They did not encourage anti-semitism which, oddly enough for a period of social crisis, seems to have been actually in decline during these years. One recognisable and none too well esteemed out-group, the Irish, were indeed quite influential within the reform movement. Nor was there any obsession with lost saviours, as had been implicit in Scots Jacobitism in the 1740s. Despite their adherence to the myth of the Anglo-Saxon constitution and their naive faith in the benefits of a reformed Parliament, the reformers were for the most part hard-headed and forward-looking in their views, and this in itself seems to confirm the suggestion of an earlier chapter, that reform politics were the politics of the upwardly dynamic, rather than of the increasingly alienated and degraded.

7

Anti-Reform Propaganda
in the 1790s

THE upheaval of French society inspired not only reformers in the 1790s, it also stimulated the development of reactionary ideology and propaganda.

Even before the French Revolution the spread of Evangelicalism, with its emphasis on the mutual obligations of all ranks of society, had had an impact on the attitudes even of the religiously indifferent. 'I have long been in the habit of believing that certain obligations or conditions or Duties are respectively attached to every station or rank of life', wrote the Duke of Portland in 1794, a few months before becoming Home Secretary.[1] The Evangelicals had, moreover, isolated the special obligation of the ruling class to set a good example. 'Reformation must begin with the *great,* or it will never be effectual. *Their* example is the foundation from whence the vulgar draw their habits, actions, and characters', wrote Hannah More in an influential book which came out in 1788, at a time when the overthrow of French society was little dreamed of either in England or France.[2] During the next few years, such ideas were bound to become even more acceptable as, faced by an immediate political threat, the ruling class took stock of its own position, and sought ways of communicating its belief in its own rôle to those lower down in society.

Two strands of conservative thinking soon emerged. Hannah More, perhaps the most successful propagandist of the 1790s, was unusual in that she combined elements of both strands, though she leaned much more to one camp, the Evangelical, than to the other, but most conservative writers used arguments characteristic only of one camp. Those who based their social code on secular foundations tended to think in terms only of a minimum framework of duties and obligations. Adherents of this view were not necessarily a-religious. In fact, even the High Church element in the Church of

England tended to take a secular view of politics. They believed that government *generally speaking* had been divinely ordained. Thus as the trial of William Winterbotham in 1793 Serjeant Rooke claimed:

'It has been laid down by divine authority, that there is no power but what is derived from the Supreme Being—therefore to cry out against the government where there is no occasion, is a crime. And for a man living under mild and equal laws, to preach sedition and discontent, is blasphemy against the majesty of Heaven.'[3]

But they no longer believed—or liked to claim—that particular forms of government were divinely ordained. At the same time they eschewed the emphasis placed on personal religiosity by the Evangelicals. For both these reasons, therefore, they left to the Evangelicals the interpretation of social duties as religious obligations. For the Evangelicals on the other hand there was no such thing as purely secular politics. For them, probity and justice on the part of rulers, and obedience and contentment on the part of the ruled, were divinely enjoined. To desire reform was wrong, for not to be satisfied with the *status quo* was a sin.

The secular ideology embraced both by High Churchmen and by the comparatively indifferent, embodied a non-dynamic view of society. It aimed at bolstering up the old, rather than at moving forward to adjust to the new. It was more concerned with criticising the subversive theories of the day than with holding up constructive theories in their place. Even Burke's most precise analysis was reserved for countering the logic of others, and though he did evoke the vision of a constantly evolving society, 'a partnership not only between those who are living, but between those who are living, those who are dead, and those who are to be born', all his writings during his last years were a warning against the mischievousness of constructing theoretical programmes for political change. Similarly John Bowles, perhaps after Burke the most impressive of the secular conservatives, made several effective points against Locke, showing for example how Locke's ideas on majority rule were inconsistent with his ideas on individual consent and were 'nothing but a paltry subterfuge to evade a difficulty which he found insuperable', and ridiculing Locke's notion of society being formed by the coming together of individuals in a state of nature,

'that is, from a state much below that of savages (for savages have always been found in society, however uncultivated) . . . . it seems that, in a state of nature, man is abundantly more tractable than in a state of society; and that civilization has only rendered him more self-willed, obstinate and impetuous. Pity that he should ever have made so disadvantageous an exchange.'[4]

But in place of Locke's theories, Bowles could only argue lamely that inequality and dependence were natural in man, 'resulting from the manner, in which the human species are produced and trained up to maturity', and that Government 'is co-eval with his existence. It is a quality inseparably connected with his nature'.[5]

Much of the secular argument was an appeal to common sense. Much reform propaganda shared this characteristic: Paine's first famous pamphlet had actually been entitled *Common Sense* and rather later, Cobbett's no-nonsense, man to man tone epitomized this line of approach. Similarly as late as 1821 one High Churchman addressed his sermon *Anti-Radicalism* to 'The *Thinking* Among the People' and claimed, 'One character of the British people, is a *soundness* of understanding'.[6] This artifice was intended to flatter, or indeed to shame, the reader into agreement. Appeals to common sense, moreover, tended paradoxically to discourage thought — 'common sense' generally being found to be received opinion — and it is possible that the High Churchmen, with their objection to the way the Evangelicals gave 'the reins to private opinion, in opposition to publick authority',[7] preferred so-called common-sense arguments to more elaborate attempts at persuasion which could only encourage the habit of reflection and discussion in those whom they believed had no duty but to obey. This is certainly suggested by Bishop Randolph's criticism of the Evangelicals that 'while they bring every thing within private suggestion, they encourage in Religion the very principle, which in Politics has proved so fatal to the peace and good government of states'.[8]

Even the Evangelical Hannah More strayed into this common-sense style in her widely distributed *Village Politics,* in which Jack Anvil, the smith says, 'I am a better judge of a horse-shoe than Sir John; but he has a deal better notion of state affairs than I; and I can no more do without him than he can do without me.'[9] The reformers were said to be trying,

'to persuade mankind, that they suffer injuries which they do not perceive, that they sustain hardships which they do not feel, that their comforts are visionary and their happiness mere delusion . . . by endeavouring to remove a due subordination, and to create contention between the several orders of which Society is composed, they tend to destroy the harmony and co-operation of the whole, and to produce evils which would fall heaviest on the lowest classes, which have the fewest resources, and are unavoidably the most dependent.'[10]

The stress on the mutual dependence of all ranks of society, described in terms of utility rather than in terms of moral or religious duty, was characteristic of this common-sense approach. Apparent unfairness was balanced out: 'the advantages which are peculiar to each station . . . prove, that notwithstanding an apparent inequality, the balance is poised with impartial justice.'[11] In *A Dialogue between a Gentleman and a Mechanic*, moreover, it was pointed out that those who supply the needs of one rich man are probably happier than that rich man:

'Each individual is gratified, and each perhaps enjoys tranquility, more unclouded and uninterrupted than the person who is the object and remote spring of their activity. The light in which I behold a man of large fortune, who confines himself to the drudgery of idle dissipation, is merely that of a victim to general expediency.'[12]

Bowles too claimed of the working class that:

'The essential blessings of health, vigour and content, seem to be particularly allotted to persons in that situation, while the luxuries to which they are strangers, and which they would be fools to covet, generally produce disappointment, disgust, and indisposition both of body and mind.'[13]

Another of the disadvantages of wealth was pointed out by Archdeacon Paley:

'in what we reckon superior ranks of life, there is a real difficulty in placing children in situations, which may in any degree support them in the class and in the habits in which they have been brought up with their parents: from which great and often-times distressing perplexity the poor are free.'[14]

John Bowdler (who on the whole did not adopt the secular view of the question) took this curiously disingenuous mode of argument to its extreme when he asserted that the ruling class was altogether worse off than the poorer people:

'Whatever you may think, the King upon his Throne has more cares and vexations than you have. Many and many a night, when you are sound asleep, he and his Ministers are hard at work, for you, and me, and all of us: And the case is the same with the Great and Learned. Some of them, indeed, like some of you, neglect their business, and waste their time in Idleness and Vice; but others work as hard or harder than you; and their work is of a worse sort—your's *preserves* your health, while their's *destroys* their health, and shortens their lives.'[15]

And in case such reasonings were not sufficient, men like Paley taught also that, 'The wisest advice that can be given is, never to allow our attention to dwell upon comparisons between our own condition and that of others, but to keep it fixed upon the duties and concerns of the condition itself.'[16]

It was also argued that the English constitution was the institutional embodiment of common sense and that the sensible English people had the right priorities:

'an Englishman loves *liberty*, but he loves it not for the sake of the mere name; he must have something substantial that results from it; something he can see and feel: this he has in the freedom of his person, and the security of his property. An Englishman, therefore, thinks more of his *civil* than his *political* Liberty; more of the end than the means.'[17]

Even the enormous inequalities of wealth characteristic of the period could be explained away as implicit in the advantages of the English constitution:

'The laws which accidentally cast enormous estates into one great man's possession, are, after all, the self-same laws which protect and guard the poor man. . . . it is rather more the concern of the poor to stand up for the laws, than of the rich, for it is the law which defends the weak against the strong.'[18]

Often, however, this pretended common-sense approach degenerated into a naked appeal to prejudice. Sometimes the finger was pointed at enemies within, the traitors who had been foolishly permitted to flourish on British soil. The Rev. William Jones, a High Court priest, picked out the Dissenters:

'Our national Debt, for which we are now paying such heavy Taxes, was doubled by the Troubles in *America*, all brought upon us from the Beginning by the Dissenters, there and here. . . . Yet these People, who brought our Burdons upon us, are they that rail most at the Expensiveness of our Government, and use it as a Handle for overturning it: just like the Devil, who drives Men into Sin, and then gets them damned for it if he can.'[19]

There were also the British Jacobins, plotting revolution:

'The existence of a Jacobin faction, in the bosom of our country, can no longer be denied. Its members are vigilant, persevering, indefatigable, desperate in their plans and daring in their language. The torrent of licentiousness, incessantly rushing forth from their numerous presses, exceeds, in violence and duration all former examples.'[20]

Thomas Paine was held up for special public loathing:

'he has not only been long actuated by, but . . . he formerly gloried in avowing, an implacable animosity and rooted hatred to this country; and *that* not merely to its Government but to its interests, its welfare, its national character, its national honour, its commercial and naval greatness.'[21]

But the most common appeal to prejudice, and in fact quantitatively the most important element in the propaganda of the secular conservatives, was denigration of the French. This did not grow out of the war with France; the peak of Francophobia was probably reached a year before the war broke out, though it abated only a little in the next eight years. Fairly shrewd analysis of the abuses of revolutionary France was employed as a commentary on reform projects in Britain, as in William Cobbett's *Democratic Principles Illustrated by Example,* or in Bowles' *Reflections on The Political and Moral State of Society at the Close of the Eighteenth Century.* The Association For Preserving Liberty and Property Against Republicans And Levellers, organized by John Reeves, published, as well as Paley's *Reasons for Contentment* and Hannah More's *Village Politics,* pamphlets like *The Mayor of Paris' Speech, The Plot Found Out* (a pretended dialogue between three members of the Jacobin club in Paris), *Ten Minutes Reflection On Late Events in France, French Kindness* (recounting French activity in stirring up the 1745 Jacobite revolt and the revolt of the American colonies) and *French Humanity* (which included references to the massacres of 1418 and 1572). Hannah More's *Village Politics* scoffed at imitation of the French.[22] William Jones' broadsides were even more xenophobic: a summary he wrote of the advantages enjoyed by Britons concluded, 'Considering all these things together; if every Man does not at this time glory in being an Englishman, why he most richly deserves to be—A *Frenchman!*'[23] In another of Jones' broadsides, his mouthpiece John Bull claimed, 'Our Poor *Moll* and *Bet* are frightened out of their Wits: for they say, if England is to be like *France,* they think they shall lose their Husbands, as Marriage goes for nothing there, now.'[24]

The same anti-French message was contained in numerous caricature prints invidiously comparing French and English conditions, such as Cruikshank's *French Happiness English Misery,* Gillray's untitled print of England and France contrasted, 1793, and his *French Liberty, English Slavery,* HB's *The Englishman and The Frenchman,* Dent's *The French Feast of Reason,* John Nixon's *French Liberty* (which was 'most Respectfully Dedicated to every True Hearted Briton who is a friend to his King and Country') and Rowlandson's *The Contrast,* which compares British 'Religion, Morality, Loyalty, Obedience to the Laws, Independence, Personal Security Justice, Inheritance, Protection of Property, Industry, National Prosperity, Happiness' to French 'Atheism, Perjury Rebellion, Treason, Anarchy, Murder, Equality, Madness, Cruelty, Injustice, Treachery, Ingratitude, Idleness, Famine, National & Private Ruin, Misery'.

Implicit in this misrepresentation of the conduct of reformers both at home and in France was the belief that reform movements stemmed from the conspiracies of small cliques of wicked men. The Evangelicals who, despite their belief in the total depravity of all humans, tended to emphasize error rather than criminality as the cause of wrong-doing, devoted less attention to this conspiracy theory of revolution. They also showed less concern for comparisons with France. Evangelical propaganda aimed much more at urging all individuals to see that the real problem was at home, within each individual: 'the only Reform which can save', Bowdler wrote, '. . . . is, *a thorough reform of principles and practices, among all ranks of people throughout the kingdom.*'[25] Not that the Evangelicals had any relish for the French Revolution; but whereas the High Church interest in the lower classes derived largely from the fears aroused by events in France, for the Evangelicals these same events were merely an instance of the dangers they had long been concerned with.

For the Evangelicals the social and political import of Christianity was central:

'Affluence she teaches to be liberal and beneficent; authority, to bear its faculties with meekness, and to consider the various cares and obligations belonging to its elevated station, as being conditions on which that station is conferred. Thus, softening the glare of wealth, and moderating the insolence of power, she renders the inequalities of the social state less galling to the lower orders, whom also she instructs, in their turn, to be diligent, humble, patient: reminding them that their more lowly path has been allotted to them by the hand of God; that it is their part faithfully to discharge its duties, and contentedly to bear its inconveniences; that the present state of things is very short; that the objects, about which worldly men conflict so eagerly, are not worth the contest; that the peace of mind, which Religion offers to all ranks indiscriminately, affords more true satisfaction than all the expensive pleasures which are beyond the poor man's reach; that in this view, however, the poor have the advantage, and that if their superiors enjoy more abundant comforts, they are also exposed to many temptations from which the inferior classes are happily extempted.'[26]

Occasionally submission to Providence was exhorted in a tone of moral blackmail. Hannah More, who with her sister Martha organized Sunday Schools and other charities in the Mendips, and as recompense assumed the right to interfere in every aspect of life in the village under their tutelage, told the villagers of Shipham in 1795,

'Let the men and women of Shipham and Rowberrow become honest and good graziers and hoglers. They are placed in this spot by Almighty direction. The very ground you walk upon points out your daily labour. Excel in that—and an honest hogler is as good in the eyes of the Almighty as an honest squire; therefore we wish to recommend you to do your duty in that state of life where God has placed and called you. Every disposition to rebellion against the highest powers would prove how little you are changed in your hearts, after all that has been done for you; and remember that rebellion against rulers first brought on the troubles in France'.[27]

In this instance, the yokels were shamed into compliance by arguments much the same as those used by the secular-High Church propagandists, and in fact Hannah More differed from most other Evangelicals in the stress she laid in her propaganda writings on good behaviour, separate from true faith; her very popular cheap depository tracts, sold at 4s.6d. per hundred for distribution by the rich, upheld the idea that sins like drunkenness, lying and improvidence would be punished on earth, perhaps by the sinner dying in a drunken fit,[28] or being struck dead for telling a lie,[29] and it is doubtful whether most Evangelicals quite approved of this emphasis. They believed good works to be less important than faith: and believed the most important good work was to set a good example, so as to assist and nourish the faith of others:

'Let the King and Queen continue to set an example of Piety, Regularity, Sobriety, and conjugal Fidelity, to their Children, their Servants and all their Subjects. Let them drive from their Councils, and their Court, all Adulterers and Adulteresses; all Gamblers; all in short, whose Characters are notoriously *bad*, of either Sex, and of every Rank.'[30]

'Let them [the rich] reform, first Themselves; their Expenses, their Wives and Children, their Servants and Dependents; and then exert all their influence, as Landlords, as Magistrates, as Friends, and as Neighbours; encouraging and protecting the sober and industrious; discouraging and punishing with Candour, but with Vigour, the lawless and profligate.'[31]

Though asserting the essential equality of all men, the Evangelicals, as such exhortations show, were anxious to utilize the effective inequalities of society for Christian purposes.

They taught not only contentment in normal circumstances, but also submission to misfortune. Even starvation could be a blessing in disguise, as Hannah More told the villagers of Shipham in 1801, following the dearth of that year:

'Let me remind you that probably that very scarcity has been permitted by an all-wise and gracious Providence, to *unite* all ranks of people *together,* to shew the *poor* how immediately they are dependent upon the *rich,* and to show the *rich* and *poor* that they are all dependent on *Himself.* It has also enabled you to see more clearly the advantages you derive from the government and constitution of this country—to observe the benefits flowing from the distinction of rank and fortune, which has enable the *high* so liberally to assist the *low;* for I leave you to judge what would have been the state of the poor of this country in this long, distressing scarcity had it not been for your superiors.'[32]

Notice here again Hannah More's adoption of a secular justification similar to that used by Bowles, though as an Evangelical she subordinated it to a religious argument. And even if there were no heavily disguised blessings, there was the whole of eternity to make up for earthly discomforts:

'God has so ordered it, that, in this life, no Man shall be *compleatly* happy; but most men, let their situation be what it will, may be *tolerably* happy, if it be not their own fault: and every Man may be *completely happy for ever* in another World.'[33]

There was nothing new in either these Evangelical ideas, or in the teachings of the secular-High Church group. Bowles' critique of Locke, for example, almost certainly derived from the writings of non-jurors like the Rev. Charles Leslie earlier in the century. The socially injurious effects of wrong opinions had been a theme developed by Hobbes during the Cromwellian era. The notion of the mutual advantages and disadvantages of wealth and poverty had been expounded in a sermon preached by Richard Watson in 1785: included in this was a seminal list of the ill consequences of wealth. This sermon was not even published till 1793, when events at home and in France gave it a topicality it had lacked eight years previously.[34] Ideas about the *social* value of religion in enforcing correct behaviour were much older; they are to be found as far back as Livy and Cicero, authors very familiar to the British ruling class in the 1790s. More recently the same ideas had been discussed by Montesquieu.[35] The emphasis on political obedience as in itself a religious duty had been a favourite notion of sixteenth century Protestant reformers.

What is peculiar about the 1790s was the energetic efforts made to lift these ideas out of the realm of abstraction, and to use them as practical bulwarks of social control. The unprecedented efforts made to disseminate them, and the real impact they had, not so much on the lower classes perhaps, as on the ruling class, distinguish these ideas from those embodied in any previous propaganda campaign. Nineteenth-century paternalism and Evangelical philanthropy did not emerge gradually from the *pot pourri* of eighteenth-century abstraction: they were forged, in a comparatively brief time, during a period when conviction, a sense of purpose, the need for missionary zeal, seemed far more vital than they had ever done before.

PART TWO: The Development of Political Conflict

1
The Addington Ministry

The Pitt Régime

IN December 1800 William Pitt the younger was at the height of his power. Still only 41, he was in his seventeenth year as Prime Minister. His management of the key issues of the day—the war abroad and the threat of subversion at home—had given him an unparalleled reputation as a statesman. The war, which had been in progress since 1793, though a failure on land, had brought victory at sea over the French, Spanish and Dutch. At home the threat of disaffection seemed to have been checked, at least for the moment. In Ireland nationalist feeling and the discontents of the Catholic majority had led to open insurrection in the south-eastern counties in May and June of 1798 but the rebels had been defeated, and on 2 July 1800 the Act of Union with Ireland received the royal assent. The separate Parliament at Dublin was abolished, 100 MPs and 28 representative peers were added to the British Parliament, and the weakest link in Britain's empire was thereby incorporated more firmly into the British political system.

The powerful party which had opposed Pitt in the 1780s had split during 1794 over the question of war abroad and repression at home, and roughly half its members, led by the Duke of Portland and including 77 MPs, had become supporters of the ministry. Portland and his associates Earl Spencer, Lord Loughborough and William Windham were now active members of Pitt's Cabinet, though Edmund Burke, the principal ideologue of the group, had since died. A reverse movement of former supporters who had defected to the opposition was less significant as it involved many fewer people and those either well-known for their difficult tempers, like the Duke of Northumberland and Pitt's own cousin, the eccentric radical Earl Stanhope, or else old men notoriously motivated by disappointed ambition, like the Duke of Grafton, the Marquess of Lansdowne (who had first made Pitt a minister in 1782) and Pitt's first Lord

Chancellor, Lord Thurlow. Earl Fitzwilliam, one of the leaders of
the Portland group, hd also returned to opposition, largely as a
result of being forced to resign the Lord-Lieutenancy of Ireland in
1795, within a few months of receiving the office.
During 1800 Fitzwilliam was renewing his former intimacy with
the Hon. Charles James Fox, the leader of those of the opposition
who had maintained their hostility to Pitt during 1794 and
subsequently. But it was not within the power of Fitzwilliam or Fox
to challenge the Prime Minister seriously, for they could muster
barely a sixth of the House of Commons to their cause. They knew
too that the mood of the country was against them, and since May
1797 Fox had rarely attended Parliament, feeling that he might as
well register his dissent by ostentatiously staying away, since making
speeches achieved nothing. Fox's admirers pretended that this policy
of non-attendance was a tactical master-stroke. 'The extreme fretful
dislike my Pittite friends express to the secession proves to me that
they have reason to fear it', wrote the Duchess of Devonshire.[1] But
in fact the secession was widely criticized as improper, even
unconstitutional behaviour in elected representatives, and cited as
an indication of the lengths to which unprincipled men dared go.
Moreover it caused divisions amongst Fox's own followers, one of
whom, George Tierney, incurred the emnity of Fox's closest friends
by continuing to attend the Commons and denouncing Pitt's measures
with such asperity that at last an exchange of hot words in the
Commons on 25 May 1798 led to a duel on Wimbledon Common.
The Foxites were supported by the Prince of Wales but this too was
of little advantage for he was a weak, vain, self-indulgent character,
and they were blamed for encouraging him in his accumulation of
enormous debts and in his ungrateful behaviour towards his father,
the King. They had lost further credit when the Duke of Norfolk, at
a dinner to celebrate Fox's birthday on 24 January 1798, proposed
the toast 'The Sovereignty Of The People', for which he was dismissed
from his post as Lord-Lieutenant of the West Riding. Norfolk had
been drunk at the time—a habitual state with him—but Fox repeated
the toast as a deliberate act of defiance at a speech in the Whig Club,
and was in consequence struck off the roll of the Privy Council.
More and more his party was assuming the complexion of a set of
frustrated demagogues, driven to extremes, and this only served to
strengthen Pitt's position.
   Pitt's dominance depended less on personal influence over the
King than on his ascendancy over MPs. He was not a personal
favourite with the King. Amongst a small circle of intimates, mostly
younger than himself, Pitt could overflow with wit and high spirits,
but towards most of those with whom he was in official contact he
was extraordinarily stiff and reserved. That George III was the

man to be charmed by Pitt's secret social talents is doubtful, but Pitt never made the experiment. They were in close touch in business, and the King relied absolutely on Pitt's control of Parliament, but, partly through pressure of over-work, Pitt never courted the King's personal affection. 'He has regularly been 6 weeks in London, without going to the Levee', recorded Earl Camden, with evident horror at such negligence. 'A long train of this conduct has certainly in a degree estranged the King from him and induced him to think of him personally with less interest.'[2]

Pitt's reserve also held at a distance most of his political supporters. A guest at the Marquis of Abercorn's noticed when Pitt was dining there with some of his followers, that 'all seemed to be impressed with an awe of him. At times it appeared like Boys with their Master'.[3] This remoteness contributed to his credit as a man quite out of the ordinary, without whom the country would be ruined. His reputation also owed much to his style as a public speaker. Without any preparation he spoke with a relentless, unreflecting eloquence quite unlike that of any other man, 'with the same deliberation and fluency as if he were reading a book. There was never a moment's hesitation for a word; the emphasis was always correct and beautiful, because it served to render the longest sentences intelligible'.[4] Philip Francis, who acknowledged 'it is but fair and honourable in me to admit that I felt a constant spontaneous dislike to him', wrote of his 'astonishing fluency and choice of correct language. . . . it was elocution perfect'.[5] It was an age when public speaking was admired as the truest index of general ability. And since he was not reserved towards all, but had an intimate coterie before whom he displayed the personal charm he was too shy, or too arrogant, to show the world, there was no lack of young acolytes ready to proclaim his virtues to the uninitiated. 'Everything that drops from him is so marked by superior virtue and superior sense that it is impossible not to love and admire in him something different even from other men', wrote one.[6] His personal ascendancy over individuals as different as Canning, Wilberforce, and Lord Grenville was a measure of his capacity to dazzle.

By 1800, moreover, Pitt had built up an impressive ministerial team. When he had taken office in 1783 his cabinet had been full of mediocrities, and his colleagues in 1800 still included some cyphers such as his extraordinarily lazy elder brother, the Earl of Chatham, as Lord President, and the Earl of Westmorland, a drunken clod given to asking absurd questions, as Privy Seal ('Only think of such a fellow as old Lord Westmorland, sitting with his dirty top-boots on the table, giving his opinions on state affairs', exclaimed one minister in later years[7]). Pitt's three Secretaries of State were of a quite different calibre however. The Duke of Portland in the Home

Department was indefatigable in his efforts to suppress Jacobinism wherever it reared its head. Lord Grenville, Pitt's cousin, in the Foreign Department, was a proud, shy, obstinate, scholarly man, generally disliked as the author of an unpopular war and unfairly suspected of being chiefly interested in amassing sinecures, but an able diplomat and a statesman thoroughly imbued with the ideas of Burke on the nature of society. Henry Dundas, in the War Department, was an uncultured, hard-drinking Scot with a broad accent and excessive self-assurance, an opportunist and a pragmatist, blind to any but short-term views, but an energetic administrator. These three men, though not as admired as Pitt, were widely respected.

Pitt's supporters were not a party, they were men who conceived their duty to be participation in the business of running the country. Politics for them concerned not policy but administration. They were, of course, committed to the preservation of the social and constitutional framework within which they had always operated, though individuals amongst them—even Pitt—had schemes for various slight adjustments of this framework. But they had no platform as such. .

This was where Fox and his followers differed. They had an ideology which they called Whiggism. This ideology was summed up by one of Fox's closest friends in an obituary tribute to the Duke of Devonshire, some years later:

'In his political principles, the Duke of Devonshire was a thorough Whig. With all due respect for the Crown, he felt that the foundation of the Whig character is laid in a love for the liberties of the People. To support the Crown in its lawful authority, he considered at all times to be proper and decorous, but he felt that his more immediate duty was to defend the People, and the popular part of the Constitution. . . . He saw, therefore, the necessity of keeping the prerogative strictly within its limitations. Against the system of favouritism and exclusion with which the present reign commenced, and with little exception, has been continued, he uniformly set his face.'[8]

This balanced and essentially issue-dodging platform was not such as to rally nation-wide enthusiasm. Moreover, the Foxite's idea of themselves as specifically appointed to defend the constitution derived from a caste exclusiveness, a belief that the long pedigree and large acreage of men like the Duke of Devonshire gave them an especial stake in the country. It was even suggested that the greater Whig families 'hold themselves distinct from the nobility in general in a political respect. Having contributed to the establishment of the present family on the throne, they claim a sort of right to extraordinary power under it'.[9] Nevertheless, the Foxite Whigs were pioneers of the idea of basing a national political crusade on an abstract code of doctrine, and if, in 1800, their doctrine seemed out of date and irrelevant to the issues that concerned most people, at least they had a certain expertise in the public manipulation of ideas which might help them in the future. Yet, as they showed by their secession, they saw little immediate hope of successfully challenging Pitt.

The Accession of Addington

At the beginning of 1801, Pitt unexpectedly resigned. Both he and Dundas had been in ill-health for some time, but the occasion of their resigning was a misunderstanding with the King on the issue of Catholic relief. The Act of Union with Ireland had, it was hoped, brought an end to the era of misgovernment and disaffection which had prevailed in the sister island for nearly a decade, but it was the opinion of Pitt and his closest coadjutors that:

'the Union with Ireland would be a measure extremely incomplete and defective as to some of the most material benefits to be expected from it, unless immediate advantage were taken of it to attach the great body of the Irish Catholics to the measure itself, and to the government as administered under the control of the United Parliament. . . . The removal of the remaining disqualifications from parliament, and from office, seemed . . . to be one indispensable feature of such a system.'[10]

The Cabinet were also to some extent pledged by Cornwallis's and Castlereagh's having held out the hope of relief to the Catholics as an inducement to support the Union. What was proposed was by no means a general relaxation of political sanctions, but the replacement of out-dated and divisive regulations by a new and more extensive system more applicable to the political issues of the day. 'The sacramental test, now notoriously evaded and insufficient for any effectual purpose', was to be replaced by

'a political test, to be imposed indiscriminately on all persons sitting in parliament, or holding state or corporation offices, and also on all ministers of religion, of whatever description, and all teachers of schools, &c. This test was to be directly levelled against the Jacobin principles, was to disclaim in express terms the sovereignty of the people; and was to contain an oath of allegiance and fidelity to the King's government of the realm, and to the established constitution both in church and state.'[11]

The penal laws against Catholics, in effect, were to be replaced by penal laws against reformers.

The Cabinet had discussed relief during the summer of 1800, in the weeks following the Act of Union becoming law, but the question had been laid aside during the autumn because of the more immediate preoccupation with the food shortages, and the expedition to drive the French from Egypt.[12] No official notice of the Cabinet's discussions was given to the King, but the Lord Chancellor, Lord Loughborough, an inveterate intriguer, spent part of the autumn in attendance on the King at Weymouth, and may have discussed the issue with him. Loughborough certainly told his relative, Lord Auckland, who in turn told his brother-in-law the Archbishop of Canterbury, and the latter wrote to the King urging him not to grant any relief to the Catholics.[13] The King needed little urging. Both in 1793, when a limited measure of relief had been granted to the Irish Catholics, and in 1795, at the time of Fitzwilliam's Lord-Lieutenancy in Ireland when the question of relief was revived, he had been worried that the grant of relief would contravene his coronation oath.

The Cabinet's discussions resumed in January 1801. Viscount Castlereagh, the Irish Secretary, had come over from Dublin expecting to help settle the details. Besides Loughborough, the Earl of Westmorland, the Duke of Portland and the Earl of Liverpool (who was ill but communicated his opinions by letter) opposed the measure, but Pitt seems to have regarded the question as settled. He had still not officially notified the King, however, when, at the levée on 28 January, the King approached Dundas and said loudly:

'What is the Question which you are all about to force on me? what is this Catholic Emancipation which *this young Lord, this Irish Secretary* has brought over, that you are going to throw at my Head? I will tell you, that I shall look on every Man as my personal Enemy, who proposes that Question to me, I hope *All* my Friends will not desert me.'[14]

Dundas tried to draw the King aside, lest he be overheard, but in vain. When Pitt learnt of the incident, he summoned a Cabinet, at which it was agreed that he and Grenville should draw up a paper to be approved by the cabinet the following day, and then submitted to the King.[15] Next morning however Pitt received a visit from the Speaker of the House of Commons, Henry Addington, who came to announce that he had been asked by the King to form a government. Addington had assured the King of his own unfitness, and had His Majesty's permission to beg Pitt to withdraw his proposals. For the next three days Addington carried messages back and forth between Pitt and the King, but to no avail.[16] Late on Saturday 31 January, Pitt wrote to the King a long, persuasive letter, setting out his reasons for being unable to give up Catholic relief and expressing his hope that the King would reconsider his opposition, failing which 'it must be personally Mr Pitt's first wish to be released from a situation which he is conscious that, under such circumstances, he could not continue to fill but with the greatest disadvantage'.[17] The tone of the letter suggested that Pitt still had hopes of the King standing down, but a letter written by Grenville to his eldest brother two days later suggests that Grenville at least was already convinced that their resignation was unavoidable.[18] Grenville was right. After a further exchange of letters the King accepted Pitt's resignation on 5 February. Grenville and Dundas, Pitt's chief lieutenants, Earl Camden, a minister without portfolio, Earl Spencer, First Lord of the Admiralty, and William Windham, the Secretary at War, also resigned.

Henry Addington, the King's choice as the new Prime Minister, had long been a friend of Pitt, Addington's father having been physician to Pitt's father. He was a 'prolix and pompous man':

'Great appearance of moderation, inward admiration, as well as outward observance of forms, an elaborate and earnest profession of all the commonest principles of morality and the tritest maxims of wisdom, uniformly distinguished him in publick. In private, he had no vice but wine; and his jokes and stories, though frequent and numerous, were inoffensive, as well as dull.'[19]

At first he was regarded merely as a caretaker minister, who would remain in office no longer than it took for Pitt and the King to resolve their differences. 'It seems still very uncertain how long the interval may be', Grenville told his brother. 'My wish, and I think the King's interest, is that it shoud be short. I trust not many weeks.'[20] It was not till a month later that Grenville acknowledged that Addington was going to be more than a temporary expedient.[21] Yet the new ministry was not a new departure, merely a reallocation of power within the ruling establishment. Several of the ministers, including Pitt's own brother, remained in office. Pitt and Grenville were friendly and helpful. The latter told the House of Lords, 'Though we may differ from them in some points, in most there is no difference between us, and while they continue to act in a firm, resolute and manly manner, they shall have our steady support.'[22] When, on 20 March the Earl of Carlisle questioned in the House of Lords whether the new ministers were sufficiently capable of directing the war against France and whether they enjoyed the public confidence, it was Grenville who defended them.[23] He also assured Lord Hawkesbury, his successor at the Foreign Department, 'I shall always be at your orders not on the footing of an ex-minister, but on that of a sincere friend and cordial well-wisher.'[24]

Pitt and Grenville also tried to prevent the resignations of several junior ministers who had not been personally compromised by recommending Catholic relief, but without success. Earl Gower resigned not only his Postmastership but also, as a sign of exceptional disapproval of the 'circumstances under which Mr Pitt has felt himself obliged to resign', his place as Lord Lieutenant of Staffordshire.[25] George Canning, the most brilliant of Pitt's protégés, resigned the Paymastership-General, even though he professed friendliness to the new ministers, but Grenville's nephew, Earl Temple, who resigned the Vice-Presidency of the Board of Trade, was frankly hostile: 'On the grounds of confidence I gave my support to the old government', he wrote, 'and from want of it I shall oppose the new always reserving "hostile and indiscriminate opposition".'[26] Temple's father, the Marquess of Buckingham, shared his views and sneered at 'the Govt. that Mr Pitt has forced upon us.'[27]

There were discontents, too, within the new Cabinet. Dundas told Pitt, 'Our friends who, as an act of friendship and attachment to you, agree to remain in office, do it with the utmost chagrin and unwillingness'.[28] Of those entering the Cabinet for the first time, Lords Eldon, Hobart, St Vincent and Hawkesbury were eager enough, but the Hon. Thomas Pelham hung back, being reluctant to take office at precisely the moment when his political friends, Spencer, Camden and Windham, were going out. He finally agreed to Addington's offer only because the King desired it.[29] A friend told him, 'it is to you alone that one can look for the infusion of any thing good into the present councils. Depend on it there is no very ardent wish to have you in the Cabinet.'[30]

In the country at large the ministerial reshuffle was greeted with consternation. Many were surprised at the promotion of the Speaker of the Commons. 'Never was a nation so insulted as the British nation in being subjected to the sway of Mr Addington, a man without birth, without connection, and without abilities', a journalist told his father. 'The King might as well make a Prime Minister of one of his beef-eaters.'[31] It was claimed later 'the Aristocracy (noble families) of the Country, were averse to Mr Addington's government not liking that a man of His degree should rule'.[32] Moreover, the King at this juncture suffered an attack of porphyria, the metabolic disorder with symptoms resembling insanity, which he had previously suffered from in 1788, and this, occurring before the out-going ministers had all had time to surrender their seals, meant weeks of uncertainty. Pitt, apparently blaming himself for the renewal of the King's illness, assured the King he would never again during His Majesty's reign bring forward the Catholic question.[33] But he made no attempt to restore himself to office, nor did he tell Grenville of his new pledge.

And so the ministry gradually established itself. Addington was helped by the evident favour of the King, once the latter's health recovered, and by a couple of successes in the war, the conquest of Egypt and Nelson's victory at Copenhagen. By dismissing Loughborough he removed the likeliest source of intrigue against his authority in the Cabinet. Many back-bench MPs moreover preferred his humanity and simplicity to the frigid brilliance of Pitt. 'The country gentlemen were for him almost to a man. . . . The mediocrity of Addington suited their mediocrity. . . . He was with them easy, frank, jovial, loved Port wine as well as the most resolute fox-hunter.'[34] Where Pitt's adherence to the Catholic cause had dismayed some of his followers, Addington's staunch anti-Catholicism was reassuring. Insofar as there was any difference between the political complexion of Pitt's and Addington's ministeries, Addington's was the more opposed to innovation, and this pleased the majority of MPs who dislikedthe newfangled expedients by which Pitt had attempted to deal with new conditions. By August 1801 Canning, who had been obstinately resisting attempts by Pitt to persuade him to resume office, at last agreed to let Pitt seek a place for him in the ministerial ranks.[35] It was an indication of the way the wind was blowing.

The New Opposition

It was only after eight months of Addington's premiership that the forebodings of his critics began to appear justified. On 4 October the government announced the preliminary terms for a peace treaty to be negotiated with France. All Britain's war-time conquests in the Mediterranean and outside Europe were to be surrendered, save only Trinidad and the former Dutch parts of Ceylon. France was to be left in control of the Netherlands, Switzerland and Liguria. Though William Cobbett the journalist reported 'I have spoken with many persons, merchants, planters and gentlemen, and I find the peace, as a matter of *terms* in particular, universally condemned',[36] the general public, tired of a war that had already lasted eight and a half years, rejoiced at the prospect of peace. The coach of General Lauriston, the French envoy, was dragged through the streets of London by a mob shouting 'Long Live Bonaparte.'[37] Cobbett had to defend his shop in Pall Mall against being sacked by rioters who resented his disapproval of the peace.[38] Amongst upper-class politicians however there was a rare unanimity in condemning the peace. George III himself had no faith in its permanence.[39] The Foxites agreed with their organ *The Morning Chronicle,* 'this country has been degraded by the Peace, though it is necessary'.[40] Pitt, Dundas, Castlereagh, Canning and Earl Camden all had serious objections.[41] There was even criticism within the Cabinet. Pelham wrote a protest to the King, and was later spoken of as 'ashamed of the peace'.[42]

The most passionate disapproval however was from Lord Grenville and William Windham. Grenville's successor as Foreign Secretary, Lord Hawkesbury, had been in close touch with him during the previous months and had already, in July, provoked his anger at the careless drafting of a treaty with Russia.[43] But Grenville's vexation then was nothing to his fury at the terms of the preliminaries of the treaty with France, and for the first 20 days after their publication he wrote off letters of condemnation to all his friends and former colleagues. To George III himself he complained that both the

Russian and the French negotiations were 'marked throughout by a tone of unnecessary and degrading concession'.[44] To Addington he wrote of his 'indispensable duty' to oppose such a treaty, and asked for a meeting to discuss it, which Addington refused. Pitt, too, was reluctant to face his obstinate cousin, and put off a promised visit to Dropmore, Grenville's country home near Beaconsfield.[45] Canning on the other hand, 'astounded and dismayed' by the preliminaries, lost no time in taking up a long-standing invitation to stay with Grenville.[46]

Windham, the gifted but impractical former Secretary at War, had even more rooted objections to the peace. While Grenville was prepared to make peace with France on the right terms, Windham opposed the very principle of treating with the republican government.[47] Amongst others opposed to the peace were the Earl of Carnarvon and his friend Earl Fitzwilliam,[48] the latter's most active nominee in the Commons, Dr French Laurence,[49] and Viscount Folkestone, who told Cobbett to pass on the information that he was willing to act 'in concert' with anyone who shared his reprobation of the peace terms.[50] All these thought in terms of actually opposing the government, once Parliament reassembled at the end of the summer recess, and even before the end of October the press was talking of 'The New Opposition' with its headquarters at 91 Pall Mall, the London residence of Grenville's brother the Marquess of Buckingham.[51] But others, equally critical, had less wish for a public confrontation. The Earl of Pembroke thought of staying away from Parliament altogether to avoid having to vote against the ministers. He told a friend:

'I may have formed an erroneous opinion but as yet I am inclined to think those are right who rank it amongst the worst measures ever adopted in this country. If I continue in that opinion, and some marked disapprobation is proposed, I shall be sorry.'[52]

Pembroke did in fact later vote against the ministers.[53] Grenville's cousin, Lord Glastonbury replied to an angry letter about the peace 'with a more vigorous pen' than his cousins expected, but he not only stayed away from London when Parliament reassembled, but persuaded his closest friend Lord Braybrooke to do likewise. Braybrooke, who had married one of Grenville's sisters, acknowledged,

'I feared the contagion of New Buckingham House, and above all that Wm [i.e. Lord Grenville] might have desired me to attend, and that if I had, common politeness or (what might happen) conviction in his arguments might have tempted me to join the family in a vote which will be looked on as factious in the extreme.'[54]

A more notable absentee was Dundas, who while in office had masterminded the conquest of the territories which were now to be surrendered. He refused either to support or oppose the peace, and seemed to wish it to be thought he had retired from politics.[55] Another member of the late Cabinet, Earl Camden, actually arrived in London to attend Parliament at the beginning of the new session, but was frightened away from the peace debate by a visit from Grenville. 'It is impossible to describe to you the violence of his manner and language', Camden reported. But agreeing with much of what Grenville said, he could not bring himself to vote for the peace, yet, since Pitt intended to support it, he could not vote against it either. 'I cannot persuade myself to vote on a different side from Pitt.'[56]

The preliminaries were debated in both Houses of Parliament on 3 November 1801. In the Commons the government was supported not only by Pitt but also by Fox and Sheridan of the opposition. There were hostile speeches from the middle Grenville brother, Thomas, from his nephew Earl Temple, from two of Earl Fitzwilliam's nominees, French Laurence and William Elliot (the latter formerly military Under-Secretary in the Irish Government, making his maiden speech at Westminster), and from William Windham. Windham's philippic was the sensation of the evening. He sat, with Temple and their friends, near the bar of the House on 'the same bench from which Mr Burke always spoke after separating from Mr Fox',[57] and indeed, according to one observer, he spoke 'like the ghost of Burke'.[58] Like Laurence, Elliot and their patron Fitzwilliam, Windham was a loyal disciple of Burke having, according to one sneer, his insanity without his inspiration.[59] Thomas Grenville had advised him against mixing with the peace 'the feverish topic of the restoration of monarchy' in France,[60] but just as Burke would have done, Windham went beyond the short-term expediency of the peace to discuss the issue of making peace with republican France on any terms. He did not however divide the Commons. In the Lords, after a less exciting debate, Lord Grenville did divide, and was left in a minority of ten to 94.

Although the opponents of the peace had been christened by the newspapers the 'New Opposition'—to distinguish them from Fox's Old Opposition—Lord Grenville claimed 'I am far enough from any idea of putting myself at the head or at the tail of what is called opposition. . . . Perhaps in the course of the session I may turn out not so factious a person as they [the ministers] seem to think.'[61] Another critic of the government, Lord Minto, who had by sheer coincidence resigned his appointment as ambassador to Vienna at the time of Pitt's leaving office, and who returned home shortly after the peace debates, differed from Grenville in the importance he

attached to Addington's opposition to Catholic relief and felt that
his objections to Addington's Catholic policy as well as to the peace
rendered impossible 'anything like connection with the Ministry',
but he too 'was not aware of any public principle depending in the
present moment which could be made the basis of a formal connection
or party in opposition to Government'.[62]

Though Addington had come in to office to avoid Catholic relief,
a measure the Foxites advocated, they approved of his peace policy.
The war had split their party in 1793-4 and had been their chief
grounds for opposition subsequently, so naturally they favoured
Addington's pacificism. 'In other respects', Fox told a supporter, 'I
feel as you do a perfect indifference to supporting or opposing
them.'[63] George Tierney, Fox's leading critic within his own party,
went further. Pitt was at last out of office and Tierney was determined
he should stay out. To ensure this Tierney wished the Foxites to
coalesce with Addington. This would also have the effect of
transforming the political complexion of the ministry. Tierney
managed to persuade Charles Grey, Fox's principal lieutenant, to
support this policy, and in October had a number of surreptitious
interviews with Addington in Hyde Park and on Wimbledon Common,
where it might appear that mere chance had brought them together.[64]
Later the Earl of Moira, the confidant of the Prince of Wales, joined
in the negotiations. 'I want security for myself', wrote Grey, 'and a
sufficient indication to the public both in the number and nature of
the appointments that the Government is to be conducted on different
principles from those which have prevailed in late years.'[65] The
negotiation was finally broken off in February 1802 because of
'insurmountable difficulties in the way of removing the Duke of
Portland'.[66]

Pitt could not have been ignorant of these furtive discussions,
nor of the degree to which they were inspired by the Foxite hopes of
preventing him from ever returning to office. His own confidants,
moreover, had begun to complain to him how Addington's financial
administration was running counter to his own former policy, and
to hint at the undesirability of being indentified with ministers
whose conduct implied criticism of his own.[67] In February, returning
to London to attend Parliament after the Christmas break, he eagerly
sought out the opponents of the peace. Thomas Grenville and Earl
Spencer were surprised at Pitt's 'unusual promptitude' in calling on
them the very next day after they had left their cards at his door.[68]
Reporting his hour's chat with Pitt to his elder brother the Marquess
of Buckingham, Thomas Grenville wrote:

> 'although he thinks war is not advisable before there shall be
> reasonable hope of our being assisted upon the continent, yet I
> think I see on his part so much nearer an approach to our sense of

danger, and so much readiness in him to seek discussion with all of us, that I cannot help wishing to forward that communication; and I much regret that William is not more at hand to improve that opportunity; although I do not look to any *quite* immediate result from it'.[69]

But William—that is, Lord Grenville—in spite of a 'very strong letter' from Buckingham, had no wish to go to London. On leaving office he had sold his town house in Cleveland Row, and he could no longer afford fruitless journeys to town, besides which he had an 'invincible repugnance to go beyond the strict line of duty in mixing myself with transactions which I think are likely to afford me nothing but unavailing disquietude'. Consequently he merely instructed his brother Thomas to keep in touch with their cousin.[70] Pitt actually visited Lord Grenville at Dropmore early in March, and they were able to discuss the international situation. Grenville found Pitt's views 'more conformable to our opinions than I had expected, but on some points we still differ widely'.[71]

The definitive treaty with France was signed at Amiens on 25 March 1802. Lord Grenville did not at first intend to do more than criticize. He told Windham, 'I could myself willingly go still further into censure but I think it very material for the public impression (which is the only real use of our proceeding) not to run too much against the feelings of our audience.'[72] In the event, however, the 'New Opposition' made a full-scale attack during the debates on the treaty on 13 May 1802. In the Lords the sitting lasted till 8 am on 14 May—'a length almost we believe, unparalleled'.[73] Only 16 peers voted against the treaty, but these included six former cabinet ministers (Grenville, Buckingham, Fitzwilliam, Earl Spencer, the Earl of Carlisle and the Duke of Richmond) four of whom were also Lords-Lieutenant of counties, four other Lords-Lieutenant (Earl Fortescue, and the Earls of Darlington, Warwick and Radnor), and two ex-ambassadors, Lord Minto and the Grenvilles' brother-in-law, the Earl of Carysfort. Lord Glastonbury and three others paired off.[74] Lord Auckland, one of the Postmasters-General, would probably have voted against the treaty, having criticized it in a preliminary skirmish on 5 May, but Addington had already asked him angrily whether it was 'the wish or intention of your Lordship to continue to hold an office connected with a government, of whose conduct you have publicly declared your disapprobation upon an occasion so important',[75] and Auckland had not dared to oppose further.

In the Commons, the debate had to be adjourned, and the House eventually divided 276 to 22 in the small hours of 15 May. Canning stayed away.[76] Tierney and Grey took exception to the Foreign Secretary's bellicose tone and abstained. The minority of 22 included one ex-cabinet minister, two friends of Canning and four independents:

the rest were relatives or protégés of the hostile members in the Lords, including five nominees of Fitzwilliam and the brother and three nephews of Lord Grenville, and the Earl of Carlisle's son, Viscount Morpeth.

Six weeks later, in order to consolidate his position while his success with the peace was still fresh in the public mind, Addington dissolved Parliament. The ensuing General Election was fought on no great public issue. Most of the critics of the peace in the Commons sat for pocket boroughs, and the county constituencies of Buckinghamshire, Montgomeryshire and Denbighshire, which returned Lord Grenville's three nephews, were too well controlled to be contested. The main upset to the Grenville family was the defeat of their nominee Scrope Bernard at Aylesbury as a result of a movement against the family's local influence, though since Bernard had not opposed the peace this defeat does not seem even to have been assisted by public disapproval of the family's opposition to the Treaty of Amiens. At Norwich, Windham's tactless arrogance led to his defeat and in his case his parliamentary conduct certainly contributed to his unpopularity and caused his local allies to withdraw their support.[77] Windham had to seek refuge in one of the Marquess of Buckingham's seats, St Mawes.

Canning secured his return at his own expense for Portarlington in Queen's County (now Leix in the Irish Republic). Previously he had owed his seat to Pitt's influence and had not openly opposed Addington hitherto for fear of offending his friend. 'The worst part of his character', it was said, 'is his love of intrigue and management'.[78] These traits made Canning a dangerous enemy for the Prime Minister, and after the General Election he felt more free to take his own line.

The Naval Reform Controversy
The major government policy departure following the peace was in the area of naval reforms. During the 1790s the naval dockyards had shown themselves to be not merely highly inefficient and hostile to innovation, but also astoundingly corrupt. The huge copper bolts holding ships together were often stolen and their heads·and tails sawn off and jammed in the bolt holes to disguise the wooden plugs which were substituted. It was believed at the time that both the 74-gun *Blenheim* and the 64-gun *York* foundered because of such malpractice.[79] At Portsmouth, artificers were not only paid at the highest piece-rate, but in some cases were paid for up to 21 hours a *day* overtime, and 2,361 more men were claimed for victuals than were actually employed.[80] A piece of cooperage at Deptford, costing £37 2s 3d, was charged at £1,020 10s 5d.[81] With peculation at such a level, it might cost more to repair a ship than to build a new one. HMS *Dedalus* cost £8,788 to build and £13,802 to repair.[82] The

Navy Board, the official body in control of the dockyards and of naval supplies, turned a blind eye to these abuses, and though its relations with its superior, the Admiralty Board, which controlled personnel and operations, were formal and often strained, under Earl Spencer, First Lord till 1801, the Admiralty discouraged publication of the service's discreditable secrets.[83] With the resignation of Spencer along with Pitt in 1801, the situation changed. The new First Lord of the Admiralty, the Earl of St Vincent, was a professional naval officer who had two hates in life. One was the Navy Board, from the inefficiency and corruption of which he had suffered while a commander at sea. The other was his predecessor, whose jobbery, ignorance of naval matters, policy of covering up abuses in the interests of decorum, and personal jealousy of St Vincent, had equally excited the latter's ire.[84] St Vincent took office resolved on changes. He was, in fact, the only member of Addington's Cabinet committed to reversing the policy of his predecessor.

St Vincent initially had little support from his colleagues, whose main concern was to establish their authority in the country. His proposed inspection of the dockyards was put off till after the General Election because 'the reforms which must take place in them would have operated powerfully against the interest of Government in all the Western Boroughs'.[85] After the Election, however, St Vincent was allowed to go ahead. Accompanied by four members of the Navy Board, the Lords of the Admiralty descended on the yards. At Deptford they were pelted with mud by the women and children of artificers who had been discharged or had had their allowances cut.[86] The visitation was followed by a heated correspondence between the Admiralty and the Navy Board on the subject of the latter's neglecting to investigate complaints made to it by Isaac Coffin, one of its commissioners, concerning irregularities at Sheerness.[87] Finally, St Vincent launched his bombshell, a statutory commission which, in the words of the Act of Parliament establishing it, was to inquire 'into any Irregularities, Frauds or Abuses, which are or have been practised by Persons employed in the several Naval Departments'. The commission was opposed in the Cabinet by Lord Chancellor Eldon,[88] in the Commons by Canning and, especially, his friend Sturges,[89] and, behind the scenes, by the two Secretaries of the Admiralty.

The difference of opinion between the Lords of the Admiralty and the two Secretaries was especially marked: Sir Evan Nepean, the Principal Secretary, hung on to office till January 1804, but his subordinate, Marsden, had been in daily expectation of an open quarrel with the Lords for over a year previously. Marsden himself wrote at the time of the Commission of Enquiry, 'the object is to get rid of the Navy Board'. He thought the dockyard visitation had been intended to discover frauds. This had failed:

'It was then tried to drive them out by the most abusive letters that ever were written from one Board to another . . . . [i.e. about Coffin and the Sheerness abuses] . . . . And now this extraordinary commission is resorted to in the hope of its operating some way (they cannot very well say how) to the end desired.'[90]

That St Vincent did not on his own authority demand the resignation of the Navy Board was apparently due to his confident expectation of their 'ignominous dismissal' by the Commission of Enquiry,[91] though he did take the opportunity of a timely vacancy in August 1803 to appoint to the Navy Board Osborne Markham, brother of John Markham, one of the Lords of the Admiralty. Osborne Markham's colleagues were soon objecting to his practice of noting down what each of them said at board meetings.[92]

In his haste to revenge a generation of wrongs, St Vincent undoubtedly went too far. He replaced a system of favouritism by a system of vendetta. Not all his coadjutors were as honest as he was, and he antagonised many sea commanders whose interests he was professedly championing. Sir Home Popham, the most brilliant commodore of the era, was told on the appointment of St Vincent that he 'had everything to apprehend, and no chance of . . . impartial consideration'.[93] On his return home from the East, he found that 'caluminous reports were circulated, in whispers and conversations, with the greatest industry, by those very persons who ought to have checked them'.[94] Popham's accounts while commanding HMS *Romney* in the Indian Ocean were investigated by one of St Vincent's protégés, Benjamin Tucker, then a member of the Navy Board's committee on stores. An enormous excess of expenditure was revealed. Soon afterwards Tucker was appointed Second Secretary to the Admiralty. Subsequent parliamentary enquiry showed that Tucker's calculations were wildly inaccurate, but on the strength of his figures, Popham's pay was stopped, and a senior petty officer of HMS *Romney* was press-ganged in the hopes of extorting from him evidence that would incriminate Popham.[95] Popham had a pamphlet printed for private circulation defending his probity: a refutation of this was drawn up by Tucker with the concurrence of St Vincent and published anonymously and copies were even distributed *gratis* to officers in the Channel Fleet.[96]

The Drift to War
In September 1802 France annexed Piedmont, and in October also invaded Switzerland. The Treaty of Amiens seemed already a dead letter. The 'New Opposition' blamed Addington, whose conciliatory policy seemed to encourage Napoleon in his aggression. Both Canning

and Lord Grenville visited Pitt at Walmer Castle (his official residence as Warden of the Cinque Ports) and urged him to resume power. But Pitt considered himself bound by the pledge he had given on leaving office to support Addington. Though he now regretted this pledge he regarded it 'as solemnly binding, not redeemable by any lapse of time, nor ever to be cancelled without the *express consent* of Mr Addington'. Nor would he ask for his release: 'my ambition is *character*, not office', he told Canning, and to ask for his release would have 'the aspect of caballing and intriguing for power'.[97] There was also the question of his support for the Peace. Grenville wrote after talking to Pitt:

'His line, *hampered as he must I presume feel himself, by what has already past*, cannot but be difficult. . . . It is a great satisfaction to us to recollect that *our line is clear*, and that we have in fact nothing more to do than to persist in the conduct we have already held.'[98]

Until his visit to Pitt at Walmer, Grenville had been willing to see Pitt join Addington in a reformed Cabinet, but after his return to Dropmore his eldest brother the Marquess of Buckingham warned his against co-operating with Addington and the Foreign Secretary, Hawkesbury, 'to whose ignorance, imbecility, and deception on the public, as well as their criminal annihilation of the internal and external political strength of the country, you have imputed and must still more strongly continue to impute the present tremendous crisis'.[99] The three Grenville brothers and Earl Spencer met at Stowe, Buckingham's country house, to discuss the matter. Lord Grenville protested 'this appearance of bustle and congress can only make us ridiculous now that nothing can result from it beyond a few angry speeches and another division of 5 or so people'.[100] Nevertheless he was persuaded both to attend the meeting, and, once at Stowe, to accede to the unconciliatory views of his brothers. He wrote to Pitt on 8 November, 'we really do feel that all our means of being of any use would be totally destroyed, and our own public characters rendered justly questionable with the country, by any such compromise as that on which you and I conversed at Walmer.[101]

Pitt answered that Grenville's decision not to co-operate with Addington caused him 'great pain'.[102] Canning, who visited Grenville at Dropmore, was also vexed at the brothers' attitude, but decided that it did not matter, as it would be easier to reintroduce Pitt to office without Lord Grenville clinging to his coat-tails.[103] In order to persuade Pitt to come forward, Canning tried to organize a canvass of Pitt's followers, but this scheme was angrily vetoed by the ex-premier himself.[104]

Windham meanwhile was developing his ideas in a different direction. Thomas Grenville and the two most active of Fitzwilliam's

members, Elliot and Laurence, met at his house, 106 Pall Mall, in
mid-November, and Windham himself, Elliot and Laurence decided
they were willing to support Fox 'if he should take the part which is
yet open to him, and Mr Pitt the contrary. We are for keeping aloof
from either till the sincerity of both is tried.' They suspected the
Grenvilles to be 'more easy in leaning to the professions of Mr Pitt'
but believed—incorrectly, for the idea had never occurred to
them—that the Grenvilles would be equally willing to join Fox's
'Old Opposition' if all else failed.[105] It would appear that Thomas
Grenville either failed to make clear the extent to which Lord Grenville
counted on Pitt's leadership at all costs, or else (having been, unlike
both his brothers, at one stage a supporter of Fox, and being still
personally sympathetic to him) held out undue hopes to Windham,
Elliot and Laurence, all of whom, like himself, had been originally
Foxites in the days before the Whig Party split of 1793-4.

Pitt had gone to Bath to take the waters after Lord Grenville's
visit to Walmer, and he did not come up to London at the opening of
Parliament. Early in December he decided to remain in Bath till
Christmas.[106] In Parliament, both Canning and Thomas Grenville
attacked Addington for not admitting the true gravity of the
international situation. A full-scale debate was planned for February
on the question of whether it was still expedient to surrender the
Cape of Good Hope to the Dutch, as provided for in the Treaty of
Amiens. Lord Grenville thought 'there really is so little prospect of
our doing anything useful'. His idea was to use the Cape issue as an
opportunity to state their general principles:

'and after that to declare that the system of concession being
decidedly adopted by the government, and sanctioned by the
parliament, we mean, though without the slightest idea of what
is called secession, to abstain from troubling the Houses uselessly
on a point which they have made up an opinion so contrary to
that which we entertain. And after this to attend as little as we
can, without giving our absence the appearance of secession, but
to attend only on the questions brought forward by government
on public business, and not on any motions of our own.'[107]

But when Thomas Grenville advised against all questions in
Parliament whatever, 'because the impression of our active hostility
will be renewed by them, and being renewed will not be explained
away by anything we can say afterwards',[108] Lord Grenville, who
was still ministerialist enough to abhor the notion of factious
opposition, gave up even the Cape of Good Hope issue.

Pitt against Addington
Meanwhile Addington was looking about him for means to secure
his ministry's future safety. He did not control a tame majority in

the House of Commons any more than Pitt had done. For his government to survive he had to maintain his credibility in the eyes of back-benchers who usually, but not inevitably, supported the ministry of the day, and by January 1803 his credibility was evaporating. No one doubted his honesty and conscientiousness, but even the country gentlemen were beginning to suspect that these qualities were not enough. Nor did Hawkesbury, the Foreign Secretary, seem the man to handle the deteriorating relations with France. The King himself later said:

'however the foreign ministers [i.e. ambassadors] might differ on other points, their dislike to, and contempt for Lord Hawkesbury was decidely unaminous . . . his Lordship always approached him with a vacant kind of grin and had hardly ever anything businesslike to say to him.'[109]

In Parliament the 'Old Opposition' had refused Addington's proposals for coalition and the only recruit from that quarter was Tierney who was, as he himself confessed, an 'outcast'. The emergence of the 'New Opposition' was no real problem in the Lords. The Lords, if not actually more ministerial than the Commons, was usually more passive. Fitzwilliam later wrote 'when I saw Ld Grenville without a following where he had been leading so many years with so great authority, I gave up all hope of an Opposition to the King in that quarter.'[110]

In the Commons, however, the hostility of Windham, Thomas Grenville and (since the General Election) Canning meant that Addington could be easily out-debated and made to look foolish before his supporters. But the most serious threat to his position was Pitt. Just as Pitt's support had materially assisted Addington's assumption of power, so the withdrawal of it would entirely undermine his command of the backbenches. Addington could not even afford to have Pitt neutral, let alone hostile. The communications between Dropmore and Walmer were well-known. Pitt's failure to attend the budget debate in December was widely interpreted as a censure of Addington's financial measures, of which Pitt was known to be critical, and in November 1802 Pitt had allowed himself to be persuaded by Canning and his other friends into requesting Addington to stop asking his adviceon foreign affairs.[111] All these things suggested Pitt was drifting into opposition. Yet if Pitt could be persuaded to join the ministry, all Addington's problems would vanish. The Commons, with the exception of 100 or so Foxites, would rally solidly behind the government. Canning and the Grenvilles would be silenced. Perhaps even Bonaparte would be checked in his arrogant course by the return to office of his greatest antagonist.

During January 1803 Pitt visited Addington on two or three occasions at the White Lodge in Richmond Park (a present from

George III to his new minister). This was their first intimate contact since Addington had taken office, though his brother Hiley Addington had visited Pitt at Bath during November. The possibility of Pitt's returning to office was not mentioned, however, till, 'within ten minutes or a quarter of an hour before their separation' after one of these visits, 'in the chaise coming into town, when they had reached Hyde Park, Mr A, in a very embarrassed manner, entered on the subject'.[112] The truth was that Addington, having tasted power, was now reluctant to surrender it, whatever its discomforts.

It was not till late in March that Addington finally brought himself to make an offer to Pitt. As his emissary he chose Henry Dundas, who had recently been ennobled as Viscount Melville, an honour for which he was indebted to Addington. Melville did not get on well with the Grenvilles (who despised him for his lack of culture) and he was eager to return to office with Pitt. He was thus an ideal intermediary. Addington's proposal was that Pitt and himself should become Secretaries of State under a nominal premier in the Lords, possibly Pitt's own elder brother the Earl of Chatham (another person who disliked his Grenville cousins). 'Mr Pitt treated this extravagant idea as it deserved.' He told Melville that he had no desire to resume office, that 'he had seen with concern and disapprobation many of the late measures, both as to foreign politics and as to finance; and that nothing but the present crisis of the country restrained him at this time from expressing in public his sentiments on the latter', and that if he did return to office 'he saw no prospect of being useful except by resuming the direction of finances' i.e. by becoming Prime Minister.[113]

Addington next sent one of Pitt's favourites, Charles Long, to the ex-minister with the desired offer of the premiership. As Long left Walmer Castle, he passed Lord Grenville on the forecourt. Grenville came to announce his refusal to join any Cabinet that included Addington or Hawkesbury—certainly not if they held 'efficient offices of real business'. Grenville also suggested a coalition with the Foxites to fight the war. Pitt was 'considerably struck' by this idea:

'and indeed it was not difficult to show him that the best hope of real success in carrying such measures not merely to a parliamentary majority, but with the general acquiescence and approbation of the country, must be by uniting all the leading men in parliament, without exception, in their support.'[114]

On 9 April Pitt and Addington met at Long's home at Bromley Hill (now engulfed in the borough of Lewisham, but then in the country a dozen miles from the London conurbation). Addington offered Pitt the premiership, and posts for Grenville and Earl Spencer. Pitt agreed and Addington returned to Whitehall to square his colleagues.

Even before seeing his Cabinet, however, he had second thoughts and sent a note to Pitt warning that he personally considered Pitt's terms unacceptable.[115] The Cabinet met, and led by Hawkesbury rejected the planned reshuffle.[116] Even Pelham, usually at odds with his colleagues, objected to the idea of Melville replacing St Vincent at the Admiralty.[117] Accordingly, Addington told Pitt no arrangement was possible.[118] Somewhat vexed, Pitt told Addington that in future he would 'receive no overtures but such as may be made by express command of His Majesty'.[119] His Majesty, to whom, at Pitt's insistence, all the relevant correspondence was shown, was not at all pleased by Pitt's attitude, and commented, 'He desires to put the Crown in commission—he carries his plan of removals so extremely far and high that it might reach me.'[120]

The episode certainly improved Addington's standing at court, where he was already a favourite, but it weakened rather than strengthened his parliamentary position, and only a month later the gossip of London was that he had to drink 20 glasses of wine at dinner each evening before going to the House of Commons, to 'invigorate' himself.[121] Grenville suspected that Addington had not given in to Pitt because he had secret reasons for believing it possible to maintain peace with France.[122] This was not the case, and the war was resumed on 18 May 1803.

Fox's attitude to the new war differed from his views on the conflict with Revolutionary France which had begun just ten years ealier. This time he acknowledged that it was France, not Britain, that was the aggressor, and he saw the need for a strong war Cabinet as clearly as Grenville. But his willingness to 'abuse Addington's pompous nonsense as it deserves'[123] conflicted with his prime concern for the political advantages of his own party:

'Some of Pitt's friends will begin opposition immediately. He himself not yet, and the first question [in Parliament] being in the nature of inquiry I must support them, and I suppose the numbers will consist chiefly of my friends. . . . What, do you mean then to bring in Pitt?—is the question I am often asked. I need not answer it to you. But, tho' the present state of things has certainly given a kind of importance to our Party which it has not had of late years, it is by no means clear how we ought to use what little power we have.'[124]

It is unlikely that Fox was party to a proposal made to Addington early in May by the Duke of Northumberland, that he should meet Fox for talks at Northumberland House. Addington declined this proposal.[125]

On 23 May there was a debate on the renewal of the war. This was the first debate Pitt had attended for nearly a year. His speech was his best ever, and he was rousingly cheered. According to one admirer:

> 'Mr Pitt's return to parliament was perhaps hailed with more interest and expectation than ever had been excited by a private individual. Exclusive of the vast pre-eminence of his abilities, the great posts he had so long filled and the phalanx of friends he was supposed to command, he came at a time unusually critical and big with fate.'[126]

It was perhaps this rapturous reception which gave Pitt the idea of showing Addington his mistake in trying to carry on without him. The Grenvilles, Canning and Fitzwilliam were concerting a plan of attack.[127] Pitt visited Dropmore but refused to join this scheme. Canning, who had got up with 'unexampled diligence' at 5.30 am to gallop cross-country to Dropmore in order to see Grenville before Pitt came down for breakfast, found Grenville criticizing Pitt's vacillation, and Pitt complaining of Grenville's rancour, especially against Hawkesbury.[128] Pitt's own plan was not to attack Addington but to upstage him, by showing that it was he, even in his retirement, who had the leading influence in Parliament. The appointment of his old antagonist Tierney as Treasurer of the Navy on 1 June made such a reminder of their relative positions all the more timely.

On 3 June 1803 Colonel Peter Patten (an obscure back-bencher discovered for the occasion by one of Canning's cronies) brought forward a motion attacking the ministers. Pitt intervened to move the orders of the day. By this simple procedural move, he meant to close the debate without giving Addington a chance to vindicate himself, thereby depriving Addington of what would have been virtually a vote of confidence, and gaining for himself the credit of stage-managing the ministerial defence. But Pitt miscalculated: only 53 MPs supported him when the House divided on his motion. On the original motion Canning, Windham and the followers of Fitzwilliam and Grenville mustered 34. Fox abstained on the second vote. Sheridan voted with the government.

Though Pitt's failure was complete, his hostility to the government was now evident. Next day one of his friends in the ministry, William Dundas of the India Board, resigned, writing to Addington,

> 'I beg very truly to thank you for the unvarying confidence and kindness, which without any exception you have ever shown me, & which setting aside only one person in the world, would have ensured in every event, any trifling support in my power to have afforded you.'[129]

That *one person* was of course Pitt. It was the first defection.

Having expressed their general dissatisfaction, the 'New Opposition' thereafter supported Addington's war measures, merely criticizing details. Despite their scheming at Dropmore, despite Minto's Whiggish opinion that 'the Ministry stands . . . securely, on the will and private favour of the Court',[130] they were still far from any thought of all-out opposition.

As summer passed into autumn however, the difficulties of the ministers increased. There was a French invasion scare, and renewed trouble in Ireland. There was mounting criticism of St Vincent's conduct of the Admiralty: during the brief peace he had run down reserves of naval stores, under-estimating the chances of war renewing and possibly imagining that the suppression of frauds would greatly reduce the rate of wastage, and even before the resumption of the war his enemies in the Navy had begun to play on public fears in a campaign to discredit him. Week after week Cobbett's *The Political Register* published anonymous letters claiming there were no warships in British ports ready for sea, that senior officers were so digusted by St Vincent's conduct that they refused to act under him, that the Admiralty Board's object was to 'get rid of persons obnoxious to themselves, and bring forward their own friends and dependents'.[131] Even St Vincent's competence as a commander at sea was questioned.[132] Another problem was Pelham, the Home Secretary, who had come to be on especially bad terms with the Lord-Lieutenant of Ireland, the Earl of Hardwicke, who was supposed to correspond officially with Pelham's department. Pelham had to be replaced, but his successor, Hardwicke's brother Charles Yorke, previously Secretary at War, was the first to admit his own unfitness for the post, claiming 'my Health & Spirits are really inadequate to the Labour & anxiety of the Department', and remarking 'you have spoiled a good Secretary-at-War and made a damned bad Secretary of State'.[133] Nor did Yorke like his colleagues, telling his brother 'with the exception of Lord Castlereagh, Lord Hawkesbury, and Lord Hobart, the Cabinet is absolutely detestable; and I cannot comprehend how it will be possible for me to get on with Lord Westmorland, his manners are so disagreeable and repugnant to my feelings'.[134]

Meanwhile lampoons on Addington, mostly composed by Canning, were being busily circulated. The loyal support given to Addington in the Commons by his brother Hiley Addington and his brother-in-law Charles Bragge was ridiculed thus:

> 'When the faltering periods lag,
> Cheer, oh cheer him, brother Bragge!
> When his speeches hobble vilely,
> Or the House receives them drily
> Cheer, oh cheer him, brother Hiley!'

Such verses could hardly have added to Addington's sense of security. When he claimed, on 10 November 1803, 'I feel very little anxiety at the approach of the meeting [of Parliament]', he must have been expressing a mood of sheer bravado.[135]

The Co-operation with Fox

At first the Grenvilles planned to attend Parliament when it reassembled in November merely to avoid the appearance of secession, and Thomas Grenville advised his nephew Charles Wynn to stay at home: 'I know not what we have to say when we are in Parliament, except to refer to the opinion which we have already delivered concerning these ministers.'[136] But the dissatisfaction with Addington, and the general belief that his policy had left Britain defenceless and without allies against an ever more powerful France was by now widespread. Lord Granville Leveson, a friend of Canning's, came up to London early because 'the discontents & murmurings of all classes of Persons in Staffordshire at the blunders, contradictions and indecision of our present Minister made me anxious to find out whether the same spirit prevailed in other parts of the Kingdom'. In London he met Pitt who told him, 'the Nobility Gentry &c in the County of Kent were unanimous in their Dissatisfaction at the Conduct of Government.'[137] The feeling seemed sufficiently unanimous to encourage the Grenvilles to make one more attempt to tell the country the real truth of the situation.

Fox had not been slow to observe the ambiguity of the Grenvilles' position. As early as June he had noticed that Lord Grenville and Pitt 'seem every day getting further distant from each other', and reflected:

'I cannot help thinking that among the different corps of the enemy, these Grenvilles are those that have preserved most of something like a trifle of reputation, and that, for that reason, they are most run down by the Court. Now ought we assist the Court in this? I think not.'[138]

By mid-October he was hoping it was possible to 'act in a manner that may lead to the forming of a party against the Court, comprised of the old and the new opposition'. For Fox the formation of a party acting 'decidedly and honestly against the Court' was 'the main object'; yet whether the Grenvilles could be induced to join such a party still seemed doubtful.[139] An added complication was that, though the Prince of Wales regarded Addington with antipathy and proclaimed 'the man, whoever he is, who rescues this kingdom from the ruin the present administration are bringing on it, will have Claims to my warmest gratitude',[140] the wing of the 'Old Opposition' most closely identified with the Prince, led by Sheridan and Erskine, preferred co-operation with Addington to alliance with either Pitt or the Grenvilles.   Late in November Lord Grenville and Thomas Grenville, who were wondering how best to challenge ministers on the question of the disturbances in Ireland, met Fox by chance in Grosvenor Square, and took the opportunity to suggest some joint action. Fox was tempted, and told his lieutenant, Grey:

'We think the measure good in a party view, as it would gain us the support of Windham, the Grenvilles and possibly other of Pitt's friends. Nay, further, if Pitt must be always considered in our deliberations, against which I protest, I think there is no measure more calculated to embarrass him and drive him to an option between acting fairly and honourably, or losing a great number of his friends, and disgusting the rest.'[141]

But Fox hesitated. He was waiting to hear from the Irish Whig leaders George Ponsonby and Henry Grattan. At the beginning of December, Ponsonby and Grattan wrote advising against any motion on Irish affairs, and Fox had to tell Thomas Grenville he was no longer interested in joint action on the issue.[142]

This episode at least showed how ready both sides were for closer links. The fact that Earl Spencer, Windham and Thomas Grenville had been followers of Fox before the party split in 1794 made reconciliation all the easier at the personal level. One of the men who had defected to the government from the Whig party in 1794 had indeed already completely returned to the Foxite fold: Fitzwilliam. Other common ground between the 'Old' and the 'New' oppositions was provided by the fact that Fox agreed with the ideas Windham was developing on Army recruitment: on 9 December Fox supported Windham in the debate on the Army estimates. A few days later, again reflecting that the Grenvilles were out of humour with Pitt, he told Grey, 'You know, I always thought that among all their faults, they had one good quality *viz* that of being capable of becoming good party men.'[143]

Yet in the end the initiative came from the Grenvilles. Lord Grenville wrote to Pitt on the last day of 1803 urging co-operation with Fox,[144] and on 10 and 11 January 1804 saw his cousin twice. Pitt refused to commit himself. 'The same ideas prevail and nearly the same course will be pursued', Grenville reported to his eldest brother. 'The most decided hatred and contempt for those who have done so much to provoke both, but view of middle lines, and managements and delicacies *ou l'on se perd.*'[145]

The three Grenville brothers therefore decided to approach Fox. There is no indication that Lord Grenville needed any persuasion by his brothers on this point, though certainly he was much under their influence, but it is probable that his attitude to Fox differed from theirs. For Lord Grenville the restoration of strong government was over-whelmingly important, and in his view a temporary alliance with Fox was a necessary expedient to rid the country of Addington. He saw no paradox in joining with those who had opposed strong government in the past, for he was confident the end would justify the means. And the alliance was to be only temporary. He insisted on calling it a 'co-operation', not a 'coalition'—an anonymous pamphlet

later in the year made great play of this studied preference for the
former term.[146] For Thomas Grenville however, and also for Windham
and Fitzwilliam, realignment with Fox meant the restoration of
congenial personal links; they had given up opposition under Fox in
order to support policies Fox denounced, but now that their principles
once more corresponded they were happy to rejoin Fox, in government
if possible, in opposition if need be. For the Marquess of Buckingham
again, Fox was a means to an end: but his aim was less the restoration
of strong government in itself, than the restoration of his family's
share in it. Ten years earlier he had led the resistance within the
ministerialist camp to Pitt's wish to ally with the recruits from
opposition, and he had been an inveterate enemy to Fox for a
quarter of a century, but now that it was a question of the restoration
rather than the preservation of Lord Grenville's position, and now
that 'the tone & language of Mr Fox are such as will justify us to
ourselves',[147] he was all in favour of co-operation.

It was not exactly the case that the Grenvilles were driven into
Fox's arms by the vacillation of Pitt. It is true that Fox initially, on
being approached by Thomas Grenville with the offer of co-operation,
believed this was the case:

'Upon their connection with Pitt, I understand them to be quite
explicit; that it is over, and that his opinions are no further to be
considered or looked to than in a prudential view, with respect to
questions in which he might or might not join us. P and Lord G
have had full discussions. The same proposal was made to him as
is now made to me.'[148]

But later Fox discovered there had been no 'decisive disconnection
with Pitt'.[149] It was merely that, by refusing to commit himself to
active opposition, Pitt opted out of a possible united opposition
front and disqualified himself from being able to influence Lord
Grenville's relations with Fox: it nevertheless remained Grenville's
chief object to restore Pitt to office.

On 27 January Fox was visited by Thomas Grenville who, as an
old friend, was the natural emissary of the family. Fox told his
crony, Fitzpatrick:

'Our friend was very distinct as to the parties to the proposal—i.e.
all of his own name and family, Lord Spencer, Windham etc. He
had seen Carlisle, and he was much for it, and thought he could
answer for Morpeth. Of Fitzwilliam of course there could be no
doubt. He knew nothing of Canning or Lord Granville [Leveson].'[150]

Fitzwilliam had apparently discussed, both with Fox and with Thomas
Grenville, schemes for a government—in Thomas Grenville's
phrase—'founded upon so comprehensive a scale as to include all
the talents and weight of the country, without exception'.[151] But
others saw other advantages in the 'co-operation'. Fitzwilliam's

friend the Earl of Carnarvon wrote, 'Whatever may be its success, it will at least give substance, union and common sense to our Efforts, it will revive Party Energy which is the Soul of our Constitution, Extinguished or Crippled for many years by little subdivisions of Men and Interests.'[152] But others of the Grenville's allies were less enthusiastic. Minto, who had not been consulted because he had been away in Scotland, explained his misgivings to Windham and Elliot when he returned to London late in February and 'staggered Windham more than Elliot who, however, admits the objection, but pleads the necessity of any effort, however objectionable on general principles, to escape the imminent ruin of a weak government.'[153] The Grenvilles' brother-in-law, the Earl of Carysfort also protested, 'when I recollect the language which has been held since the peace by Fox and the monstrous lengths he went before, I cannot but shrink from a very close connection with [him].'[154]

Pitt was also against the 'co-operation'. He had been among the first to learn of it: Grenville wrote to him on 31 January, and the letter included the official statement, so to speak, of the Grenvilles' position—as distinct from whatever speculations Lord Grenville's brothers may have privately indulged:

'What I have therefore to state to you is, that an opportunity has been taken to explain to Mr Fox, that we hold (and, as we believe, in common with him) two principles of action as indispensable to any reasonable hope of saving the country from its present danger. First, that the government which now exists is manifestly incapable of carrying on the public business in such a manner as the present crisis requires, and that persons sincerely entertaining that opinion are bound to avow and actively pursue it; and secondly, that if, now or hereafter, there should arise any question of forming a new Government, the wishes and endeavours of all who mean well to the country should be directed to the establishment of an administration comprehending as large a proportion of the weight, talents, and character to be found in public men of all descriptions, and without any exception. To this was added our decided opinion that it was not necessary, for the purpose of acting on these two principles, to extend the communication to any other matters whatever, or to enter into details of any kind not relating to the Parliamentary business which may from time to time be brought forward; and above all, that anything leading to compromises of former opinions, or engagements for future arrangements, was to be carefully avoided, in order that it might be at all times and with the strictest truth, distinctly and publicly denied.'[155]

It was thus purely an *ad hoc,* temporary alliance. There was no justification for a pamphleteer's sneer that the mob would soon be shouting, 'Grenville and the rights of man', or, 'Canning and no bastile'[156] — not that Canning had agreed to the 'co-operation' anyway, he was still waiting for a lead from Pitt. Pitt himself told Grenville that his chief objection was that the 'co-operation' might increase the 'unfavourable impression' of the King, who might then refuse to have Grenville in any future Cabinet, thereby forcing Pitt to form a ministry on too narrow a basis;[157] but privately Pitt feared that Grenville's belief that he had not actually committed himself irrevocably to Fox was 'delusive'.[158]

The new alignment was also unwelcome to many of Fox's followers. Charles Grey, his principal political adjutant, thought,

'They certainly are able men: their conduct is direct and open ... But on the other hand, their Opposition has appeared to proceed rather from personal disappointment than from public principle: they are extremely unpopular, and it is not till they have failed, first, in their endeavours to set up Pitt as the only man who can govern the Country, and next to gain the Country and inflame it in support of a War which they hoped to conduct, that they have recourse to us.'

He advised 'expressing a general inclination to support — promising it on certain occasions — but declining a regular and systematic attendance'.[159] The section of the party most closely associated with the Prince of Wales was even more hostile. Sheridan was in almost daily contact with Addington,[160] and probably only his uncertainty about the Prince's attitude restrained him from publicly throwing in his lot with the ministry. Early in March the Prince's friends met at Norfolk House and drew up a remonstrance to Fox, signed by the Dukes of Norfolk and Northumberland, the Earl of Moira, Erskine, Sheridan, and many others.[161] On 15 March Sheridan, Erskine and MacMahon, the Prince's secretary, voted with the government against Pitt's motion on the Navy which Fox supported.[162] Sheridan and Erskine were soon afterwards offered posts in the government, but the Prince being unfavourable they had to refuse.

How the new grouping of parties struck the country at large is hard to say. Grenville's nephew Charles Wynn assessed the 'general sentiment' as 'contempt mixed with pity for Mr A. dislike and respect for Ld G. admiration and distrust of Mr F. and for Mr P. veneration confidence and desire'.[163] Carnarvon too thought that 'Fox & the Grenvilles are not at this moment as popular in the Country as I could wish them to be, the first from various little indiscretions, the last from an unfounded notion that war at all Events is his [sic] Object.'[164] In a letter to Southey discussing the nature of Addington's support Wynn wrote, 'Many of them are country Gentlemen & from personal respect & attachment to the person of the King & from a sense of the alarming situation of the country are afraid of doing anything in opposition or at all thwarting the executive govt, and he added as an afterthought, 'Many who do not approve of them dislike their opponents still more.'[165]

Thus the Grenvilles at least had no illusions about their own unpopularity. Addington, on the other hand, had achieved considerable public respect at the time of the Peace of Amiens and had established himself in the public mind as a sound, honourable, straightforward man dedicated to the service of his country and his King: a man with whom, almost because rather than despite the contempt shown for him by his political rivals, honest-minded squires and burgesses felt they could identify. In later years Addington used to boast of the 'almost unanimous support of the country gentlemen' which he enjoyed at this time.[166] One of his friends even assured him afterwards that he had been 'the only peaceable & truly constitutional Minister except Pelham since the accession of the House of Hanover'.[167]* *The Times*, the main press organ of the ministry, carefully exploited this aspect of Addington's popular image, partly by setting up his opponents as possessing very different and less acceptable characteristics. For example, it described the co-operation of the 'New' and the 'Old' opposition as:

'a singular mixture of the *Aristocratical arrogance* of the *Grenvilles* and the *Democratic Insolence* of their new allies. . . . Few men who may aspire to office would like to subject themselves to the ministerial tyranny of men, proverbially grasping and imperious; the rashness of the one party will but ill brook the overbearing formality of the other.'[168]

Much play was made with the inconsistency of the united opposition, in contrast with the plain dealing of Addington. 'What then', it was asked, 'will the adherents of the House of *Grenville*, without doors, say to their union with a party, whom they have been accustomed to execrate as the enemies of Monarchial Government, and the Constitution of their country?'[169] It was probably this apparent inconsistency that most struck the public, and Warren Hastings (admittedly an admirer of Addington) claimed that everyone he spoke to was 'disgusted at the effrontery of so unnatural a combination of discordant interests, connexions, and opinions'.[170]

Pitt on his Own

Without formally acceding to the Fox—Grenville alliance, Pitt soon joined them in all-out opposition. In order to show his independence, however, he constantly vacillated over parliamentary tactics. Thomas Grenville complained 'he does not seem to know his own mind for 2 days together', and Fox was 'worried and disconcerted by having always to pursue a concurrence wh. he never obtains'.[171] Fox, who considered Pitt to be 'a mean, low-minded dog', would have been as happy to act without him as with him,[172] but such was not the

*The reference was not to Thomas Pelham but to Henry Pelham, Prime Minister, 1743-54.

attitude of the Grenvilles, nor of the Prince of Wales. The latter actually wrote to Pitt via the Duchess of Devonshire and Lord Granville Leveson, offering his support.[173]

The first full-scale assault in the ministry was Pitt's motion on naval affairs on 15 March 1804, the climax of a long press campaign against St Vincent. (It was rumoured that his fellow ministers were as anxious as the public to get rid of him, but that his 'obstinacy has defied and baffled the efforts of his trembling colleagues in administration to turn him out, for these last twelve months'.[174]) The debate ended in only a small division, 128 to 107, but over 120 former supporters of the government went away without voting, and Wynn remarked:

> 'Unless they can get better speakers it will be absolutely impossible for them to keep their party together. Young men especially never will support those who have not argument enough at least to save their supporters from the ridicule of those whom they live with.'[175]

A larger turn-out was expected for a debate on defence on 23 April, and Addington, knowing his ministry could not survive much longer, made one last effort to win Pitt to his support. At his instructions Castlereagh (since July 1802 President of the Board of Control) gave Earl Camden a message for Pitt, asking 'whether he was willing to state, through any common friend, what his opinions are as to the present state of things, and the steps to be taken for carrying on the King's affairs.' Pitt refused to give any advice, beyond that he was willing to be consulted on the formation of a new ministry, and told Fox and Grenville of the message.[176] He did, however, write to the King, under cover to the Lord Chancellor, urging that Addington should be removed.[177]

The debate on 23 April was mainly notable for a vitriolic attack by the Attorney-General, the Hon. Spencer Perceval, on Fox and Windham—the first time since the crisis of Lord North's ministry 25 years earlier that one of the law officers of the Crown had taken on himself to make a major speech on a non-legal issue. Addington's majority was 52 (256 to 204). Two days later, on a motion from Pitt on the Army of Reserve, it was 37 (240 to 203). These were much smaller government majorities than had been usual for many years, and far from there being any likelihood of their holding up, it seemed probable that there would soon be a mass desertion of pro-ministerial back-benchers. According to Wynn, the ministry 'was reprobated and ridiculed without doors by many of the very persons who had sanctioned it by their votes within'.[178]

Addington could not even trust his own ministers. As early as the previous December, the Hon. William Eliot, one of the Lords of the Admiralty, had warned that he was uncertain how to behave 'in the present strange commixture of Parties & opinions', and that he would probably follow Pitt if he were ever to oppose the government. Soon afterwards he had resigned.[179] By late March, even the Lord Chancellor, Eldon, was securing his retreat, inviting Pitt to dinner, apparently to discuss future prospects, and not telling Addington.[180] Addington had no wish to proceed to a clear defeat in Parliament, for this would discredit the King's government altogether. He was anxious to spare the King 'the outrage of having a Minister forced upon him rudely and violently, to the degradation of royalty',[181] as had happened in 1782-3 in the period of constitutional confusion before Pitt had become Prime Minister. At the end of April, therefore, he warned George III he would have to resign.

> 'The Doctor is Dishd
> Huzza
> In we go.'

wrote Grenville's nephew Charles Wynn jubilantly.[182]

Pitt was instructed through the Lord Chancellor to give his proposals for a new government in writing to the King.[183] Pitt's letter, dated 2 May 1804, argued strongly for coalition with Fox. In keeping with the then current notions of the fatal effects of party strife, he claimed that the eradication of parliamentary conflict would enable the country to persevere against any misfortune, without the danger of being 'thwarted or embarrassed by any powerful opposition in Parliament or in the country'. He also suggested that by uniting the parties he could prevent the revival of the Catholic issue.[184] The King's reply set a new standard of royal rudeness. After praising Addington he described the proposal of Catholic relief in 1801 as ' the most ill-digested and dangerous proposition . . . brought forward by the enemies of the Established Church' and claimed that Grenville's motive for supporting the Catholics was 'obstinacy, his usual director'. He added that in view of Fox's past conduct he was astonished:

> 'that Mr Pitt should one moment harbour the thought of bringing such a man before his Royal notice. To prevent the repetition of it, the King declares that if Mr Pitt persists in such an idea, or in proposing to consult Lord Grenville, His Majesty will have to deplore he cannot avail himself of the ability of Mr Pitt.'[185]

In his cover note to the Lord Chancellor, George III described Pitt's letter as an 'essay, containing . . . many empty words and little information.'[186]

In spite of such a harsh rebuff, Pitt asked for an audience to discuss the matter further. He saw the King for three hours on 7 May. The conversation was more cordial than the tone of the King's letter may have led Pitt to expect. The King

> 'objected a good deal to Lord Grenville, but gave way completely

about him:— to Lord Spencer he made no objection at all, only said he thought a better First Lord of the Admiralty might be found:— to Mr. Windham, in like manner he did not object, but he said he thought he better not be placed in any situation of business "though if he had been in the House of Commons, he should have voted with him on some of his questions." On Mr. Fox's name being suggested, the King digressed a good deal, but returning to the matter he said he could not possibly take him into his Cabinet.'

It was after all only six years since the King had had Fox ignominiously struck off the roll of the Privy Council. On the other hand he was willing to employ Fox on some diplomatic mission abroad. 'On the whole, the impression was very strong in Mr Pitt's mind that he could have easily prevailed with the King to admit several of Mr Fox's friends into office, some in the cabinet.'[187]

After the audience Pitt sent Canning to Grenville and Lord Granville Leveson to Fox with the bad news. To Fox at least it was not unexpected. The previous night he had left a note at Thomas Grenville's house in Charles Street, Berkeley Square, saying,

'My *opinion* (but it is only an opinion) is that Pitt will accept on the most humbled Plan. . . . If an offer is made to him [Lord Grenville] and his friends, it is for him and them to consider it, and you will see it is a point on which I *can* offer no advice, but I wish you and them to understand most distinctly that I have not the smallest notion of any engagement either express or implied or anything like engagement with me that ought to influence them against accepting any offer which if I were dead or had never existed, they would otherwise deem worthy of their notice.'[188]

On the evening of the day on which Pitt saw the King (7 May), Thomas and Lord Grenville, Earls Spencer and Fitzwilliam, and Windham met at Camelford House, a mansion on the corner of Oxford Street and Park Lane which Lady Grenville had recently inherited as a result of her brother Lord Camelford being killed in a duel.* There was a simultaneous meeting of Fox and his friends at the Prince of Wales' residence, Carlton House, on the other side of the West End. Fox urged his followers to join Pitt, but both at Camelford House and at Carlton House the decision was the same: they would join no government without Fox.[189]

Next day Lord Grenville wrote to Pitt enclosing a letter which he wished to be laid before George III in a last attempt to reconcile the King to Fox. Copies of this letter were also sent to the Prince of Wales and many of the Grenville allies. Despite injunctions to the various recipients to avoid multiplying copies of it,[190] unauthorized copies were circulating around London within five weeks[191] and

*This house was demolished before the First World War.

eventually it was published in *The Annual Register.* The letter, so
eloquent of Grenville's anxiety for the submerging of all party strife
in a united government, was as follows:

May 8, 1804

'My dear Pitt,

I have already apprised you that all the persons, to whom, at
your desire, I communicated what passed between us yesterday,
agreed with me in the decided opinion, that we ought not to
engage in the administratiion which you are now employed in
forming.

We should be sincerely sorry, if by declining this proposal, we
should appear less desirous than we must always be, of rendering
to his Majesty to the utmost of our power, any service, of which
he may be graciously pleased to think us capable. No consideration
of personal ease or comfort, no apprehension of responsibility, or
reluctance to meet the real situation into which the country has
been brought, have any weight in this decision: nor are we fettered
with any engagements on the subject, either expressed or implied;
we rest our determination solely on our strong sense of the
impropriety of our becoming parties to a system of government,
which is to be formed, at such a moment as the present, on a
principle of exclusion.

It is unnecessary to dwell on the mischiefs which have already
resulted from placing the great offices of government in weak
and incapable hands. We see no hope of any effectual remedy for
these mischiefs, but by uniting in the public service "as large a
proportion as possible of the weight, talents, and character, to be
found in public men of all descriptions, and without any exception"
. . . .

An opportunity now offers such as this country has seldom
seen for giving to its government, in a moment of peculiar difficulty,
the full benefit of the services of all those who, by the public voice
and sentiment, are judged most capable of contributing to its
prosperity and safety. The wishes of the public on this subject,
are completely in unison with its interests, and the advantages,
which not this country alone, but all Europe and the whole civilized
world might derive from the establishment of such an
administration, at such a crisis, would probably have exceeded
the most sanguine expectations.

We are certainly not ignorant of the difficulties which might
have obstructed the final accomplishment of such an object,
however earnestly pursued. But when in the very first instance
all trial of it is precluded, and when this denial is made the
conditon of all subsequent arrangements, we cannot but feel,
that there are no motives of whatever description, which could

justify our taking an active part in the establishment of a system,
so adverse to our deliberate and declared opinions.
> Believe me ever, my dear Pitt,
> > Most affectionately yours,
> > > Grenville.'

It is hardly surprising that Fox's own followers should refuse to
desert him, but the motivation of the 'New Opposition' was less
simple than they themselves pretended. As Pitt told Grenville
when he wrote refusing to pass on his cousin's letter to the King,

> 'that part of his letter in which he stated that an administration
> formed on the principle of excluding Mr Fox and his friends
> would be weak and inefficient . . . would appear strange to his
> Majesty who could not but recollect that Lord Grenville had
> formed a leading feature in the administration formed on that
> principle during the most alarming period of his Majesty's
> reign.'[192]

Canning believed that it was the generosity of Fox's note of 6 May
which persuaded the Grenvilles to stay out, and quoted Lord Grenville
as saying the note 'was so very noble, that in his mind it obliged him
to stand steady by Fox'.[193] Minto, though sneering at this 'point of
honour'[194] gave his son an explanation that was the testimony of a
man who was no friend to Fox, and an admirer of Pitt, and the
considerations which occurred to him must surely have weighed
even more with the Grenvilles, who were far more committed to Fox
than Minto was. Minto wrote of the 'co-operation' with Fox:

> 'This measure was resorted to in my absence, and I confess was
> neither sanctioned by any opinion of mine at the time, nor acceded
> to by any subsequent act of mine. I stated my objection to it, on
> my arrival in town, to my friends, as forcibly as I did privately
> and all the world felt them. But I did not deliver these sentiments
> publickly, nor took any steps to distinguish myself from those
> with whom in the publick eye I stood connected, on this point'.

He now accepted the 'co-operation' because Fox had agreed to the
suspension of 'those measures in Parlt or out of which could alarm
or distract Govt or country'; and he asked his son 'If they who
form'd this connexion with Fox had accepted the fruit of their
common victory, and had cast Mr Fox by as soon as he had served
their turn, what would have been the language of all the world
today?'[195] So Minto submitted to the Camelford House decision.
The Earl of Carlisle, another Grenville supporter who had been
absent from the Camelford House meeting, visited Pitt to make one
last effort to persuade him to include Fox in the ministry[196] but his
attempt failed and so he and his son Viscount Morpeth also decided
to follow the Grenvilles.

Pitt was left to form his new government out of his other friends and the serviceable fragments of Addington's régime. The Earl of Euston, his colleague in the representation of Cambridge University, who had favoured a comprehensive ministry, turned down the Mastership of the Mint.[197] (The post was given instead to Earl Bathurst.) Canning too hesitated at taking office. He was probably one of the ring-leaders in a scheme for a meeting at the house of the Marquess of Stafford (who, as Earl Gower, was one of the junior ministers who had resigned with Pitt in 1801) aimed at putting pressure on Pitt to seek a broader-based government. 'Mr Pitt immediately had it communicated to these gentlemen that he could not consider those persons his friends who attended such a meeting'.[198] The Marquess of Stafford's half-brother, Lord Granville Leveson, later recalled, 'He flattered us at the time, I remember, with the Hope that by habitual intercourse with the King, he should acquire influence sufficient to persuade HM to agree to the formation of the broad admin. he had originally recommended.'[199] But others were pleased at the separation of Pitt and Grenville. The Earl of Malmesbury claimed 'this *emancipation from Pitt,* strange as it may seem, has, I have for many years perceived, been the ruling wish in Lord Grenville's mind', and he congratulated himself on his own superior loyalty to Pitt with the proverb *'un bon ami vaut mieux que trois mauvais parents'.*[200] *The Times* wrote on 11 May:

'We cannot believe that Mr Pitt can feel extremely sorry at the intended secession of the House of *Grenville* and Mr *Windham.* We know how he was thwarted and perplexed by some of these Gentlemen in the Cabinet during his former Administration; and he will now get rid of the only unpopular and obnoxious party with whom he was connected.'

Even Pitt is said to have exclaimed resentfully 'he would teach that proud man that, in the service and with the confidence of the King, he would do without him, though he thought his health such, that it might cost him his life.'[201]

Lord Grenville certainly gained no popularity from the episode. He remained one of the most generally disliked individuals in public life, with his existing reputation for arrogance and self-seeking enhanced. Yet Pitt gained nothing in public credit from his separation from his proud and charmless cousin. His own ambiguous conduct had rendered him an object of suspicion. At the parliamentary and administrative level, which chiefly concerned these men, the three-way rift between Pitt, Addington and Grenville, meaning as it did a three-way division of the personnel who had governed the country prior to 1801, was a personal and public tragedy. Yet the effect on public opinion of the ministerial camp breaking up into factions was even more significant. Addington emerged as a deeply wronged man. Pitt and Grenville as the men who had wronged him, and perhaps each other. One of Addington's friends wrote to him from Dorset:

> 'My Bailiff, who is a very honest man, assures me there is not one in a hundred in these parts who is not sorry for the change of ministry—they all say you were very honest, that the nation was very well governed, & as well defended as it could—he adds as his private opinion that Mr Pitt is very like Bonaparte, allways [sic] restless & not knowing what he would be at.'[202]

Probably many others thought likewise. Before 1801 Pitt, having been for so long Prime Minister, had been a fixed point in public affairs, a fact of life, not perhaps well loved, but certainly reliable, reassuring, and looked up to. At the same time the Foxites had type-cast themselves in an opposite role, as the perpetual trouble-makers, impotently factious, opposing every measure of government in rash disregard for public necessities. By the time Pitt resumed power in 1804, this comfortingly simple black and white picture had been obscured. All politicians, excepting only Addington, were revealed as the same under the skin, self-seeking, factious, contemptuous of public feeling. If anything, the Foxites gained in public opinion. At least they had supported Addington for a while, and now that Fox was no longer to be condemned out of hand by a public opinion that was now more free of Pitt's tutelage, perhaps a few of those who had formerly abhorred his conduct began to wonder if there was not some justice in his cause. Of course, there was no sudden revolution in the public mind. The political situation was too confused for that, but old prejudices had been shaken, and new possibilities suggested. Addington had inherited a political system in 1801 which in 1804 could no longer be handed back intact.

2
The Second Ministry of Pitt

Ministerial Weakness

ON resuming power Pitt had two priorities. One was the vigorous prosecution of the war. The other was to heal the mutual animosities amongst the supporters, both actual and potential, of his government. Addington and a group of his friends and relatives seemed intent on unfriendly neutrality. The Grenvilles were pledged to support Fox. Both groups had sympathizers actually within the new ministry. Because Addington was especially bitter against Lord Grenville for leading the cry against him since 1802, there was no immediate prospect of the factions combining but, by the same token, their sympathizers within the new ministry were at loggerheads.

Portland, Chatham and Westmorland, whom Addington had inherited from Pitt's Cabinet in 1801, continued in place. Of those raised to the Cabinet by Addington, Eldon and Castlereagh retained their posts and Hawkesbury was transferred from the Foreign to the Home Department. The only Cabinet ministers who resigned in 1801 to follow Pitt back into office were Melville, who replaced St Vincent at the Admiralty, and Camden who succeeded Hobart in the War Department. All the others who had resigned in 1801 were now in opposition. Lords Harrowby and Mulgrave, friends of Pitt who had remained loyal and well-behaved during the Addington Ministry, now entered the Cabinet for the first time. Canning, who of course had favoured the inclusion of Grenville in the ministry and who seems to have felt that Pitt's turning against Grenville marked a decline in his own influence, was at first dubious about accepting office, but in the end decided that his appointment as Treasurer of the Navy 'will be considered by everybody as a complete triumph for me, & will refute and bring to shame a crowd of lies & calumnies that have been circulating with incredible industry'. But it was with difficulty that he concealed his resentment at not being offered a

Cabinet post. 'A pretty set they make altogether', he sneered of the Cabinet ministers, 'I would not be the thirteenth, as the thing now stands, for any consideration.'[1] Canning particularly objected to Hawkesbury who seemed to retain some loyalty to Addington and who, in effect, led a pro-Addington group within the ministry, just as Canning, outside the Cabinet, led a pro-Grenville faction. Canning and Hawkesbury had been at Christ Church together, but the length of their acquaintance merely served to embitter their rivalry. An allusion made by Canning to Addington's ministry in a Commons speech on 18 June so upset Hawkesbury that he resigned. Canning was obliged to apologize, and Hawkesbury agreed to stay in office, but mutual recrimination on the subject continued for eight months.

The fragmentation of the old ministerial grouping had its effect on the problem of the war. Pitt felt obliged to repeal Addington's army legislation, which was bound to provoke Addington to outright opposition. And as Britain stood totally alone against France (as had not been the case in 1793) he needed to pursue a course of vigorous diplomacy, and for that he could ill do without the expertise of Lord Grenville and the diplomatic experience of Thomas Grenville, Lord Minto or even of the Earl of Carysfort. Yet Pitt, with his 'over sanguine temper, which never would allow him to contemplate the possibility of a defeat in any project which he undertook',[2] refused to be dismayed. 'The appearances of difficulty have diminished every day, and I think we shall on the whole start with a very fair prospect', he assured Bathurst on 12 May.[3] He even, in a euphoric gesture, revenged himself on Lord Auckland for his lobbying against Catholic relief in 1801, by dismissing him from his Postmaster-Generalship. Auckland, whose daughter Pitt had at one time courted, was flabbergasted: as late as December he was still writing dolorously to Pitt offering to take all blame for 'the misconceptions, or the cause of grievance, real or imaginary'[4] —but in vain.

The Foxites, meanwhile, were equally optimistic, and with better cause. Fox thought they had won a substantial victory: 'Pitt lowered, and, what is of more consequence in my view, the cause of *Royalism* (in the bad sense of the word) lowered too'.[5] The opposition had also gained considerable parliamentary and administrative strength. 'It combines an extent of property, and talents, unknown before in the political world', claimed the normally non-partisan *The Morning Herald* on 11 May. Fox thought opposition seemed 'now restored, at least to what it was before the Duke of Portland's desertion'.[6] Not that all the recruits were happy. Lord Grenville abhorred faction, and with Windham assured Minto that 'nothing like a professed and systematic opposition should take place'.[7] The Earl of Carlisle claimed that the 'New Opposition' was still 'a middle party' and that

'there is no marriage between that party and that of Fox'.[8] They
were more a section of the government establishment in exile, than
an opposition. Even Lord Auckland, having been cast off by Pitt,
thought it safe to attach himself to such a middle group.

In Parliament, Pitt's first trial of strength with the new array of
enemies was on the Additional Forces Bill which replaced Addington's
ill-conceived army legislation by provisions scarcely less chaotic.
The ballot for Addington's Army of Reserve was replaced by locally
organized levies, bounties were reduced and became payable by the
government rather than by the parish, and the troops raised were to
be formed into second battalions to the regular Army regiments.
Shorter terms of service in regular Army regiments, to encourage
recruitment, and the extension of civilian training—the two ideas
Windham had been advocating for over a year—were not provided
for, and Addington's clique, supported by over 30 country gentlemen,
naturally wished to vindicate their own legislation, so both the
Grenvilles and the Addingtons joined the Foxites in opposing Pitt's
bill. Pitt's majorities were up to 60 less than he had expected.[9] The
largest division was 265 to 223. Thus, at the very commencement of
his new ministry, Pitt found himself no stronger in the Commons
than Addington had been when he resigned.

Pitt and Addington

During the recess Pitt set on foot negotiations with the Prince of
Wales' friends. The ostensible object was a family reconciliation
between the Prince and his father, but Pitt also hoped for political
advantages. The Prince had been very pleased by the reinforcement
opposition had received. He had invited all the Grenvilles, even the
neutral Lord Glastonbury, to various of the large political dinners
held by himself and Earl Fitzwilliam in May and June—not that the
Grenvilles were grateful for these invitations,[10] but an invitation
from a Prince was a command—and he had pointedly engaged both
Auckland and Addington in lengthy conversation at a party at the
Duchess of Marlborough's on 22 June.[11] But the Prince's chief
adviser, the Earl of Moira, condemned the conduct of the Foxites
and Grenvilles in refusing to take office without Fox as 'highly
impolitic',[12] and he worked without success throughout the late
summer and autumn to bring about the family reconciliation.
Meanwhile George Rose, a veteran amongst Pitt's admirers, who
was honoured by a visit from the King to his country home, Cuffnells,
in October, tried as hard as a subject could to persuade His Majesty
of the necessity of admitting Fox to his councils, even describing
Fox, with rare penetration, as 'a determined Tory'. But the King
said he would prefer civil war to making Fox a minister.[13] Pitt had
to look elsewhere, therefore, and, as Grenville still seemed inseparable
from Fox, that left only Addington and his 40 or so followers.

Charles Long, the intermediary of 1803, again urged reconciliation, though expressing no very high opinion of Addington's abilities.[14] Hawkesbury, too, was keen on the idea, and it was through him that the approach to Addington was made. A touching interview between Pitt and Addington at Coombe Wood, Hawkesbury's country home, settled the business. Addington was motivated by zeal for the King's service, hostility to Fox and Grenville, and a 'Determination to resist Those, who are labouring to subvert [the government], for no other Purpose but that of forcing themselves upon the King'.[15] After some hard bargaining he accepted the Presidency of the Council and a peerage. The Earl of Buckinghamshire, formerly Lord Hobart, who had been Secretary of State in the War Department between 1801 and 1804, was to have the next vacancy in the Cabinet, and three of Addington's back-bench followers were made Privy Councillors.

Canning was furious, and thought of resigning.[16] His friend Viscount Lowther left London 'sadly dissatisfied' and the eight MPs he returned to Parliament stayed away from the Commons for two months after Parliament reassembled.[17] The Hon. J. C. Villiers told Pitt that their connection was at an end, and that he might soon retire from politics.[18] Pitt ignored these signs of discontent. Harrowby, the Foreign Secretary, was ill after a fall downstairs and needed to be replaced, and instead of appointing Canning, who expected the post, Pitt gave it to Lord Mulgrave, whom George III had earlier thought unfit for that near-sinecure, the Chancellorship of the Duchy of Lancaster.[19] And instead of giving a Knighthood of the Garter which was then vacant to the Marquess of Stafford, another supporter disgusted by the reconciliation with Addington, Pitt gave it to the Marquess of Abercorn, with the result that Stafford went over to the Grenvilles, though it was reported, he 'is not violent, nor will he have anything to do with Fox.'[20] Even the normally docile Harrowby grumbled to Bathurst about the coalition:

'in the form in which I first heard of it, I felt much as you do, that there might be advantages sufficient to counterbalance the numerous objections. But, when it came, clogged with Lord B.[Buckinghamshire] in a great place, and with three Privy Councillors (of whom the two last Sulivan and P. Carew, are of a description absolutely unexampled) I confess I was staggered.'[21]

Addington's followers, who naturally regarded his return to office as a vindication of their leader, hardly improved matters by spreading it around 'that the thing was settled with the King before Mr Pitt knew of it; that he had no choice left but resignation or compliance'.[22] Yet not all Addington's friends were pleased by the reconciliation. When Addington asked Lord Rous to second the Address in the Lords at the beginning of the new session, Rous refused and warned

'He was aware that you alone stood high enough in Character
with the People at large to cheque his Insolence and Ambition:—He
was aware that in case of his offending the King, you were the
only Man his Majesty could have recourse to, to rescue Himself
from Insult; it therefore became Mr Pitt's first and immediate
Interest to unite with you in such a Situation as would leave Him
nothing to fear from so powerful a Rival.'[23]
But Pitt's alliance with Addington was triumphantly vindicated in
the first major parliamentary confrontation of the new year, the
debate on 11 and 12 February on the question of the resumption of
war with Spain. The united Foxites and Grenvilles ran ministers
close on arguments but the 313 to 106 vote in the Commons left no
doubt that Pitt had secured his position for the time being.

The Melville Scandal

Yet, unsuspected by anybody, the events which were to reveal the
junction with Addington to have been a major blunder were already
in train. Within hours of the government victory in the lobbies at 6
am on 13 February there was published the tenth report of the naval
enquiry set up by St Vincent in 1802. Scarcely anyone attached
much importance to this publication, though Viscount Folkestone
called on Windham before he had breakfasted, to urge him to attend
the Commons when the report was laid on the table. He found
Windham, who was subject to fits of melancholy, 'all despair', and
refusing to stir.[24] It soon became known, however, that the report
contained evidence of misappropriation of public funds by Alexander
Trotter, Paymaster of the Navy, during the time that the Treasurer
of the Navy had been Henry Dundas, now Viscount Melville, the
First Lord of the Admiralty.

The Foxites quickly saw an excellent opportunity to embarrass
Pitt, especially as the Addington group having, however reluctantly,
sponsored St Vincent's naval enquiry in the first place, now wished
to pursue the matter with the utmost vigour. Lord Grenville was
much less enthusiastic. It was contrary to his political instincts to
make party capital out of individual mistakes. Earl Spencer, knowing
as he did the complexities of naval administration, also sympathized
with Melville, especially as there was a good chance the enquiry's
eleventh report would show him up just as badly.[25] Lord Minto was
even more directly involved, as the delinquent Paymaster, Trotter,
was originally his own protégé; he spent a morning with Trotter
going through the Navy Pay Office papers and concluded that there
had been irregularity but no fraud. 'Indeed', he told his wife, 'the
whole of the inquest seems so much the effect of party rancour, and
so venomous agt Dundas personally that I don't sympathize with
it.'[26] Of the 'New Opposition', only Thomas Grenville, true to his

Foxite past, and the Earl of Carlisle were 'violent' against Melville.
What Trotter had done was to pay government money into his
own bank account to facilitate his private transactions. This was
illegal by the terms of the statute 25 Geo. III c. 31, passed only 20
years previously, but the justice of the situation was somewhat
confused. It was by exactly the same process that Fox's own father
had made his fortune at the Army Pay Office in the 1760s. Such
abuse of public money in the Army Pay Office had been subsequently
prohibited by 22 Geo. III c.81, three years before the passage of the
statute covering the Navy Pay Office. The same thing was still legal
however in other departments, such as those of the Deputy
Remembrancer of the Exchequer and the Registrar of the Court of
Admiralty. The latter sometimes had £200,000 of suitors' money
employed at interest, yielding £7,000 personal profit.[27]
    In the particular instance of Trotter's misappropriation of funds,
moreover, Melville's knowledge and concurrence were problematical.
Nevertheless on 8 April 1805 the Foxite Samuel Whitbread moved
that Melville should be censured. Lord Grenville feared the motion
'may take a more personal turn than can easily be controlled', and
advised his brother Thomas and his three nephews to stay away.[28]
This advice was originally accepted but in the event Thomas Grenville
attended the debate and spoke in support of Whitbread, as did Fox.
Fox expected a large vote against Melville, perhaps 160, but still a
minority,[29] but Pitt spoke badly, and Wilberforce, the most influential
back-bencher normally supporting the government, came out in
condemnation of Melville, thereby it is said altering 40 votes.[30]
They were on their trial, he told the Commons, before the moral
sense of England. At 5 am on 9 April the House divided 216 to 216.
After sitting ashen-faced for ten minutes, the Speaker, Charles
Abbot, gave his casting vote against Melville.
    Melville's resignation followed as a matter of course. This was a
serious blow to Pitt. It is not clear what Melville's role had been in
the ministry. In May it had even been said, 'Dundas is the man who
gives away everything. He rules Pitt, and is thus the first man in
England.'[31] Others believed that Pitt had never forgiven him for his
dealings with Addington in March and April 1803. Wilberforce, for
example, thought the two men were 'scarcely on speaking terms'.[32]
Contemporary accounts that after the Speaker had given his casting
vote, Pitt left the House of Commons with his cocked hat pulled
down over his face to hide his tears, seem to be quite untrue.[33] 'In
truth', Wilberforce wrote, 'Pitt was chiefly led into supporting Melville
by that false principle of honour, which was his great fault—he
fancied himself bound in honour to defend one who had so long
acted with him.'[34] Perhaps it went further than that. Perhaps Pitt
felt that his own personal credit was at stake, both as an individual

long associated with Melville, and as Prime Minister. Perhaps he
saw that it would be difficult to separate himself from the political
ruin of his oldest colleague. Little can be deduced from Melville's
official position at this time as to the relationship of the two men.
Though he had always been interested in naval matters, Melville's
appointment to the Admiralty in May 1804 had been odd since at
that time the First Lord of the Admiralty was in an essentially
subordinate position in the Cabinet, mainly executing policy made
by the War Department. Pitt, envisaging that the new war would
be largely naval in character, may have appointed Melville with a
view to strengthening Admiralty control of policy. (Camden the
Secretary of State in the War Department was, after all, a mere
cypher.) But Pitt's intention may equally have been to fob Melville
off with hard work and patronage, but no real independence.

At any rate, Pitt now found himself without his most experienced
coadjutor. Nor were alternative First Lords easily to be found.
Castlereagh and Yorke were spoken of for the post, the latter being
passed over because of 'want of temper and of nerves' and because of
'his partiality to Lord St. V[incent]'s ideas'.[35] Hawkesbury was actually
offered the job but turned it down.[36] Melville himself recommended
his own confidential adviser, the octogenarian Sir Charles Middleton,[37]
and it was he who was appointed, with a peerage as Lord Barham.
Yorke wrote:

'I was not aware that his advanced age his health and faculties
were equal to such a post: if they are he is indisputably the fittest
man that could be chosen to occupy it at this time. His abilities
were always considered great, his exprience is consummate, and
he has few equals in application and method in business.'[38]

But Addington, now known by the title Viscount Sidmouth to which
he had been promoted as part of his deal with Pitt, was displeased
by the appointment, and even the King was dubious and requested
that 'Middleton should only attend those cabinet meeings dealing
with naval affairs.'[39] Middleton was mainly interested in the peerage
that went with the job, for he had long wanted that honour. He told
Melville, 'I have no other wish towards the admiralty but to secure
the peerage to myself and family, and to be assistant in carrying
into execution the many salutary measures you have begun and
which must be lost if not followed up with zeal and perseverance',
but in private he confessed that if he could have had the peerage
without the Admiralty he would have happily left Melville's 'many
salutary measures' to face the future on their own.[40] In fact he was
too old and infirm to do much more than draw his salary. He never
attended board meetings, leaving it to the junior Lords to do most
of the business, and when the two Sea Lords Gambier and Lord
Garlies quarrelled, instead of sorting out their differences himself,

he wrote to Pitt requesting his intervention.[41] But he did remove St Vincent's protégé Osborne Markham from the Navy Board, sent another troublemaker, Samuel Bentham, to Russia on a mission, and established a Commission for Receiving and Digesting the Civil Affairs of His Majesty's Navy, which drew up endless lists of standard requisition and account forms, and tables of instructions for use in the royal dockyards. He also had the good fortune to be First Lord of the Admiralty when the Battle of Trafalgar was fought and won.

More important than the loss of ministerial strength was the opening up of a serious rift in the government's parliamentary following. Wilberforce's defection could be forgiven. His consistent high-mindedness was recognized by Pitt as a political asset which must, occasionally, be paid for. Even Melville forgave Wilberforce, as the latter recorded:

'We did not meet for a long time, and all his connexions most violently abused me. About a year before he died, we met in the stone passage which leads from the Horse Guards to the Treasury. We came suddenly upon each other, just in the open part, and at first I thought he was passing on, but he stopped and called out, "Ah Wilberforce, how do you do?" and gave me a hearty shake by the hand. I would have given a thousand pounds for that shake. I never saw him again.'[42]

With Sidmouth (late Addington) and his followers it was different. They wished to cash in on the popularity of the cry against Melville, not least because it reflected credit on their own former administration which had instituted the naval enquiry. Hawkesbury, who was at this stage turning against Sidmouth, subsequently complained of his old chief:

'his ruling passion was vanity; that vanity, and regret at having missed all the popularity which he would have acquired in consequence of the discoveries against Lord Melville (which was his work), and which made him often intimate to Mr Pitt what he renounced by joining him—all this made him take the part he did.'[43]

Sidmouth wished to have the belated success of his naval enquiry acknowledged by the concession of more influence in the present government. Though he discussed with Pitt the possibility of Hawkesbury taking over the Admiralty, he really wanted the post to go to the Earl of Buckinghamshire, in keeping with Pitt's earlier promise to give Buckinghamshire the first Cabinet vacancy. The appointment of Middleton was therefore most vexatious and Sidmouth complained:

'to select an individual who has little professional and no political importance, and thereby to forego the means of making an arrange-ment conformable to the pledge given to me in December last, and which would have been at the same time far more satisfactory to parliament and the public, is to declare that any expedient is preferable to the admission into office of those with whom I am connected.'[44]

Sidmouth was also, quite unjustifiably, nervous that Canning was regaining the intimacy he had once had with Pitt. The truth was that Canning's influence was almost at its lowest point, and he was in the position of standing by helplessly while Pitt battled on manfully, virtually unsupported by any colleague or private friend. But Sidmouth could not forget Canning's industry in writing lampoons and otherwise whipping up opposition while Sidmouth had been Prime Minister, and his fear of Canning's capacity for intrigue was almost pathological. He confided to his brother:

'Observing, as I do, that the Intercourse with a certain Person, who is more imprudent, & obnoxious than ever, is growing more & more forward, & that He is allowed to appear in the H. of C. more & more as the prochain Ami; I look with Uneasiness & Distrust to the Relation in which I stand to the Government, & with great Apprehension to what appears to be impending over the King, & Country.'[45]

Taking all these circumstances into consideration, Sidmouth decided to abandon ship. To Pitt he wrote on 22 April concerning Middleton, 'I deplore the choice which you have made. It will, I fear, have the effect of weakening and lowering the government at a time when it is peculiarly important to give it additional strength, and to raise its character.' And he added: 'To me it is a decisive proof that my continuance in office could neither be useful to the public nor honourable to myself: an opinion to which I have long been compelled to incline.'[46] Pitt knew he could not afford to lose the votes of Sidmouth's followers. It is also possible that he was personally distressed by Sidmouth's attitude. After all, they had once been as close friends as Pitt could be with anyone. The two men talked over the situation on 27 and 28 April, and Pitt persuaded Sidmouth to remain in office. But Sidmouth did so, as he told his brother, merely as 'an experiment'.[47]

The third, and ultimately the most significant consequence of the vote against Melville, was its effect on middle-class opinion. The middle class had been startled and confused by the junketing of politicians during the previous four years. By 1805, though Pitt was still the most widely respected politician, many of his former admirers were discontented and perplexed. Fox's supporters in the country at large had gained if not considerably in numbers, at least in confidence. Those generally suspicious of politicians, who had welcomed Addington's accession in 1801, had been confirmed in their hostility to Pitt and Fox equally by the events of May 1804. In

November of that year Addington—of course somewhat biased—and noted 'a growing ill-humour and distrust in the country. The government, though strong in connexions, had no hold whatever in the opinion or affection of the people.'[48] The vote against Melville (the first majority over any government for 20 years, if one discounts snap votes in ill-attended Houses) was the signal for the widespread anxiety and discontent to manifest itself. Public meetings at Westminster, Southwark, Salisbury, St Albans, York, Reading, Southampton, Coventry and of the London Livery, and county meetings in Surrey, Middlesex, Norfolk, Hampshire, Hertfordshire, Bedfordshire, Berkshire, Northumberland, Cornwall, Essex and Kent all drew up petitions urging the Commons to press on with its investigations. The Southwark petition said:

> 'We implore your honourable House to pull down guilt however protected; to save from rapacity, from peculation, and fraud, a people who contribute cheerfully to the real wants of the state, and who never complain but when their generous temper is abused and imposed upon: so shall the Commons of England take the most efficient course possible to vindicate the sullied honour of government; to confirm the public confidence; and to plant in all good hearts the most unfeigned admiration of the British Constitution.'[49]

At a Wiltshire county meeting, delayed by the absence of the sheriff till after Melville's impeachment had been decided, Henry Hunt, afterwards notorious as 'Orator' Hunt the demagogue, made his political *début*. Resolutions denouncing Melville were carried by acclamation.[50] At the Middlesex county meeting there was an even more auspicious episode: the veteran reformer Major Cartwright was dissuaded by the Duke of Bedford from moving resolutions proposing parliamentary reform, but he referred to parliamentary reform in his speech, to rapturous applause.[51] It was the first public ventilation of the topic for nearly ten years. Within the next few months Cartwright, and the Rev. Christopher Wyvill, the architect of the Yorkshire reform movement of the early 1780s, began reconstructing the reform campaign of a generation earlier, and began to renew their pressure on Fox. To an extent that none dreamt of at the time, reform was once more becoming a live issue. In the short term this public clamour about Melville merely served to strengthen the hands of the Foxites, and of Sidmouth's followers within the government. But it was in fact the commencement of a new phase in politics.

The Resignation of Sidmouth

Attention was temporarily diverted from the Melville scandal by the arrival in London of a petition for relief drawn up by the Irish

Roman Catholics. The Irish Catholics originally hoped that Pitt would present the petition to Parliament. Pitt had of course resigned on the Catholic issue in 1801 but when, shortly afterwards, George III had been ill he had offered to resume office and never raise the question again. Grenville heard of this by chance only in October 1803,[52] and it was still not widely known. Now Pitt refused to present the petition. The opposition was then applied to.

The Prince of Wales and many of his closest associates were, as became increasingly apparent, adverse to the Catholic claims, and the Prince's attitude was reinforced by circumstances in the last degree personal and private. His mistress, Mrs Fitzherbert, herself a Catholic, had adopted the daughter of Lord Henry Seymour, and both she and the Prince were devoted to the child. Unfortunately Lord Henry had chosen this juncture to sue for the child's return on the grounds that Mrs Fitzherbert, as a Catholic, was not a suitable foster parent. The matter was about to come up before the Lord Chancellor, and the Prince was afraid that the public sensation aroused by the Catholic petition would jeopardize Mrs Fitzherbert's case. The Prince spoke to Windham and to Thomas Grenville personally in an attempt to postpone the petition, and the latter warned Lord Grenville, 'My conviction is that in persisting you will make the future possessor of the Crown as adverse to it as the present.'[53] Windham, Earl Temple, and Grey were also in favour of the petition being put off, but they could not prevail against Lord Grenville, Fox, and the Irish Whig junta of Henry Grattan and George and William Ponsonby. Grattan himself secured his return to Parliament in order to be able to speak in favour of the petition: Earl Fitzwilliam's nephew the Hon. Charles L. Dundas resigned his seat for Malton (one of Fitzwilliam's close boroughs) to provide the vacancy.

When the petition was presented, the debates in both the Lords and the Commons lasted two nights. Grattan's speech alone lasted a record five hours. But the defection of the Duke of Northumberland's members and other friends of the Prince left the opposition in a minority of 124 to 334. In the Lords the petition was defeated 178 to 49. This marked the public affirmation both of the Foxite and Grenville support for Catholic relief, and of the general hostility to the measure of the majority in both Houses of Parliament.

Afterwards the Melville issue returned to the fore. The Earl of Darnley's motion on the state of the Navy on 24 May (which could be seen as reflecting on naval administration prior to 1801 when Melville had been Treasurer of the Navy and Earl Spencer First Lord of the Admiralty) was the occasion of Lord Grenville washing his hands of the whole factious business:

'I did not approve Pitt's conduct in the formation of his government last year, and am willing on all occasions to express that sentiment, and act up to it; but I cannot think this (or, indeed, any other feeling) a sufficient reason for my concurring to fix upon him charges of which I know him innocent, much less for sacrificing to the views of those who want to run him down, my own character, and that of Lord Spencer. . . .

P.S. You will see by Lord Spencer's decision, which was taken without concerting it with me, that I am not singular in the opinion that it is high time for us to pull up, if we do not mean to be hurried away into courses precisely the reverse of the whole tenour of our lives.'

He urged his eldest brother, 'For God's sake, consider this more than you seem to have done yet.'[55] After his brother's unhelpful reply, Grenville wrote in veritable agony, 'I am so unhappy as to differ in my whole view of the present state of things from those with whom I am most nearly connected, and as far as I can judge, from every individual with whom I have been acting, except Lord Spencer.' He might have added that it had been their aim a year previously to end party strife, not to make it worse by joining in. But he confined himself to arguing at his customary pragmatic level. He refused to follow others

'in hunting down the measures and character of a government of which I certainly was no more the head than I am of the opposition now, but of which I could not well deny that I was often considered as the next responsible member . . . to add to the distractions of the country when the very foundations of its safety are shaken both within and without, to play (as you expressed it) the Duke of Orleans's game, without even the wretched motive of personal ill-will or resentment, or false ambition which ever it was, that actuated that wretched criminal*—why should I do it? How can I justify it to myself, or to others? or think that when I am doing it I can hope that I am doing otherwise than evil?

Where I think the government wrong as I did in the Spanish and the Catholic questions, I am most ready to take my part. When the question is on the original formation of the government, I have declared, and will continue to declare my decided resistance to the principle of exclusion, and to the wretched system of a cabinet of cyphers, and a government of one man alone. But what friend of mine can wish me to add to the clamour against them on points where I am satisfied they are innocent, or to concur in measures for reviving that agitation, discontent, and popular

*Louis-Philippe-Joseph, duc d'Orléans, cousin of Louis XVI of France, supported the Third Estate during the French Revolution and, as a member of the National Convention, voted for Louis XVI's death. He was himself guillotined on 6 Nov. 1793.

commotion in the country, which it was my only merit, if I have any merit, to have contributed to allay, and set at rest as I had hoped for the remainder of my life.'[56]
These objections gradually prevailed in the minds of his relatives. On 12 June, in the long debate which decided Melville's prosecution, Thomas Grenville and his nephews did not speak, though they voted for prosecution, and two days later, when Whitbread made another motion arising out of the tenth report of the naval enquiry, they stayed away altogether. But when it was decided to impeach Melville rather than have him prosecuted in the ordinary courts, as had originally been decided, the 20 MPs who were elected to draw up articles of impeachment included two of Grenville's nephews, Wynn and Temple, and four other regular supporters, French Laurence, Henry Holland and Lords Porchester and Folkestone.

Meanwhile the internal difficulties of the ministry continued. The Sidmouth group showed themselves unco-operative in the debates on the Melville issue. Nathaniel Bond was particularly bitter against 'the Delinquent', as they called him. Patience was running out on both sides, and Sidmouth, while still dreading the suspected influence of Canning, discovered that he had a new, more formidable and altogether unexpected enemy within the ministry—none other than his own lieutenant while Prime Minister, and the architect of his return to office, Lord Hawkesbury. Whether Hawkesbury had originally worked to secure Sidmouth's reconciliation with Pitt to strengthen his own position, and vindicate his own former involvement with the man, or whether he had acted only for what he thought was the good of the government, is not clear. But whatever Hawkesbury's original motives, he had not been able to avoid the realization that Sidmouth was now a liability. He blamed Sidmouth for the growing coolness betwen them, telling his father early in July, 'I have not word from Lord Sidmouth on any confidential subject for two months; and in truth he is wholly in the hands of other persons'.[57] But Sidmouth blamed Hawkesbury.

On 24 June 1805, Lord Grenville received a visit from Earl Camden, the Secretary of State for the War Department. Camden came to grumble, on his own and on Pitt's behalf, about Sidmouth, and to try to sound Grenville on the possibility of his rejoining Pitt. Though he had been feeling so painfully isolated in opposition, Grenville was obliged to reply that it was a 'matter into which I could not enter individually, being engaged in a party, separately from which neither any of my immediate connections nor myself would listen to any suggestions on the subject'.[58] Pitt also arranged an approach to the lower echelons. On 27 June, Sturges Bourne, one of the Secretaries to the Treasury, chatted to Earl Temple in the Commons for half an hour on the same subject.[59]

On 30 June and again on 4 July (just over a week before the
parliamentary session ended), Sidmouth saw Pitt to discuss the
worsening rift between them. After the second interview he resigned,
telling his brother-in-law, 'I am sure that Mr Pitt expected and
intended that such should be the result.'[60] The immediate cause of
the rupture seems to have been Pitt's refusal to give Bond office
because of his behaviour in the Melville business.[61]

Sidmouth left office in a tide of resentment. Taking official leave
of George III on 7 July he told the King that he blamed Canning and
Melville for what had happened.[62] Nor did he spare Hawkesbury.
When he tried to give back to the King the key which all Cabinet
ministers had to open the boxes containing confidential papers, the
King said he should return it to Hawkesbury, to which Sidmouth
replied 'Sir, I am not on speaking terms with Lord Hawkesbury.'[63]
George III afterwards confessed, he 'had never been so fatigued
with any audience' since the time of Lord Grenville's father.[64] It was
against Hawkesbury that Sidmouth's anger was strongest: 'From
all my former Colleagues I have met with every Demonstration of
Kindness, & Regret', he wrote to Bragge, and as an afterthought
inserted after *Colleagues* the words 'Ld Hawkesbury excepted'. He
went on:

> 'Ld H knows that thro' his Coldness, & Neglect, Opportunities
> have been lost of cementing the Union, which He has been chiefly
> instrumental in accomplishing, & in counteracting the Machinations
> of those whose object it was to dissolve it. On this He must reflect
> with Self-Reproach, & Shame, as I do with some Degree of
> Resentment, I fear, & certainly with strong Feelings of Disap-
> pointment as far as He is concern'd, & Disgust.'[65]

As for Pitt, Sidmouth announced, 'I will be deceived by Him no
more, setting Him down as a consummate Hypocrite, and as a Man
whose affections are on all occasions deliberately made subservient
to his Interests.'[66] In fact, however, the two men parted on relatively
good terms. Sidmouth quickly repudiated an approach by Bond to
the Foxites on the subject of co-operating to prosecute 'the Delinquent',
and at the end of September Pitt even visited Sidmouth at Richmond
Park.[67]

The Last Days of Pitt

By delaying his resignation till a week before the end of the
parliamentary session, Sidmouth softened the blow of his desertion.
Fox complained:

> 'Had he stuck to his resignation in April, he must have destroyed
> Pitt: even three weeks ago he might have done it, but to wait for
> the close of a session, and to go out at a season when his retiring
> is rather an ease to his enemy than any additional difficulty, it is
> too foolish'.[69]

As in 1804, Pitt had arranged for Parliament not to reassemble till the following January, and so he had six months' respite. The Marquess of Buckingham and Fox suspected he would try to soldier on alone. As Fox pointed out, 'the Ministry with which this very Pitt set out in the year '84 was in all respects as weak and contemptible as the present'.[70] Moreover, Fox thought Pitt would apply for assistance, if at all, only to Lord Grenville, and that he would not himself be involved as it would 'break off upon preliminary points'.[71] Nevertheless, he prepared his terms, just in case. First, Pitt could not remain Prime Minister—'any proposal ought to be, and would be, rejected in which he was to be head',[72] and Hawkesbury, Castlereagh, Camden etc. were to be sacked from the Cabinet. 'Our first principle ought to be *exclusive* (and in that sense only will I use or admit the idea) of underlings of all sorts. To this rule the retaining of Lord Chatham, if P. wishes it, should be the only exception.'[73]

As early as 11 July, Sturges Bourne had told Wynn that an offer was imminent, and that the reallocation of places in the ministry to fill the gaps left by the resignation of Sidmouth and his friends was only a necessary preliminary to negotiation.[74] Earl Bathurst called on Grenville and encouraged his hopes, apparently at the request of Pitt.[75] Even reactionaries like Westmorland and Mulgrave seemed to favour an approach to the opposition.[76] Indeed the only opponents of coalition within the Cabinet were Hawkesbury, Eldon, the Lord Chancellor—and Pitt himself. For Hawkesbury and Eldon, personal antipathy for both Fox and Grenville were combined with fear for their policies and a belief that the objections of George III should be mandatory on his ministers. Pitt cared less tenderly for the King's personal susceptibilities—he was on particularly cool terms with the King in this final phase of his career—but he naturally feared that the recommending of unpopular realignments would further weaken his influence. He also feared rivals in the Cabinet (one Foxite wrote of 'the impossibility of Pitt's going on with any set of Ministers who are not his own mere creatures and tools'[77]), and he realized that Fox and Grenville were in a less docile mood than they had been in May 1804. Nevertheless, he had to hide his real sentiments from the majority of his followers who were anxious for coalition, and as usual he managed to find an excuse to put off making any public decision. As August drew on he began to put it about that he was only waiting for the latest news from Austria and Russia, who had resumed hostilities against France as Britain's allies, the intention being to settle his foreign policy before consulting the opposition. Camden was afraid Pitt would procrastinate till too near the next session, but Pitt promised to see the King early in September.[78]

At the beginning of September the Foreign Secretary, Lord Mulgrave (presumably acting on Pitt's instructions) visited Lord

Minto, whose uneasiness in opposition had been even more marked than that of Lord Grenville, and who was especially concerned with making a fortune in politics with which to endow his heirs.[79] Mulgrave offered Minto the embassy at St Petersburg, and made it clear that there was definitely not going to be a general offer of coalition.[80] Minto's refusal forced Pitt finally to come to a decision to discuss the matter with the King.

George III have been virtually blind since July. Still weak from a recurrence of porphyria in May, and now increasingly isolated by his old age and the loss of sight, he had spent the summer at Weymouth with George Rose and Lords Eldon and Hawkesbury attending him. Rose took the opportunity to speak frequently on behalf of the proposed coalition. Eldon and Hawkesbury, with better success, as frequently hinted their objections. Eldon, who had few political skills beyond that of being a perennial survivor, had long been a favourite of the King, but it was only now that Hawkesbury, on some ways much stronger minded, began to worm his way into the royal confidence.[81]

Pitt went to Weymouth and saw the King on 20 September 1805. The King took two days to think matters over. His final decision was a victory for Eldon and Hawkesbury. He said there was no need for a coalition and that he refused to have either Fox or Grenville in his Cabinet.[82] The opposition were not directly informed. Final confirmation that there would be no union of parties came only on 4 October, in a letter from Charles Long, newly appointed Irish Secretary, to the Marquess of Stafford.[83] Pitt was not forced to fall back on the possibility of adding Canning and Yorke to his Cabinet,[84] but in this too he was dilatory. He talked things over with Canning on 23 November but in the event the matter was never finally settled.

During November and December the opposition experienced internal difficulties of its own. Fox was convinced that the continental alliance on which Pitt had pinned his hopes would crumble before Napoleon, and proposed to denounce Pitt's foreign policy when Parliament reassembled in the new year. Lord Grenville was not so sure, and actually rather approved of Pitt's alliances.[85] Windham and Thomas Grenville had originally, while the European situation was still uncertain, agreed with Lord Grenville that there was no occasion to plan any attack on Pitt's diplomatic measures, but the persuasions of Fox, and the tremendous French victory over Russia and Austria at Austerlitz in December 1805 changed their minds.[86] Windham pretended that the dispute was of no crucial importance and suggested fancifully that they 'move in two or three separate columns; all, however,' he hoped, 'assisting each other, and tending to one point' — at which suggestion Grey commented drily, 'instead of meeting in one point, it will end in some of them joining him [i.e. Pitt].'[87]

The fact was, however, that this difference of opinion brought to a head, on the one hand, all Lord Grenville's fear of involvement in faction politics, and on the other hand, the eagerness of his two older brothers to see him take a leading part in an onslaught on Pitt that would lead to his own coming into power. 'I never had from the beginning any other object than that of uniting the leading parties, and healing the distractions of the country', he complained bitterly to Buckingham. But he had been thwarted on all sides, 'by the great misconduct of Pitt', and by his own friends 'some of whom (Fox's party) never wished the thing to succeed; and others feel so much resentment at its failure, as to be ready to overlook the danger of the country, in their view of making war against its administration'. He had opposed Addington in the hope that a coalition government would be set up, and had continued in opposition to Pitt because it was not; but now that a union of all parties in government seemed impossible, he could see no purpose in continuing:

'If then, after a struggle that shall tear the country to pieces, we now make it impossible for Pitt to carry on the government, who is to succeed? Another experiment of shreds and patches like Addington's, to be composed of Hawkesburys and Castlereaghs; will that mend our case? a joint government of Fox's friends and ours, who the very first day we meet in Cabinet, shall probably differ on the leading question of our whole policy—that of resistance or submission? or, lastly, which, indeed, is the only thing probably, a separate government of the Foxites reinforced by the Addingtons . . . if it were any satisfaction to have foreseen justly the course in which the operation of the passions and interests which govern the parties of this country, were bringing on its ruin, that satisfaction to be sure I should enjoy. But can I with these feelings lend myself as an instrument to inflame all those passions already roused to such reciprocal violence, and to perpetuate the very distractions to which I attribute all our evils?'[88]

But Buckingham was not in the least impressed by all this: his opinion was that Lord Grenville's 'partiality to Mr Pitt has & will cost the country & him personally very dearly'.[89] Both he and Thomas Grenville were anxious for Lord Grenville's differences with Fox to be resolved so that they might, if events turned out as hoped, be able to co-operate in forming a ministry.[90] In the end Fox's conciliatory attitude won through. He had confided to his nephew, 'I have a dread of arguing much with obstinate men, lest one rivet them faster in their absurdities',[91] but with Thomas Grenville acting as intermediary he was able to persuade Lord Grenville there would be no future disputes about policy.[92]

This reconciliation was achieved just in time. It would have required strong personal reasons for Lord Grenville to free himself from his brothers' tutelage and from his own sense of obligation to Fox, but just such a personal reason had recently come to hand, with the return of the Marquess Wellesley to England after his brilliant viceroyalty in India. Wellesley had been Grenville's friend since their time together at Eton and Christ Church; together they had been foremost amongst the clever young men who had rallied to Pitt after 1784. Under his particularly ungracious exterior Grenville possessed a heart constructed for passionate loyalty, and Wellesley, like Pitt and the two older Grenville brothers, was one of the few objects of this hidden ardour, though it would be difficult to say what, apart from their love of the classics, they had in common. There had been considerable speculation whether Wellesley would side with Pitt or with Grenville on his return to London,[93] but it was naturally to be expected that his first efforts would be directed to reconciling his two dearest friends. This was precisely what happened, but not at all in the sense anticipated. When Wellesley called on Grenville on 15 January after a visit to Pitt the message he brought was that the Prime Minister was on his death bed.

Pitt was still only 46. He had been suffering from a stomach disorder since 1802. The tradition that he ruined his constitution by excessive drinking of port (recommended by Addington's doctor father to keep up his strength), and by too many hasty meals snatched after exhausting late-night debates in the Commons, is probably ill-founded, for his symptoms seem to have been those of cancer, a disease that cannot necessarily be attributed to his diet. After he had seen the King at Weymouth in September, he had returned to Downing Street, but had gone to Bath for his health on 7 December. By the beginning of January 1806 it was evident that he was very ill. He returned to his villa at Putney on 11 January and within three days it was evident that he was dying.

Grenville received Wellesley's 'fatal intelligence with the utmost feeling, in an agony of tears'.[94] At the suggestion of Wellesley and Lord Auckland the foreign affairs debate was postponed—to the annoyance of Windham who was not consulted, and of Fox who was not even convinced that Pitt was really ill, but who had to pacify those of his friends who had come up early for the expected division.[95] In spite of Fox's suspicion that the illness was a ministerial stratagem, Pitt expired at 4.30 in the morning of 23 January 1806. 'The sun is indeed Set, and what can now follow, but the blackest night!' wrote the young Earl of Aberdeen.[96] Melville next day declared 'that if he lived a hundred years, it would be impossible to remain an hour without having the image of Mr Pitt in his mind.'[97] The Earl of Essex thought that 'with that last breath expired the last hopes of this country.'[98] Even Fox felt 'as if there was something missing in the world—a chasm, a blank that cannot be supplied.'[99]

Certainly the loss could not be supplied by Pitt's own ministerial subordinates. Pitt had probably put off all thoughts of what might happen after his death, and either from egoism or from disinclination to face issues, had actually constructed his ministry so that it could not survive without him, for example by giving the Foreign Department, normally occupied by the premier's heir apparent, successively to two light-weights. At his death the King had no one to turn to but Hawkesbury, who had been rising steadily in both Pitt's and the King's confidence for over a year, but who was still, in Pitt's opinion, though 'by no means a contemptible adviser' not 'a man to whose decisions, singly, I would commit a great question of policy.'[100] Hawkesbury refused to carry on, and at his advice the King sent for Lord Grenville.

3
The Ministry of All the Talents

Formation of the Ministry

GRENVILLE, in succeeding Pitt as Prime Minister, acted as the head of a Foxite—Grenville coalition. But that this should be so by no means seemed inevitable at the time. Few contemporaries realized how inextricably Grenville was committed to Fox. Canning and other Pittites regarded Grenville 'as the direct and lawful inheritor of the support of Mr Pitt's friends, provided he continued Mr Pitt's system, and provided he showed himself disposed to call for our aid'.[1] They actually seem to have hoped Grenville would take over the leadership of Pitt's ministerial team. Equally, many in opposition expected—and hoped for—a speedy dissolution of the Fox-Grenville 'co-operation', and protested bitterly when they learnt the two men were going to take power together. The Duke of Northumberland complained that he had opposed the Grenvilles for 17 years 'from a conviction that the measures they pursued were founded on principles inimical to the constitution', and asked, 'Can they or can any man expect that I shall blindly give my support to an Administration of which this noble Lord and his friends form so considerable a part?'[2] Burdett, Cobbett and other reformers subsequently looked back on Fox's entry into office with Grenville in 1806 as the beginning of the Foxite Whig betrayal of reform.[3]

Sidmouth was also included in the coalition ministry. This is nowadays considered the most remarkable aspect of the new government but it attracted less attention at the time. Sidmouth's political stature had declined since 1804, and as he did not hold a leading office in the new Cabinet there was a tendency to disregard him. The initiative for his inclusion seems to have come from the Prince of Wales, who instructed Sheridan to contact Sidmouth as soon as Pitt died.[4] Five months earlier Grenville had written, 'There are none of the public men of the present day towards whom I entertain, or have reasons to entertain, any feelings that should prevent my co-operating with them in any course I thought useful to the public.'[5] But those closest to Grenville, including Windham, Elliot and his own brother Thomas were hostile to the inclusion of Sidmouth.[6] Nor was Sidmouth himself enthusiastic, though he was prepared to take part for the King's sake. One admirer described him as a 'faithful old steward .... watching new servants lest they should have some evil design against the old family mansion',[7] but another friend later described him as being 'treated by his brother Ministers as a sort of Lepidus'.[8]

With the exception of Charles Long, the Irish Secretary, and of Lord Charles Spencer, one of the Postmasters-General, not one member of Pitt's government was asked to stay in office. Nor does it appear that the possibility was even discussed. According to Lord Holland's supercilious phrase, the Pittites were a 'disunited rump' of 'clerks and secretaries',[9] and since they included a dozen ex-cabinet ministers it was obviously easier to exclude them altogether rather than waste time discussing their pretensions to offices which Fox and Grenville anyway considered them unfitted to hold. Grenville may also have thought they would be reluctant to stay in office without Pitt; after all Long did turn down the offer to be continued as Irish Secretary,[10] and Earl Bathurst, whom Grenville had not been intending to continue in office, actually wrote in expectation of being asked to remain Master of the Mint, expressing his wish to retire.[11] Eldon later claimed that many of Pitt's colleagues resigned in the belief that Grenville would reinstate them.[12] It is possible that Grenville was stampeded by Fox, in the pressure of events after Pitt's death, into overlooking the Pittites: Lord Charles Spencer, who was promoted to Bathurst's place at the Mint, may have been excepted as a personal friend of Fox. At any rate, the men who actually attached most importance to Grenville's role as Pitt's heir were entirely excluded from the inheritance, a fact which Grenville certainly regretted subsequently. It was also rather vexing for the Canningite group amongst Pitt's followers, as it represented nothing less than 'the adoption of a principle of exclusion which for the last two years we have by various modes been endeavouring to overcome, & to overcome in favour of those who now adopt it'.[13]

In 1801 and 1804 there had been only a limited replacement of ministers, and 1806 saw the largest changeover of office-holders for over 22 years. According to Sidmouth, 'Lord Grenville and Mr Fox were nearly inundated by the pretensions which poured in from their respective connexions.'[14] Except that Fox and Grenville refused Sidmouth's demand for a Cabinet place for the unfortunate Earl of Buckinghamshire, and Grenville refused Fox's request for Cabinet office for the Earl of Lauderdale, the struggle mainly concerned the lucrative posts below Cabinet rank. The Marquess of Buckingham thought Grenville had been careless of the pretensions of his immediate followers and that they had no 'friend or connexion in office' in the Commons who could channel patronage in the family interest, except Wickham, made a Lord of the Treasury, and Earl Temple, made Vice-President of the Board of Trade.[15] But Fox complained to Thomas Grenville:

'There does not seem to be a proper feeling that having conceded the enormous point that the Treasury should be in your hands, I have a right in return, to everything in arrangement that can tend to take off the unfavourable impression this circumstance will make among my friends. There has been always something in the manner of receiving my proposal of Grey for the Treasury that I do not like . . . What your objections to Derby for Ireland are, is to me inexplicable . . . . Besides there is this general difference, that I recommend a Man because he is a Grenvillite, you seem to accept a Man *though* he is a Foxite.'[16]

Next day Fox was even more bitter:

'Pray tell me what places I have to give in the H of C. They will be much more easily counted than those I have not—Besides I must own that after giving up Lauderdale's Seat in the Cabinet, I did expect that at least I should find some notion that somebody else would give up something, but that province is left wholly to me.'[17]

The following week, having failed to secure the next Garter for the Duke of Norfolk, and a place for the Earl of Albemarle, Fox came close to hysteria. 'Indeed my dear Grenville', he wrote desperately 'I cannot bear it, I can not.'[18] To Earl Fitzwilliam he wrote the same day, 'I *cannot* give up Lauderdale if it is left to me, and Ld. Grenville *will* not I believe give up Ld. Carysfort if it is left to him—Entre nous the Grenvilles are neither very modest or conciliating.'[19]

Yet the Grenvilles were far from greedy. Both of Lord Grenville's brothers were satisfied without office. Sir Watkin Williams Wynn, their nephew, asked to become a Privy Councillor, but cheerfully withdrew his request and later refused the earldom to which his wealth and pedigree gave him fair claim.[20] Despite Fox's opposition, Carysfort became a Postmaster-General. Sir John Newport, one of Grenville's oldest friends, was appointed Chancellor of the Exchequer for Ireland, despite the opposition of Sheridan.[21] Temple became Vice-President of the Board of Trade under Lord Auckland as President, and Earl Spencer, the new Home Secretary, made Charles Wynn his Under-Secretary of State. This was the sum of the family's jobbing. The pretensions of their political followers were left entirely to the care of Fitzwilliam and Windham.

Fitzwilliam, the new Lord President of the Council, secured the

Mastership of the Horse for his close friend Carnarvon. He also tried to provide for his brother-in-law, Lord Dundas, who wished to regain his former electoral influence in Scotland which had been undermined during the Pitt era by his own kinsman, Viscount Melville. Dundas thought that if he became a Postmaster-General, the patronage at his disposal would assist his purpose, besides which he doubted if the Postmastership could be occupied 'by any man who has stronger claims upon *our* Friends than I have'.[22] Dundas was unlucky, however. Meanwhile Windham, the new Secretary of State for the War Department, had brought forward the names of Elliot and of Lords Minto, Folkestone and Kensington.[23] Minto had his eye on the Cabinet and had determined to refuse a foreign embassy on the grounds that 'I should be sent there merely to make room for somebody else at home'.[24] He became President of the India Board of Control. His kinsman Elliot, though not eager for employment, became Irish Secretary. Folkestone, despite Windham's repeated recommendations to Grenville, was also reluctant to take office,[25] but Kensington became a Lord of the Admiralty. Having forgotten French Laurence and Sir John Coxe Hippisley in his first batch of recommendations, Windham pestered Grenville about them throughout April.

With the new government coming into office after a period (for the Foxites a whole generation) in opposition, it was natural enough that there should be so much eagerness in the scramble for places. Appointment to a vacancy was not merely the recognition of one's position in the party hierarchy, or at least of one's place in the friendship of a party leader. It was also the means of establishing the importance of too-long neglected public services. Whitbread, who had led the campaign against Melville, was furious at not gaining his reward: 'I feel that I have lost all the Reputation my Consistency & Effort of fifteen years, added to the Triumph of Last Session had procured for me', he told Grey, who replied sympathetically that he had not had 'a moment's happiness since this cursed arrangement began'.[26] Office was even regarded as a compensation for past political injustices: Dundas pressed his claim to a Postmastership by asserting, 'no man has suffered more from Political attachment than I have, having been persecuted by Lord Melville and his adherents, not only in my political concerns but in my own private concerns',[27] and Philip Francis thought, 'the Government of India is the only real reparation that can be offered me for all my Sufferings in that Country, and for the Slight and Injustice I have met with in England from the Year 1781 to this Hour'.[28] Even Fox was anxious to make up to the Duke of Norfolk for his dismissal from the Lord Lieutenancy of the West Riding in 1798, and asked Fitzwilliam, Norfolk's successor as Lord Lieutenant, to resign in Norfolk's favour, urging 'you know the claims he has upon me on that score'. Fitzwilliam refused, leaving Fox to lament 'if the Lieucy of Herefordshire or Sussex were vacant it would be all easy'.[29] With such considerations prevailing in the minds of, especially, the Foxites, the actual fitness of certain ministerial appointees was rather lost sight of.

Though soon christened 'The Ministery Of All The Talents' on account of the Grenvilles' reiterated claim that they sought to unite all the talents of the country, the ministry was in fact of very uneven calibre. The Duke of Bedford was an undistinguished Lord-Lieutenant of Ireland, and Fitzwilliam continued the tradition of *fainéant* Lords President. Windham, the new Secretary of State for the War Department, possessed a brilliant intellect, but tended to live in his own private world of grandiose schemes and sweeping generalizations; and he was certainly too unmethodical and too much an individualist to make a good departmental head. The new Lord Chancellor, the Hon. Thomas Erskine, now created Lord Erskine, was an outstanding advocate, but he was scarcely learned enough to be a judge in the King's Bench, in which he practised, let alone fit to preside in a department of law of which he had no experience; Romilly, the new Solicitor-General, confessed, 'The truth undoubtedly is, that he is totally unfit for the situation.'[30] In the event Erskine turned out better than expected as a Chancery judge, even though his decisions were later known as the Apocrypha, but he had little political weight in the Cabinet, and even less at the King's court. The new ministers were, moreover, unable to find a candidate suitable to replace the second Chancery judge, Sir William Grant, who caused considerable administrative inconvenience by boycotting the sittings of the Lords Commissioners of Appeals in Prize Causes.[31] Another odd appointment was the virtually unknown, 26-year-old Lord Henry Petty, the new Chancellor of the Exchequer. This post had been held with the Treasury by both Addington and Pitt while they were Prime Minister, but on this occasion, Grenville being in the Lords it was necessary to appoint a separate finance minister in the House of Commons. It was possibly hoped that Petty would reveal extraordinary talents—in fact, be another boy-wonder, like Pitt—though he had as yet given no indication of possessing any such qualities, and it is difficult not to suspect that his title was not the least of his recommendations. In office, his ministerial statements, even his budget speeches, seem to have been based on the ideas of Fox—scarcely the best model since Fox boasted of his ignorance of economics.

Two of the appointments were widely considered as *jobs*. So that Sidmouth should have an ally in the Cabinet, the Lord Chief Justice of the King's Bench, Lord Ellenborough, was appointed to the

Cabinet. One Pittite, Charles Yorke, regarded Ellenborough
'as one of the most valuable Men in that same Cabinet, which wd
be in my opinion little worth without him; & as we must submit,
& make up our minds to be governed by it for the present at least,
I cannot help relying upon his Lordship a good deal for the
prevention of Mischief.'[32]
But the propriety of the appointment was doubted even by some
Foxites: Francis Horner thought it 'a foul stain upon the new system
of government',[33] and it was made the subject of motions in both
Houses of Parliament, this being the first sign of opposition from
the Pittites. Fox's speech in the Commons debate, in which he
argued that the Cabinet was merely a committee of the Privy Council,
of which Ellenborough was already a member, sidestepped the real
issue of whether the confusion of judicature and executive was con-
stitutionally desirable, and there was really no answer to Spencer
Perceval's jibe that had Fox been in opposition he would certainly
have denounced such an appointment.[34] Later Grey is supposed to
have said, 'of all the acts of the administration of 1806, there was
nothing he so deeply regretted as having ever consented to let Lord
Ellenborough into the Cabinet.'[35] At the same time it was decided
that the sinecure post of Auditor of the Exchequer which Lord
Grenville had held since 1794 was not fully compatible with his
being First Lord of the Treasury, and a bill was rushed through
Parliament providing for the appointment of a deputy auditor. The
Pittites had no objection to this, and George Rose actually helped
draft the bill, but many reformers in the country were scandalized
by Fox's allowing such a thing. It was bad enough that he should
have joined forces with Grenville at all, but 'to commence his
administration with them in sanctioning a system of equal notorious
corruption with any that has before signalized them' was even worse.[36]
As a result of this measure both Cobbett of *The Political Register*
and White of the newly established *The Independent Whig* began
systematically to criticize the new government as maintaining the
corruptions of the Pitt régime.
    Finally, the changeover, for all the frantic competition in the
upper echelons, extended only a little way down the structure of
administration. Many former supporters of opposition, who had
suffered from the petty tyrannies of ministerial underlings, looked
for a wholesale purge. They could argue that the ministers who
made policy were scarcely more important than the persons who
executed it. But either because they feared the disruption which
such an upheaval would entail, or because they lacked a sufficient
body of men to replace ousted officials, the ministers did little in
this direction. Wynn later wrote:
    'The change of the inferior Officers of Government at the coming

in of Ld Grenville & Fox did not extend near so far as at any
former total change such as that when Sr R. Walpole went out in
1742. When Ld North went out in 1782 or when the Coalition
came in in 1783. Indeed from what I had an opportunity of seeing
myself the great fault was that it was not sufficiently
extensive.'[37]
Only in Scotland, where over a period of 20 years the entire
administration had been filled with personal clients of Viscount
Melville, was there much idea of a total overhaul, and there it was
less with a view to improving administration in the future, than to
repaying past political debts. Thus Lauderdale told Fox:
'I am aware that all the patronage which is left at the immediate
disposal of Government . . . . is very inadequate to reward our
Friends, or indeed, to make a decent compensation for the continued
severe persecution they have suffered, that can alone be effected
by a steady attention to their interests, as vacancies in the different
departments give an opportunity.'[38]
The Scots purge soon took on the complexion of a vendetta tempered
by gentlemanly humanity. A manuscript booklet entitled *Officers
holding Places in Scotland during Pleasure, Proposed to be removed.
1806*, which was circulated amongst some of the ministers, contained
entries such as the following:
'[re John Campbell, Receiver-General of Customs]
If Mr Campbell is allowed to retain his office, the President,* his
brother, must agree immediately to withdraw Mr Connel from
the contest for the Procuratorship, & to give what support he can
to the measures of government. Mr Campbell is poor, & Lord
Moira requests that he may be retained in office under this
arrangement.
'(re Henry Mackenzie, Comptroller of the Tax Office—and novelist)
This Gentleman is author of the Man of Feeling & other works.
He is brother-in-law of Sir James Grant; & if it is thought proper,
that he shall continue in office, it is very necessary, that there
should be explanations concerning his future conduct.
Upon the whole it may perhaps be better not to touch the Lieuten-
ancies; reserving the Principle of Removal to be exercised if
provoked by any Act of marked Hostility on the Part of any
Person holding the Office.'[39]
Indeed, for many of the Foxites, the chief satisfaction of their
coming into office was not the opportunity they now had of reversing
policies of which they disapproved, but merely the chance of settling
old scores.

*Ilay Campbell, Lord Succoth, was President of the Court of Session, the Scots
High Court of Justice.

Policy
The Foxites had at no stage elaborated a positive programme of policy. They were pledged to oppose the extension of the royal prerogative beyond its constitutional limits — whatever that meant — but on all other points their creed was merely to be deduced from their criticisms of what they called the Pitt system. What this signified in practical terms had never been made clear. Their entry into office was welcomed by the veteran reformer Wyvill who, discussing the need for men of public spirit and zeal for constitutional liberty, wrote in March 1806,

> 'power is fortunately lodged in the hands of men who are unquestionably of this last and honourable description, and who posses, with the influence of their station and of their common talents, the confidence of the public, at least in a very considerable degree.'[40]

But what were these zealous and public spirited men actually going to do? Wyvill believed that Fox would naturally take the opportunity to reform Parliament. He seems to have realized that Sidmouth and Grenville would be adverse to such a measure. When Cartwright planned a Middlesex county meeting to call on Charles Grey to renew his former parliamentary campaign for electoral reform, Wyvill acted on Fox's request that it should be postponed so as not to jeopardize the formation of the new ministry, but he hoped 'a more favourable opportunity than the present will occur in the course of the next twelve months; I mean, that in that time a change of political circumstances, and consequently of opinions, probably may take place, which will be advantageous to our views'.[41] In other words, Wyvill expected the Foxites to oust their conservative allies and then show their true reforming colours. In reality, despite their encouragement of Wyvill, none of the Foxites regarded themselves as pledged to parliamentary reform, and had no more idea of bringing in a reform bill than they had of ousting Grenville and Sidmouth. Both their own, and the Grenvilles' commitment to Catholic relief was clearer, but on this issue, too, they had no immediate plans. In many respects, the defects in the composition of the new ministry were matched by defects in its conception of the tasks before it. A generation of rhetoric in opposition, while giving little guidance to conduct in office, had nevertheless woken expectations in their supporters which the new ministers had no notion of meeting.

Even in the most immediate problem of all, the war with France, the ministers had no plans worked out in advance, with the exception of Windham's scheme to reform the army. The situation inherited from Pitt was unfavourable in that Britain's allies Austria and Russia had been crushed at Austerlitz, but it did have the advantage that Britain was relatively free from overseas commitments. The troops Pitt had sent to the Elbe had been withdrawn after Austerlitz and the bulk of Britain's Army, apart from a force in the Mediterranean, was at the disposal of the new ministers. But it was some months before the ministers hit on a scheme to utilize these troops. At the same time they were unable to prevent a further deterioration of Britain's diplomatic situation. Prussia acceded to Napoleon's demands for a defensive alliance, by the terms of which Prussia seized control of Hanover and closed the ports of north Germany to British trade. The Prussian minister at London assured the British government that Prussia had only signed the treaty under compulsion, and Fox considered the idea of war with Prussia 'quite wild', but he saw no means of avoiding it.[42] Fox also embarked on preliminary correspondence with Tallyrand on the possibility of a new peace with France. Early in January Grenville had written that a peace policy would lead to 'a ruin more certain, and more rapidly accelerated than can come upon us by any possible military disasters, even by defeats in our own country',[43] but his inability to see how the war could possibly be maintained without effective allies led him to fall in with Fox's plans.

Owing partly to the opposition of the King, it was not till June that negotiations began to get under way (by which time the ministers still had not hit on a military strategy should peace be impossible). Fox's first choice as negotiator was the Earl of Yarmouth. Yarmouth had been on a visit to France at the outbreak of the war, had been interned, and had only been released in order to carry a message from Talleyrand to Fox in June. He was young—29—inexperienced, thought to be clever but notoriously unprincipled, and it is difficult to explain his appointment. It was not even a piece of political favouritism, for Yarmouth's father, the Marquess of Hertford, had been one of those dismissed by the ministers on coming into office. He soon proved himself inattentive to his instructions, and the Earl of Lauderdale was sent to Paris to advise him. On arriving Lauderdale discovered that Yarmouth was using his inside information to speculate on the funds, and Yarmouth was recalled. The negotiations dragged on with Lauderdale in charge till the beginning of October: the ministers had little faith in their ultimate success but were reluctant to take the initiative in terminating them. Napoleon had his own reasons for keeping up the charade. The negotiation diverted Fox from the necessity of making a separate peace with Prussia and offering her an alliance against France. Lauderdale was still engaged in fruitless talks with Talleyrand, and Britain was still officially at war with Prussia, when Napoleon left Paris to begin the campaign that culminated in his overwhelming defeat of the Prussian army at Jena.

The chimerical hope of peace with France also had an unfortunate influence on the ministers' aggressive strategy when they finally embarked on an overseas involvement. The scene of operations was in no way of their own choosing. They were committed to it by the initiative of local commanders of relatively junior rank. On 24 June 1806 they learnt that a small expedition had been despatched from Cape Town to attack Buenos Aires. The Cabinet's first reaction was to recall the responsible officers, Sir David Baird and Sir Home Popham, for court-martial. The news that Buenos Aires had fallen to Popham completely transformed the situation. Windham, who during the 1790s had been the chief advocate of a direct body blow against France, suddenly came round for favouring a policy of attacking Napoleon on the peripheries of his power, with South America the key area of operations:

> 'a footing once obtained there, the rest would do itself by a mild and gradual operation . . . with discontents in France described in Lord Lauderdale's letter, and with the establishment on the continent of South America followed by a hearty support of the war in this country, the period may not be far distant . . . . when the power of Bonaparte may begin to totter, and, if once thrown out of its balance, fall to the ground with every little struggle.'[44]

Perhaps of more influence on the Cabinet was the pressure that had been building up in the commercial sector for the opening up of a South American market to counter the ill-effects of the closure of European ports against British trade. As early as February Nicholas Vansittart, one of the Secretaries to the Treasury, had discussed the matter with Sir Francis Baring '& other great merchants', and 'found the commercial body impressed with very great, & possibly too sanguine, expectations of the immense advantage to be derived from opening the trade of the Spanish Colonies to our manufacturers'.[45] When the news of the fall of Buenos Aires arrived, one peer wrote 'it appears to me almost a miraculous interposition of divine Providence to frustrate the malignant designs of the Corsican for the destruction of our Trade.'[46] Such considerations had considerable weight with Grenville, Moira, Sidmouth and some of the others who 'were not insensible to the censures lavished already on our defensive system of warfare, which they foresaw would be much augmented and aggravated if Sir Home Popham's expedition were to fail for want of further support from home'.[47] Grenville also hoped they would be able to use Buenos Aires to barter for Naples in the peace negotiation,[48] but the chief ill effect of the unfortunate peace policy was that the Cabinet instructed the British commanders in South America to avoid committing Britain by pledging protection to any colonials who might assist them. Since the fact that the Spanish colonies were on the brink of revolt was Popham's original reason for invading a populous province with an army of less than 1,000 men, and since (as even most of the Cabinet realized eventually) the reinforcements hurriedly gathered and shipped out to South America were quite inadequate to withstand a hostile populace, the instruction to avoid any treaty with the colonials, and to act as invaders rather than as allies in the colonials' struggle for independence, virtually doomed the whole enterprise.

The South American débâcle and the various other military blunders of the ministry did not reach their climax, however, till after the ministers resigned, and it was two pieces of domestic policy which first made a public impact. The first was the budget in March, raising income tax to 10 per cent. A year earlier, when Pitt had raised the rate from 5 per cent to 6.25 per cent Fox had objected,

'This time 25 per cent are added, possibly there will be next time 25 per cent more put on it; after that possibly, it will be doubled, then, possibly, trebled, until the principle is silently, but fatally established, of taking the money of the subject wherever and however it may be found.'[49]

Fox's objection was, basically, to 'a tax that had no natural limit in itself',[50] and when on 28 March 1806 Petty announced the 10 per cent rate, he cunningly explained, 'A gradual rise would have led to the supposition that this was a fund to be drawn upon to an indefinite extent, but being raised at once to its natural limit, there will be less suspicion of future augmentation.'[51] This ingenious excuse failed to render the measure popular with the public, and it was bitterly criticized even by members of Fox's own party, Francis and the Earl of Thanet.

The second measure was the implementation of the Army reforms Windham had been proposing since 1803. This was even less popular than the budget, because, by way of justifying his own proposed training scheme, Windham scathingly denounced the ineffectiveness of the Volunteer system. The Volunteers were a cherished hobby of numerous country squires and local magnates and they performed a useful social function for their rank and file members. Men were proud of their uniforms, enjoyed feeling patriotic, and recognized the variety of non-military advantages of belonging to the movement. Windham's remarks provoked a storm of abuse, but when Grenville asked him to 'counteract' the effect of his out-spokenness, he refused, leaving Grenville to complain of 'Windham's utter unacquaintance with militia and county affairs'.[52] If the budget alienated friends, the Army reforms provoked enemies, and it was during the Commons debates on Windham's proposals that the Pittites first began systematic opposition.

The Pittites

Though Canning for one considered the new ministerial arrangements 'more disgusting than it was possible to believe',[53] Pitt's followers had not at first any idea of organized opposition. On the contrary, it seemed likely their group would break up for want of a leader.[54] On 20 February 1806, however, there was a meeting of Pitt's friends and it was decided to stick together and support the new government except

'upon any measure brought forward by them either in derogation from Mr Pitt's system, or in discredit of his memory, and upon any measure originating with them in itself really objectionable and felt to be so by the country and still more by the K [King]—to feel no difficulty in stating our opinions broadly and plainly, and (if the matter should be of moment enough) to take the sense of Parliament upon them.'[55]

Though they meant to 'abstain from *creating* any division of sentiment by questions *sought out* for that object', it was noted that 'there was certainly no appearance of a wish to support whenever at least there was an opportunity to oppose fairly given by the Ministry themselves'.[56] Charles Yorke thought there was a general feeling that

'the circumstances of the country *require a strong Government,* & party disputes & personal dislikes & differences ought to be laid aside in this conjunction, if ever. It is of the first importance that the King should not be induced to withdraw his support from these men, *suddenly* or *rashly;* such a step might risque everything.'[57]

Nevertheless the appointment of Lord Chief Justice Ellenborough to the Cabinet was regarded as so objectionable that 64 Pittites voted in condemnation of it in a Common debate on 3 March, and thereafter they rapidly assumed to themselves the title of 'the Opposition'.

They were far from united. Castlereagh, Hawkesbury and Mulgrave were as hostile to Grenville as they were to Fox, and Castlereagh had great influence on his stepmother's brother, Earl Camden, 'not the most decided character in public or private matters'.[58] Earl Bathurst, though disliking Fox, was a a friend of Grenville. Others, like Yorke and Canning, responded less to personal feelings than to concern for their own political futures. But they all recognized that Grenville was the best Prime Minister available, and they all disapproved of the Foxites more than they did of the Grenvilles. They all recognized, too, that Lord Grenville himself was closer politically to themselves than he was to Fox.[59] He shared their loyalty to Pitt's memory and, like themselves, disliked Fox's anti-royalism. Both Canning and the Duke of Portland hoped Grenville would ditch Fox and assume his future role as leader of a Pittite ministry,[60] and Canning even talked of vigorous opposition, 'looking to Lord Grenville *at the same time* as the person really at the head of the party'.[61]

Despite his initial neglect of the Pittites, Grenville set his face against any posthumous vilification of Pitt himself. He persuaded Fox 'as a personal favour' not to oppose a motion in Parliament that Pitt should be buried at the public expense in Westminster Abbey, though he failed to prevent the opposition of Windham.[62] In February he objected to a revenue motion drawn up by Petty which embodied criticism of Pitt: 'My idea has always been that persons who have differed however widely as to past transactions may agree in prospective measures for the public service . . . .', he told Fox. 'But this can only be done by carefully abstaining from retrospect'. He described Petty's motion as 'a contravention and breach of the fundamental principle upon which our union rests'.[63] Though Fox agreed they should not attack Pitt's first ministry, of which Grenville had been a member, he refused to 'decline inquiring, where necessary, into the acts of Pitt's last ministry, to which we were *jointly* adverse'.[64] He believed they could not afford *not* to attack Pitt:

'We are not, nor can be safe in *character,* perhaps not even in other respects, if we do not shew that the present state of affairs is in a great measure owing to the absurd and, in the event, ruinous line of conduct pursued by the late administration.'[65]

In office no less than in opposition, Fox saw the need for a good public image, based on favourable comparison with his political rivals; probably he saw, too, that as newcomers to office, they would be the ones to take the blame if things went wrong, unless they could train the public in advance to blame everything on the misgovernment of Pitt.

The question of Pitt's posthumous reputation was soon overshadowed by the problem of the Marquess Wellesley. Wellesley had no sooner returned to England than he was accused of wholesale aggression, acting without consulting his council, and other unconstitutional acts in India. He was eager to be in the new Cabinet, 'whether with or without office',[66] but Grenville side-stepped his numerous hints on the subject. Nevertheless they remained the closest of private friends; Wellesley's brothers supported the new ministry in the Commons, and Wellesley himself moved into Grenville's London residence, Camelford House, once Grenville had established himself at 10 Downing Street. Wellesley's accuser, James Paull, MP for Newtown Isle of Wight, had little support from the Foxites. He later claimed Fox had bargained to cover up for Wellesley in return for Grenville's agreeing to Lauderdale becoming Governor-General of Bengal.[67] But Paull was backed by some of Grenville's closest associates, Windham, Laurence and Minto. They probably thought they were maintaining the tradition of Burke, whose disciples they were, in denouncing Wellesley as Burke had denounced Warren

Hastings. In June it was rumoured that Nathaniel Bond was resigning the post of Judge Advocate, and Windham urged that Laurence should succeed him.[68] Grenville refused on the grounds of Laurence's hostility to Wellesley. This resulted in an acrimonious correspondence, and the deterioration of relations between Windham and Grenville.[69] Thus, with Fox's attitude to Pitt, and Windham's to Wellesley, Grenville found himself by June 1806 with some reason for regretting he had not looked more favourably on the Pittites.

The Pittites meanwhile had become increasingly discontented. The weeks passed, and still Grenville made no overtures. Melville's impeachment began on 29 April. Each day's proceedings increased their resentment. They objected to the repeal of Pitt's Army legislation, regarding their opposition on this question 'as a sacred duty'.[70] By the end of May it was clear they had to adjust and elaborate their political position. They had been holding opposition dinners for some weeks, and, at the dinner on 4 June, Viscount Lowther, the most powerful borough patron in the group and previously an influential advocate of neutrality, announced that 'the hope deprived from Ld Grenville's influence has been so long and so entirely disappointed, that unless some change, which was now hardly to be looked for, manifested itself, in the whole, in Ld G. very speedily', he would embark on open opposition.[71]

Within a week however it seemed that most Pittites were preapred to join Grenville,[72] and Lowther and Bathurst were actually planning a rapprochement with the Prime Minister. Having written to Grenville concerning a bill designed to clear up abuses in official expenditure in the West Indies, Bathurst called at 10 Downing Street, and they 'had some general conversation . . . in which Grenville expressed a very great desire of seeing more of, and having more communication with Mr Pitt's friends, who are not embarked in opposition'.[73] On 12 June, a major source of vexation to the Pittites was removed by the acquittal of Melville. Soon afterwards, Lowther himself called on Grenville and, taking an aggressive line, told him that the government was generally considered as belonging to Fox, and that apart from Fox the debating power of the Commons 'was wholly on the side of opposition', who were now a formidable party wanting only a leader.[74]

After some thought, Grenville instructed Wellesley to sound out Canning. Fox was at this time ill, but Wellesley seems to have received his instructions before Grenville learnt that Fox was actually dying, and Grenville was probably not motivated by any desire to find a replacement for Fox, still less for all the Foxite ministers. He merely wished to put an end to an opposition which, in accordance with his invariable principles, he deplored as weakening national unity. Canning was approached because he was better placed than

Bathurst and Lowther to carry out an active canvass of opinion amongst the Pittites, though he was not actually eager for a coalition.[75]

Wellesley found him at his most slippery. While Wellesley tried to discover which of the ministers the opposition most objected to, Canning tried to discover which of the Pittites Grenville disapproved of. Canning told his wife that Wellesley admitted, 'Ld G. liked Ld Camden & the D of Montrose—I said nothing. He had always felt the same sentiments towards me as ever. I said still less if possible—for I looked nothing'. Canning concealed from Wellesley what he freely confessed to his wife: 'For my own part, with the exception of Ld G and Ld Spencer, I objected to *all* the present people, as the persecutors of Ld Melville, & consequently the slayers of Mr Pitt'.[76] Led astray by Canning's evasiveness, Wellesley gave Grenville a report sufficiently encouraging for the latter to write to Canning asking to see him. Canning's reply made it clear that he would not join the ministry on his own, and after a discussion with Castlereagh, Hawkesbury and Spencer Perceval he told Wellesley at a second meeting that he required a total dissolution of the government so that it could be formed anew. He also asked if Grenville had the King's sanction for any changes.[77] After hearing this, Grenville wrote putting off any interview with Canning for the time being.[78]

On 4 July 1806 there was a large meeting of Pittites which had been arranged some days earlier at Lowther's initiative. Canning gave only a brief mention of his negotiation with Grenville as it seemed now in abeyance: 'the most important object was the pledging two or three persons who had *not* as yet had any direct communication with us'.[79] Nevertheless, Canning was able to take stock of the situation now that Grenville's first advances had failed. 'Ld Cam[den] is reclaimed, Ld L[Lowther] is fortified', he congratulated himself. He listed the Duke of Portland, Rose, Huskisson and Lords Harowby and Boringdon for compromise with Grenville, and Perceval, Eldon, the Earls of Malmesbury and Chatham and HRH the Duke of York against—though he suspected Chatham might be bought off.[80] His own sympathies were with the latter group (to whom Castlereagh and Hawkesbury should perhaps be added). This siding with the reactionaries against his own former ally may seem strange, especially in view of subsequent events, but Canning was playing a larger game than any of his associates. He had a dream of an organized party dedicated to the upholding of Pitt's principles, and he knew that a premature settlement with Grenville on the terms of a total end to party strife would mean the end of this dream.

The negotiation was soon renewed. On 27 July the Earl of Carysfort passed on to Grenville the information proferred by the Bishop of Lincoln, that 'Lord Castlereagh, Canning and Rose are to be had, if you think it worth while to buy them'.[81] Grenville was sceptical[82]—with perfect justice, for Canning was at this juncture busy egging on Eldon to make a direct approach to the King urging a change of government.[83] Nevertheless Wellesley renewed his approaches. He made Canning 'a more direct and pressing *personal* offer, and such a one as, if personal objects alone were in question, must have come up to any of the most exaggerated wishes or pretensions of *mine*'. Openings for others were also mentioned.[84]

By now Grenville knew that Fox was dying, and it was the government leadership of the Commons, rather than the ending of party strife, which was now his chief concern. Grenville knew Canning would be a much more satisfactory leader of the Commons than anyone in the existing government. He also hoped to silence Perceval, one of the most outspoken critics of the ministry, by giving him legal preferment, and to persuade Sir William Grant to end his boycott of sittings of the Lords Commissioners of Appeals in Prize Causes by conferring on him some honour, perhaps a peerage.[85] Though it was a meagre offer to the Pitt party as a whole, Canning personally was offered an enviable prize, yet he decided he would do better still by sticking to his friends in opposition. Accordingly he complained to Wellesley about the Bishop of Lincoln, who was trying to organize a separate negotiation between Carsyfort and Rose,[86] and privately condemned Camden, another, though less obstreperous independent, as 'an empty, shabby fellow', who wanted 'to be a sort of out-port, separate from the main body and more accessible to the enemy'.[87] Canning dared not let control of the negotiations pass from his hands. Though he despised or disliked nearly all his associates, he wanted above all to keep them together. The choice before him was office without credit or real power if he joined Grenville, or a leading position in a powerful party if he refused—providing he could keep the party from melting away behind his back.

Concerning his prospects in the government Canning had no illusions:

"To be plunged *alone* in the midst of the present Cabinet, constituted as it now is, and *that* not in consequence of any general arrangement on either side, but by Lord G.'s individual selection of me individually, and without the K.'s previous knowledge; in these circumstances to have had the labour of the House of Commons to devolve upon me in Fox's absence, and (what would be worse) under F.'s occasional superintendance, would, I really think have formed altogether the most undesirable, the most discreditable, and the most helpless situation into which any man ever was misguided by an inconsiderate precipitancy of ambition.'[88]

That Canning's fears derived not from any mistrust of Grenville, but from a belief that Grenville was virtually powerless within his own Cabinet, is shown by a letter to Rose on 2 September:

'I have most distinctly declared that Fox's occasional appearances (for such is the plan—the Foxite plan . . . I doubt whether it be Ld G.'s also) and a viceregal or vice-minsterial authority excercised by T.G. [Thomas Grenville] in his absence, will not at all do away in my mind the impression that this is Fox's Government; and that the admission of Tierney, Whitbread &c would do away every notion of forbearance, and extinguish all consideration for Ld G. as much as it would infallibly extinguish his authority'.[89]

Canning in fact believed, as did the other Pittites, that Grenville really had nothing in common with the Foxites, who were only biding their time before completely taking over the government. Consequently, for the Pittites to join Grenville would be merely putting themselves in the power of the Foxites.

In the second week of September, with Fox having only days to live, Canning and Wellesley's discussions entered their final phase. Wellesley gave the impression that Grenville had to choose between Canning, Rose and Perceval, whom he would have preferred, and the Foxites Tierney and Whitbread, and Bragge Bathurst, Sidmouth's brother-in-law. 'If his preference for the former be as strong as he states it, why cannot he make some exertion to render it practicable?' Canning wondered.[90] Finally, on 12 September, Wellesley played his last trick. He asked outright what it was that Canning demanded. Canning answered that the various other Pittite leaders should be consulted as to what terms they would jointly accept. Next day Wellesley told Canning that Grenville was against this, and so the negotiation ended. Fox died the same day. 'Who would have imagin'd', wrote Viscount Howick, '. . . that C would sacrifice himself and his country not to be separated from Ld Hawy and Castlegh.'[91]

In Canning's view the failure of the negotiation was due to Grenville's 'determination of not displacing for that purpose any one of the persons who had come into office with him',[92] but this was merely Canning's disingenuous way of saying that Grenville refused to change the whole complexion of his ministry by replacing as many Foxites as possible with Pittites. Canning also wanted the dismissal of Windham whose attacks on Pitt, on Wellesley, and on the Volunteers had made him widely disliked. Canning described Grenville's reluctance on this point as 'a determination of itself almost sufficient to defeat and certainly to discredit any compromise between us and the Government'.[93]

The breakdown of the talks was a relief to some Pittites, especially Perceval, Castlereagh and Hawkesbury, but it was a disappointment to others. Charles Long thought Grenville 'would have found opinions much more congenial with his own in Mr Pitt's friends than in those of Mr Fox or Lord Sidmouth',[94] and Mulgrave still spoke of Grenville as 'the first of the surviving statesmen of the country . . . the favourite Elève and most distinguished associate of Pitt'.[95] Altogether the business did nothing to unite the party. Canning, though still regarding Grenville as the best available Prime Minister, and 'the natural head of an administration of which Mr Pitt's friends should form a part',[96] argued with his usual tortuous logic, 'The only road to an union with Ld G is by a vigorous opposition for which there is ample enough ground. An abatement of zeal in attack would not facilitate a junction, but impede it.'[97] Robert Ward, the friend of Mulgrave and protégé of Lowther, on the other hand pointed out, 'I do not see that we are either strong, or the ministry bad, enough to attempt their destruction by regular war.'[98] The Earl of Euston and Lord Carrington, two men closely associated with Pitt in private during his lifetime, actually moved over to supporting the government, as did William Dundas,[99] while Charles Yorke encouraged his brother the Earl of Hardwicke to think of taking office, and, presumably, bring him in too.[100] Wellesley, who, despite his rôle as mediator, was regarded by the Pittites virtually as one of themselves, was also thinking of office, and wondering about financing a newspaper and getting as many of his friends into Parliament as possible, with a view to building up his influence.[101] It was not long before Canning was regretting that he had refused the individual offer that had been made to him.

The Replacement of Fox

By 1806 Fox had long since given up the debauchery that had made him notorious as a young man, and having settled into a quiet domestic routine with his wife, the ex-prostitute Mrs Armistead, had devoted himself to gardening and literature. This tranquil existence had not prevented the progress of a serious heart condition, and within a few weeks of his taking office following the death of his great rival, it became evident that his own health was failing. His increasing bulk was identified, not as the healthy corpulence favoured by the medical knowledge of the day, but as dropsy. In June, having achieved two immediate ambitions by setting on foot the peace negotiation with France and by conducting through the Commons resolutions proposing the abolition of the slave trade, he began to withdraw himself from his public duties. At first it was thought his semi-retirement would be merely temporary, but on 29 June 1806 Grenville learnt from the Marquess of Buckingham that Fox was dying.

Though Buckingham had not claimed any office in January, he had since then begun to grow restless in the sidelines, and perhaps not a little jealous of his youngest brother. Early in May he had written to Grenville spitefully rebuking him for 'his change of manner'

since becoming premier. Grenville had written back:
> 'It would be useless for me to attempt to describe either the pain
> or the astonishment with which I received your letter this morning
> . . . .
>
> My visits at your house have been fewer than when I had my
> whole time to myself. Is this a fault, or a misfortune to me? I
> considered it as the latter, but I think your own feelings for me,
> as well as for the country, would have made you regret instead of
> rejoicing, if when I have occupation pressing upon me for forty-
> eight hours out of every twenty-four, I had added to the mass of
> business daily falling in arrear, by visits for the purpose (I really
> should have hoped an unnecessary one) of convincing my own
> brother, and that brother you! that my head was not so turned
> with my situation as to lead me at near fifty years old to forget
> those whose affection I have cherished all my life, and to whom I
> never have ceased to acknowledge the greatest obligations.
>
> I hope the time is not distant when we shall cease to have
> political subjects to discuss; because . . . I cannot conceal from
> myself, that my continuance where I am, can do no good to
> anybody, and will only destroy my own happiness without object
> or motive of any sort. In the meantime, let us, in the affection of
> brothers (which on my part has never been interrupted or suspended
> for a moment in the whole course of my life) forget for the moment
> that one of us has had the misfortune to accept stations for which
> he is totally unqualified, and let me cultivate in the peace of
> private life that happiness which it is but too manifest public life
> can never leave me. A soon as it is possible, and but barely
> possible for me to do it, I shall place myself again in circumstances
> in which neither my manners, nor the number of my visits, nor
> any drudgery to which I am subjected, can lead you to doubt
> whether the first, almost the only gratification of my life is not
> the cultivating the affection of my brothers. . . .'[102]

But Buckingham had not been impressed by this agonized
outpouring,[103] and continued to fret and imagine slights.

Buckingham regarded the death of Fox as an opportunity to
transform the ministry, and especially, to increase the family influence
within it. As a preliminary step, he bullied Grenville into making
his own confidant, William Henry Fremantle, Secretary to the
Treasury, and it was probably the result of his urgings that when
Thomas Grenville succeeded Minto at the Board of Control after the
latter had been appointed Governor-General of Bengal, the middle
Grenville brother was also given a place in the Cabinet, from which
Minto had been excluded. But Buckingham's real ambition was to
see Thomas Grenville succeed Fox as Foreign Secretary and
government leader in the Commons. This was impossible for two

reasons: the Foxites wanted one of their own number, preferably Fox's nephew, Lord Holland, to succeed Fox at the Foreign Department, and Thomas Grenville himself refused to become leader in the Commons on the grounds that his health would not stand up to it. The easiest solution would have been for Grey (now known as Viscount Howick owing to his father's promotion to an earldom) to succeed Fox in both his offices. This would vacate the Admiralty for Thomas Grenville. The latter had no intention of remaining at the unprestigious Board of Control, but he refused the Admiralty:

> 'partly because it would entirely bury me, and make me perfectly useless in the House of Commons, but chiefly because the public have been so justly satisfied with Lord Spencer in that situation, that it would seem imperfect indeed to make any change there without putting him there.'[104]

By the beginning of September Thomas Grenville and Buckingham had plumped for an arrangement whereby Howick should replace Fox, Spencer should replace Howick at the Admiralty, and Thomas Grenville should replace Spencer at the Home Department. The only difficulty about this was that it was illegal for all three Secretaries of State to sit simultaneously in the Commons. Thomas Grenville was too poor to support a peerage, besides which Buckingham wanted him as the family representative in the Commons; Howick was needed as Commons leader, so it was Windham, the Secretary of State for the War Department, who stood in the way of the arrangement. There was a further objection to Windham: when Howick's ailing father died, he would himself go to the Lords, leaving the Commons lead to Thomas Grenville, and Buckingham regarded Windham as in the way of Thomas Grenville's establishing his authority in the Commons. Accordingly, Buckingham urged Lord Grenville to make Windham a peer. Reluctantly Lord Grenville wrote to Windham asking him to accept a title. Windham refused.[105] Fox died two days later, on 13 September. After a few more days of thought and discussion, Lord Grenville wrote to Howick, urging him to join in putting pressure on Windham to accept a peerage: it was either that, or a substantial offer to the Pittites, or the resignation of the whole ministry. Howick replied, 'I feel we are not acting kindly to him [Windham], and if he should reject this proposal, I cannot concur in pressing it to his exclusion from office.'[106] Windham again refused. Lord Grenville talked of resigning, was persuaded against it by his brothers,[107] and finally swallowed a compromise. Fitzwilliam resigned the Lord Presidency to Sidmouth, allowing Holland to enter the Cabinet as Privy Seal. Howick went to the Foreign Department, and Thomas Grenville, much to his own disgust, replaced him at the Admiralty. The main effect of the episode was to increase Grenville's uneasiness in office, and his posture of submission to his brothers, and to exacerbate Windham's growing irritation against the whole Grenville family.

The End of the Grenville Ministry
The ministry having been reconstituted, and the Paris peace talks having broken down, Lord Grenville dissolved Parliament at the end of October 1806. The General Election was intended as a kind of announcement that the trial period was over, that the government was established in the royal confidence, and that it was here to stay. In this respect the election was a great success. There were some defeats of stage management, as when the Grenvillite William Praed ran successfully against the Foxite Dudley North at Banbury, and when John Calcraft, supported by the influence of the Ordnance Board, beat the Grenvillite candidate Sir Sidney Smith at Chatham, but on the whole it was a well orchestrated parade of ministerial influence. The Pittites were depressed, first by the King's agreeing to a dissolution at all, and secondly, by the efficiency of the ministerial campaign. The Talents had already been stronger than Pitt had been in May 1804, and the election consolidated their position.

	Pro-govt	Independent pro-govt	Independent anti-govt	Opposition
Old House	260	176	110	108
New House	308	151	102	90[108]

It was a quiet election. One newspaper remarked, 'It is a remarkable trait of this Election that, except in the places where notorious democrats have been rejected, political principles have scarcely been heard of in the severest contests.'[109]

The election increased the disunion amongst the Pittites, and by January 1807 there was a widespread feeling that the whole notion of a Pitt party was defunct. Long wrote to Huskisson,
'Rose and Hawkesbury I think talk of this person having joined, & another having left us, but I confess that is language I do not understand, nor ever shall untill we have a head to us as a party, and some distinct intelligible System to act upon as contra-distinguish'd from that of the Government —without this we are no party, & whether we are in a state to form one is to me very much a Subject of doubt.'[110]

Even Canning regarded the party as dissolved by the General Election.[111] He suspected Perceval and Castlereagh of having some scheme from which he was excluded, and he resented the suggestion of Eldon that he was no longer pulling his weight in opposition.[112] Grenville meanwhile had not given up his dream of abolishing party strife, and he told the Bishop of Lincoln on 6 February, 'my own feelings are not satisfied while persons for whom I have so much regard—and Pitt's best friends . . . are estranged from me'.[113] When the Bishop told Canning of this, he decided to approach the Grenvilles again, and this time he was determined to act for himself alone: 'They shall not catch me again', he told his wife, 'no pledge—no engagement—no putting out of my own hands the management of anything that may be likely to come into them.'[114] He made contact with the Grenvilles through Pitt's niece, Lady Hester Stanhope.

On this occasion, Grenville conceived the chief problem to be, not settling terms with Canning, but persuading Sidmouth and Howick, and whereas in July and September they had not been consulted, this time Grenville asked their consent before making an offer to Canning. Almost everyone save Grenville's own brothers objected to the idea of recruiting Canning.[115] Nevertheless Grenville met Canning secretly on 5 March 1807. Canning gave serious thought to whom he would nominate if offered a Cabinet seat besides his own, taking into consideration, '1st. Who would carry most of *Pitt?* 2ndly. who would be going to satisfy most people? 3rdly. who would feel the most obliged to me? 4thly. whom would the K. like best? 5thly. whom would Ld G?' and weighing against these factors the questions of 'Inefficiency—Unpopularity—Mischievous intrigue'.[116] Later he decided to demand that Perceval should be Attorney-General, that Huskisson should be Secretary to the Admiralty, and that a seat on each of the Treasury, Admiralty and India boards should be placed at his disposal. 'Who will venture to say that you have not done more for Pitt's friends, than ever one individual had it in his power to do for a party?' he asked his wife rhetorically.[117] Yet his scheme in reality involved the dispersal of the Pitt party, the course he had opposed five months earlier. In the event his *volte face* was only prevented from proceeding to its conclusion by the unexpected collapse of the ministry in the third week of March, before arrangements for his joining the Cabinet had been finalized.

As Canning's willingness to join the ministry indicated, the ministers did not embark on a more reformist course after their success in the General Election, but rather the opposite. They had espoused a number of overdue minor innovations: auditors of public accounts had been established in June 1806; an enquiry had been set on foot by Charles Wynn, Under-Secretary at the Home Department, into the provision for confining lunatics; and in the second week of March a bill to reform the Scots judicature was introduced into the Lords. Grenville and Howick were also active in securing the passage of the bill abolishing the slave trade through Parliament in February and March 1807, though it was opposed by Sidmouth and was not, as Howick readily admitted, a government measure.[118] Grenville and Howick exerted considerable pressure on many peers—especially the bishops—and MPs to support the bill,[119] but it does not seem the issue was as controversial as it had once been; only 16 MPs opposed and there were only 35 present at the third reading of the bill on 17 March. The abolition was however the most popular act of the whole ministry and was proudly claimed as such in later years—much to the derision of Grenville's and Howick's opponents, who knew they had not been responsible for it in their ministerial capacity.

The ministers' chief preoccupation remained the war. Peace had been belatedly made with Prussia in November 1806, after the Prussian army had ceased to exist, and Britain's only effective ally on the continent was now Russia. The ministers ignored urgent demands from St Petersburg for the use of British credit to raise a £6m loan on excellent security, and for British coastal raids on France and Holland that would serve to draw off French troops from Poland. Instead, the British ambassador was instructed to pester the Tsar to renew an expiring Anglo-Russian trade treaty, and 60,000 muskets and a paltry £500,000 subsidy were sent to Russia as a token of Britain's friendship. Coastal raids on France were impossible, as most of Britain's disposable troops were on the way to Buenos Aires, but in order to prevent Russia from being distracted by a war which had just broken out on her southern borders with Turkey, the ministers sent a fleet to Constantinople and an army to Egypt, neither of which achieved anything; though the full extent of the debacle of the ministers' military policy was not to be revealed till after they had resigned. Lord Grenville himself devoted less attention to the details of the war than to the problem of financing it. He devised a complicated and inadequate plan for a new system of public finance which was announced in the Commons by Petty on 29 January 1807, and which provoked instant opposition.[120]

The ministers' failure to implement any substantial reforms had caused discontent amongst former supporters. On 2 November 1806 *The Independent Whig* denounced them as 'Men, whose measures are bold and uniform only on a system of subversion, repugnant to every popular principle of the Constitution'. Even within Parliament itself restlessness was growing on the back benches. On 10 February 1807 Robert Biddulph proposed a finance committee to investigate sinecures and official fees. Petty, on this occasion the government spokesman, agreed that 'the strictest economy should be preserved in the management of the public money, and that all places, offices, and pensions should be reduced to the smallest charge, consistent with the proper administration of the affairs of the nation', but argued that sinecures were 'necessary' to supplement low salaries.[121] Though widely welcomed in the Commons, the finance committee extremely distressed Grenville who belonged to the greatest family

of sinecurists of the period. He spoke of the committee as
'one of the many evils inseparable from the station which we fill
in the country, and one of many causes which makes me daily and
hourly sigh for the moment when my friends will allow me to
think that I have fully discharged (by a life hitherto of incessant
labour) every claim that they, or the country can have upon
me.'[122]

In spite of subsequent claims by Perceval that the committee was
packed by the Talents,[123] it is clear that Grenville recognised it as a
political threat, to himself and his family especially.

But more important than the rumblings at home were the growing
discontents amongst the Catholics in Ireland. In 1800 the Catholics
had been expecting a further measure of relief as a complement to
the Act of Union. Apart from Robert Emmet's abortive rising in
1803 and occasional outbreaks of rural terrorism, there had been
general acceptance of Addington's, and later Pitt's subsequent refusal
to grant relief, but the Irish Catholics had increasingly looked to
Fox and Grenville for redress should they ever take office. When
Fox and Grenville did become ministers at the beginning of 1806,
Fox persuaded the Catholic committee in Dublin to put off any
further agitation, such as a revival of the petition of the previous
year, and to rely on the Cabinet to instigate reforms once it had
finally consolidated its political position in England. Some Catholics
fell in with this policy. 'Every means should be tried to keep back
the imprudent & hasty from an open application, which if brought
forward against their [the ministers'] opinion, can produce nothing
but mischief', wrote Sir John Throckmorton to the leading Catholic
layman, the Earl of Fingall.[124] But other Catholics were impatient
of further delays. Fox's principal contact amongst the Irish Catholics,
John Ryan, the secretary of the Catholic committee, began to lose
influence because of his support of Fox's policy. Nor was the new
Irish government designed to have much moderating influence over
the Catholics. The Lord Lieutenant, the Duke of Bedford, was shy,
inexperienced and confused by Irish conditions. William Elliot, the
Irish Secretary, had a bland and distant manner which seemed to
signify indifference and standoffishness. He suffered, moreover,
from the stigma of having been an Under-Secretary in the Dublin
government during the 1798 rebellion, and his return to the Dublin
scene was not popular. George Ponsonby, the Irish Chancellor, had
allowed his promotion to go to his head, and alienated many former
friends by his sudden assumption of a reserved, pompous demeanour.
Curran, one of the most popular of the Irish Whigs, had expected to
made Attorney-General, but was fobbed off with the more prestigious
but much less influential post of Master of the Rolls for Ireland. He
had been vaguely implicated in Emmet's rising in 1803, and

Ellenborough refused to countenance his holding any office which gave him responsibility in criminal matters. Bitterly disappointed, Curran took every opportunity to whip up discontent amongst his Catholic friends.[125] Baffled by and alienated from its potential supporters, the Irish government failed to implement any policy that would foster its popularity with the Catholics, and its attempts to allay the fears of the Orange party created far more discontent amongst Catholics than confidence amongst Orangemen. By January 1807 the government was being described as 'a feeble, neutral compromising one that wants to keep a balance between all parties',[126] and Lord Ponsonby, the Chancellor's nephew, denouncing the government's failure to foster friends at the expense of enemies, claimed that 'by the Misconduct of our Government we have lost Ireland'.[127]

On 4 February 1807 Bedford informed the Cabinet in London that the Irish Catholics intended to petition for relief again, and only some immediate concession would persuade them to give up this idea. Most of the Cabinet had, while in opposition, supported the 1805 petition and were therefore committed to supporting a new petition, and as there was no doubt of the King's dislike of the idea of Catholic relief, a petition would force the ministers into a public confrontation with His Majesty. This was the more embarrassing because, as Howick claimed, 'We came in on an implied, tho not an express understanding, that we should not promote it's [the relief] being brought forward.'[128] There was also a group within the Cabinet who objected to relief, consisting of Sidmouth, Ellenborough and Erskine, the Lord Chancellor. When the Cabinet met on 10 February to discuss Bedford's report Erskine

'betrayed ignorance as well as weakness, mistook the policy of the question, confounded the state of the law, and forgot every circumstance that had attended its enactment or its amendments. When the moment of decision approached, he played with pencils and pens, took up books, and pretended even to sleep with the hope of not being committed in any resolution we might adopt.'[129]

The concession which was finally decided upon was the opening up to Catholics of commissions in the armed forces. This was no more than the revival and extension of the Irish statute of 1793, which enabled Catholics to hold commissions up to the rank of colonel in regiments on the Irish establishment. This concession was so limited that it was doubtful whether it would be sufficient to prevent the Catholic petition, but in the event it was never carried through because the King, having at first seemingly accepted the proposal, suddenly came out with a complete veto.

On 15 March 1807 a depleted Cabinet met to discuss what to do next. Sidmouth, Ellenborough and Erskine stayed away because of their disapproval of concession. Spencer and Fitzwilliam were both absent through illness. Howick, Holland and Windham argued for immediate resignation, and had they been present Spencer and Fitzwilliam would probably have supported them. As it was, Petty, Moira and the two Grenville brothers carried the decision to drop the concession but to advise the King that when the Catholic petition was presented they would express their true views on the question. The King replied with a demand that the ministers should pledge themselves never to raise the Catholic issue again. Spencer, still ill, posted down from the country to join the discussion, and after four hours of discussion at his London house, the ministers finally decided to resign on 18 March.[130]

It was thus, seemingly at the height of their power, that the Talents ministry threw away the reins of office. Only two days before the decision to resign was made, Thomas Grenville had announced to Buckingham that he would relinquish the Admiralty to Canning, once the Irish business had been settled, and that Canning would probably accept;[131] and next day, alluding to the possibility of resignation, even the pessimistic Lord Grenville had written:

'I do not pretend to be indifferent either to the interruption of a course of public service which I really believe was likely to be useful to the Public, & creditable to myself — or to the sudden disappointment of the views & prospects of so many persons of every description who had embarked with us, & from whom I have experienced so much assistance & kindness of every kind.'[132]

But the real truth was that the ministers were in serious difficulties, and even without the crisis brought about by the ineffectiveness of their Irish policy, they faced major problems which, by resigning, they shifted on to the shoulders of their successors. The select committee enquiring into sinecures, for example, posed a serious risk, involving as it did the probability of further back bench revolts. The ministers would also have had to face the consequences of their military policy if they had remained in office. Both the army sent to the River Plate and the smaller force sent to Egypt (which landed only the day before the ministers resigned) had to be withdrawn after ignominious defeats, within weeks of the ministers' leaving office. Even at the time of the ministers' resignation it was remarked:

'So there is an end of the administration of all the talents and all integrity. They have shown themselves eminently deficient in both. Their own bad measures and their easy yieldings to Mr Windham have been most fatal'.[133]

Later it was said, 'They did so many absurd things for such wise men, and committed suicide in so many ways in 1806.'[134] The ministry was in fact a setback for the Grenvilles and Foxites. It left a legacy of bitterness and division, and without rendering the Pittites any more popular, markedly increased the unpopulaarity of the Grenvilles and Foxites in the country at large.

4

The Portland Ministry

The New Ministers

WITH the advantage of hindsight it might seem that the Pittite ministry which took office late in March 1807 was particularly well-constituted, with three such men as Hawkesbury, later Earl of Liverpool, Castlereagh and Canning as Secretaries of State. But it did not seem so at the time: 'there can be but one opinion', Sidmouth claimed, of their 'inadequacy to the situation in wh they are placed.'[1] Charles Wynn wrote, 'I cannot believe that even after dissolving Parliament, such a compound of Vanity and incapacity without talent character or property as the present administration can continue to govern this Country for a twelvemonth.'[2] Southey, by no means unsympathetic to their politics, thought they 'held their places less by their own strength than by the weakness of their opponents, for of all administrations, that to which they had succeeded, had been the most unpopular.'[3] Of the three Secretaries of State, Hawkesbury had been tried and found wanting, Castlereagh, though a businesslike administrator, seemed an uninspired plodder, and Canning, who had so narrowly escaped being involved in the wreck of the preceding ministry, had no Cabinet experience at all, and was appointed to the Foreign Department only because the Marquess Wellesley, the first candidate for the post, turned it down.[4]

Canning's jealousy of the other two Secretaries of State made it imperative that there should be a strong head to the Cabinet, but the Prime Minister, the Duke of Portland, was virtually a cypher. Spencer Perceval later explained,

'There never can be the sort of acquiescence amongst us in control as there was naturally and necessarily to Mr Pitt. Mr Pitt . . . had himself such comprehensive talents and powers that he was himself essentially the Government in all departments . . . But the present Government is constituted with so many of equal or nearly equal pretensions that it . . . must, to a great degree, be and remain a Government of departments. It is not because the Duke of Portland is at our head that the Government is a Government of departments: it is because the Government is and must be essentially a Government of Departments that the Duke of Portland is at our head.'[5]

In private, Portland was capable of asserting his opinions with some vigour, but with his official colleagues he preferred to exercise 'the talent he possesses in an eminent degree; that of dead silence'.[6] Moreover, failing health caused him increasingly to withdraw from business. He required the attendance of his secretary each day from 11 am to 8 pm or 8.30 pm, and again from 11 pm to 'till one, two, or three in the morning',[7] but it is by no means clear what the fruits of his labour were. During 1807 and 1808 he managed to attend only ten of the 196 meetings of the Treasury Board at which, theoretically, he presided.[8] In the Cabinet he was probably the least vocal member.

Most of the responsibility for directing the nation's finances at this particularly difficult juncture were left to the new Chancellor of the Exchequer, Spencer Perceval. As a financial minister Perceval was another weak link in the government. He had previously had so little interest in such matters that it had been Castlereagh who had taken the lead in opposing Grenville's finance plan. Initially he wanted to be Attorney-General. Having a wife and 12 children, and no private fortune to support them, he needed the fees of about £9,000 per annum which he could have counted on as Attorney-General. It took three days to persuade him to take the Exchequer, of which the salary was 'so low that it would be absolute ruin to me to accept it'.[9] He finally succumbed to the offer of the Chancellorship of the Duchy of Lancaster for life, in addition to the Exchequer, but this grant of the Duchy for life was condemned by a Commons resolution on 25 March 1807, the majority of 208 to 115 against the new government including Perceval's Evangelical friends Wilberforce and Thornton. Perceval soon established himself as an influential voice in the Cabinet, but the real business of his department was done by Huskisson, one of the Secretaries to the Treasury, who took the worst possible view of Britain's financial prospects, and disapproved of the measures Perceval undertook on political grounds because they conflicted with his Adam Smithian analysis of economic realities.

Perceval was also the Cabinet's spokesman in the Commons. Charles Abbot thought that 'though by no means an eloquent speaker, [he] was the ablest debater in the House'.[10] If not as brilliant as Canning, he was fluent and perspicuous. Perhaps because he feared that intransigence could lead to disaster, he was less rigorous in

controlling the Commons than he might have been: 'His treatment
and management of the House of Commons was by no means
satisfactory to me', complained the Speaker.[11] Charles Long, who
was one of the joint Paymasters-General in the new government,
thought,

> 'He was the most candid man in the world, but of a disposition
> too yielding, which causes Him to grant papers when moved for,
> which causes vast expense, at the Pay Office there is in consequence
> as much business on that account as the regular business of the
> Office requires.'[12]

Yet in view of the fact that Perceval, when he later became Prime
Minister, survived more lost divisions than any British government
leader before or since, complaints that he was too conciliatory are
not perhaps to be taken too seriously. More damaging was his lack
of personal prestige. His evangelical views made him popular with
Wilberforce and his friends in and out of Parliament, and he had
been prominent in opposition to the Talents' ministry, but he had
yet to establish himself as a major political figure. Physically he was
an insignificant little man, quite without presence. His corpse-like
pallor and facial resemblence to Robespierre were calculated to repel
rather than to inspire confidence. Also it was held against him that
he had been a lawyer. The Foxites sneered, 'what was to be feared
from a man who had not business enough to employ a clerk.'[13]
Whitbread called him 'an adventurer from the bar'[14] and even a
colleague noted, 'He did not pass for a very learned or a very sound
lawyer.'[15] Romilly who had been on circuit with him as a young
man, was more charitable to him than most other Foxites:

> 'With ... very little reading, of a conversation barren of instruction,
> and with strong invincible prejudices on many subjects, yet, by
> his excellent temper, his engaging manners, and his sprightly
> conversation, he was the delight of all who knew him.'[16]

But even in this description it was implied that Perceval made up in
facility what he lacked in depth. The lawyer taunt was not merely a
snobbish jeer at a man who had had to earn his own living, it also
conveyed the idea that he was a man accustomed to speak from a
brief, with no time to ponder on abstract questions of statesmanship.
    Eldon, Westmorland, Camden, Bathurst, Chatham and Mulgrave
occupied the other Cabinet posts. It was not much of a team to
guide the policy of a nation staggering towards the brink of
collapse.

The Constitutional Crisis

Though they made relatively little impact on the public consciousness,
the circumstances in which the new ministers came into office marked
a watershed in British politics. Within a few days the issues of the
next 20 years were clarified and defined. The Grenville ministry's

proposal to encourage Catholics to join the Army, originally only a tactic of expediency, was quickly blown up into a great confrontation between the Grenville-Foxite alliance and the King on the question of Catholic relief. Their consequent resignation bound the Grenvilles and the Foxites all the more closely to the Catholic cause, and to each other, and tied the succeeding government, though it included many pro-Catholics, to the view that relief should never be agitated against the King's will. Thus the new government was even more specifically anti-Catholic in its basic principle than the Addington ministry had been in the similar but less dramatic circumstances of 1801. This re-emphasizing of political divisions led to realignments of personnel. Sidmouth and his followers split entirely from their former colleagues and supported their successors, but the Earl of Hardwicke, who had been appointed Lord-Lieutenant of Ireland by Sidmouth (then Addington) in 1801, and superseded by the new ministers in 1806, sided with them after they left office, much to the vexation of his younger brother Charles Yorke, who intended to support the Portland ministry and was unable to see why Hardwicke felt 'bound in point of consistency' to support men 'who have no claim whatever upon you, & with whom you had continually differed while they were in office'.[17] Hardwicke's former Attorney-General in Ireland, William Plunket, who had been unexpectedly continued in office by Grenville, and who was asked to stay on by the Portland ministry, actually resigned in protest at Catholic relief being shelved.

The Catholic issue tends however to conceal the real significance of the crisis. Catholic relief was only the occasion for the conflict. It was not itself the issue at stake. The real dispute was over whether the government should serve the King actually or only nominally. It was because men like Canning and Castlereagh were willing to be the King's servants in more than name that they gave up their personal commitment to Catholic relief and co-operated with the anti-Catholics in order to oblige the King; and it was because men like Grenville and Howick were not willing to give up their principles, and conduct an administration along a course they believed doomed to catastrophe, merely a please their monarch, that they resigned. Amongst those who resigned with them were at least two men, the Earl of Carysfort and Lord Auckland, who shared the King's prejudice against Catholic relief but could not accept his insistence that it was his right to dictate in advance the advice his ministers were to give him. It was the question of the King, rather than of the Catholics, which inflamed tempers during the succeeding years.

Lord Grenville, as might have been expected of a man who had been a minister for most of his adult life, had not originally shared the Foxite abhorrence of the Court and all its works, and it was only after March 1807 that he began to think in terms of personal hostility towards George III. In 1801 he had accepted the propriety of George III's stand on the Catholic issue. 'We cannot blame his Majesty', he had then written, 'or complain of his conduct towards us, when he resists decidedly a measure, which in his conscientious opinion involves a breach of his engagements with his people, and a violation of so solemn an oath [i.e. the Coronation Oath].'[18] But the sense that he had been cheated by the King in March 1807 subsequently caused him to see matters differently. He came to believe

'a man must, indeed, be of a most depraved ambition, to wish for the appearance and responsibility of governing the country, with the certainty that a Court intrigue would be incessantly at work with ample means of depriving him of all power to be of real use.'[19]

A reluctance to be again trapped and deceived by George III (and later by his son) henceforth characterized the remainder of his political career.

Amongst the Foxites, the anti-royalism normally fashionable amongst them had retreated into the background during their 14 months in office. During 1806 generous grants were secured from Parliament for the King's younger sons; foreign-held funds were exempted from the property tax, thereby saving the King (as elector of Hanover) £70,000; and an Act was passed authorizing the increase of the number of Hanoverian troops in England. These measures, which caused some surprise to reformers outside Parliament, were evidently adopted at least in part in order to woo the King, and in general relations between the King and his Foxite ministers were unexpectedly harmonious. It was only afterwards that they saw cause to accuse George III and his courtiers of 'secretly undermining them in the very unequal warfare of stratagem and intrigue'.[20] With the fall of the ministry in March 1807, all their former prejudice against the King revived at more than its former strength. The King versus Whig system of politics which had prevailed in the 1770s and 1780s was renewed: 'The old struggle, which began with the Reign — which adornd the Middle of it dignifies the Close.'[21]

The first confrontation between the new ministers and the old was on 9 April on the motion of the Hon. Thomas Brand that

'it is contrary to the first duties of the confidential servants of the Crown to restrain themselves by any pledge, expressed or implied, from offering to the King any advice which the course of circumstances may render necessary for the welfare and security of any part of His Majesty's extensive dominions.'

The opposition were confident of winning, but when the Commons divided at six the following morning the result was 258 for the government and 226 against. 'I own I did not think they would have brought quite so many', wrote the Grenvillite Fremantle, 'but there was no exertion and promise, and no threat they did not use.'[22] On 15 April, the Hon. W. H. Lyttleton moved that the House regretted the change of ministers, and the government won 244 to 198. As a result of these narrow majorities the ministers asked for a dissolution of Parliament, which the King granted on 25 April. This had been predicted more than a week previously, and there was much consternation amongst MPs faced with the expense of a third election in five years. Fremantle, who as Secretary to the Treasury had orchestrated the Talents' electoral campaign in 1806 reported:

'Nothing can be more disagreeable than the applications which are made to me on the subject of the parliament. Having nominated so many persons, they of course are dreading the loss of their money, and for which, of course, I can give them no redress. In general, they have stood very stoutly, and I can only except a very few, who have ratted.'[23]

The ensuing general election enabled the government to shift the controversial emphasis from the King's demands for pledges to the Talents' demands for Catholic relief. More than any previous election, with the sole exception of that of 1784, this was an election fought on a clear national issue. It was the 'No Popery' election. 'The cry is what must form their whole reliance', wrote Lord Grenville. 'It will certainly operate much in their favour; more than one could have thought possible in this age.'[24] The voters had been well prepared. There had been 197 loyal addresses to the King on the fall the late ministry, hurriedly organized by Pittites and opponents of Catholic relief; 31 of these addresses came from county meetings.[25] The Foxites responded by centralizing their propaganda, and the advertisements both of Viscount Howick in his campaign for Northumberland, and of Whitbread at Bedford were widely disseminated beyond their own constituencies, effectively the first time a party campaigned with a nationally distributed manifesto. The 'No Popery' cry defeated Viscount Duncannon at St Albans and the Hon. Laurence Dundas at York, and caused the withdrawal of William Roscoe at Liverpool, of Sir William Paxton in Carmarthenshire, and of Sir Gilbert Heathcote in Lincolnshire.[26] In Yorkshire, Walter Fawkes declined to stand because of the unpopularity of the Catholic cause, and Earl Fitzwilliam, Fawkes' main backer, ran his own son, Viscount Milton, in his stead. Lascelles, the 'No Popery' candidates, afterwards attributed his defeat by Milton to the odium attached to him by the accusation that he had raised the 'No Popery' cry for party reasons.[27] At Bristol, Bragge Bathurst, Sidmouth's brother-in-law, who was implicated as a supporter of the late ministry even though he was opposed to Catholic relief, was received by the voters 'with hissings, hootings, and peltings, and abused from one end of the town to the other as a most determined abettor of Popery if not himself an obstinate Papist'.[28] Yet the influence of the 'No Popery' cry should not be exaggerated. Its chief significance is that it was one of the first attempts to fight an election on a national platform, but as a matter of practical results it influenced only 29 out of 100 contests, and these 29 included the Co. Tipperary election where the Catholic freeholders indignantly voted the pro-relief candidate to a handsome victory.[29]

Of more importance was the government's negotiations with, and application of pressure on, the patrons of closed boroughs. Having less time for preparation than their predecessors had had in 1806, the ministers interfered in 39 constituencies and secured from 25 to 32 returns, as compared to 58 constituencies interfered with by the government in 1806, and from 42 to 50 returns (six of them of MPs who deserted the old ministry for the new).[30] It is significant that of the 138 MPs elected for the first time in 1806, 95 were supporters of the then government, and 49 of these lost their seats in 1807; but of the 43 who were not supporters of the Fox—Grenville government, only ten lost their seats in 1807.[31] These 49 MPs who lost their seats as soon as the government which had brought them in left office were for the most part MPs for boroughs particularly vulnerable to government influence (either directly, or through the venality of patrons). They were also, for the most part, particularly loyal partisans of the Grenville and Fox factions, and their elimination was a serious blow to the groups now so recently restored to opposition.

	Pro-govt	Independent pro-govt	Independent anti-govt	Opposition
1806 election	308	151	102	90
1807 election	216	154	71	213[32]

As can be seen, in addition to electoral changes, about 50 constant supporters of the old ministry, and a rather larger number of independents who had usually supported it, had transferred their allegiance to the new ministers, on the principle of supporting the government of the day, rather than the principles of the men who composed it. But the most significant fact was that, despite these switches of allegiance, and despite the decimation of the new recruits brought in by the Fox—Grenville ministry in 1806, they still had almost as many partisans in the Commons as the government. To a greater extent than ever before, the government relied on a floating vote, which meant that, at the first serious crisis, its majority would evaporate. It was not an encouraging prospect.

Thus the election, as well as being a pioneer, though not very successful, attempt to fight on a national platform, was also as near to a ministerial defeat at the polls as ever occurred before 1834. But it had one further distinction. It was the occasion of the return of the term 'Tory' to common use. At the beginning of the eighteenth century the description of one party as 'Tory' had seemed as inevitable as the description of the other party as 'Whig'. By 1800 however all public men assumed their political inheritance from the makers of the Revolution of 1688 and the architects of the Hanoverian succession, and the term 'Whig' was used by men on both sides of politics, even though it was jealously claimed by the followers of Rockingham and later of Fox for their own exclusive use. The opposite term 'Tory', on the other hand, had dropped out of use except to disparage men or attitudes that were regarded as anachornistic. The statement of the second Lord Kenyon in March 1804 that 'on the subject of Emancipation and everything relating to the Church and State he never would join any party but on Tory principles',[33] is possibly the earliest instance of a man of this period himself professing to be a Tory, as distinct from being accused of it, and even then there was possibly some self-consciousness in his choice of the term. In August 1806 Cobbett pointed out that the so-called Whigs

'had no principle different from that of Mr Pitt and his set. Mr Pitt himself was a Whig. In fact, there has been no Tory principle existing amongst public men for the last seventy years: the *name* of Whig was kept up merely for want of another wherewith to attract a crowd of empty-headed partizans.'[34]

'Pittites', the Whig—Tory dichotomy that eventually re-established cry was added the slogan 'Royal Prerogative'. The revival of the issue of royal prerogative in connection with the position of the Church of England, after a century in abeyance, naturally encouraged the revival of the party labels of an earlier era when 'No Popery' and 'Church and King' had been the general cry. After this election 'Tory' became more frequently used, and though it remained more common to speak of 'Government' and 'Opposition' or 'Foxites' and 'Pittites', the Whig-Tory dichotomy that eventually re-established itself must be dated from this period.

Leadership Changes in the Opposition

The new Parliament met on 22 June 1807, and the King's speech was read out on 26 June. There was a record attendance during the Commons debate on the customary address in answer to the King's speech and after 12 hours the House divided 350 to 255. This minority was much larger than the opposition had expected. The day before the debate Fremantle had been congratulating himself on the certainty of 150, and told Buckingham:

'I think we may satisfy ourselves that, if notice is given of some notion tomorrow, to be made a week hence, we shall divide one hundred and seventy. Such a division in such a Session is infinitely more than any government can stand; and it is not only the prospect of this division, but, you may rely on it, the cry of the public is with us.'[35]

Equally the number of MPs voting for the government was far beyond expectations; furthermore it held up, whereas the opposition vote rapidly fell away. A motion by Whitbread on 6 July on the state of the nation was defeated by 322 votes to 136. Thereafter the opposition seemed to have lost impetus and there was no major clash during the remainder of the session, though there was a considerable degree of sniping from the more extreme opposition MPs. Three weeks before Parliament was prorogued, Wynn confessed despairingly:

'we appear to me to have extremely mismanaged our game since the meeting of Parlt. The more I see the more I am convinced that deeply & generally as the inefficiency & weakness of the present administration is felt, nothing but the demise of the Crown or great & overbearing calamity can restore us to power. For the Catholic question *per se* the Public care nothing, but the great majority of the Country is so engrossed by a sentiment of besotted attachment & adherence to the King personally that while he lives & till they set the Country upon the apparent & manifest verge of Ruin they will not consent to force upon him either a measure or a Minister against his inclination.'[36]

Parliament was prorogued till the following Spring on 14 August, and within three months there was a crisis in the opposition leadership.

It is probably true to say that the Whig party never recovered from the death of Fox. Though his aristocratic Whiggism did not fool people like Horne Tooke or Cobbett, he had managed to establish himself as a popular hero in the eyes of a considerable number of reform-minded persons in the country at large, while at the same time holding on to the allegiance of great landed magnates like the fifth and sixth dukes of Bedford, and the fifth Duke of Devonshire. The secessioin of Portland, Burke and their sympathizers in 1794 should not conceal the fact that even when his party's fortunes were at their lowest ebb in the later 1790s, Fox still presided over a very broad spectrum of opinions, and after his alliance with Grenville in 1804 he had managed to reconcile political ideologies of very conflicting tendencies. How long he could have maintained this tight-rope cannot be said. Some reformers were already turning against him in the last months of his life, angered by his failure to implement in office the policies with which he had flirted in opposition. But after his death there was no one who could even *try* to maintain his influence. Some MPs such as Whitbread and Brand, who had still looked to him for guidance despite the first murmurings of discontent, felt obliged after his death to assume a more reformist stand.

The first indication of this was in January 1807 when Whitbread bitterly denounced the government for breaking off the peace talks with France. The finance committee established on 10 February 1807 was an even more serious indication of the growing rift between the then government front bench and its back-bench MPs. On the fall of the ministry six weeks later claims such as that in *The Morning Chronicle* of 25 March that the fallen ministers' 'real crime is their having been enemies of jobbers in whatever situation, and their being determined to suppress extravagance by whomsoever practised, and to check abuses by whomsoever protected', were not only quite untrue, but were also at variance with the actual political views of the ministers themselves. To some extent the fall of the ministry enabled its reformist supporters to go much further on the subject of abuses than they would have dared had their faction remained in power. The issue of the suppression of abuses was kept alive during the first months of the new ministry, first by a bill on the grant of offices in reversion, founded on the first report of the February committee (this bill was eventually rejected by the Lords) and secondly by a motion from Lord Cochrane for a new committee to investigate offices and pensions held by MPs. In terms of parliamentary votes the question of the suppression of abuses gained little attention; but outside Parliament reformers watched with growing interest.

Significantly the economic reformers attracted support from the pro-ministerial benches, often from men of mercantile origins representing large urban or urbanized constituencies, such as Wilberforce of Yorkshire, Calvert of Hertford, and Henry, Robert and Samuel Thornton, respectively MPs for Southwark, Colchester and Surrey. These men were social 'outsiders', not native members of the ruling class, and their power base was the electoral support of men of their own sort, social outsiders, solid bourgeois folk, who increasingly resented the abuses and inefficiency of the aristocratic system. Wilberforce and the Thornton brothers were of course Evangelicals, and were known in politics as 'The Saints', but on this issue they co-operated with two spectacularly unsaintly reformers, Sir Francis Burdett and Lord Cochrane, who represented the largest urban constituency of all, Westminster. Though it was scarcely appreciated at the time, a formidable campaign was building up with widespread national support, especially in the towns, aimed not at replacing one party in power by another, but at reforming and purifying the power structure. Fox, during the Lord North era, had managed to unite the two causes in a single programme. Had he lived he might have done so again.

But the death of Fox had not only deprived the opposition of the one man who could transform his party's struggle for office into a national crusade, it had also deprived it of the one leader who actually believed in struggling for power. His successors not merely had a much narrower concept of the opposition's public role, they even had doubts as to whether it had a role at all. As Prime Minister Lord Grenville had come increasingly to hate office. He was a natural chief lieutenant, but he was too shy and too easily discouraged to enjoy overall authority. As early as 10 February, over a month before his actual resignation, he had written the epitaph of his administration:

'We have at least the satisfaction of having done some good, and certainly not disgraced ourselves or our friends by our twelve months administration, and you know that to me as the task was from the beginning most irksome, so the release cannot but be pleasing, provided I should have weight enough with my friends to keep them, as I am fully resolved to keep myself, out of even the appearance of struggling for a fresh representation of this short-lived piece.'[37]

When he finally resigned, and contemplated the prospect of opposition, he asked, 'Why should I feel myself included in a struggle, the success of which is to put my fetters upon me again, which when on I felt so galling?'[38] He was anxious only to do his duty, and that this duty was best performed by fruitless opposition he doubted. So did Lord Auckland, who told Temple:

'I am not sanguine as to any immediate or early result of the struggle; nor can I feel certainty as to any result, except that the empire is subjected, for a long period of time, to all the mischiefs of divided parties, and popular animosities, much beyond what the perilous circumstances of the age can admit, and such as with the addition of a weak ministry, cannot fail to create a predicament of public affairs of the most calamitous description.'[39]

Viscount Howick, who had succeeded Fox as the acknowledged leader of the Foxite section of the opposition, may not have altogether shared these views, but with his love of rural seclusion he had even less taste for active opposition than Grenville or Auckland had.

The opposition was thus divided between two mutually conflicting attitudes. On the one hand there were those who desired a vigorous campaign against the abuses of the political system, on the other were those who, with much less enthusiasm, thought merely of replacing their rivals within the system as it existed. It may be argued that the resulting two decades of confusion made possible the development of a genuine reform party, working less on the basis of short-term parliamentary advantage than on the basis of a long-term nationally co-ordinated strategy. In fact, of course, the Whigs never did fully reconcile the conflict, as the rift between

Whigs and Radicals in the 1830s demonstrated. All that happened in those two decades was a shift of balance within the party, but it was not a very permanent or a very solid shift, more part of a process of oscillation; and what began to become apparent in 1807 was merely the first sequence of the oscillation. Had Fox lived this disequilibrium might well have been converted into a genuine progressive compromise.

The real extent of the division within the opposition was still not apparent when, on 19 November 1807, in the middle of the parliamentary recess, the long expected death of the first Earl Grey and the succession of his son Viscount Howick to his peerage deprived the opposition of Howick's leadership in the Commons. The ensuing struggle between George Ponsonby and Samuel Whitbread for the leadership was more a question of personalities than of principles, but it did contribute to the increasing alienation of the Whig extremists from their official leaders. It was not, however, the case that the point at issue was whether the opposition should follow a true Foxite line, or whether it should kowtow to the Grenvilles. This is the view taken by the leading authority on the politics of the period, Michael Roberts, who saw Ponsonby as the Grenville candidate and Whitbread as the Foxite candidate and truest exponent of the principles of Fox himself. Roberts claims:

'The Grenville alliance made reasonable political development impossible. Ponsonby was the symbol of this sterility . . . he was the link between two parties, rather than between two sections of the same party. . . . The true policy of the true Whigs was to have chosen Whitbread, and sloughed off the Grenvilles.'[40]

Roberts' basic premise that there was a substantial difference between the political views of Lord Grenville on the one hand, and of the Foxite leader Grey (formerly Howick) and of Fox's nephew Holland on the other, is unsound. On all the key issues of the time they were generally agreed: not only on Catholic relief which they favoured, but on Parliamentary reform of which they were wary.[41] It is worth quoting at length a statement of belief by Lord Holland, the principal Foxite ideologue, written in 1811 or 1812:

'1st. I will support in Parliament any reform which without subverting Parliamentary Government offers a fair prospect of reducing the Influence of the Crown in the Commons house of Parliament.

2dly In an abolition of Sinecures, whatever I may think of the insignificance of the saving, I will cheerfully concur to gratify the people provided such rights of property as the Courts of Law allow in the present possessors, be preserved.

3dly The absolute suppression of what is miscalled the splendour of the Crown, Bedchamber Lords, Keys, Staffs, and such like trumpery I would earnestly and eagerly recommend, and I should enjoy exceedingly to see that worthless tawdry kind of ware *smashed* at once.

4thly I consider a reduction of the army as a *sine qua non* to my support of any government.

5thly A relinquishment of our Continental system I consider equally so, because in my conscience I think that to insist on the reduction of the army and at the same time to maintain a system which can only be upheld by force is as absurd as Bankes's famous conduct in voting *for* a war and *against* the supplies for carrying it on—Moreover for my private satisfaction the abandonment of that system would give me more heartfelt pleasure than the accomplishment of any one political object that I now do, or have for years pursued in publick life.

6thly Such measures as by conciliating Ireland would enable us to reduce our establishment there, I think consistency as well as good sense, justice, and policy calls upon us to propose.'[42]

Holland's programme, in short, consisted merely of a vindictive scheme to dismantle the apparatus of monarchy, while fobbing off the lower classes with minor reform, the abolition of sinecures, which he himself regarded as insignificant. Probably this degree of anti-royalism was uncongenial to Grenville, and Grenville also disliked the proposal of abolishing sinecures when their present incumbents died, as this would reflect unfavourably on those incumbents (including himself and both his brothers). But even Grenville came to acknowledge the necessity of allaying public discontent by some small concession in the direction of reform, and there was nothing in Holland's programme which tended towards the kind of sweeping transformation of the political system such as the real reformers demanded, and against which Grenville steadfastly set his face. Even in the sphere of parliamentary reform Holland wished for no more than the weakening of crown influence, and he later wrote:

'The nearer I look to Parliamentary reform the less I own I like it & even when I saw it at a distance I was none of its most fervent adorers. . . . Any Reform that entirely new modelled it, & altered the whole basis of the representation would make it much worse & in no particular more, than in increasing instead of reducing the influence of the Crown.'[43]

Holland, Grey, and the Foxite establishment in fact substantially agreed with Lord Grenville's views, and the real divide was not between Foxites and Grenvillites, but between the majority of Foxites, supporting the Grenvillites, and a small minority who became known as the 'Mountain', whose reform views were actually far in advance of what Fox's had been.

Fox of course had been a great compromiser on the subject of reform: it was his powers of conciliation, of lending an air of decisiveness to compromise decisions, which had made him such a successful leader. Whitbread was very far from being his heir in this respect. No one had less capacity than he for uniting other men. He was a vehement, cross-grained man, with the annoying nervous mannerism of laughing mirthlessly whenever he spoke, and a propensity for believing himself injured by all and sundry. Thomas Grenville wrote of 'the unpopularity and impracticability of the man';[44] Lady Holland referred to 'the unpopular and odious manners of Whitbread, whom unfortunately all parties concur in hating, however they may respect him as a public character'.[45] Only the new Earl Grey was anxious for Whitbread to take a more prominent role in the party, and that was solely on personal grounds. Whitbread was not only married to his sister, but was his 'oldest & dearest friend',[46] and, as he told Whitbread at a later period, 'My own disgust at Politics can never make me indifferent to any increase of your reputation, and even when pursuing a course that I cannot approve whatever adds to the opinion of your talents is gratifying to me'.[47] And even Grey acknowledged that there would be 'a great deal of prejudice' against Whitbread as a parliamentary leader.[48]

Grey, then still Viscount Howick, had suggested making the then Chancellor of Ireland, George Ponsonby, leader of the Commons in September 1806, after the death of Fox.[49] His reason for being interested in Ponsonby was that he was Lady Howick's uncle. Both he and Thomas Grenville had thought about future openings for Ponsonby during the summer of 1807.[50] Tierney reported to Grey a conversation he had had with Thomas Grenville:

'With respect to G. Ponsonby, he told me that his motives for thinking of him were personal to yourself, and that he had been induced to mention him because he thought that, from his near connection with you, the selection of him would be an atonement to you for the opposition which he felt it would be necessary to make to the nomination of Whitbread. Beyond that he professed he had no view, having no personal knowledge of G.P. and no decided opinion as to his fitness or unfitness for the vacant Situation.'[51]

The Grenvilles really did know nothing of Ponsonby, beyond that he had led the opposition in Dublin to the Marquess of Buckingham (then Earl Temple) as Lord-Lieutenant of Ireland during the Regency Crisis in 1788. They merely favoured him as the alternative to Whitbread most acceptable to Grey.

Lord Grenville himself was actually against the whole idea of nominating anyone to replace Howick. He certainly had no idea of nominating a 'safe' leader in the Commons in order to straitjacket the reformers. He believed that leaders had to emerge, rather than

be created, and he was personally reluctant to pledge himself formally
to having his 'character and opinions' committed to the care of a
stranger.[52] Holland, too, objected to a formal nomination, and would
have preferred

'a small council of war . . . trusting that the natural necessity of a
leader will at the end of the Session place one of those members in
that situation without the invidiousness of an election or *promotion*
which I am convinced will not in the present circumstances be
borne by the army.'[53]

In the event the opposition, its leaders included, were confronted
with a *fait accompli.* Ponsonby, at home in Ireland and far away
from these discussions, decided to take the lead if offered before he
actually knew of the first Earl Grey's death and Howick's succession
to the peerage. His letter to Thomas Grenville notifying him of his
decision had a postscript indicating that he had heard the news only
after he had written the main part of the letter.[54] Having heard
Ponsonby's decision, the other opposition leaders merely acquiesced
in the arrangement, for the truth was that apart from the ineffectual
Petty they had no other suitable candidate.

The Decline of the Portland Ministry

The two principal ministerial acts of the recess were the bombardment
of Copenhagen by an expeditionary force under Lord Cathcart,
between 2 and 5 September 1807 at a time when war had not been
declared between Britain and Denmark, and the issue on 11 November
of Orders in Council prohibiting neutral shipping from trading with
France or her allies. The Grenvilles were against 'a renewal of the
disgraceful and disgusting recriminating debates which took place
last Session . . . to the entire discredit of all public men of every
description and character',[55] and when Parliament reassembled there
was no division on the address to the King. During the following
weeks however there were six divisions on the Copenhagen expedition,
but the government won them all with ludicrous ease, 100 to 19, 253
to 108, 157 to 73, 184 to 85, 224 to 64, 216 to 61. The opposition was
equally ineffective in denouncing the Orders in Council. And it was
noticeable that Ponsonby was not on his feet significantly more
often than half a dozen other opposition MPs — Whitbread, Tierney
and Windham in particular — nor were his speeches the most
impressive. He was indeed a solid, intelligent, but uninspiring and
rather charmless man, not at all a worthy successor to Fox. The
opposition was further discouraged by the conclusion of the Buenos
Aires expedition, their major military venture while in office.
Lieutenant-General Whitelocke, the commander appointed by Windham
to make way for one of his own friends in an appointment at home,
had met heavy resistance from the rebel colonials and on 7 July 1807

agreed to evacuate his troops. Both his own troops, and the people at home, who had had such extravagant expectations from the opening up of South America to British trade, were enraged by this capitulation. Whitelocke was court-martialled, and, on 18 March 1808, sentenced to be cashiered.

Perceval, who had not shone in debate during his first session as government spokesman, did rather better during 1808. There were some disputes within the Cabinet over Irish policy, though a report which reached the Grenvilles in December 1807 that the ministry was actually about to break up on the Catholic issue is not confirmable from other sources.[56] By the early summer of 1808, therefore, the Portland ministry could congratulate itself on having survived longer than its predecessor, with less internal strife and more external success. The arrival at Falmouth on 6 June 1808 of six Spaniards changed all this.

During May 1808 Carlos IV of Spain resigned his throne under pressure from Napoleon, who had been establishing large French garrisons both in Spain and in Portugal. The presence of French troops, and the unpopularity of and uncertainty concerning the government sparked off risings in many parts of Spain. In Asturias the local hidalgos and clergy declared themselves at war with France, and six delegates set out for England to request aid. It was they who reached Falmouth on 6 June. They were received with raptures. After the failure at Buenos Aires and at Alexandria the public was hungry for a military triumph, a great and successful adventure on a grander scale than the attack on Copenhagen. The rising in Spain, moreover, seemed in itself a major blow against the Napoleonic system, perhaps the first stage of its collapse. Even reformers rejoiced. Campbell the poet enthused:

'here are my hopes, that what the French Revolution has failed in, the Spanish will achieve; and that we shall hear, in the language of Cervantes, all the great principles of British liberty laid down in the future writings of Spain; that they will become a free people, and have, like us, their Sydneys and Chathams.'[57]

It was not appreciated to what extent the rising was by the obscurantists, the ignorant, the reactionaries, the vested interests of Church and petty property, against the progressives, the *philosphes*. As so frequently during the remainder of the nineteenth century, British liberals (to use the later term) were blinded by their own complexes and mistook reactionary xenophobia for nationalist idealism. But it did mean that all sections of British opinion found something to admire in the Spanish: 'a common *focus*', as Coleridge put it,

'which made us all once more Englishmen by at once gratifying and correcting the prediliections of both parties. The sincere reverers of the throne felt the cause of loyalty ennobled by its alliance with that of freedom; while the *honest* zealots of the people assumed a more winning form, humanized by loyalty and consecrated by religious principles.'[58]

The now habitually pessimistic Lord Grenville (still smarting from the Buenos Aires débâcle) was almost alone in thinking 'it will all end ill'.[59]

Castlereagh rapidly prepared the despatch of troops to assist the Spanish. He had already sent Sir John Moore and 12,000 men out of the country to help Sweden, which was hard-pressed by France's Russian and Danish allies. (Though this force had arrived off Gothenburg on 17 May it had not yet received permission to land owing to a disagreement between Moore and Gustav IV of Sweden). There were however more troops available, and the Hon. Sir Arthur Wellesley, the Irish Secretary, was appointed to their command. His army of less than 11,000 men sailed from Cork on 13 July. Sir John Moore's expeditionary force was also soon on its way. Though ordered by Gustav IV not to leave Stockholm without permission, Moore had finally fled to his army at Gothenburg disguised as a peasant and arrived back in the Downs on 15 July. From there he was sent on with his troops to Portugal. The population of Portugal had also risen against the French, and Wellesley's troops began to go ashore at the Mondega estuary, on the Portuguese coast, on 1 August.

Moore, a self-opinionated prig, was on bad terms with Castlereagh, partly because of the Swedish business, and at their last meeting before his departure for Portugal he harangued Castlereagh on 'the unhandsome treatment' he had received:

'Had I been an ensign it would hardly have been possible to treat me with less ceremony. . . . Why I should be the object of such obloquy I cannot guess . . . I have a right, in common with all officers who have served zealously and well, to expect to be treated with attention. . . .'[60]

Moore may have also at this interview forecast the failure of the Peninsula expeditions.[61] A letter from Moore to Castlereagh complaining of 'unhandsome and unworthy treatment' was discussed in the Cabinet and shown to the King, but it was too late to replace Moore. Instead, to avoid his having the supreme command, Wellesley being his junior in the Army, it had already been arranged that Sir Hew Dalrymple and Sir Harry Burrard, lieutenant-generals senior to both Wellesley and Moore, should follow the troops to Portugal. Burrard arrived off the Portuguese coast and assumed nominal command of Wellesley's force on 20 August. Next day Wellesley defeated the French General Junot at the Battle of Vimiero; the day after that Sir Hew Dalrymple arrived and took over the supreme command from Burrard. 'Sir Hew, having never had the experience of command, seems quite at a loss how to work the different heads of departments', noted Moore. Later he decided, 'Sir Hew Dalrymple was confused and incapable beyond any man I ever saw head an army.'[62] Soon after Dalrymple assumed command, a flag of truce arrived from the French, proposing a convention for a French withdrawal from Portugal, and anxious to be relieved of his embarrassment as a front-line general, Dalrymple decided to accept.

The Convention of Cintra, as it was called, was concluded at Lisbon on 30 August 1808. It provided for the peaceful evacuation of the French troops, with all their property, public or private, to France. Wellesley, who agreed to the principle of the evacuation though objecting to several of the details, signed on Dalrymple's behalf. This was at the suggestion of the French representative, General Kellerman. Wellesley later explained:

'I signed it, notwithstanding my objections to it, because I would not, in the face of the whole army, set myself up in opposition to the commander of the forces on the very day he joined his army ... My refusal to sign would not have prevented the execution of the instrument, and would only have tended to raise my character, at the expense of others; and probably at that of not a little outrage and want of discipline in the army.'[63]

The significance of Wellesley being the one who signed was that, although only the third most senior British officer on the spot (Moore was still with his troops further along the coast), and although acting at the request of Dalrymple, he nevertheless assumed a degree of responsibility for the terms of the convention.

It was with horror and disbelief that the government heard the first news of the convention. Castlereagh at first thought it 'a base forgery',[64] but on 15 September the first reports were confirmed by Dalrymple's official despatch. The ministers, trying to put a good face on the situation, ordered the guns of the Tower of London to be fired in celebration, and published the terms of the convention in an extraordinary *Gazette*. It was to no avail. 'The public indignation this day is at its height', it was reported on 17 September. '. . . the people seem quite wild. In the city, the discontent and murmur is not in the least restrained.'[65] It was noted that 'papers of all parties concurred in execrating the measure.'[66] People in all walks of life, feverish with enthusiasm for the latest news from Portugal, were appalled by the betrayal of their hopes. Their reaction, Moore heard, was 'beyond even that which was occasioned by the misconduct at Buenos Aires.'[67]

'Wherever the tidings were communicated they carried agitation along with them—a conflict of sensations in which, though sorrow was predominant, yet through force of scorn, impatience, hope and indignation, and through the universal participation in passions so complex, and the sense of power which this necessarily included—the whole partook of the energy and activity of congratulation and joy. Not a street, not a public room, not a fireside in the island which was not disturbed as by a local or private trouble; men of all estates, conditions, and tempers were affected apparently in equal degrees.'[68]

These words of the poet Wordsworth, which might appear the exaggeration of one habituated to oracular statement, are confirmed by the sober phrases of Viscount Castlereagh, writing to Wellesley on 26 September:

'Charles [Castlereagh's brother] will probably have told you how strongly I myself felt upon the nature of the arrangements made with the enemy, when it first reached us, and was disbelieved. Since the definitive arrangement was received officially, we have tried to reconcile ourselves to it in some degree, but without effect.

You will learn from others the deep impression it has produced on the public mind, much beyond any former occurrence, at least in my recollection.'[69]

The London Common Council petitioned the King for an enquiry, and Cobbett attempted to bring about a county meeting in Hampshire. Canning, six months and two crises later, attributed to the Convention of Cintra the beginning of the ministry's loss of credit with the public. As the convention was soon overshadowed by events even more dramatic and nearer home, Canning's diagnosis cannot be confirmed. What is certain however is that the convention was the first of the train of events which led to the break up of the ministry. It was the convention which led to Canning's alienation from his colleagues, which was the cause of the ministerial crisis a year later.

Canning saw, very clearly, all the most objectionable elements in the convention, and how far it threatened not merely the prestige but even the trustworthiness of Britain in the eyes of potential allies. He saw, for example, that the French soldiers' being permitted to leave Portugal with their 'lawful property' would, even in theory, allow them to take away items purchased from looters and, in practice, would protect all booty acquired in any fashion whatever. His conclusion was the 'the result of this convention is to make the expedition to Portugal the most disastrous that I remember'.[70] He was absent from the Cabinet meeting which decided there were no grounds for repudiating the convention, but afterwards wrote a protest to the King, and while his colleagues attempted to salvage what they could from the disaster, he gave himself over to bitter carping, his favourite form of self-indulgence.

Canning may have wished to put all the blame on Sir Arthur Wellesley though to Wellesley himself he expressed not the least disapprobation.[71] Castlereagh on the other hand stressed the importance of rescuing Wellesley's reputation, telling Perceval,

'we ought well to weigh how we can best save, together with our own characters and that of the country the *Instrument,* which of all others seems capable, if we can rally round him the requisite amount of support, of consoling us and the world for any fault either he himself or others have committed.'[72]

To Wellesley himself Castlereagh wrote, 'My first object is your reputation; my second is, that the country should not be deprived of your services at the present critical conjuncture.'[73] In the event Castlereagh succeeded in preventing Wellesley being sacrificed to the public outrage, but at considerable cost to his own public standing. Temple reported, 'The universal cry in London is against Ministers. Our crimes are all forgotten, and the indignation of the public is now solely directed against government, especially against Castlereagh.'[74]

Dalrymple and Wellesley were recalled to face a court of enquiry and were soon followed by Burrard. This left the command to Moore. Castlereagh had wanted to avoid this, not because of any doubts as to Moore's capacity, but because he knew Moore would do everything to make trouble for the ministers. In Spain, Moore's quarrel with Castlereagh was described as 'a circumstance notorious here, and much talked of'.[75]

Advancing into Spain in accordance to instructions from Castlereagh, Moore reached Salamanca on 13 November 1808, four days before the court of enquiry opened at Chelsea. A separate British division was advancing by a more southerly route, and a force under Sir David Baird, which had landed at Coruña, was coming down from the North. On all sides it was reported that Spanish resistance was collapsing before the French army, and Moore, having virtually decided on retreat, only continued his advance on Madrid under great pressure from the British diplomatic envoy, John Hookham Frere. By the time the separate British divisions had united, Madrid had fallen, and the Spanish armies had been routed. Moore had no choice but to fall back. His united command now consisted of about 23,500 men. Pursued by much larger French forces he began a nightmare retreat to Baird's base at Coruña across the snowbound highlands of northern Spain:

'The soldiers, barefooted, harassed, and weakened . . . were dropping to the rear by hundreds, while broken carts, dead animals, and the piteous spectacle of women and children, struggling or falling exhausted in the snow, completed a picture of war, which, like Janus, has a double face.'[76]

At home, the government, with no up to date information, could only conclude that Moore had led his army into a trap, and their apprehensions of another disgrace led to further recrimination:

'Each of the Ministers begins to extend the circle of his confidential communications, which are full of complaints of each other, and which announce, beyond all disguise, the bad opinion they entertain of their own permanence. They all agree of falling foul of Lord Castlereagh.'[77]

Yet even Canning warned Castlereagh 'the whole of the efforts of opposition & of Moore's faction (which are pretty much the same thing) will be employed to throw the blame off him and upon you.'[78] To Portland he wrote of Moore:

'I take shame (my individual share, I mean, of the shame belonging to us all) for our having so pusillanimously shrunk from facing the inconvenience of removing him, at a period when his removal might have prevented mischief.'[79]

Having reached Coruña, on 16 January 1809 Moore turned on his pursuers to cover the embarkation of his troops. During the ensuing battle Moore was fatally wounded. 'I hope the people of England will be satisfied! I hope my country will do me justice!' he exclaimed just before he died.[80] He was buried in the citadel by the officers of his staff:

'But half of our heavy task was done
    When the clock struck the hour for retiring:
And we heard the distant and random gun
    That the foe was sullenly firing.
Slowly and sadly we laid him down,
    From the field of his fame fresh and gory;
We carved not a line, and we raised not a stone,
    But we left him alone with his glory.'[81]

Because of the victorious outcome of this final engagement, the retreat to Coruña, initially occasioned less stir than the Convention of Cintra, though it contributed to a further decrease of public enthusiasm for intervention in Spain and Portugal. This was fostered by 'the very decided opinions expressed by every officer who has returned'.[82] Within the Cabinet, however, it was the cause of yet more bitterness. The British envoy in Spain, Frere, was an intimate of Canning's, and Canning supported his view that Moore should have acted much more boldly in his advance. His instinct of loyalty to Frere was strengthened by his discovery of how little faith Moore had had in the success of the expedition. When Castlereagh mentioned how, at the end of his last interview with Moore, the latter, having already left the room and closed the door, returned to say, 'Remember, my Lord, I protest against the expedition, and foretell its failure', Canning exclaimed, 'Good God! and do you really mean to say that you allowed a man entertaining such feelings with regard to the expedition, to go and assume the command of it?'[83] Canning was surprised therefore to find that Castlereagh, merely out of a sense of fairness, intended to give up the political advantage of denigrating Moore, and meant instead to defend Moore at the expense of Frere, who was responsible for pressurizing Moore into continuing the advance on Madrid at a time when the latter had already seen the necessity of retreat. For Canning the logic of making a scapegoat of a dead enemy rather than of a live friend was irrefutable, and the fact that in the particular circumstances the insufferable Moore had been altogether in the right meant nothing to him. When Castlereagh permitted the publication of the relevant correspondence between More and Frere, which revealed Frere's lack of judgment to the full, Canning's patience with his colleague ran out.

The opposition meanwhile had been observing the fruits of the ministry's war policy with increasing disgust. After the collapse of the Spanish armies only the hispanophil Lord Holland retained any faith in the Spanish venture, and Lord Grenville sneered at the 'silly notion that Don Somebody with the Peasants of Galicia was to overturn Bonaparte'.[84] Nevertheless they saw little to be gained from opposition. 'The Ministry are certainly a good deal lower than when I saw you, but is the Opposition in the least raised?' Tierney asked Whitbread: 'Is there any Symptom of the Country having more confidence in us?'[85] Whitbread himself confessed,

'I am fully aware of the apathy of the Publick and of their indifference towards the proceedings of the House of Commons, and of their Distrust of all Publick Men; and I cannot but agree with you that poor Fox did overset the Publick opinion with regard to Statesmen. The last administration completed the job.'[86]

Furthermore, the ineffectual leadership of Ponsonby in the Commons meant that it would be difficult to keep opposition back-bench criticism of the ministers within the confines of general principles. As Grenville told Grey:

'The present circumstances and temper of the Country seem to render the pursuit of minute and harassing opposition less justifiable in itself and less creditable to those engaged in it than ever. And yet it is but too plain that there is not one of our friends in the House of Commons who possesses sufficient authority there to restrain the eagerness of individuals who are imperceptibly led on into such a course by the warmth of their own feelings, and by the unusual weakness of the Government'.

Grenville suggested that they should make a statement of their views at the beginning of the new session, but move no amendment to the address on the King's speech, and thereafter attend only on exceptionally important issues.[87] Grey agreed. He even seemed to believe that Ponsonby's failure to control the back-benches was not his own fault, but was to be blamed on 'the strange conduct of the weakest & most unprincipled Administration that ever existed'.[89] There was some objection from Ponsonby and from Petty to the idea of suspending opposition, but Tierney wanted to go further and favoured 'breaking up the party' altogether.[90] It was finally decided they should confine themselves to criticism of the Peninsular operations.[91] Later the basis of attack was broadened to include the deterioration of Anglo-American relations, and Grenville called Portugal, Spain and America 'the three great *vital* questions of the day', and hoped that 'the exertions of those who are actively disposed in Parliament' would be directed to them rather 'than to desultory motions on points of minor interest'.[92]

But as a result of developments by no means foreseen by the party leaders, the session of 1809 turned out very differently from what either the opposition leaders or the ministry intended.

5
The Revival of Reform

The New Style of Reform

IN order to understand the events of 1809, it is necessary to step aside for a moment from parliamentary politics to examine the revival of political activity amongst the lower classes.

By 1803 the reform movement of the 1790s had completely faded away. The publicly organized institutional framework of reform, seriously weakened by prosecutions and legislation, had been finally abolished by law in 1799. The activities of extremists, mainly from the lower classes, unco-ordinated and virtually unorganized, had continued sporadically till 1802, before petering out. The trial and execution of Despard and his associates in 1803 was the postscript to a chapter of failures, and later in that same year the country re-entered upon the war with France far more united than it had been at any time during the previous decade.

During the next few years lower-class political activity revived, but both the personalities and the environment were different from what they had been in the 1790s. Some of the former leaders, such as Muir and Gerrald, had died in exile. Others, such as Margarot and Binns were still abroad. Others again, such as Thelwall and Hardy, though still in Britain, had given up the unequal struggle and retired from politics. But the two ablest men of the 1790s, Francis Place and John Horne Tooke, were still prepared to take a lead, and those who had dropped out were replaced by new men. It was the different personal qualities of these new men, as compared to Thelwall, Margarot and company, and their different relationship to the aristocratic politics of Whigs *versus* Tories, which was the major factor in the difference of style of political dissent. Where the reformers of the 1790s were inspired by faith in future possibilities, the reformers of the 1800s were inflamed by disgust at present actualities. Southey the poet wrote in 1812:

'There was a wild cosmopolite character about the democracy of the last generation. Old men of warm hearts and sanguine spirits sung their *Nunc dimittis;* and young men of ardent mind and generous inexperience became enthusiastic disciples of a political faith which ushered itself into the world with the lying annunciation of Peace on earth, Good will among men. Their talk was not merely of the rights of men; but of the hopes and destinies of the human race, of rapid improvement and indefinite progression.' The new generation set their sights lower: 'They understood the temper of the vulgar too well to preach to them of fine fabrics of society, the diffusion of general knowledge, and the millenium of wisdom and philosophy.'[1] The impractical idealists had been replaced by opportunist demagogues.

William Cobbett, the leading new propagandist, had much more and much wider personal experience than Thelwall ever had, and in particular he knew the workings of public institutions, of government, and even of Cabinets at close hand. As an NCO in the army, he detected some of his officers in peculation, and on being discharged, had them court-martialled. When his prosecution failed, Cobbett went to France and from there to America. In America, having unsuccessfully solicited a post in a government department, he established himself as a leading pro-British journalist. He returned to England expecting to edit a government paper, only to find that his ministerial contacts were going out of office. Instead, under the auspices of Windham, he became an opposition spokesman. He remained particularly closely associated with Windham for six years, and through Windham's friends received valuable insights into government. Through the playboy reformer Viscount Folkestone, whom he introduced to Windham, he learnt about the raffish *beau monde.* Through his own continuing interest in country matters (he was the son of farming folk), and through his own establishment as a yeoman farmer in Hampshire, he improved his knowledge of the *Realpolitik* of rural England. Cobbett was certainly not unique amongst journalists in this multiple exposure, but it was something that had never been experienced by Thelwall, whose knowledge of affairs was confined to what he had picked up as an attorney's clerk in London.

This difference of background was reinforced by a difference of temperament. Where Thelwall and his associates prided themselves on their espousal of abstract reason, Cobbett wallowed unashamedly in the prejudices of the age. For example, even as a reformer he preached that war was not only necessary but actually 'conducive to the elevation of human nature, to the general happiness of mankind'.[2] Where Thelwall was a rhetorician, a lover of empty phrases, Cobbett was a lover of facts, a political pedant who devotedly exposed, not in sweeping generalizations, but little detail by detail, all the petty intricacies of the political structure he knew so well. Cobbett made politics alive, personal, particular. His genius was for the concrete. His distaste for theory extended even to the great abstract ideal of the day, parliamentary reform, which he opposed till 1816. In 1806 he wrote:

'Of what has been denominated *Parliamentary Reform*, I have always disapproved; because I never could perceive, in any one of the projects that were broached, the least prospect of producing a *real reform*. Of universal suffrage I have witnessed the effects too attentively [i.e. in America] and with too much disgust ever to think of it with approbation. That the people of property, I mean *all* persons having real property, should have some weight in the election of members of parliament I allow; but, even if this were provided by the law, the funding and taxing and paper system still continuing in existence to its present extent, I should be glad to hear the reasons, whence any one is sanguine enough to conclude, that . . . the evil of leaving the making of laws in the hands of men of mere money, who have little or no connection with or feeling for the people . . . is to be gotten rid of . . . When the funding system, from whatever cause, shall cease to operate upon civil and political liberty, there will be no need for projects of parlimentary reform. The parliament will, as far as shall be necessary, then reform itself.'[3]

It was thus that again and again he cut through the illusory benefits of theoretic reform to gauge the absence of practical advantages beyond. To some extent this concentration on detail was also shown by his great coadjutors Sir Francis Burdett, who first made a name for himself by his carefully researched exposure of the conditions in Cold Bath Fields prison in 1798, and Thomas, Lord Cochrane, who campaigned against abuses in the Navy.

It was in Burdett and Cochrane that lower-class politics found the heroes it had lacked in the 1790s. Burdett, who had a baronetcy dating back to 1619 and who had married the daughter of Coutts the banker, was a stiff, handsome, aloof patrician; 'a fine-looking man on the whole, of lofty stature, with a proud but not forbidding carriage of the head. His manner was dignified and civilly familiar; submitting to rather than seeking conversation with men of our class', recorded one lower-class reformer.[4] He was neither especially intelligent nor well-informed. 'His education had been neglected, and he had no depth of knowledge. He boasted of his ignorance of all authors but Shakespeare and Horace.'[5] He had early shown his contentious independence, having been expelled from Westminster School in 1786 for leading a revolt against the headmaster. (Horne Tooke, from whom he derived most of his ideas, had done even better: he had been expelled from both Westminster *and* Eton.)

Burdett had entered Parliament in 1796 for the venal constituency of Boroughbridge being told on that occasion 'a Rotton Borough perhaps is the best Soil for an Independent Member'.[6] He came under Horne Tooke's influence in the late 1790s and also admired the reforming Earl Stanhope, to whom in 1799 he wrote a long essay on their common views.[7] In 1807 he was returned head of the poll in the largest urban constituency in the country, Westminster. With his lower-class supporters he had little social contact. His snobbish demeanour was distasteful to the more self-assured lower-class reformers, and held the less confident at bay. Surrounded as it were by a non-conductive medium of class distinction, he preserved himself from being much influenced by his supporters and equally, having few ideas of his own, gave little in terms of ideology or inspiration. He was the perfect figurehead.

Cochrane, who was elected MP for Westminster at the same time as Burdett, was a more formidable specimen. He was heir to an even a grander title than Burdett's, though the families of the two men were connected. Cochrane was distantly related to the Coutts family, and his father, while a schoolboy at the Hackney Academy, had been a sweetheart of Burdett's future mother-in-law, then a nursemaid in the household of James Coutts.[8]

Whereas Burdett was one of the idle rich, Cochrane was one of the greatest naval heroes of the day. His father, the ninth Earl of Dundonald, had ruined himself in his industrial projects, but Cochrane had made a fortune for himself from prize money as captain of the Royal Navy brig *Speedy,* and later of the frigate *Pallas.* In the *Speedy* he had in 13 months captured over 50 ships including a Spanish frigate four times the size, with six times the crew and much heavier guns than his own vessel. Victory in war always makes for interest. The war itself, after its resumption in 1803, was far more popular than it had been in the 1790s, and it was as a great war hero that Cochrane entered Parliament.

In personality he was more attractive, if less imposing than Burdett: 'A mild, very gentleman-like, agreeable man', Hobhouse thought him.[9] Where Burdett was stiff, Cochrane was 'cordial and unaffected in his manner'.[10] There was a pleasant aura of the man of action about him: 'He stooped a little, and had somewhat of a sailor's gait in walking; his face was rather oval; fair naturally, but now tanned and sun-freckled . . . . the expression on his countenance was calm and self-possessed.'[11] He was also much cleverer than Burdett. But his true interests, and consequently his real expertise, lay in gadgets and ingenious stratagems of warfare. His parliamentary speeches showed competence and verve, as far as they went, but they were chiefly on the esoteric subject of abuses in the Navy, and especially in the Prize Courts. He devoted no time to political theorizing. Indeed he had little sense of public duty. When new regulations came into force which allocated a larger share of prize money to naval ratings at the expense of their captains, Cochrane told the Commons, perhaps jokingly, 'it was the diminution of the prize money by the recent regulations which principally induced him to leave the profession for the last two or three years.'[12] At about the same period, while publicly crusading for the suppression of political and administrative corruption, Cochrane was co-operating with his uncles the Hon. Basil Cochrane and the Hon. Andrew Cochrane Johnstone in their campaign to suborn the borough of Grampound. Cochrane's help included using his influence in the Navy to transfer one Grampound voter who was a naval seaman to his own ship, giving the man unlimited leave of absence, and then, after five years, when the fellow had the temerity to support the Cochranes' rivals, having him arrested as a deserter.[13]

In 1814 Cochrane was implicated in a fraud on the Stock Exchange perpetrated by his uncle Andrew, and was sentenced to a year's gaol, a £1,000 fine, and was dismissed from the Navy, stripped of his Order of the Bath, and expelled from Parliament, whither his loyal constituents promptly re-elected him. Cochrane was eventually restored to all his honours and became a full admiral and it is generally believed that he was innocent of the fraud.[14] Nevertheless, detailed re-examination of Cochrane's trial suggests that he was in fact guilty.[15] Even the Earl of Dundonald seems to have had no doubt of his son's guilt, though since Cochrane had refused to give his father money, had surreptitiously patented some of his inventions under his own name, and had once actually knocked Dundonald down for calling Cochrane Johnstone, 'an *unprincipled Villain Swindler* and *Coward,*'[16] it may be that the head of the family was a little prejudiced. Cochrane Johnstone was not the only one of Lord Cochrane's uncles to be a shady dealer (Dundonald thought, 'the most of the Cochrane family are a set of Damned Scoundrels'[17]) and it may be that dishonesty ran in the blood at this time.

It would be disingenuous to pretend that, because Cochrane was brave and resourceful in war, and a reformer in politics, he could not have been capable of baseness. He had effrontery enough to be capable of anything. If guilty of nothing else, he was guilty of bribing the electors of Honiton at the rate of ten guineas a head to vote for him in 1806, and of later boasting to the House of Commons that he had sent the town crier through the streets to tell the voters to collect their money from his banker. He even offered to show the vouchers he had received in return.[18] Possibly Cochrane's own corruption, and his scornful denunciation of the corruption of others, are best to be seen in terms of his being a *frondeur,* opposing the powers that be, by fair means or foul, out of resentment for their treatment of him personally, and disgust at their manifest weakness, while all the time himself partaking of the vices he denounced in the system of which he was a part. Whatever the dark secrets of Cochrane's psyche, his preoccupation with matters outside politics meant that his impact on popular politics was even more negative than that of Burdett. Neither took the least pains to capitalize on their status as demagogues, neither took advantage of their position as darlings of the mob to turn reform poitics in any new direction, constructive or otherwise. Moreover, it was precisely in this negativeness that the achievement of Burdett and Cochrane lay. Their presence in Parliament helped focus public attention on the parliamentary stage.

The reformers of the 1790s, who were so much larger in their views and more free in the rein they gave their imaginations, were able to be thus because they had no leaders in Parliament save the eccentric Earl Stanhope in the Lords. This exclusion from the world of upper-class politics was a means of emancipation as well as a measure of their impotence. The ideas of the 1790s about national conventions, and revolution, and the infinite benefits to be derived from parliamentary reform, could be taken seriously even though each reformer was equally powerless to bring about the Millenium, precisely *because* the political leverage that seemed necessary for achieving their aims was lacking. But after 1807, with radical reformers for the first time in Parliament, the rank and file began to sit back and look to their upper class parliamentary leaders for guidance: guidance which was not forthcoming. The most powerful reform organization after 1807, for a period of nearly ten years, existed not so much to disseminate ideas and theories, but to secure votes for the borough of Westminster. The conceptual horizons had shrunk. Obviously disillusion with the fantasies of the 1790s played a part in this. There was now a more modest notion prevailing of what was possible. But Cochrane and Burdett were also important, for they satisfied aspirations without actually nourishing them. By lending themselves to a political campaign against the class to which they belonged, they effectively channelled off much popular energy which, if denied a parliamentary outlet, might have manifested itself in a much more dangerous extra-parliamentary organization.

The New Ideology
The revived political dissent had two mutually supporting strands. One strand was the growing criticism of abuses in high places; the other was the campaign for free elections.

With regard to their general political programme, Burdett and Cochrane differed little from the left wing of the Whig party, led by Whitbread. In fact Burdett and Whitbread were often mentioned in the same breath. But to regard Burdett and Cochrane merely as a splinter group on the Whig left is totally to misconceive their political position. They were not on close terms with Whitbread and his circle, and on one fundamental nexus of issues they differed. This nexus of issues can be most conveniently covered by the phrase *free elections.*

The Burdett—Cochrane view of the Whigs was that they were a self-interested faction, like the Tories, who were working to undermine the position of both the Crown and the people while concealing their purpose by talking about the rights of the people. This belief that there was no difference in the ultimate political aims of government or opposition was at least as old as the reign of George III. As long ago as 1765 a political writer had warned, with corroborating evidence from classical antiquity, that 'The Leaders of Faction (being naturally of the higher Ranks) would aim to establish an *aristocratic Power* and inslave both Prince and People to their own Avarice and Ambition.'[19] Horne Tooke had revived this idea in the 1790s, at a time when most reformers looked up to the Foxite Whigs because of their opposition to the war and because of their admittedly moderate proposals for parliamentary reform. By 1807 the Foxites had lost credit with the reformers because of their recent conduct in office, and Horne Tooke's views, in the mouth of his disciple Burdett, became much more widely acceptable. But it was Cochrane who gave them their virtually definitive expression in an address to his electors in 1812:

'Gentlemen, no part of the cant of the times seems to me more hypocritical than the declamation of party-men against what they call the "over-whelming influence of the Crown"; when the fact is notorious to us all that the ruling faction in Parliament seize the offices of state and share them amongst themselves. . . . Our liberties in these days are not in danger from violent and open exercise of regal authority; such acts, because free from the deception practised by the mock representatives of the people, would not be tolerated for an instant. No, Gentlemen, it is by the House of Commons alone that the Constitution is subverted, the prerogative of the Crown usurped, the rights of the people trampled on.'[20]

This association of Crown and people as joint victims of oligarchic usurpation also became a commonplace of Tory propaganda. In 1807 the Grenville—Foxite party was described as 'An Ambitious Aristocracy, engrossing both the power of the Crown, and of the People'.[21] Their political activities were denounced as 'an attempt on the part of the Aristocracy to acquire such a permanent interest and influence, as to enable it to influence both King and THE PEOPLE.'[22] This last accusation was quoted approvingly by Cobbett,[23]

who later described the Foxites as
'if possible more hostile to reform than the followers of Pitt and
Perceval themselves. . . . They hate one another, they would
destroy one another; but they love the public money more than
they hate one another, and, therefore, when the *system* is in
danger, they always unite. They cordially unite also against
every man who is hostile to the system. They hate him more than
they hate each other; because he would destroy the very meat
they feed on.'[24]

In 1815 the Whigs were characterized by another journalist as
'dull and pompous Aristocrats, who, assuming a popular title for
private purposes, despise equally popular feelings and popular
sentiments; who, bolstered up with heaps of wealth, and stiffened
into one compact mass by family alliance, with cold selfishness
turn their backs at once on the Monarch and the nation.'[25]

Even the followers of Thomas Spence, the most isolatedly extreme
reform group of the day, believed in the aristocratic threat:
'Both king and people now find themselves paralized and subjected
to one of the most unfeeling powers that can exist, namely an
oligarchy, that degrades the crown by granting or withholding at
their pleasure, and questioning, calling upon, and compelling its
agents to account for very shilling in its expenditure; while they
engross, possess, and enjoy the country, uncontrolled and unlimited
in their acquisitions, destroying the people by their exactions to
gratify their lust of power, corruption, and oppression, wallowing
in wealth, and grasping at the command and plunder of the
world.[26]

The Whigs counter-attacked feebly, boasting that they
'understood nothing of the modern popular jargon of the
Independence of the Crown; by which those who have elected
themselves to be leaders of the people are seeking an alliance with
the Court against the Whigs, in order more effectually to destroy
the Crown itself, after depriving it of its true constitutional defence.'[27]

The reformers however seem genuinely to have placed considerable
faith in the institution of royalty. Cartwright, thought that 'whatever
may be the language of partizans, from either direct selfishness or
egregious folly, the nation at large has no hope whatever, in respect
of its liberties, from either party,'[28] and even went so far as to petition
the King on the subject of reform, much to the disgust of George III
who informed the Home Secretary 'that the impertinent attempts of
such individuals as Major Cartwright cannot be too positively
checked.'[29] Indeed the only extreme reformer of the period who
made much of his hostility to royalty was Jeremy Bentham, who
had little influence at this time.

Despite the rhetoric about 'aristocrats', the Whig and Tory leaders were viewed merely as leaders of rival factions rather than as spokesmen of the ruling class — they were of course both one and the other — and men of their own class like Burdett and Cochrane saw nothing incongruous in allying with the lower classes to attack them. This objection to the Whigs and Tories as mere factions was related to an old-fashioned rejection of the very idea of party. Thus the Essex reformer, Montagu Burgoyne argued:

'I cannot pledge myself to support any particular set of men, without running the risk of deviating occasionally from those principles which from my earliest years I have never changed, nor can ever desert. These principles are, as I conceive, the principles of the British constitution, as settled at the Revolution of 1688.'[30]

Such appeals to the past, with all the conservatism they involved, were the foundation of the reform ideology of the 1800s to a much greater extent than had been the case in the 1790s. Burdett for example claimed:

'A scrupulous adherence to the Common Law of this land, and the wise provisions of the ancient statutes declaratory of that Law, which together form what I understand by the Constitution, raised our Country to an unexampled height of happiness and prosperity; and in an exact proportion to the invasion and neglect of them has the country declined.'[31]

Reform was conceived as restoration rather than progress. It was no coincidence that the two most prominent reformers were a Scots lordling and an English baronet, and that of the numerous men of title who embraced reform in the 1790s and 1800s only two, Stanhope and Camelford, were peers entitled to sit in the House of Lords. All the rest had baronetcies or Scots peerages, relics of former eminence that had not kept abreast of the expansion of wealth and titles in the later eighteenth century: men like Lords Selkirk, Daer and Sempill Sir John Throckmorton, fifth baronet, Sir Bellingham Graham, seventh baronet, Sir William Wolseley, sixth baronet — his family went back to the reign of William Rufus — Sir Thomas Ham, sixth baronet, Sir William Pilkington, eighth baronet. All these men belonged to families which had merited titles under the Stuarts, but had been unable to secure peerages under George III, and perhaps they felt left behind by a changing society, and were embittered by their relative loss of status. Similarly, Henry Clifford, the aristocratic Roman Catholic barrister, nephew of the fourth Lord Clifford, who was the most prominent lawyer amongst the reformers, was reputedly motivated by 'Impatience of the unjust disabilities under which his sect labours [which] had reconciled him to violent opinions in politics.'[32] Clifford even denounced Pitt in open court for degrading the House of Lords,

'by inundating it with a crowd of low born persons devoid of talents or respectability, and with no pretensions but their venality to the peerage—Thus outnumbering and weighing down the ancient and hereditary nobles of the land, and rendering them mere cyphers in the state.'[33]

He confessed, 'I entertain as high a reverence for ancient, as I feel contempt for upstart nobility.'[34] Such views were not unique in this period,[35] but in the mouth of an aristocratic reformer like Clifford they do help to explain the reactionary element in reform thinking at this stage.

Where the Burdett—Cochrane reformers were on the side of the future was in their detailed diagnosis. They saw (as did subsequent generations of more truly progressive reformers) that the key to the system of aristocratic subversion was electoral corruption. They saw that it was by means of treating and bribery that 'party men' had themselves returned to Parliament there to work to undermine the Constitution. Since Whigs and Tories were equally involved in the buying and selling of votes, they objected to Whigs and Tories equally. It was for this reason that they had little to do with the Whig 'Mountain' who, though eager for any number of reforms, were also participators in the borough-mongering system, and were working to further the Whig cause by trying to set up the Whig party as the champions of popular rights. Thus fundamentally different political orientation led to an open quarrel between Burdett and Whitbread in 1806.

Central to the Burdett—Cochrane objection to bribery and treating was the realization that such practices diverted attention from political issues and actually contributed to keeping the voters in a state of ignorance. The corollary of no treating was the attempt to fight elections solely on a platform of public issues.

Yet though after 1807 Burdett and Cochrane were the only two MPs elected on the professed principle of no treating, there was a certain disingenuousness in their attitude. Both had bought their way into Parliament when they first became MPs, Burdett having spent £4,000 on his election for Boroughbridge in 1796, and Cochrane having bribed his Honiton voters at ten guineas each in 1806. Burdett had later spent £100,000 bribing and treating the electors of Middlesex, and his disgust with corruption seems to have originated from his failure to get any return on this investment. Nor, after their election free of expense for Westminster in 1807 did the two men disdain co-operation with other independents such as Viscount Folkestone, Colonel Wardle, and Cochrane's own wicked uncle Andrew, all three of whom owed their places in Parliament to greater or lesser degrees of corruption.

The Westminster Election of 1807

Horne Tooke had stood for Westminster in 1790 on the platform of strict hostility to both government and opposition, and of no treating. He had polled 1,679 votes at a cost of £28.[36] In 1796 when he ran again he asked the voters to give their second votes to Fox, the Whig candidate, because of his opposition to the war, and this time he received 2,819 votes. In the 1802 general election, Horne Tooke did not stand, clergymen having been recently excluded from the Commons by statute following his entry into Parliament for Lord Camelford's rotten borough, Old Sarum; but an obscure Westminster citizen John Graham offered himself as a candidate on Horne Tooke's principles and was defeated by an alliance of Fox and the government candidate. In the same general election, in the contiguous Middlesex constituency, Burdett was bribing and treating on so massive a scale that he was unseated by the parliamentary committee formed to investigate the petition of his unsuccessful opponent. This general election also saw the return of one Joseph Birch, on no-treating principles at Nottingham. Nottingham had both a freeman and a freeholder vote. Birch, the candidate of the notoriously reformist corporation, was supported by the freemen, mostly poor artisans, against the richer and more conservative freeholders. His lavish victory parade allegedly included a Tree of Liberty, a totally naked woman representing the Goddess of Reason, and people wearing French cockades.[37] Like Burdett, Birch was unseated as a result of a petition: not for treating, but because the rioting of his supporters interfered with his rivals' voters.

There were two elections in Westminster in 1806, one a by-election caused by Fox's death in September, the other the result of the dissolution of Parliament. Both elections were characterized by a vast amount of treating, especially in the September canvass when profuse expenditure by the Duke of Northumberland on behalf of his son Earl Percy obliged the other candidate, Sheridan, to withdraw. Francis Place, the former Corresponding Society leader, who was then living quietly at Charing Cross busy with his tailoring trade, was disgusted to see

'the servants of the Duke of Northumberland, in their showy dress liveries, throwing lumps of bread and cheese among the dense crowd of vagabonds they had collected together. To see these vagabonds catching the lumps, shouting, swearing, fighting, and blackguarding in every way, women as well as men, all the vile wretches from the courts and alleys in St. Giles and Westminster, the Porridge Islands,* and other miserable places;

*St. Giles was the area between what is now New Oxford Street and Charing Cross Road; the Porridge Islands were the slums on the south side of St Martins-in-the-Fields, on the site now occupied by South Africa House and the north-east part of Trafalgar Square.

to see these people representing, as it was said, the electors of Westminster, was certainly the lowest possible step of degradation.'[39]

In the November election there were three candidates: the Whig Sheridan, the Pittite Sir Samuel Hood, and James Paull, who had recently become famous for his campaign against the Marquess Wellesley, and who was regarded as an embarrassment both by the government and by the opposition. Paull's committee was led by the London Corresponding Society veteran Lemaitre, who had earlier been active in Burdett's struggle in Middlesex. Paull was beaten narrowly into third place, with 4,481 votes, of which no less than 3,077 were plumpers, a sign that the majority of his voters refused to use their second votes for candidates as corrupt as Sheridan and Hood. Burdett, who had nominated Paull for Westminster, again offered himself for Middlesex, but this time, instead of lavishly treating his voters, he ran on independent principles, announcing 'I desire no seat, but by the unbiassed votes of intelligent and uncorrupt Freeholders.'[39] He polled only a sixth of the votes cast.

The two elections at Westminster had not only shown the worst excesses of the borough-mongers, but had also revealed a degree of independent spirit in the constituency. This, together with the Whig's extraordinary loss of favour with the reformers as a result of their record in government, offered the conditions for a new departure. The unexpected dissolution in April 1807 provided the occasion. Paull again wished to be the reformers' candidate, but his popularity had declined, and he was suspected of misuse of supporters' donations.[40] A group of electors including Francis Place called on Burdett after the dissolution had been announced. Burdett refused to put himself forward and reommended in his stead Lord Cochrane, at that stage an unknown quantity in politics, but he signified that if elected he would accept the honour.[41] Burdett's reluctance to participate actively in his election was soon confirmed by physical incapacitation. Resenting Burdett's refusal to nominate him a second time, Paull persuaded himself that he was being cheated out of an easy electoral victory, at the instance of Horne Tooke, 'The fiend of Mischief', and so he challenged Burdett to a duel. They met on 2 May, and at their second fire succeeded in shooting each other in the leg, so that both had to spend the period of the election recovering from their wounds. On the same day another, less comic opera, meeting took place at the 'Ship Tavern', Charing Cross, the meeting of what was to be known to posterity, though not at first to contemporaries, as the 'Westminster Committee', that is, the self-nominated committee for managing the election of Sir Francis Burdett. Place boasted afterwards,

'We were all of us obscure persons, not one man of note among us, not one in any way known to the electors generally, as insignificant a set of persons as could well have been collected together to undertake so important a public matter as a Westminster election against wealth and rank and name and influence.'[42] In fact, some of the committee were already notorious for their activities in the 1790s. The original gathering of 20 men consisted of Lemaitre, the watchmaker who had been tried for treason in 1796, a currier, a solicitor, a mercer, a bootmaker, a broker's man, two tailors, a shoemaker, a coachmaker, a clerk, Cobbett's assistant, a wine-merchant and seven others of unknown occupation. They were later joined by William Frend, the Unitarian expelled from Cambridge University in 1793, Joseph Clayton Jennings, a barrister from the West Indies who had stood unsuccessfully for Gatton on independent principles in a by-election in 1803, and four others.[43] Eight of the 26 had served their political apprenticeship in the Corresponding Society or the Society for Constitutional Information. Their aim was to organize canvassing, to disseminate propaganda, and to raise money for printing handbills and posters. As Burdett was now unable as well as unwilling to speak from the hustings, it was arranged that Jennings should speak for him. Although Paull had been nominated by some of his few remaining supporters, the committee aimed solely at Burdett's return, and voters were urged to plump for him.

Besides Burdett and Paull there were three other candidate, Sheridan the Whig, Elliott the ministerialist, and Lord Cochrane. Despite Burdett's recommendation of him, and despite the fact that he had first stood for Honiton in 1806 on independent principles,[44] Cochrane was regarded as politically uncommitted, and there was confusion about his political views and even his motives. Admiral Markham thought he was merely out to make trouble for the Admiralty and everyone else: 'His foolish & reprehensible conduct appears to have been guided by envy, hatred, & malice, & all uncharitableness.'[45] No one knew whether he would support the new government if elected, or the Whigs, and throughout the election Paull's spokesmen Gibbons and Power denounced him as the principal ministerialist candidate, a notion Elliott, the real ministerialist, was never able to deny as he was invariably howled down on the hustings. At the same time Sheridan, who did most of the speaking on the hustings, referred amiably to Cochrane on frequent occasions, and even Jennings, speaking for Burdett, announced that 'he considered it much to his [Cochrane's] honour to have declared sentiments similar to those of Sir F. Burdett',[46] though he did express the wish that Cochrane should pledge himself not to support the new ministers.[47] Cochrane spoke mainly on naval abuses and did not clarify his general position.

As a result of this confusion Cochrane was able to share 1,432 votes with Burdett and 1,264 with Elliott, and came in second with 3,708 votes to Burdett's 5,134. Sheridan polled 2,645, Elliott 2,137 and Paull a mere 269. Paull's candidature had been withdrawn several days before the end, but his spokesmen had continued to denounce Cochrane, apparently to the latter's advantage.* Historians have generally emphasized the significance of the Burdettite success, apparently based on careful organization and publicity, though Cochrane's election, with neither an organization nor a coherent programme to recommend him, was surely a much greater personal achievement. A curious factor was that there was rather a low turn-out. Possibly the reluctance of Tory electors to vote for the feeble Elliott kept many of them at home. Nearly a thousand fewer voters polled than in the 1806 general election.

The Duke of York

The years that saw the emergence of political consciousness amongst the Westminster electors also saw the build-up of disaffection in some sections of the Army against the Commander-in-Chief.

HRH Frederick, Duke of York and Albany, the second son of George III, had become Commander-in-Chief of the Army in 1795 though he only received the official title as such in 1798. He had quickly set himself to correct the abuses that had flourished under his predecessor, Lord Amherst. He put an end to the situation where inexperienced youths could buy their way in and out of regiments, without regard to merit or seniority, and having by this means reached the rank of lieutenant-colonel, could find themselves commanding brigades in action owing to the unofficial absences of their seniors. System and order were re-established. Naturally the new regulations were inconvenient to some and irritating to others, but many admitted that the Army was far better administered than during Amherst's régime, and the respect the Duke of York obtained as the son of the King made his efficiency seem all the more estimable.

But of course the Duke of York made enemies, and two in particular were men of prominence. His own younger brother HRH Edward Duke of Kent had been in command of Gibraltar at the time of a mutiny there. Addington's government, suspecting that the Duke of Kent's unnecessary strictness had provoked the outburst, had him replaced. In the Duke of Kent, George III's painstaking industriousness manifested itself almost as psychosis. In 1806 alone, for example, at a time when he had almost no official duties, he personally drafted 3,876 letters.[48] This morbid attention to detail,

*Paull, overwhelmed by gambling debts, cut his own throat nearly a year later. On hearing the news, the Marquess Wellesley remarked, 'Mr Paull could not have died by a more ignoble hand.'

which led him into a minute concern for the appearance and behaviour
of his troops, had rendered him so unpopular that it was said he
would have been shot in the back had he ever risked leading his men
into battle.[49] Consequently, when he demanded a court-martial in
the hope of vindicating his conduct at Gibraltar, his brother the
Commander-in-Chief refused. Possibly the Duke of York objected
to the very idea of a prince being put on trial, even as a formality.
But the Duke of Kent and his adherents chose to believe that the
Duke of York was actually jealous of his brother.

Then there was Colonel the Hon. Andrew Cochrane Johnstone.
Cochrane Johnstone had been MP for Stirling boroughs from 1791
to 1797, and had married the niece of Henry Dundas' wife. Dundas
had appointed him governor of Dominica in the West Indies. Cochrane
Johnstone was thus well-connected and apparently had a brilliant
career ahead of him. In order to impress Dundas' successor at the
War Department he drew up a cogent, enthusiastic, though not very
exciting memorandum proposing numerous improvements in West
Indian administration.[50] In 1803 however he was recalled. His troops
had been discontented at having to work as labourers and at not
receiving their pay in time, owing to Cochrane Johnstone's negligent
and possibly criminal handling of official money, and they had
finally mutinied. Cochrane Johnstone put the blame on his subordinate,
Major John Gordon, who was court-martialled. On being deservedly
acquitted Gordon made his own charges against Cochrane Johnstone,
and the latter was tried on four counts, two regarding financial
irregularities, one concerning his use of troops for unpaid labour,
and the fourth relating to his ordering the wrongful arrest of civilians.
While the charges were still pending, Cochrane Johnstone was omitted
from a brevet promotion. The court-martial acquitted him, and he
expected his promotion to be granted. When this was not done he
resigned his commission. He published a vindication of himself in
1805, and his case was sympathetically taken up by Cobbett. He
seems also to have gained the confidence of Burdett.[51] When Fox
and Grenville came into office his hopes revived. In May 1806 he
wrote to the Duke of York's secretary Colonel Gordon saying he had
heard his resignation had been cancelled and that he was to be
promoted. Gordon denied this.[52]

Cochrane Johnstone, described by one associate as a 'confounded,
mawkish, pompous braggart',[53] was soon involved in numerous
shady deals. His brother Vice-Admiral the Hon. Sir Alexander
Forrester Cochrane rashly appointed him agent for the captors of
Ste Croix and was soon complaining to another brother that he felt
'hurt and vexed beyond measure, at the conduct of Andrew, who
must have taken leave of his Senses', and that 'contrary to my
advice, and his duty as an Agent, [he] has been buying Estates at St

Croix, Gardens Vessels &c; all of which must have been done, with the Captor's money or his credit thereon.'[54] Amongst other transactions with which his name was linked, there were reports that he was hired by the South Americans to ransom the Pope from Napoleon.[55]

The grumblings of Cochrane Johnstone and of the Duke of Kent's entourage were an encouragement to smaller fry to circulate rumours which in a different climate no one would have dared repeat. In particular there was gossip concerning the Duke of York's mistress, and it was hinted that members of his household were selling commissions which were subsequently gazetted as without purchase. As early as January 1806, at the formation of the Fox-Grenville ministry, it was said that the Duke of York 'was so terrified at the expectation of impeachment for disposal of commissions in the army gazetted "without purchase" that he prevailed on his father to make his own non-impeachment the only stipulation'.[56] During 1806 the Cochrane Johnstone case received considerable publicity in Cobbett's *Political Register*. In August Cochrane Johnstone claimed that the Earl of Moira had had several interviews with the Commander-in-Chief on his behalf and that HRH had eventually agreed to promote him, and that John McArthur, Judge Advocate General of the Navy, had written to him that Colonel Gordon had said at a dinner party that the promotion would soon be announced. Both Moira and McArthur denied these statements,[57] which gave the impression (such was the circumstantial detail of Cochrane Johnstone's lies) that Army HQ was busily covering its tracks after some further chicanery. It was not till the following year, however, that the scandalous rumours began to become public property. During 1807 two extraordinary pamphlets were published, boldly denouncing the Duke of York. One, entitled *Mentoriana,* took the form of 'A Letter Of Admonition And Remonstrance To His Royal Highness The Duke Of York Relative To Corruption, Oppression, Cowardly Revenge, Agency-Monopoly, Meretricious Influence, And Other Subjects Connected With The Army'. The Duke of York was not actually accused of anything, but the hints were sufficiently broad. For example, referring evidently to Cochrane Johnstone the anonymous writer suggested 'You *might,* if evilly disposed, cause a brave and experienced officer to be dismissed His Majesty's Service, even though he had been declared guiltless by a court-martial.'[58] It was implied that the Commander-in-Chief favoured the Army agent Greenwood to such an extent that he gave colonelcies of regiments only to those who agreed to give Greenwood the agency,[59] that he allowed a harlot *'to prostitute your patronage, in return for the prostitution of her person',*[60] that he mutilated court-martial reports 'by erasing all honourable mention of prosecutors to whom you had any personal dislike', and by suppressing charges against others, and that he robbed meritorious officers of credit by suppressing their names in despatches.[61] The writer also cited an instance 'Not *many centuries* ago' of an officer passed over for promotion who had been driven to suicide by the disgrace and asked, 'what would be the agony of your soul had *you* been the author of such deplorable events.'[62] The other pamphlet, *A Letter to His Royal Highness, or, a Delicate Enquiry whether He be more Favoured by Mars or Venus,* also referred to Cochrane Johnstone; it also mentioned the Duke of Kent but only as an accomplice in concealing the facts of Cochrane Johnstone's case. There were various references to the Duke of York's sexual exploits, and one 'Clarke', described as an 'artful, vain, flippant, mercenary giglet'[63] was numbered amongst his mistresses. The threat was made that in a subsequent publication:

'I shall proclaim by whose influence, for what money, and upon *whose* recommendation *certain* persons have been honoured with commission—rank, and promotion in the army; *who* received the money; *how* and by *whom* it was paid; what claims *they* had; what active service the *beautiful creatures* had done the state &c. &c. My quotations from particular *original letters* will make even the bench of bishops smile.'[64]

Another pamphlet, not published till 1808, though the preface was dated 7 August 1807, was *The Agent, And His Natural Son* which purported to be a fable about one Charles Evergreen, an agent ('whether a military agent, or a navy agent, or a commercial agent, is not recorded') to whom 'a gay, thoughtless—perhaps dissipated—youth of some birth, and *great* expectations' became so heavily indebted, that the agent, assisted by his illegitimate son, was able to sell his patron's protection at pleasure. Charles Evergreen was of course the Army agent Greenwood previously mentioned in *Mentoriana.* A postscript identified Greenwood by name and claimed that he had the agencies of 194 out of 357 line, militia and fencible regiments.[65]

Not much attention to these hints was paid by the upper-class political world, though a rather dull defence of the Duke of York was published with the title (more intriguing than the content) *A Bonne-Bouche of Epicurean Rascality. The Agent, and His Natural Son* actually congratulated the Duke of York sarcastically for not prosecuting any of the pamphleteers, doubtless from consciousness of his own innocence.[66]

Scurrility was of course a sufficiently usual polemical device at this time. The play with Cochrane Johnstone's name suggests that he was involved, though systematic vilification does not seem to have been his usual brand of villainy. Burdett, too, as was soon to transpire, was well aware of the discontents in the Army. Otherwise all the indications are that the anonymous authors had nothing to do with the usual political arena. They were certainly not friendly to the Whigs. The author of *A Letter to His Royal Highness* had previously written a pamphlet denouncing the Prince of Wales, and in his discussion of the Cochrane Johnstone case he sneered at Fox's friend General the Hon. Richard Fitzpatrick, who had defended Cochrane Johnstone while in opposition but had abandoned his cause on becoming Secretary at War in the short-lived Fox—Grenville ministry:

'See General Fitzpatrick's speech on the 28th June, 1805. He was then in opposition, seated on hard and inconvenient benches — restless — and a great Patriot: — he was afterwards translated to the Treasury-seats; but, like an escape from fire, or Dunkirk,* he fled so precipitately, that he left his memory — resentment — motion — justice — all behind him; but providence is very good to him and us too, in sending him so soon back to look after them: the poor General had a place, and just time enough to say, "Hail and farewell" — hail to the place, and farewell to his own character.'[67]

The same author warned of the horrors of the poison of 'the tree of French liberty', and reminded the Duke of York, 'The profligacy of the French Princes hastened the French revolution; — an awful truth I must and will impress upon the memory of your Highness and your brothers'. *Mentoriana* referred to 'that artful, eloquent, but deceitful statesman, Charles F-x', and even attacked Burdett, suggesting that his object was 'the downfall [*sic*] of a King, and the destruction of a kingdom'.[68]

Burdett was, in fact, aware of the discontents in the Army and on 14 March 1808 during the debate on the Mutiny Bill, he proposed an amendment to prevent the dismissal of officers except by court-martial. There is an anonymous letter amongst his papers, beginning 'Dear Wharton' and dated 20 March 1808, referring to a bill Burdett was planning to protect officers. Evidently this letter had been forwarded by Wharton to Burdett. It claimed that Major-General Fawcett and Lord Amherst had been virtually turned out of the service, that General Sturt had been unfairly passed over for promotion, that a lieutenant-colonel and 12 or 15 subalterns of the 83rd Foot had been placed on half-pay because their troops had been in a riot, and the colonel dismissed for 'want of energy'. The letter ended, 'you know the Duke of York has already gone very much out of his way to injure me. I therefore rely on the honour of Sir Francis in not using my name, and beg this letter may be burned.'[69] Burdett's amendment had received little encouragement in the Commons and had been withdrawn. In June a separate bill to the same effect was proposed by the Hon. W. H. Lyttelton and supported by Burdett, but was soon given up.

*A reference to the Duke of York's abortive campaign in Flanders 1793-4.

But there was no giving up on the pamphlet front. During 1808
the pamphleteers so gained in boldness that they did not scruple to
reveal their identities. The fury within the Army by the Convention
of Cintra—regarded as a betrayal of the Army's honour by two
incompetents who owed their commands to the Duke of York's
favour—added a new bitterness. A pamphlet by Thomas Hague, a
friend of the Duke of Kent's secretary, Major Dodd, described
Dalrymple as 'a creeping, watchful sycophant, with just industry
and talents enough to do mischief, to assist, *if necessary*, in circulating
whispers against the Duke of Kent and his friends'.[70] Kent was
described as 'a man (although a Royal Duke) of solid acquirements
and great intellectual capability . . . brave, sober, and attentive,
unstained by any vice', and it was hinted that it was precisely
because of those qualities that the Duke of York avoided appointing
him to the chief command in the Peninsula. 'The strong political
claims of some, and the real qualifications of others, gave the command
to Sir Hew.'[71] Again there were references to the strange influence of
the agent Greenwood, and it was suggested that the Duke of York
consorted with 'actors and actresses, play writers, wit crackers and
would be managers . . . spies, black legs and harlots.' His evening
amusements were compared unfavourably with those of the Cabinet
ministers: 'I have not heard that *their* dinners are bacchanalian
feasts, polluted by every varied introduction of ribaldry, licentiousness
and excess.'[72]

An even more serious attack was *Observations on H.R.H. the
Duke of Kent's Shameful Persecution since His Recal from
Gibralter; together with an Enquiry into the Abuses of the Royal
Military College,* published in December 1808, by a parliamentary
reporter named Pierre Franc McCallum, whose grudge against the
Duke of York stemmed from the belief that he was protecting Major-
General Picton who, as governor of Trinidad, several years earlier,
had had McCallum flung into jail without trial.[73] McCallum partly
derived his information from Major James Glenie, a mathematician
and Fellow of the Royal Society, who had cut his own controversial
teeth a generation earlier by denouncing the Duke of Richmond's
coastal defence schemes, and who was currently employed as an
instructor by the East India Company and as inspector of fortifications
in the West Indies. McCallum rehearsed the details of the Duke of
Kent's case ('that cruel, unbrotherly, and dirty business'), repeated
the fiction that the Duke of York was 'anxious about fixing himself
with greater security in his present situation, by an attempt to
destroy the military reputation of his brother', and denounced the
Royal Military College as 'this Barefaced JOB . . . more a school for
vice and dissipation, than for useful military tuition.'[74] McCallum
went far beyond any earlier pamphleteer (and far beyond the truth)

in his denunciation of the Duke of York's régime as Commander-in-Chief:

> 'We see a military establishment, maintained at the enormous expense of twenty millions per annum, reduced almost to a state of ruin, for want of discipline and proper arrangements with regard to men and officers. Under his management, essentials have been totally neglected, and the whole of the art (military) has been frittered down into folly, frivolity and nonsense. . . .
>
> No nation on earth was ever before saddled with such a generalissimo as we have at the head of our military establishment; who has never led any troops without exposing them to disgrace and discomfiture—who could not abstain from intoxication even in the face of the enemy—who, independent of his want of martial skill and his total inattention to his duty, is, through his debaucheries, incapacity and dissolute life, an absolute reproach to his profession.'[75]

McCallum took up a staunchly conservative constitution line, claiming that he sought 'to expose the iniquitous system pursued by those who have picketted-in the throne, and are in exclusive possession of the royal ear, to the manifest violation of the constitution, and the ruine of the country',[76] and he concluded with the warning:

> 'there are advisers about the throne unknown to the constitution . . . the baneful influence of the late Lord Bute is still scourging this unfortunate, and we much fear devoted, country, in the mushroom family of the Jenkinsons.'[77]*

This language indicated that he shared the essentially conservative reformist ideology of Horne Tooke, but McCallum also evinced a xenophobia not at all fashionable in reform circles of any complexion. His denunciations of the Royal Military College, especially in a later work *The Rival Queens* made much of the French and German instructors employed there, the 'illiterate foreigners', and included the accusation that one of the German professors was originally a cobbler.[78] Equally illiberal was his complaint that both the major and the adjutant of the senior department at the RMC had risen from the ranks and were 'therefore mere drill-judges, who perform their official duties like common ploughmen'.[79] Horne Tooke, or Burdett, would not have lowered themselves to such abuse.

Much less sweeping in its accusations, but more striking from its wealth of circumstantial detail, was the pamphlet of another parliamentary reporter, Peter Finnerty, published under the name of the man whose tribulations it described, Dennis Hogan. Hogan, a captain, acting major, in the Army, had applied to the Duke of York to purchase a majority in May 1805. He had purchased his captaincy

---

*Bute was, of course, George III's favourite at the beginning of his reign. Jenkinson was the family name of Lord Hawkesbury, who succeeded his father as Earl of Liverpool in 1808. The first Earl of Liverpool had been a close associate of Bute.

in 1796, had served seven years in the West Indies, and had testimonials from three generals. Despite repeated applications and his recruitment of 155 soldiers following the Commander-in-Chief's order of 8 December 1806 which hinted at promotion for officers who recruited large numbers of men, Hogan was constantly put off and by July 1808 40 captains had been promoted without purchase over his head. He was informed that it was possible to gain promotion without purchase by the payment of a rather smaller sum to the right persons. Hogan then decided to sell out, but as there was no record of his having purchased his original rank of ensign, he was permitted to sell out only at half-price—£750. On advertising his pamphlet, he was visited by a woman in a barouche who gave £400 in banknotes to his servant, presumably as hush money. It was suggested, in the by now familiar vein, that 'the allurements of Venus are suffered . . . to interfere with the interests of Mars'.[80]

Even Cobbett regarded Hogan's story with scepticism,[81] but the pamphlet roused considerable interest. A refutation entitled *A Short English Answer to a Long Irish Story; or, a Key to the Mystery of the Barouche and the Bank Notes, Proving Brevet – Major Hogan's Accusations against His Royal Highness The Duke Of York to be Barefaced Calumnies,* went through at least five editions in a few weeks. The Attorney-General was interested too, and *ex officio* information were filed against Hogan's publisher, and against Leigh Hunt for some remarks on the pamphlet in his paper *The Examiner.*

The authorities in fact were beginning to be worried. At the Royal Military College pressure was put on the Lieutenant-Governor, Colonel Le Marchant, to take the onus of denying McCallum's charges.[82] Le Marchant had been excepted by name from McCallum's general abuse (a piece of uncharacteristic generosity which McCallum later made up for in his posthumous *The Rival Queens* which referred to Le Marchant's 'very scanty share of knowledge and military science'.[83]), and there was some suspicion concerning his part in the whole business. Another pamphlet, *A Plain Statement of the Conduct of the Ministry and the Opposition, towards His Royal Highness The Duke Of York,* was investigated by the Attorney-General. This was a vindication of the Duke of York, and claimed that he was defended neither by the government nor by the opposition because he kept aloof from both parties. The Attorney-General decided not to prosecute its publisher because the case might fail and thereby further discredit the Duke of York.[84]

Colonel Wardle and Mrs Clarke

Meanwhile a new protagonist was emerging on the scene, Gwyllym Lloyd Wardle. Wardle was a Flintshire man who had distinguished himself during the Irish troubles in 1797-8 when he had commanded a Volunteer regiment raised by Sir Watkin Williams Wynn, known officially as the Ancient British Light Dragoons but called by the Irish 'The Bloody Britons'. Wardle had made himself especially hated in Ireland. One Irishman wrote 'You *Major Wardle* have swam in streams of *Human Gore*—while the more Timid hounds of your Infernal pack were scarcely Knee Deep in Blood!'[85] After the rebellion, Wardle and his men offered to serve in Europe,[86] but this offer was refused. This refusal was probably the origin of the North Wales tradition (possibly not current in 1809) that the cause of his personal animus against the Duke of York was the latter's refusal to incorporate the Ancient British Light Dragoons into the regular Army.[87] Even after the Ancient Britons were disbanded Wardle styled himself 'Colonel' Wardle. He later became a partner of William Madocks, the reformist Whig MP for Boston, who had built a clothing factory at Tremadoc. They hoped to secure contracts for Army uniforms, and it seems to have been the disappointment of these expectations which led Wardle to attack the system of privately negotiated tenders. It was on this issue that he first came before the public as a critic of Army administration.[88] There is a local tradition that Wardle and Madocks made up for the lack of Army contracts by smuggling their cloth from Tremadoc to France, for sale to the French Army.[89]

Wardle entered Parliament at the 1807 general election, defeating the proprietor of Okehampton and his dependent freeholders or 'faggot' voters to the cry of 'Wardle and the Independence Of Our Oppressed Borough' and 'Honest Freemen Against Dishonest Faggots'.[90] The story that Wardle helped Peter Finnerty concoct Hogan's *Appeal* is probably untrue. McCallum's account was that he met Wardle in August 1808, and that when Hogan's *Appeal* came out they together introduced themselves to Finnerty to ask for further information, of which Finnerty had none to give, Hogan himself being by then in America.[91]

McCallum was by this time on the trail of the Duke of York's discarded mistress, Mary Anne Clarke, who had been named in print over a year previously and who, it was supposed, could give definitive details of the illicit traffic in commissions in which she had allegedly participated. Mrs Clarke was not easily found, for she was penniless and lodging in a cottage in unfashionable Haverstock Hill, and news of her whereabouts came to McCallum only chance.[92] McCallum interviewed Mrs Clarke for the first time on 17 December 1808, and introduced Wardle to her next day. Mrs Clarke was a natural liar, chiefly concerned to feather her own nest. She herself freely admitted that she did not expose her ex-lover merely *'from pure* PATRIOTIC ZEAL TO SERVE THE PUBLIC'.[93] She claimed that she had told Burdett of her trafficking in commissions more than two years previously. McCallum thought Burdett had not proceeded with the matter because he saw that Mrs Clarke would tell any lie for the sake of money.[94] Mrs Clarke undoubtedly knew that other leading reformer, Viscount Folkestone, for she had slept with him while still under the Duke of York's protection,[95] but apparently Folkestone had been reluctant to denounce the Duke for fear of compromising himself. Wardle thus found a scandal more than ripe for exposure, and his chief ambition was to gain the credit for the act. Charles Wynn, whose brother Sir Watkin knew Wardle intimately, thought him 'a headlong & indiscreet man. . . . a wrong judging man run away with by his own violence & really not aware of the impropriety of his own conduct'.[96]

Wardle sought the co-operation of no other MP, though presumably he mentioned his discoveries to Madocks. The only persons party to his investigations apart from Mrs Clarke were McCallum, Glenie and Major Dodd, military secretary to the Duke of Kent. Mrs Clarke later claimed that the Duke of Kent was behind the whole business from the beginning, meaning to revenge himself for his Gibralter disgrace by ruining his brother and supplanting him as Commander-in-Chief. But the Duke of Kent denied any prior knowledge of Wardle's investigation and spoke of Dodd's 'highly culpable' imprudence.[97] The Duke was so excessively active in anything he undertook that if he had been involved, there would have been ample evidence of it, in default of which his innocence seems indisputable, and it is not even clear how much Wardle consulted Dodd, whose own rôle was probably limited to indiscreet hints that the Duke of Kent would welcome his brother's disgrace.

The Public Enquiry

Wardle, Glenie, Dodd and Mrs Clarke settled the details during a trip to look at the Martello Towers on the south coast, and on 27 January 1809 Wardle charged the Duke of York in the Commons of conniving at the unofficial traffic in commissions. Such was the general concern, even the ministers agreed that Wardle's allegations should be investigated, not privately by a select committee, but publicly by the whole House of Commons sitting in committee. Consequently the lengthy examination of Mrs Clarke and other witnesses took up nearly the whole of MPs' time till 20 March when, after the Duke of York had resigned his post, the enquiry came to an end. The opposition's plans for a systematic attack of the ministers' war policy was completely thrown into the shade. A motion by Petty, delayed till 21 February, which blamed the Convention of Cintra on insufficient preparation by the government, was defeated 203 to 152, whereas houses of nearly 500 divided on some of the debates on the Duke of York.

For both the ministers and the opposition the enquiry was a

disaster.' The ministers were blamed for their incompetent management of such an explosive issue; even members of the opposition thought that 'the whole Enquiry and the manner in which it is pursued is both mischievous and disgraceful.'[98] It was reported that 'the King is violently angry with them [his ministers], and that:

'All power and influence of Perceval in the House is quite gone by; he speaks without authority and without attention paid to him; and Canning has made two or three such rash declarations that he is as little attended to . . . . There is no government in the House of Commons. You may be assured the thing does not exist, and whether they can ever recover their tone of power remains to be proved.'[99]

Yet the opposition altogether failed to profit from the disarray of the ministers. 'The Whigs as a body took no distinct or manly tone whatever upon this embarrassing situation.'[100] The leaders were chiefly preoccupied by the effect on the public of such a scandal in high places, and resentful that it had diverted attention from topics which they conceived to be more important. The Earl of Rosslyn lamented:

'the Progress of the French, the Ruin of Spain, and the Disasters & Disgraces of our own Arms together with the total failure of every plan are as much banished from the Memory & Thoughts of almost all people in & out of Parliament, as if they had no real existence.'[101]

And Lord Auckland complained 'Our Countrymen are quite lost in the silly business of the enquiry into the conduct of the Duke of York, & are stupidly indifferent to all the Misdirection of the gigantic Interests now afloat in Europe & in America.'[102] Ponsonby was described as 'sunk in the estimation of the party, and the party sunk yet more in the estimation of the public'.[103]

All the enormous political capital to be made from Wardle's revelations was cornered by the opposition extremists and their extra-parliamentary supporters. Some of the young men on the conservative wing of the opposition, Ward, Horner and Viscount Althorp, were also active. Althorp, the son of Earl Spencer, had been previously principally concerned with fox-hunting, even while a Lord of the Treasury under Lord Grenville, but now he became closely involved with Cobbett's friend and parliamentary mouthpiece Viscount Folkestone, an intimacy which was welcome to Folkestone's father the Earl of Radnor who told Folkestone that the Whigs were 'preferable to some of the Acquaintances You have had' — particularly, it may be assumed, Cobbett — ' . . . Obscurity of Birth, & situation in one's Acquaintance is evidently less creditable, & desirable, than that with Persons of your own Condition'.[104] Spencer was less pleased by the budding friendship, but thought under the circumstances it was better for his son to go too far than to do nothing.[105]

Some of the older oppositionists were horrified. 'The consequences are incalculable', wrote Fremantle, 'for it involves now the very existence and security of the monarchy and the parliament, and I may add of every constituted authority.'[106] The opposition leaders had, after all, no quarrel with the ministers on the subject of the class structure of politics: their dispute had been on the relatively minor issue of the King's rôle within that upper-class dominated structure. The attack on the Duke of York represented an assault on the whole framework of society. Some of those who joined in the attack realized this, regretted it, but still felt obliged to persist in denouncing wrong-doing. Others looked only to the discredit of a government which had identified itself with the royal offender by seeking to defend him. Many, perhaps, were simply intoxicated by the public support which rallied behind them. Thus Charles Wynn could write subsequently:

'I consider myself the dismissal of the D of York as one of the greatest triumphs ever yet exhibited by the British Constitution. The King's favourite son after fourteen years command of an army of 12,000 Officers connected with every family in the kingdom, was overthrown by the exertions of an individual unconnected with & unsupported by any party, unknown even by name & without any distinguished abilities. When this can be done things are not as corrupt or the voice of the people of as little effect as has been supposed.'[107]

No one in Parliament, not even Burdett or Folkestone, had more than a vague notion of what kind of society they might be promoting by undermining the existing structure. Certainly there was nothing very far-sighted about the more vocal critics of the Duke; perhaps the moderates who regretted their involvement had more prescience. The split down the middle of the opposition was widened, the split between those committed to the old-style politics of disputing about power within the existing system, and those who, however blindly, wished to join the popular cry against that system.

In the country at large, Wardle's revelations were greeted with an excitement besides which even the furore over Viscount Melville four years earlier seemed insignificant. As with the Melville case, the public interest reflected the increasing concern for higher standards of probity in official circles, but there was more to it than that. The Duke of York was after all the King's son. By virtue of his position, by birth and by appointment, he personified the symbiotic relationship of Crown and aristocracy which was the essence of British government. By attacking him the middle class, the third and most neglected part of the British political system, was able to give full expression to its discontents. Even those MPs who played only a secondary part in the parliamentary enquiry became household names, were regarded as champions of the people against the forces of corruption, and were deluged by votes of thanks from the provinces. Wardle himself was hailed as 'Another Hampden'.[108] There were county meetings in Berkshire, Cornwall, Dorsetshire, Fifeshire, Hampshire, Herefordshire, Hertfordshire, Huntingdonshire, Inverness-shire, Middlesex, Monmouthshire, Norfolk, Radnorshire, Renfrewshire and Wiltshire, and meetings of townspeople at Annan, Bedford, Berwick, Beverley, Bolton, Boston, Bristol, Calne, Canterbury, Carmarthen, Chippenham, Christchurch, Coventry, Deal, Doncaster, Dover, Durham, Glasgow, Godalming, Guildford, Highworth near Swindon, Huddersfield, Holbeach, Hull, Hythe, Ipswich, Kilwinning, Kendal, Kilmarnock, Kirkcudbright, Lewes, London, Manchester, Maidstone, Norwich, Nottingham, Oldham, Okehampton, Paisley, Plymouth, Pomfret, Radford near Nottingham, Reading, Rochester, Salisbury, Shaftesbury, Sheffield, Shrewsbury, Southampton, Southwark, Stafford, Warwick, Winchester, Worcester, Wrexham, and Wycombe. Of course, the reformers did not have everything their own way. At the Cornwall county meeting, which only 200 freeholders attended, 50 or 60 of those present voted and signed a protest against the resolutions of the reformist majority.[109] At Oxford, at a Common Council meeting, a motion of thanks to Wardle was withdrawn when it was argued that the Duke of York had been taught his lesson, and that the King's feelings should not be hurt unnecessarily.[110] At Northampton a requisition for a meeting to thank Wardle was signed by 17 people but a counter-requisition was signed by 71, so that only an unofficial meeting could be convened.[111] At Montgomery, the supporters of the town's MP, Whitshed Keene, 'aware of the current which popular opinion was taking', put it about that Keene had supported Wardle. As a result some of Keene's partisans thought it would be right to sign a requisition for a meeting of the Common Hall to propose thanks to Wardle, but when the meeting took place they were disabused of their error and the address to Wardle was negatived by all present save the proposer and his brother, who seconded him.[112] At Liverpool the mayor refused permission for a town meeting, though a large public dinner was held instead on 21 April 1809, and the details of the speeches made on that occasion were afterwards printed as a broadsheet. Elsewhere, however, the public meetings had all the appearance of a revolt against the local patricians who had hitherto held sway. At the Hampshire county meeting, for example, the cautious Whiggish motions proposed by the Hon. Powlett Powlett and the Hon. William Herbert were thrown out in favour of a more violently anti-Establishment address proposed by Cobbett (making a rare personal appearance). Nor were the supporters of such addresses the lowest riff-raff, but as at the

Hampshire meeting 'the principal tradesmen and yeomanry from all parts of the county, persons able to spare the time and afford the expence of carriages and horses . . . sober, intelligent men of property—fair representation of the sense and integrity of this county.'[113]

The upper-class politicians had in fact lost the confidence of the majority of the middle classes, whose complaisance, as voters and tenants, they relied on. There was widespread disgust at the Duke of York being allowed to expiate his offence merely by resigning: Southey thought:

> 'The majority of the House of Commons stand now towards the people of England in the predicament of Jurors who have given a false verdict wilfully and corruptly. They have betrayed their trust, and a dismal thing it is to think with what a dead palsy it will strike all honest men, except those who are prepared to welcome the day of revolution come when and how it may.'[114]

The opposition was blamed as much as the government. Wardle himself turned down his election to the Whig Club, to which he had been proposed by Madocks and seconded by Whitbread,[115] and he told a meeting at 'The Crown and Anchor' on 23 May 1809 that 'in the avowal of corruption, the great factions, "The Talents" and "No Popery" were quite agreed.' At the Liverpool dinner one of the speakers, Colonel George Williams of the Liverpool Volunteers proclaimed:

> 'I divide the nation into two great parties—those who fatten upon corruption and those who are a prey to corruption— *(Applause)*—All other subdivisions of parties I disregard: for experience has shewn that the opposition come forward upon pitiful and trifling objects: but that when any question of vital importance is agitated, they desert the cause of the people;—*(loud Applauses)*—What did the late ministers do? they who were 'the talents', when out of office; but who proved to have no talents when in?—what did they do but copy their predecessors in dividing the public plunder, and in fostering abuses? *(Applauses)*—Late events, Gentlemen, have proved that the people must, for the redress of grievances, rely upon their own exertions.'[116]

But at the same dinner the greatest applause was reserved for a clergyman who, referring to the French Revolution in the course of a particularly violent anti-Establishment speech, went on to say:

> 'I am persuaded that for the tranquility which we have enjoyed in very critical times, we are in a great degree indebted to the sense which the nation at large has entertained of the private virtues of our beloved sovereign.'[17]

Such distinctions betweeen the King personally, and the rest of the upper class, which were at the base of Horne Tooke's political philosophy, boded ill for the established political parties.

The Break-down of the Reform Offensive
It is possible that with the public mood so favourable to reform, a well-organized campaign might have achieved a great deal in the way of legislative change, but in the aftermath of the Duke of York scandal no such well-organized campaign developed. Wardle had done well, speaking from a brief, but he had not the talent to exploit the situation he had helped create. Before the year was out he was totally discredited as a result of Mrs Clarke taking him to court to make him pay for furniture which, apparently, he had promised her as the price of her evidence. Folkestone took his former mistress's part, and when a subscription was launched to collect money, he refused to support it.[118]

Folkestone himself seems to have looked around for some new grounds for attacking the Establishment. He toyed with the idea of exposing yet another of the King's military sons, HRH the Duke of Cumberland, who was guilty of ordering a Berkshire militia unit to buy meat from a regular contractor at a price higher than was available from other suppliers.[119] There was also a plan for a bill to exclude members of the royal family from all official posts.[120] But none of Folkestone's contacts encouraged these schemes. His new friend Althorp warned:

'What is generally called the thinking part of the community, but which I should rather call the prejudiced part, have not sufficiently recovered from the influence of Pitt's diabolical doctrines, not to be on the constant alarm for fear of some attempt at Jacobinism.'[121]

One or two other MPs attempted to expose other scandals. Sir Charles Pole (one of the Earl of St Vincent's most loyal partisans) attacked the arrears and inefficiency of the Victualling Board on 21 March 1809, but his motion was defeated *nem. con.* A motion by the Foxite Lord Archibald Hamilton accusing Viscount Castlereagh of abusing Indian patronage for electoral purposes while President of the Board of Control in 1805 caused some public sensation but was defeated 217 to 167 on 25 April, and a motion by Wardle's partner Madocks accusing Perceval as well as Castlereagh of malpractice in parliamentary elections was defeated 310 to 85 on 11 May. Folkestone proposed a general enquiry into abuses on 17 April, but it was generally felt that such an enquiry would only serve to maintain popular excitement, and it was defeated 178 to 30. On 8 May Henry Martin proposed several resolutions arising out of the third report of the finance committee appointed in 1807, on the subject of reducing public expenditure. The government at first seemed favourable but when Martin proceeded to practical details and on 8 June proposed the suppression of sinecures, he was defeated without a division. It would appear that the party leaders now felt that public support for reform was already on the wane.

During the debate on Madocks' motion, Tierney accused all the supporters of reform of having ulterior motives. He spoke of a ' "no-party" party' who generally supported government because 'a weak administration might be more valuable to those who had such views', and said, 'One of the most remarkable characteristics of this party was the attention which it paid to stage effect, in carefully concealing the ultimate object at which it aimed'.[122] These sneers were aimed at the various independent MPs, from Wardle, Folkestone and Martin to Wilberforce, Bankes and the Thornton brothers, who had come forward as critics of public corruption, and thereby upstaged the Fox-Grenville opposition. At the same time, while even the conservative Grenvilles wished to be thought 'not so intolerant as to put down every man for a Jacobin who entertains the question of the possibility of any reform',[123] the opposition was virtually siding with the government in trying to fend off reform. And yet, in order to maintain their claim to be a populist party, the Whigs had to be supposed to be at the forefront of reform. It was for this reason that Grey informed the House of Lords, on 21 April,

'To the principles of reform, to a temperate, intelligible and definite reform I have been always and still continue, a friend. To promote that desirable end was, I contend, the study of the last Administration, and I can answer for it that no man is more friendly to such an object than my noble friend near me'.[124]

His noble and adjacent friend was of course the tremblingly reactionary Lord Grenville.

The only far-ranging proposal of reform made during these weeks was a motion by Madocks on parliamentary reform. Madocks had consulted no one in drawing up his motion, and even Burdett was displeased.[125] Folkestone objected to Madocks' motion as 'particularly dangerous, both to the Cause of the overthow of Corruption & to the Country'.[126] The critics of abuses feared that such a theoretical issue would divert public attention away from more practical matters. As Viscount Milton wrote:

'I cannot conceive anything more acceptable to Government & all the other protectors of corruption than the discussion of Parliamentary reform, for it is sure to engross public attention to a very great degree & consequently to draw it away from the other object.'[127]

In addition, even Folkestone objected to parliamentary reform on principle. He explained to a London reformer,

'My objections apply solely to a Reform of the Representation — & by no means to a Reform of the Members such as the exclusion of Placemen Pensioners &c — or to any Reform . . . such as the shortening of Parliaments.'[128]

In the end the motion was taken over by Burdett, with Madocks seconding, and was easily defeated on 15 June.

Just such a reform of details as Folkestone approved was proposed early in May by a Foxite back-bencher, John Christian Curwen. Curwen did not consult the opposition front bench before announcing his bill; he claimed he had discussed it only with Thomas Coke, who, like himself, was a county MP, leading agricultural improver, and in some respects an embodiment of the old 'Country Party' mentality of the previous century.[129] Curwen's proposal was to prohibit the purchase of parliamentary boroughs. He claimed that the measure would tend to 'the re-establishment of this house in the good opinion of the people', and that,

'By the alterations I propose, a larger proportion of the landed interest would appear among us. . . . the peculiar advantage of having the landed proprietor in the house, is that each individual brings with him the affections and the confidence of a portion of the people. . . . It would give a different tone to our councils. It would check the rage for foreign commerce, and the acquisition of fresh colonies. It would turn our efforts and our attention to domestic improvements.'[130]

In other words, he conceived his bill as a restorative one. Like many opposition MPs he believed that the emergent industrial and commercial sectors were more favourable to the Pittite than to the Foxite tradition, and he hoped to strengthen the opposition at the same time as placating the reformers. His ideal of a House of Commons of independent country squires was very much in keeping with the 'Country Party' ideology of 80 years previously — rather oddly in view of the fact that as well as being an improving landlord he was the second largest colliery owner in the thriving Cumberland coalfield, and therefore involved in the new commercial system.

At first Curwen's bill was generally supported in the Commons, though it was bitterly criticized by Windham who, since leaving office, had developed a 'systematic repugnance to every proposition that savours of reformation which turns all his wisdom to foolishness'.[131] In committee, however, the bill underwent extensive surgery at the hands of Perceval, who, according to Ponsonby, left only three and a half lines of the original draft.[132] His crucial alteration was in suppressing the phrase 'or implied' in the clause prohibiting contracts for money 'express or implied'. This favoured the government, whose powers of patronage enabled them to pay in kind as well as in cash. The bill was then carried through thin

Houses by government majorities, and was actually introduced into the Lords by the government leader in that house, the Earl of Liverpool (the former Lord Hawkesbury). Thus the session, which had been so unfortunate for both the government and the opposition, ended with a substantial tactical victory for the government.

6
The Collapse of the Portland Ministry

Canning and Castlereagh

BOTH within the government and the opposition it was realized that the existing party organization was inadequate to resist the new pressures, and towards the end of March 1809, in both the government and the opposition, preparations began to be made to replace weak links.

In opposition the weak link was the uninspiring Ponsonby. It has been argued that the opposition leaders wished to retire Ponsonby to placate Whitbread who was jealous of him.[1] It is true that Whitbread had been irritated at Ponsonby's promotion, and his share in the debates on the Duke of York scandal had confirmed his own standing as a major figure, but Grey and Grenville looked beyond the need to conciliate him. They wished to retire Ponsonby in order to bring forward Lord Henry Petty, who they believed would have more success as a Commons leader, if given 'both the means and the desire of opposing himself steadily to the new standard that is raising.'[2] But Ponsonby was reprieved because Whitbread decided at this juncture to declare all party connection between himself and the opposition at an end,[3] thus enabling Ponsonby to argue that with Whitbread separated from their party he would in future be better able to control the back-benchers.[4] Grey and Grenville had been so embarrassed at having to ask the leader they had created to step down that with characteristic weakness of purpose they agreed to Ponsonby's arguments. As Fitzwilliam pointed out, 'Everything is due from the Party, or at least from the Principal persons in it, to Geo. P. He did not thrust himself into that situation.'[5] Ponsonby therefore remained leader, even though the grounds for his retention did not materialize, as Whitbread soon gave up the idea of breaking off contact with the party.

Within the government the weak link was identified as Castlereagh, and whereas the position of Ponsonby was canvassed in private, the attempt to oust Castlereagh ended in such a blaze of publicity, and was so much more complex in its underlying causes, that it deserves lengthy consideration.

On 24 March 1809 Canning sent an ultimatum to the Duke of Portland. He attributed the government's loss of credit in recent months to its readiness to take blame for circumstances out of its control, 'a conduct . . . which . . . appears to me to have arisen from a spirit of compromise, from a desire to avoid meeting difficulties in front, and a hope of getting round them by arrangement'. He asked that the cabinet should be reconstructed:

> 'If that should be impracticable, my next wish is, that your Grace may not take it unkindly if I desire to withdraw myself from a share in the responsibiity for a system in my judgement, so little adequate to the crisis in which the country and the world are placed.'[6]

The letter did not mention Castlereagh specifically, though it is possible Canning had already voiced his dissatisfaction with Castlereagh in the course of talks he had had with Portland during the previous November and December. But in the discussions with Portland resulting from this letter, he made it clear that Castlereagh had to go, and that the Marquess Wellesley should replace him at the War Department.

It is true that Castlereagh could be blamed for the disasters in the Peninsula, which had begun the government's loss of credit, and it was true, too, that Lord Archibald Hamilton's attack on Castlereagh's abuse of Indian patronage stood to embarrass the ministry further. In a subsequent letter to Portland on 5 May Canning claimed that Hamilton's revelations in themselves would have been sufficient grounds for Castlereagh's removal. But since Castlereagh was not responsible for the government's failure to moderate the violence of back-benchers in the Commons, it is difficult to see what improvement of the parliamentary situation Cannning expected from his replacement, especially by a peer. Canning himself later said that he had not himself suggested Castlereagh's removal but had merely acquiesced in it, '*not* because I had any personal liking to it, *not* because I thought it cured all the evil, but *simply* out of deference to a suggestion of *the King's*'.[7] This was mere equivocation: Canning wanted any number of changes, but he certainly regarded the replacement of Castlereagh by Wellesley as the first priority.

It seems clear that Canning imagined the excitement aroused by the Duke of York case was just a passing frenzy and that having no understanding of how substantial the grounds were for popular discontent, he supposed that all that was needed to restore the ministry in public esteem was a more brilliant war minister. In spite of his courting of middle-class opinion in the 1820s, it is quite evident from his private correspondence that Canning had not the least sensitivity to, or even curiosity about the public mood, and his sense of political realities was in this respect much more limited than was the case with most of his colleagues. His intimate correspondence is almost unique amongst that of public men of the period in that it contains not one reflection or speculation on the popular ferments of these years. Even during the Burdett riots all he had to discuss with his wife was how he could best exploit the crisis to better his political position. To his friends and especially to his wife he wrote enormously long self-revealing letters, every page of which proclaimed his passionate self-centredness. Few men can have risen to positions of such power and responsibility and remained as single-mindedly obsessed with their personal careers as Canning was, and this was undoubtedly a factor in his desire to have Castlereagh replaced, for he had long regarded the latter as a rival.

Castlereagh was only ten months older than Canning, and only slightly more elevated in social rank, being heir to a brand-new Irish marquisate whereas Canning was brother-in-law to the heir of a long-established English dukedom. They were in fact quite closely connected by marriage, Castlereagh's half-sister being married to Canning's first cousin and namesake, later Lord Garvagh. The two men on one occasion joined in soliciting the Irish government for a post for their relative.[8] Personally two men could not have been more different:

> 'Lord Castlereagh was an obscure orator, garnishing his speeches with confused metaphors. . . . He had no classical quotation, no happy illustration, no historical examples with which to adorn argument and enforce conviction. . . . He was, as a man of business, clear, diligent, and decided. His temper was admirable—bold and calm, good-humoured and dispassionate. He was a thorough gentleman; courteous, jealous of his own honour, but full of regard for the feelings of others. No one doubted his personal integrity, however much they might dislike his policy.'[9]

He was also remarkably handsome and brave. No one was better suited to the taste of the majority of MPs, squires of commonplace intellects, businesslike in the management of their estates, fond of hunting and shooting, and too unimaginative to be anything but as brave, frank and honourable as the ethos of the time required.

Canning was the complete opposite. He lacked Castlereagh's manly open-air demeanour. He seemed bred for the drawing room. He *did* have the apposite metaphors, the apt quotations, the happy illustrations. He had also the arrogance, prickliness and bad-temper which Castlereagh lacked. Moreover, he was jealous of Castlereagh, jealous because Castlereagh had been a Cabinet minister while Canning himself was still in subordinate office, jealous because in the last months of Pitt's life Pitt had treated Castlereagh with more confidence than he had shown his old favourite. As early as 1802 Canning had complained of his rival, 'He has taken precisely that line in Parliament which P laid down for *me*.'[10] In the spring of 1804 Canning had hoped for Castlereagh's ruin along with Addington's, gloating after a talk with Pitt, 'No shabby tenderness, except for Cast. —& for him in a much less *whiny* way than before.'[11] Yet when Addington resigned, Pitt continued Castlereagh in office. Perhaps at this stage Canning was more jealous of Hawkesbury, but during the Grenville ministry Hawkesbury dropped behind in the race for influence and it was Castlereagh whom Canning began to recognize as his chief competitor. Unable to appreciate his qualities, Canning both despised and envied the other man. Perhaps curiously, for they sometimes appear as two antithetical figures in Tory politics, especially because of a pretended distinction between their foreign policy in the 1820s, their views on fundamental issues like parliamentary reform and catholic relief seem to have been similar, but these issues were never at dispute between them. It was frustration at the failure of their joint war policy, and a belief that Wellesley, that other drawing-room genius, would be a more creditable colleague and would contribute more to 'the well doing of the Govt & .... *my* personal weight & consequence in the Cabinet' that persuaded Canning to act.'[12]

Having talked to Canning about his ultimatum, Portland turned for advice first to Earl Bathurst and then, at the latter's urging, to Earl Camden. Canning meanwhile canvassed Wellesley, Rose, the Speaker of the Commons, and the Hon. Robert Saunders Dundas.[13] As the person in the Cabinet most closely bound to Castlereagh by ties of kinship and mutual obligation, Camden was made responsible for safeguarding Castlereagh's interests pending the decision to tell Castlereagh himself. Camden asked Canning whether he thought Castlereagh should resign before Lord Archibald Hamilton's motion on abuse of Indian patronage came up in Parliament. Canning, not wishing to commit himself or to seem too eager, replied, 'upon such a point a man must judge for himself.'[14] Unfortunately Camden took this as an excuse not to say anything at all to Castlereagh. Eldon was told on 24 May.[15] News of the intrigue leaked out to the opposition at about the same time,[16] possibly through Canning's intimates, Lord Granville Leveson or Lord Boringdon, both of whom knew by early April and both of whom were friends of Lord Holland.[17] But Castlereagh had not the slightest inkling of what was going on.

We now come to the by-plot. Three days before his ultimatum to Portland, Canning had suggested to Castlereagh the seizure of the

French fleet at Flushing.[18] During preliminary discussion of this project Canning began to see in it a particular advantage. Portland was thinking of retirement, and had already mentioned the possibility to the King.[19] Canning did not want Portland replaced by too active and too dominating a leader. He saw that the best candidate for the role of figurehead premier would be the Earl of Chatham; but though Chatham was by now the father of the Cabinet, his indolence was such that he had not the least public reputation save as Pitt's brother. He needed to be brought forward. The Flushing expedition (known to posterity as the Walcheren expedition) seemed an ideal opportunity, and so Canning 'fully persuaded that the Walcheren expedition must succeed. . . . urged Lord Chatham's appointment to its command.'[20]

Meanwhile, disturbed by Portland's tardiness in dismissing Castlereagh, Canning offered his own resignation to the King on 31 May. It was refused.[21] In his next letter to Portland Canning again spoke of resignation, and returned to the matter of the Indian patronage, which in his opinion required Castlereagh's 'atonement'.[22]

It was now three months since Canning's ultimatum to Portland, and Portland had still not decided to act. On 21 June Parliament was prorogued and the Walcheren expedition was finally approved by the Cabinet. Next day Portland told Perceval of the plan to remove Castlereagh. Perceval found a new reason for further procrastination. As he wrote to Canning on 25 June,

'that Castlereagh should have been permitted, by those who knew how this discussion was likely to terminate, to be preparing and arranging one of the most important and extensive military expeditions which this country ever set on foot, and that he should be told, just as it is about to be executed, that he must resign his situation, remaining responsible, in great part at least, for the arrangement, and being deprived of the superintendance of the execution, is what I think cannot be intended.'[23]

Though Portland promised to tell Castlereagh after the expedition had sailed, he changed his mind later. Canning, vainly offering up his own resignation once again, was forced to acquiesce. As a sop to his patience, Lord Granville Leveson, his bosom friend, and a man personally hostile to most of the other ministers, was appointed to the Cabinet as Secretary at War on 7 July, without any consultation by Portland of other ministers.[24] Tierney later thought it was this appointment which 'laid the foundation of all that has happened'.[25] At the same time, as a counter-weight to Lord Granville Leveson, Lord Harrowby was reappointed to the Cabinet as President of the Board of Control.

Liverpool, Chatham and Harrowby were told of the scheme to

oust Castlereagh in the second week of July. Liverpool immediately
lent his weight to the view that it would be 'an act of manifest
cruelty and injustice' to dismiss Castlereagh so long as the Walcheren
expedition was in the balance.[26] Like Bathurst and Camden before
him, Liverpool offered to resign to facilitate a reshuffle. At this
point Canning, after one last remonstration on 18 July, gave up
badgering Portland and settled down to await the event of Chatham's
great expedition.

Chatham sailed on 28 July, and his troops began to go ashore on
the dunes on the north coast of Walcheren early in the morning of 30
July. The expedition was almost instantly bogged down in its advance
on Flushing. The opposition were at first inclined to attribute the
blame to the 'total want of arrangement, of information, of common
precaution on the part of our Ministers',[27] but the real reason was
the dilatoriness of Chatham himself. The news of the Hon. Sir
Arthur Wellesley's victory at Talavera, which also occurred on 28
July could not conceal the fact that the ministers were faced with
yet another disgrace. But that was not all. On 11 August Portland
suffered a bad stroke.

The Break-up of the Ministry

Portland was too ill to remain premier, but there was now no question
of Chatham succeeding him. At first it was supposed that Harrowby,
or possibly Bathurst, would become Prime Minister.[28] Harrowby
was semi-invalid, and 'lost ground amongst his friends by crotchets,
and too much doggedness in his own views',[29] but in other respects
he was well qualified: 'His Talents, His Character and above all the
Cordial affection which for so many years united Him with Pitt as a
private & political Friend, would point him out equally to the feelings
& to the Judgement of Pitt's other Friends.'[30] But neither Harrowby
nor Bathurst were sufficiently malleable for Canning's taste and
after some reflection he insisted that Portland's successor should be
a member of the House of Commons.[3] Portland did not resign
immediately however.

On 2 September the Cabinet decided on withdrawal from Walcheren,
and Canning wrote to Portland (now somewhat recovered) insisting
that the promised change—that is, Castlereagh's removal—should
at last take place. Portland consulted Perceval who advised that a
total reconstruction of the Cabinet was now necessary, and persuaded
Portland to resign. Perceval saw Canning next day, and the latter
again insisted that the new premier should be in the Commons.[32]
Perceval had already told Canning he refused to give up his own
leadership in the Commons to serve under Canning.[33] To his own
brother Perceval explained:

'Public men are, for their means of public utility, the creatures, in great measure, of public opinion; and if, as I much fear would be the case, such a sacrifice would be felt by my friends and the public as a degradation which I ought not to submit to, the submitting to it might much abridge my means of future service to the King and the country.'[34]

Canning in fact was insisting that *he* should be Prime Minister, and Perceval was no less determined that he should not. When Bathurst discussed the matter with the King on 6 September, the King said, 'He was anxious to keep Mr. Canning, who he thought essential to his Government, but if he was driven to choose between the two, he would choose Mr. Perceval, who was the most straightforward man he had almost ever known.'[35] Canning did not know George III's opinion, of course. He was confident that his threats of resignation would eventually force his colleague into line.

On 6 September Portland announced his resignation. There was a Cabinet meeting the same day, which Canning refused to attend, accusing Portland of resigning 'only from a desire of retaining Lord Castlereagh'.[36] At the Cabinet meeting Castlereagh asked the reason for Canning's absence, and now at last Camden brought himself to blurt out the truth. Castlereagh was dumbfounded. He had suspected nothing. Thomas Lawrence of the Royal Academy, who called on Castlereagh next day to paint his portrait, found him in the depths of depression:

Lawrence never saw any man who appeared to be more sunk in His spirits than His Lordship appeared to be. — He spoke very little, quite unlike what He had done before, — and while He stood for Lawrence to look at His figure, He seemed to be a figure of woe; & Lawrence observed Him more than once to wipe His eyes.'[37]

On 8 September he, too, resigned.

For the next three days it was an open question whether Canning would after all accept a nominal replacement of Portland and stay in the ministry. 'There is no doubt that Lord Bathurst is silly enough, and I should say bold enough to agree to stand in the Duke of Portland's shoes', reported Fremantle.[38] On 12 September, however, Canning wrote a letter to Portland, to be shown to the King. In this he insisted on the necessity of an active Prime Minister, and refused categorically to serve under Perceval:

'I trust indeed that neither your Grace nor His Majesty would think the worse of me, if I avow those ordinary feelings of human nature which would preclude my remaining in office [under Perceval]. But I should carry out of office with me the most sincere and undiminished personal goodwill towards Perceval . . . amongst the alternatives which I have stated, far from preferring that which motives of personal ambition might be supposed to recommend to my preference, my sincere wish is to be enabled to retire.'[39]

Next day Canning saw the King and though he spoke in some detail of his hopes of being Prime Minister, George III gave him no encouragement. The King's decision was already made. Though this last letter of Canning's had been meant only as yet another ultimatum, the King chose to accept what Canning had mentioned only as a threat—Canning's own resignation.

For the next week the situation was confused. Canning looked to his personal followers. Rose, to whom he had broached the question of Castlereagh's replacement in April, now refused to play the game. 'Old Rose came to me today—cried, & remains Treasurer of the Navy.'[40] Fortunately for Canning's scheme, Huskisson one of the Secretaries of the Treasury, and Sturges Bourne, one of the Treasury Lords, had been anxious to resign for some time, though a letter written by Sturges Bourne to Rose suggests that disapproval of Canning was one of their reasons for disliking office:

'I see much of management in political matters that disgusts me. I need only instance that ruinous appointment by which the safety of a large army has been hazarded, the success of an important enterprise, and the credit of the country sacrificed, by selecting, for indirect motives I am sure, a man to conduct an expedition whom *all* those who consented to his appointment must have felt to be the most unfit for that special service.'[41]

Whatever their motives, however, Sturges Bourne and Huskisson were in effect backing up Canning. Their resignation, along with Canning's, would certainly render the ministry too weak to survive. The rump of the Cabinet, meeting on 18 September, decided that there was no hope but to apply to the opposition, but as the King still set his face against Catholic relief there was no prospect of any such application succeeding. Beyond that there was no alternative but capitulation to Canning.

But Canning's prospects of ultimate success were shattered by an unexpected development on 19 September. A few days earlier Canning had remarked complacently to his wife, 'Castlereagh has disappeared, as through a trap door.'[42] Castlgh had in fact been brooding, and the result of his brooding appeared on 19 September in the shape of a challenge to Canning. This was not altogether fair on Canning. As his second was later to remark, 'Canning has been fighting the poor old Duke's duel, or Lord Camden's, or that of any of the different friends of Castlereagh who insisted on concealment rather than his own.'[43] Yet Castlereagh saw clearly enough that the business had originated with Canning, and he felt that Canning's not demanding his removal by *name* involved an empty distinction, as Canning's objective had been evident enough: 'It may have been intended to convey the idea, that the person who supplied the name concurred in the measure.'[44]

But to say that Castlereagh had grounds for blaming Canning is not sufficient explanation for his challenging him to a duel. According to Lord Holland, 'The conduct of Lord Castlereagh, who was an excellent marksman, and had practised with pistols to qualify himself for the Irish House of Commons, seemed dictated by a thirst of vengeance, rather than by a sense of wounded honour.'[45] Wilberforce called the challenge 'a cold-blooded measure of deliberate revenge'.[46] Canning's wife seemed to feel this too, and complained bitterly of Castlereagh who, she said, knew himself 'to be the best shot in the country'.[47]

Perhaps these accusations will seem less startling when it is remembered that in the United States at this time there were frequent duels between public figures (all of them originally British subjects by birth) in which the homicidal intention was too evident to be denied. For example, there was the duel between Aaron Burr and Alexander Hamilton in which the latter was killed. Possibly Castlereagh, finding himself apparently betrayed by all his colleagues, regarded his political career as over, and with his natural outrage exacerbated by the possible triumph of his rival, decided to involve that rival at least in his own destruction. He had certainly shown himself thicker-skinned on many other occasions, and he must have known that the duel, rather than vindicating his honour, would guarantee the publications of the extent to which he had been his colleagues' dupe. Yet perhaps the disapproving Wilberforce was right in thinking that the challenge was merely the stock response of the hard-living country gentleman that Castlereagh was, who naturally turned to his pistols as 'an expedient for restoring him in some degree to his level, and putting him in good humour with himself, as a man who had obtained satisfaction for the insult'.[48] Certainly, it was in keeping with current attitudes that Castlereagh should suppose that the activities of public men were guided by the same rules of honour and straight dealing as governed private conduct.

Canning for his part, frustrated by the way events were turning against him, accepted the challenge with alacrity. Characteristically, he tried to capitalize on the duel in order to make sure of the Marquess Wellesley, whose participation in any future government would be vital. On receiving the challenge he sent for the Hon. Henry Wellesley, youngest of the Marquis' brothers, and Huskisson's fellow Secretary to the Treasury, and asked him to be his second. 'I have always been at a loss to account for Canning's motive for applying to me on this occasion', recorded Henry Wellesley, 'for although I had known him all my life we had never lived in great intimacy. I have sometimes thought that he might have a political motive.'[49] Indeed it is inconceivable that Canning did not. Wellesley sagely refused and Canning turned instead to an old friend, Charles Ellis.

Canning and Castlereagh met on Putney Heath two days later. Castlereagh, true to his breeding, showed impeccable sangfroid. On the way to the meeting he discussed opera with his second, the Earl of Yarmouth. 'I conclude it is not your wish to render this Business more desperate than is necessary', Yarmouth told Ellis when they arrived at the Heath, and they marked out 12 paces, which the experienced Yarmouth claimed 'was the longest distance of which there was any precedent'[50]—in fact Lord Camelford had been shot dead at 30 paces less than six years earlier.[51] At the second fire Canning was hit in the thigh: 'a very good wound, as wounds go', commented Ellis, 'but an inch more to the right would have killed him.'[52]

George III heard about the duel on the same day 'but was not affected, though he thought it very silly and wrong'.[53] Amongst the public at large the duel caused a sensation. It naturally raised the question of who was at fault, the challenger or the challenged, and for the most part it was Canning who was blamed. This added to his already established reputation for intrigue. Later, when he sent a justification of his conduct to the Earl of Lonsdale (the former Viscount Lowther and a one time close ally) 'and afterwards called on him having begged to explain himself', he was refused admittance.[54]

Having vindicated his honour Castlereagh held aloof from further discussion. 'I have declined any confidence, having quite enough to do to save my reputation from being buried in the ruins of Intrigue, Shabbiness, and Incapacity', he told his brother Lord Charles Stewart.[55] Camden naturally hastened to make his peace:

'After the duel he came to my house in a state of great agitation and broke into my room in tears, condemning himself and stating his wretchedness. Under these circumstances, I gave him my hand and told him I must acquit him of any motives deliberately unkind to me, but that I never could forget the political injury he had exposed me to, and I stated to him in the strongest terms what I felt both of the determination to sacrifice me to Canning, and of the danger to which my character and honour had been exposed by the delusions practised on me.'[56]

Probably several other of the ministers shared Camden's sense of shame, but they had no time for tears and breast-beating, for the country was now in its third week without a proper administration.

Attempts at Reconstruction

On 24 September Perceval wrote to Grey and Grenville asking them to discuss with him the future government of the country. Grey refused even to leave his home in Northumberland. Grenville, wondering whether the King 'repents of the dark intrigues in which he engaged against us',[57] posted up from Cornwall, but on discovering that Grey was not coming to London, wrote to Perceval from Camelford House expressing the impossibility of joining what was left of the Cabinet. 'My objections are not personal', he wrote, 'they apply to the principle of the government itself, and to the circumstances which attended its appointment.'[58] For the next week the opposition amused themselves debating whether Grenville should have stayed in Cornwall or whether Grey should have come down from Northumberland. There was little discussion of whether they actually wanted to return to office. Thomas Grenville argued that 'without complete liberty of choice both as to men & measures, I do think it would be an act of the most absolute folly & madness to take the responsibility of government in such a state of things as now prevails',[59] and Windham probably spoke of the majority when he wrote it was 'difficult, indeed, to say what good we could do, if we had the affair all in our own hands. . . . for great and beneficial measures I know not what they are to be'.[60]

The Cabinet meeting of 18 September had decided that Sidmouth's group was too weak to offer any worthwhile reinforcement, especially as its accession might antagonize Canning's friends, but with the hope of an alliance with the opposition lost, and with further application to Canning now put out of the question by the scandal ensuing from the duel, the rump of the Cabinet had nowhere else to turn. On 5 October Chatham called on Sidmouth and told him that though he could not be offered any office himself, he was requested to prevail upon his friends to join the ministry.[61] Staggered by this proposal Sidmouth could only recommend a renewed approach to Grey and Grenville.[62] Next day Perceval wrote to Sidmouth what the latter called 'a most extraordinary Letter' again stating the impossibility of including Sidmouth in any Cabinet, for fear of bringing down the wrath of Canning, but offering the Secretaryship at War and a seat in the Cabinet for Sidmouth's brother-in-law Bragge Bathurst. Perceval's real object was to secure the services of Vansittart, another Sidmouthite, as Chancellor of the Exchequer, but Sidmouth turned his offers down.

The rump of the Cabinet had by now decided to carry on as best they could with the stubborn but uncharismatic Perceval as Prime Minister, but with Huskisson gone Perceval was desperate to have a Chancellor of the Exchequer to assist him at the Treasury, and there were also two Secretaryships of State and several minor offices to dispose of. The Exchequer was offered to Viscount Palmerston (who had only ever spoken *once* in Parliament), to Pemberton Milnes, and finally, late in October, to Rose. Rose refused on the grounds that he was needed at the Board of Trade, and that he was too old at 65 to make his début as a Cabinet minister, besides which, believing as he did in the 'absolute and indispensable necessity' of reducing public expenditure, he feared Perceval would allow him no scope to carry out the policies he desired.[63] Finally, Perceval retained the Exchequer himself. Other posts went begging, such was the general conviction that the ministry was too weak to survive. Lord William Bentinck turned down the Secretaryship at War which was afterwards claimed by Palmerston as more to his taste than the Exchequer. Sir Evan Nepean, Earl Percy and Lord Brooke all refused seats on the Treasury Board.[64] The Earl of Powis, when asked, refused to urge his son to accept office.[65] The Hon. Frederick Robinson turned down the Under-Secretaryship of State in the War Department, or a seat on a board, because 'by embarking in a crazy vessel, I may chance to go to the bottom with the rest, for wrecked I believe they will be at the commencement of the Session'.[66]

Perceval was a little lucker with the vacant Secretaryships of State. Since the Marquess Wellesley had been brought forward by Canning to succeed Castlereagh, Canning's partisans hoped initially that the Marquess would hold aloof from the new arrangement, but Wellesley's own entourage of sycophants had lost no time in making sure that their patron would not side with the ruined minister. Colonel Sydenham wrote several letters to Wellesley (then on an embassy to Spain) putting the worst construction on Canning's behaviour, not failing to point out, for example, that Canning's insistence that the next Prime Minister should be in the Commons 'must operate to the exclusion of your claims, as well as those of all the nobility'.[67] Sydenham was commissioned by Perceval on 5 October to convey to Wellesley the offer of the Foreign Department. Wellesley had no hestitation in accepting. With regard to his obligation to Canning, he told his brother, the Hon. William Wellesley Pole:

'It is not difficult to perceive the distinction between a disposition to serve with a Minister and an engagement to act with him in or out of office, for the purpose of forcing him into any particular station against the wishes of his colleagues of his party, of his Sovereign, and even against the opinion of all those in my own favour.'[68]

The War Department was offered to the Hon. Robert Saunders Dundas. There had been some talk of Saunders Dundas' father, the ruined Viscount Melville, returning to office, but Perceval had been advised against this by Rose and Long.[60] Nevertheless Melville's support was counted on, and Perceval wrote to him frankly confessing the impossibility of giving him a Cabinet post but offering him an earldom.[70] Melville's response was to write a bland acknowledgement to Perceval, and to advise his son privately not to support the ministers.

Consequently Saunders Dundas withdrew his initial acceptance of the seals on 24 October, to the 'utter disappointment and dismay' of his prospective colleagues.[71] This was doubly unfortunate as Charles Yorke had earlier refused to join the Cabinet except as Secretary of State, and had had to be turned down because the post was on offer to Saunders Dundas.[72] Saunders Dundas finally accepted the Board of Control, and Liverpool moved from the Home to the War Department. His successor as Home Secretary was the Hon. Richard Ryder, the brother of Lord Harrowby and one of Perceval's closest friends, but a man deficient both in talent and experience.

Two and a half years previously the Portland Ministry had taken office with a certain enthusiasm for its task of defending Church and King from the Whigs, and with confidence in its claim to be vindicating the policy of Pitt. The new ministry had no such enthusiasm or confidence. Lonsdale, described earlier in the year as a 'principle & indeed solitary ... buttress' of the Portland Ministry[73] regarded its successor with coldness. The new ministers seemed insignificant men: 'In the whole of the list there is no one man of old property, weight & influence in the country but that ideot Lord Westmoreland', complained Wynn.[74] Wellesley, new to the Cabinet and soon to be estranged from his colleagues, had his own private sense of mission. The others saw themselves only as the last ditch defenders of a lost cause. They realized that the crisis 'would break up, if not destroy, the remains of the Pitt party'.[75] It was doubtful if Perceval and Liverpool, who had first risen to prominence under Addington, could even be regarded as *pure Pittites*.[76] As Perceval explained to Melville,

'We are no longer the sole representatives of Mr Pitt. The magic of that name is in a great degree dissolved, and the principle upon which we must rely to keep us together, and to give us the assistance of floating strength, is the public sentiment of loyalty and attachment to the King.'[77]

In the aftermath of failure abroad and scandal at home, with an opposition of unprecedented strength, and with half of Pitt's disciples at odds with the government, it seemed little enough to go on with.

7

The Perceval Ministry

The Marquess Wellesley

SHORTLY after becoming Foreign Secretary, Wellesley told a friend:

> 'I state fairly that I expect some strength from my own name; and I have no reason to doubt that I shall have a principal lead in the Government, sufficient to justify those who think favourable of me in supporting the system as being assentially mine.'[1]

Largely as a result of Wellesley's notions on this score, his colleagues found the new Foreign Secretary even more trouble than the old.

Canning had been insidious and intriguing, but, even taking the worst view, no more could be said than that he proceeded on a principle of divide and conquer. Wellesley's style was different. He took a high horse and met his antagonists head on. He tried to overwhelm rather than, as with Canning, to undermine. If, as his enemies said, vanity was Canning's secret motor, with Wellesley vanity was his leading public principle. He concealed it from no one. He even wore make-up while sitting to Lawrence for his portrait.[2]

George III complained of Wellesley, while still in India:

> 'demanding ceremonious respect much beyond what was due to his station. . . . when he had been more than once reminded that he was exacting from those about him more than the King did, his Lordship replied, "Then the King is wrong; but that is no reason why I should improperly relax also".'[3]

Even his fellow ministers sneeringly referred to him as 'The Grand Lama'. Previously there had been mixed with this enormous conceit an ingenuous self-awareness which enabled him to joke at his own vanity.[4] But after the death of Pitt, and with his increasing estrangement from Grenville after 1807, he found himself in a world which contained none that he regarded as his equal, and surrounded by a small circle of sycophants led by Colonel Benjamin Sydenham, who fostered his monstrous pride till it had far outstepped the acceptable norms of behaviour. In this respect he was extraordinarily different from his rather conventional younger brothers, William, Arthur and Henry. Of the dissimilarity between himself and Arthur, the later Duke of Wellington, it was said, 'If Virgil and Caesar, Pope and Cromwell, had been brothers, the contrast could hardly have been more striking.'[5]

Perceval, the shrimpish, skull-faced common-place Perceval, Wellesley of course despised. Amongst the other ministers he had no friend except, to begin with, Earl Bathurst who was described as 'most devoted to him'.[6] He had initially counted on as Secretary of State in the War Department the Hon. Robert Saunders Dundas, 'who was a particular friend of Lord Wellesley, and who, as a young statesman, would gladly consult Lord Wellesley's opinion on all things: so that in fact both departments would be constantly under Lord Wellesley's superintendance'.[7] Whether Wellesley's expectations of Saunders Dundas' compliance would have been fulfilled is unlikely. Saunders Dundas had a prior allegiance to his interferring father, at whose instructions he anyway refused the War Department.

Wellesley however expected his other colleagues to accept his tutelage as readily as Saunders Dundas might have done. 'None of them had acquired much fame either as war ministers or as diplomatists, and Lord Wellesley flattered himself that he would have little difficulty in persuading them to adopt *his opinions*.'[8] As anyone but Wellesley might have predicted, his attempts to lay down the law to his less fortunate colleagues were not welcomed, and as his views were often in direct conflict with those of the majority of the Cabinet his opinions were frequently over-borne. To Wellesley this was intolerable. He had taken office 'expecting confidently that he was not invited to be a mere assessor of Lords Camden, Westmorland &c'.[9] He was, moreover, passionately committed to the views he put forward, which chiefly related to the concentration of the utmost effort on the war in Spain and Portugal, and his intransigence was increased by the sense that the fortunes of his family and himself were inextricably bound up in the Peninsula War, he himself having been ambassador to the Spanish, and having been succeeded by his own brother Henry, and his brother Arthur being in command of the British troops in that theatre.

This conflict of views soon developed into personal alienation. By the end of April 1810 it was reported 'that he hates, despises, and is out of friendship, or even intimacy with every one of his colleagues'.[10] He did not cultivate his colleagues: 'He attended the Cabinet dinners pretty regularly; but he did not enter into their daily society so much as was desirable.'[11]

Wellesley's isolation within the Cabinet was aggravated by two circumstances which no one had in the least expected. One was his sex life. Prior to his leaving for India in 1797, his sexual activity had been at least monogamous, in that he had lived with, and had several children by, a Frenchwoman named Hyacinthe Gabrielle Roland. (The eldest son, Richard Wellesley, was appointed a Lord of the Treasury in January 1812). He had married Hyacinthe before his departure for India, but had left her in England and after his return they had quarrelled bitterly, and finally, early in 1810, separated. Thereafter Wellesley became increasingly involved with *demi-mondaines*.

This sort of behaviour was no longer quite as fashionable as it had once been and it is doubtful whether the Evangelicals Perceval and Ryder much approved, but it was not totally unprecedented, and in fact the Earl of Westmorland subsequently paid Wellesley back for objecting to his dozing through Cabinet meetings with his muddy boots on the table, by enticing away Wellesley's principal whore, Poll Raffles.[12] What was unprecedented was the excess of Wellesley's self-indulgence. One of his toadies, Meyrick Shawe, advised him to scotch the more scandalous rumours by going out more in society, so that 'they would not accuse him of keeping bad company when he was passing a quiet evening at home.'[13] In fact Wellesley does not seem to have spent many quiet evenings at home, let alone in his office, and his official paperwork soon fell extraordinarily into arrears. Even his brother Arthur, who may be supposed not to have paid undue attention to gossip against the head of his family, was brought to burst out:

'I wish that Wellesley was castrated, or that he would like other people attend to his business and perform too. It is lamentable to see Talents and character and advantages such as he possesses thrown away upon Whoring.'[14]

Wellesley's total inefficiency as a minister was the other thing no one had expected of him. Perhaps it was less the case that his inefficiency was the result of his debauchery than that both stemmed from his bitterness and frustration at being perpetually checked within the Cabinet. As an example of the chaos prevailing in the Foreign Department during his régime may be quoted the case of Stratford Canning, a young ambassador under great strain as minister at Constantinople where he was striving desperately to keep Turkey out of Napoleon's Continental System. In two years he received no instructions at all from Wellesley, and only 16 despatches, including seven routine acknowledgements, a request to use thicker envelopes when writing and (the most important communication of all from Wellesley) an enquiry about 'some manuscript copies of classical works supposed to have been stored away in the seraglio.'[15] In other instances, Wellesley totally ignored the usual procedures of consultation, sending out despatches and even ambassadors without telling his colleagues. Perceval learnt only by chance that Sir Robert Wilson was being sent to the Levant on a mission, 'whether to Egypt, Constantinople, Palestine or elsewhere', he did not know till he questioned Wellesley.[16] Sir James Saumarez was authorized to treat with Russia in August 1811 at such short notice that only Perceval could be told in advance.[17] This haphazardness made Cabinet meetings difficult, especially with regard to fixing the agenda. Ryder complained that as Wellesley 'lets everything go its own way, professes himself ready to bring one, two, or three points forward, not being ready on any one, there is no knowing beforehand where one is as to state of business.'[18] Yet any interference in his departmental concerns was resented. In July 1810 Perceval altered a draft despatch to the Hon. Henry Wellesley, who had to be cautioned against drawing on money for the Spanish government which was needed for the British army in Spain. The Marquess Wellesley thought the corrections were 'much stronger than the occasion requires. Indeed, all the necessary suggestions of caution appear to me to be quite clearly expressed in the original draft'.[19] What Wellesley objected to was less the bullying of his little brother by an outsider, than the fact that anyone could dare to tamper with his perfect prose style. According to Mulgrave the main cause of Wellesley's eventual resignation was 'his jealousy of having his despatches commented upon or altered by the Cabinet . . . . [he once said] he thought he was among a Cabinet of statesmen, but found them a set of critics'.[20] In this respect Wellesley differed enormously from Canning who not only was orderly and indefatigable as a head of department, but also showed, despite his competitiveness, not the least reluctance in adopting other people's suggestions at Cabinet meetings. When this was pointed out by Bathurst, Wellesley replied, 'that it might be so, but that his habits in India had not accustomed him to this.'[21]

Under almost any circumstances internecine strife with Wellesley would have absorbed much of the Cabinet's attention so long as he remained in office, but his involvement with the conduct of the war, one of the two major public issues of the day, was an added guarantee that he would hold the centre of the stage. What Wellesley failed to appreciate was that, besides the war, there was one other matter of concern to his colleagues—literally, their survival as a government. Sitting as he did in the Lords, and not even attending there very assiduously, contemptuous of all events in which he did not play a leading part, and to a great extent not identifying himself with the fate of colleagues whom he despised and expected to outlast, Wellesley never realized how insecure the ministry was in the House of Commons, nor as time went on, appreciated how far Perceval's increasing personal domination of the parliamentary situation entitled him to be a dictator within the Cabinet.

The Opposition

At the beginning of the parliamentary session of 1810, the ministry defeated an opposition amendment to the Address by a gratifying 263 to 167 votes. Three days later, however, they went down 195 to 186 on a motion for a committee of enquiry on the Walcheren campaign. This was the first defeat of a government in what was effectively a full house since 1805. Two days later, the Commons divided three times on the membership of a new finance committee. The government, not helped by the recent revelation that owing to 'too negligent a confidence in his clerk', George Villiers, the Paymaster of Marines, had defaulted on his account for 1804 to the tune of £280,000,[22] was defeated 107 to 98, 108 to 103 and 117 to 104. There were further government defeats on the Walcheren issue on 23 February, when a motion for the production of papers was carried 178 to 171, and on 6 March when Perceval tried to end the debate and was defeated 221 to 188.

These defeats were partly due to the Sidmouth, Canning and Castlereagh factions rallying to denounce Chatham, and Canning noted with regard to Perceval, 'the very helpless state in which he stands in the House of Coms without one single soul to help him in debate (for Saunders [Dundas] is dumb, & R. Ryder worse than if he were so).'[23] Chatham's bungling of the Walcheren expedition had enraged so many people both in and out of Parliament that there seemed no hope of preventing further defeats in the Commons, and a further loss of public credibility, so long as Chatham remained in the Cabinet. Chatham, however, long resisted his colleagues' pressure to resign, till Wellesley finally persuaded him 'in a long harangue'.[24] His resignation largely restored the parliamentary situation. At the end of the fourth night of the debate concluding the enquiry, in the small hours of 31 March 1810, the government defeated a motion censuring the expedition 275 to 227 and carried three motions approving the expedition 272 to 232, 275 to 224 and 255 to 232.

Having refused to resign following his defeats, as might have been expected, and having fought on to this triumphant vindication, Perceval had showed the extent of his resolution not to give way to the opposition. The opposition, having done their utmost on an issue where the government was so especially vulnerable were by the beginning of April spent and demoralized. At the beginning of the year Lord Holland had urged on Grey the revival of the issue of Catholic relief. 'The agitation of it & the preserving it as the badge & standard of the party seems to me the only means of keeping us permanently united—for on what other point do our friends agree?'[25]

Grey responded, 'As to the advantage of it as a *cause* I have only this to say that it is a cause on which you have both the King & the People against you.'[26] Holland also recommended praising the reformers when they did right and saying nothing when they did wrong: 'Nothing is so gratifying to the old & Common Enemy as seeing the Democrats and Whigs at variance and as the former have no power we are never obliged to meddle with them at all, unless we like it.' But Grey thought otherwise: 'I cannot admit that Wardle's proceedings last year did anything but the greatest mischief. It is not by such means that I shall ever wish to see the influence of the Crown reduced.' He thought the reformers 'the best friends of the Court':

> 'By directing the public attention from all useful and practicable objects, they provide the best means of escape for the Ministers from those difficulties in which their folly & wickedness have involved them.'[27]

The opposition, as this correspondence showed, seemed to be fumbling around for a new strategy, and was failing to find one.

Grey's words about the activities of reformers relieving the pressure on the ministers turned out to be prophetic. In an ill-considered attempt to reduce the public interest in the Walcheren enquiry, Charles Yorke had moved on 2 February for the exclusion of strangers—including reporters—from the gallery of the Commons. When the former Corresponding Society spokesman, John Gale Jones, advertised his attention of discussing this in a London debating society known as the British Forum, he was arrested for breach of privilege. Burdett protested against his arrest in the Commons, and published his views in Cobbett's *The Political Register* on 24 March. This, too, was regarded as a breach of privilege, and the Commons voted to have Burdett committed on 6 April. For three days he refused to submit himself to arrest. His resistance aroused tremendous public excitement. A mob ran riot, breaking the windows of many of the ministerialist party. Troops were poured into the capital. Never since the Gordon Riots had London been in such a turmoil. Finally, on 9 April, Burdett was taken into custody by main force. On the way back to their barracks after escorting him to the Tower the troops were stoned and shot at in the streets and opened fire, killing at least two rioters.

Though Burdett's imprisonment brought to an end the three days of rioting, it did not allay public excitement. Slogans were chalked up on walls in London proclaiming, 'Reform in Parliament and we shall then be Masters', 'No King', 'The Foot Guards are our Friends', 'Soldiers fight for Burdett', 'The good old Cause and no King', 'Burdett for Ever' (to which in some instances had been added 'and a Knife in his Liver').[28] Areas outside London caught the infection. From Fenstanton, Huntingdonshire, a progressive landlord reported, 'I hear my labourers discussing the subject every day; and what surprizes me is, that they all seem perfectly to understand it, and regard the cause in which he is engaged as their own.'[29] In Birmingham at the end of May, the high price of potatoes occasioned rioting, during which a hand-bill was circulated saying:

'If you want Bread Potatoes support Sir Francis Burdett and you will soon have bread potatoes beer Clothes and every thing else on reasonable terms while you permit such men as Wel--y and party at the head of Government you will be robbed of your rights and at last be starved
God save the King.'[30]

The Burdett riots and the debates in the Commons consequent on them not only distracted the opposition from any further assault on Perceval but also showed up rifts within their own ranks. Whitbread, who during the previous weeks had waived his objections to Ponsonby in order to support him on the Walcheren issue, spoke out strongly in favour of Burdett at a London Livery dinner. Lord Grenville wrote to him expressing his 'deep concern' at his speech, especially its tendency to discredit the Commons:

'From Parliament alone all the Principles of our Freedom have flowed and by Parliament alone in my judgement can they be revived and secured. . . . to weaken the authority of Parliament or to lesson its respect and confidence with the Country is not only not to promote these objects but essentially to counteract them.'[31]

Whitbread replied to this promptly enough but unhelpfully, and thereafter his separation from the rest of the opposition became an acknowledged fact. Yet amongst the more conservative of the opposition there were still misgivings at Whitbread's continuing influence. Earl Temple decided:

'I feel my attendance in Parlt cannot be of any use untill a party is formed united in itself, and acting upon defined, ascertained and fixed principles. The present Opposition is evidently not so constituted, and I do not think it necessary to furnish by my attendance fresh proof of division and difference of opinion.'[32]

At the same time, the riots rallied support to the government. Wynn remarked, 'Nothing but Burdett's violence & unprincipled folly has kept them in to the end of this Session.'[33]

An attempt to seize the middle ground was made on the initiative of Grey. On 1 May Grey, commenting on Whitbread's response to Grenville's rebuke, insisted 'The necessity of some proceeding to mark our line of conduct clearly to the public remains undiminished; on the contrary it is much increased by the progress which false principles are making in the country.'[34] Grey's plan was for a motion in both Houses 'to mark equally the line of distinction between us and the Ministers on the one hand, and those who are urging these popular questions in such pernicious modes on the other'.[35] The disarray in the Commons was such that nobody could be found in that House with the temerity to take up the idea, and when, on 13 June, in pursuance of his scheme, Grey moved for the Lords to go into committee on the state of the nation he was defeated by 71 votes and 63 proxy votes to 43 and 29 proxy votes.

Wellesley and the Cabinet Reconstruction

When Parliament was prorogued a week later Perceval could congratulate himself on having successfully confronted his parliamentary enemies. Wellesley, however, with his different perspectives, measuring success not by votes, but by Grey's debating points, and less concerned with the practical cohesion of government than with less ponderable factors such as a valid Pittite pedigree, was anxious for the Cabinet to be reconstructed. Whether Wellesley was primarily concerned to reunite as many as possible of Pitt's former followers merely because they had been Pitt's followers, or whether he primarily wished to repay his debt to Canning who had in some sense sacrificed himself to enable Wellesley to enter the Cabinet, and was unable to restore Canning to office save as part of a broader arrangement made under the guise of Pittite sentiment, is not clear.

Wellesley first broached the idea in March.[36] When discussion of the measure got under way in April the idea was 'to propose to all those several parties (Canning, Castlereagh and Sidmouth) a junction with us, upon the principle of collecting again all the remains of Pitt's friends'.[37] Eleven years later, in 1822, Castlereagh was to place the same emphasis on a scheme for a junction with the Grenvilles, in which ulterior, or indeed any practical motives, cannot easily be seen, demonstrating thereby the importance attached by Pitt's followers to the idea of uniting his shattered party.[38]

Wellesley was to approach Canning, with whom he had had a 'complete reconciliation' at the beginning of April.[39] Yorke, though not a member of the government, was commissioned to approach Sidmouth. It was only if Sidmouth was favourable to the plan that any advance was to be made to Castlereagh, as Perceval thought it 'quite impossible that he would consent to come to us with Canning except upon the principle of such an extended arrangement'.[40] Yorke's overture to Sidmouth on 24 April was 'instantly declined'.[41] Sidmouth had no wish to sit in a Cabinet with Canning. The idea of making an offer to Sidmouth and Castlereagh only was rejected by Wellesley.[42] The idea of Canning alone was barely mooted, but instantly negatived by ministers, and, surely, very wisely, for this step would instantly have thrown his declared personal enemies, Sidmouth and Castlereagh, into open opposition.[43] There was at this stage one vacancy in the Cabinet, the Admiralty, Lord Mulgrave, the First Lord, having moved to the Ordnance to replace Chatham. The Admiralty was first offered to Saunders Dundas, who felt obliged to refuse it 'unless there had been an arrangement of office in view of more strength'[44] — he had in fact resigned from the Board of Control two weeks earlier but had been persuaded to stay on at Perceval's request. The Admiralty was then offered to Yorke: a poor choice, as Wellesley pointed out, for the mediocre Yorke was already a ministerial supporter and brought with him no additional strength.[43]

As the parliamentary session drew to a close, Wellesley renewed his efforts, a reinforcement being necessitated, as he argued, by 'the present crisis, when Lord Grey has opened such an attack upon those leading principles which constituted the basis of Mr Pitt's government.'[46] Both Wellesley and Perceval met Sidmouth in a vain attempt to persuade him to withdraw his opposition to Canning, and it was finally decided, in late July, to leave Sidmouth out and make a joint offer only to Canning and Castlereagh. It took Perceval nearly three weeks to draft the letter of invitation to Castlereagh. Camden, though intending to resign if Canning came into office because he objected to the way Canning had tried to throw the blame on to him for his quarrel with Castlereagh,[47] pressed his friend to accept the offer. To Camden Castlereagh replied:

'he had left his personal animosities on Putney Heath [the scene of his duel with Canning], but . . . he could not resume office with Mr Canning without loss of character with the public which would render him less capable of assisting Government.'[48]

A less personal statement to the same effect was sent to Perceval on 4 September. It later transpired that Canning had been preparing difficulties of his own. A statement he sent to Perceval on 25 September indicated that he would have insisted on his return to the Foreign Department (in which case Castlereagh would certainly have demanded his own reinstatement in the War Department) and that in addition he would have wanted the Exchequer for Huskisson, who was at that time vocally critical of Perceval's financial policy.[49]

The failure of this negotiation was not calculated to improve Wellesley's temper. He was said to have told Perceval that 'as government had no longer any hopes of that efficient strength and aid he had sought for, so the greater weight of labour and responsibility would be thrown upon him', and that consequently Perceval would have to make up his mind to concede to Wellesley 'a far greater share of patronage, and in the conduct of the war'.[50] Equally, Wellesley's colleagues could not have been pleased by his anxiety to shuffle them around in their posts. Perhaps, too, they began to wonder precisely how far his schemes really went. Wellesley's own brother Arthur, before the end of the year, was confiding that he did not write to Wellesley because,

'I have always expected he would quit the government, at which period it would have been reported that he and I had been intriguing to increase the power of our family, and I wished to be able to say that I had not written him a line since he went into office.'[51]

The Regency Crisis

Parliament was due to reassemble on 1 November. The ministry had more to fear from the continuing endeavours of Wellesley than from the demoralized opposition, and as there was little parliamentary business to transact, the Cabinet decided to postpone the reassembly till after Christmas.

During the second week of October, the King had been under great strain from attending the death-bed of his favourite daughter, Princess Amelia. He was now elderly and blind. This was the fiftieth year of his reign and, while Perceval had been desperately patching up his ministry, the jubilee had been celebrated by illuminations, parades, and a lavish fete at Frogmore. Now, however, his anxiety for his daughter brought on an attack of porphyria, and he was himself placed under medical supervision on 28 October 1810. He was thus unable to sign the commission for the further prorogation of Parliament. Parliament accordingly reassembled on 1 November and was adjourned without opposition for two weeks, all parties being anxious to await the progress of his illness before deciding what course to take. Princess Amelia died the next day, but the King had still not quite recovered when Parliament met according to the adjournment on 15 November. A further adjournment was proposed and this time there was a division, 343 to 58 in favour. The following week, the King's condition deteriorated, and a third adjournment was opposed by a larger minority of 129 MPs. Perceval now decided that further adjournments were impossible, and that Parliament should proceed to make some more workable arrangement, according to the precedent of 1788.

Because of George III's eventual recovery, the regency crisis of 1788-9 is generally regarded as a dramatic episode full of constitutional import. Equally, because he did not recover in 1811, the second regency crisis of 1810-11 seems in retrospect to have been an excessive fuss about a foregone conclusion. In terms of party politics, however, it was the second crisis which was the more significant and the more complex. As in 1788 the desire of the opposition was to proceed so that, if the King recovered, they would have enjoyed a temporary party advantage, and humiliated the ministers, and if the King did not recover, they would be able to enter as quickly as possible into their inheritance as the friends of the Prince of Wales. The government, similarly, aware that their survival was no longer in their own hands, wished to deny the opposition any temporary advantage, and also the satisfaction of humiliating them. Their resolve in 1810-11 was strengthened by the eagerness of Perceval to model his conduct as far as possible on Pitt's behaviour in the earlier crisis. He later said that 'he spoke from a brief (meaning Mr Pitt's brief).'[52] Befall what may, he desired the credit of having behaved worthily till the last.

Where the situation differed from that of 1788 was in the disposition of the opposition leaders. Ponsonby and the rank and file, in keeping with the party's policy in 1788, desired that the Prince of Wales should be invited by an address from both Houses to assume the regency as an indefeasible right. Lord Grenville, on the other hand, thought himself bound by the precedent he had himself helped to establish in 1788, and felt obliged to support Perceval's policy of establishing the Prince as Regent by parliamentary bill. Temple was similarly disposed, in order to be consistent with his father's conduct as Lord-Lieutenant of Ireland in 1788 when he had resisted the address to the Prince by the Dublin Parliament. Moreover, as Lord Grenville explained, 'Chas. W. Wynne will probably vote for the address exactly for a similar reason, because *his* father did so 20 years ago, and because he knows that it is sincerely a matter of indifference to me which way the question is carried.'[53] Grey seems to have been neutral, too, for he did not even come down from Northumberland to attend the debates. Subsequent events indicate that neither Grey nor Grenville was as anxious to hound the government from office as their followers were, or as Fox had been in the similar circumstances of 1788.

Perceval in fact had little trouble in re-establishing the principle of proceeding by bill rather than by an address. Ponsonby was defeated 269 to 157 when the Commons divided on the measure on 17 December. But it was not expected that he should maintain control of the situation thereafter. 'We shall have a compromise. . . .' wrote Brougham, 'very few restrictions, just enough to *save the principle,* as it were.'[57] Others thought likewise. But they had underestimated Perceval. His Regency Bill, the details of which were communicated to the Prince on 19 December, proposed that the Prince should be restricted for the first year of his regency from creating peers, granting reversions or bestowing pensions, and that the care of the King's person should be entrusted to the Queen. The Prince, confidently expecting a total concession of royal powers, was flabbergasted by this attempt to circumscribe his actions. His reply to Perceval was restrained, but he also summoned his six brothers and his cousin His Highness the Duke of Gloucester to a meeting at Carlton House, and these seven, at midnight on 19

December, issued a 'solemn protest against measures that we consider perfectly unconstitutional, as they are contrary to, and subversive of, the principles which seated our family upon the throne of these realms.'[55] Over the Christmas break Perceval and Ponsonby rallied their forces for the great confrontation. During the night of 31 December-1 January Perceval won three divisions in the Commons, on the principle of restriction, on the limitation of the power of creating peers, and on the granting of pensions and reversions. Though Canning and some of his friends joined Ponsonby, Perceval's majorities were 224 to 200, 226 to 210 and 233 to 214. Next day, however, on a motion giving the Queen control of the Royal Household, the desertion of Castlereagh and Wilberforce in addition to Canning left Perceval in a minority 226 to 213. 'I do not think there are many rats, only a few mice', said Perceval cheerfully.[56] Despite this reverse, the indomitable little man's reputation was never higher. His resolute opposition to what appeared inevitable, and the vigour of his speeches, filled his back-benchers with admiration. They were not looking forward to the regency of the self-indulgent, Whiggish Prince of Wales any more than Perceval was. A friend wrote:

'Many country gentlemen told me they disagreed with him on the resolution, and knew he would be beaten, but devoted themselves to him on account of his manly firmness, his integrity, honour, and courage. . . . It is pleasant, if you must fall, to fall with such a leader, and in such a cause.'[57]

Perceval was also helped by the conscientious scruples of Lord Grenville. In the debate in the Lords, Grenville first of all supported the Marquess of Lansdowne in a successful amendment to the government resolution establishing a restricted regency, but then voted against his friends on the crucial restriction, the limitation of the Prince's power to create peers, so that the government won the most vital division of the debate by 106 votes to 100.

Having by these resolutions in both Houses established the provisions of the Regency Bill, the rest of January was taken up with the progress of the Bill itself through Parliament. There were six divisions in the committee stage in the Commons, all victories for Perceval. This, though it did not make him any the more acceptable to the Prince, strengthened the allegiance of his own partisans. 'The superiority he has assumed and keeps is confessed by everyone; by none more than opposition, some of whom (the younger men), as Sir George Warrender and Brand even cheered him', confided one junior minister to his diary;[58] and another remarked, 'This crisis will now make the world understand and approve Perceval as those only who know him have hitherto done.'[59]

The opposition meanwhile were making plans for their assumption of power, which was expected to take place as soon as their friend the Prince of Wales was legally invested with the regency. Their discussions soon extended even to the appointment of under-secretaries. As Thomas Grenville and Earl Spencer were no longer willing to take office, and Francis Horner (one of the Marquess of Buckingham's rotten borough members) refused to be joint Secretary to the Treasury,[60] the projected ministry quickly took on a more Foxite complexion than that of 1806. This circumstance threatened to sabotage the ministry before it had even been formed. Grey was anxious for the participation of Whitbread ('There is no anger—no ill will in any of them, all *piano*—all upon their knees. Is not this a triumph?' chortled Whitbread's friend Creevey).[60] But the possibility of having the government officially represented in the Commons by Whitbread was too much for the Marquess of Buckingham, who wrote:

> 'I could not be brought to enrol my family flag and friends under Mr Whitbread's standard. . . . I know not why the idea of Mr Canning, or of Mr Percival [sic], or even of that contemptible animal Lord Sidmouth is to be abandoned as hopeless; anything is better than such an attempt on principles wholly indefensible.'[62]

Thomas Grenville likewise urged that Canning should be First Lord of the Admiralty:

> 'There are, I am persuaded, many who will start in the House at the three original names [i.e. Grey, Holland and Ponsonby as Secretaries of State] who will be reconciled to them by the addition of C. If I do not much deceive myself, it is not over estimating the point to say that the certainty of success turns upon it.'[63]

The Foxites saw clearly, however, that the Grenvilles wanted Canning not so much as an assistant to Ponsonby in the Commons but rather as 'an organ of their own'. This Grey would not permit, especially as there was a great deal of back-bench distrust of Canning as a person. Grey argued that with Canning they would gain ten votes and lose 30 real friends.[64] Grey also, under pressure from Whitbread (himself advised by Creevey), objected to Lord Grenville's proposal that he should again take the Treasury while retaining his Auditorship, thereby repeating one of the most unpopular arrangements of the 1806 ministry. Whitbread had recently attacked Yorke for becoming First Lord of the Admiralty while still retaining his sinecure as one of the Tellers of the Exchequer, and did not wish to be associated with a similar piece of pluralism within his own party.

Grenville was too touchy to like being dictated to on his personal concerns by Grey, and did not relish the prospect of being represented by potential critics in the Commons. He sent Grey 'a sort of manifesto of fifteen pages' arguing that they could not form a government without Canning and that if he could not himself have the Treasury and keep his Auditorship, he wanted to be Home Secretary but with all the Treasury patronage at his disposal, and the lead in the Cabinet. Grey considered this paper 'endangered our connection'.[65] Grenville soon regretted his letter. Auckland was sent to recover it while Thomas Grenville 'begged Grey not to be offended at any dryness and formality in the style of Ld Grenville's letters, as official habits early in life makes all he writes upon topics of business seem as dry as a chip'.[66] In fact Lord Grenville was probably correct in supposing both that he would be uncomfortably isolated in the projected Cabinet, and that the government would lack security in the Commons without the support of some recruit like Canning.

What neither Grenville nor Grey realized was that, by the time this dispute took place, they had virtually forfeited any chance of forming a government at all. The Prince of Wales had asked them to draft an answer to the resolutions of both Houses. This draft, dated 9 January 1811, was rejected by the Prince, who adopted instead a draft by Sheridan. Grey and Grenville protested that they had been originally 'consulted with as the public and responsible advisers' of the Prince's answer, and expressed

'deep concern in finding that their humble endeavours in your Royal Highness's service have been submitted to the judgement of another person, by whose advice Your Royal Highness has been guided in your final decision in a matter on which they alone had, however unworthily, been honoured with your Royal Highness's commands.'[67]

To Adam, one of the Prince's confidants, Grey expressed himself even more boldly, objecting to 'having the advice which we were called upon to give thus subjected to another interior council, and [stating] very plainly that it would be in future impossible. . . . to offer any if such a practice was to continue'.[68] This was hardly calculated to conciliate the Prince. A memorandum of 21 January informed him that they were prepared if necessary to take office, and a second memorandum to the same effect, but more peremptory in its terms, had actually been sent to Adam on 2 February for transmission to the Prince, when Grey and Grenville learnt that the Prince had decided not to dismiss Perceval.

'They were in the very act of forming the Administration, filling offices, &c., &c., when Adam came to them from the Prince. They said they could not be disturbed; he said he must disturb them, for he had a message from the Prince; they replied that it was for the Prince they were at work, for they were making the Government; Adam told them to spare all trouble, for no Government was to be made.'[69]

It is true the Prince was a weak, self-indulgent, histrionic character, but it was Grey's and Grenville's own bullying attitude, their refusal to behave diplomatically to the Prince or to his clique of personal advisers, which was as much to blame for this *volte face* as any treachery or lack of conviction on the Prince's part. (The usual explanation of the day was that the Prince expected his father's imminent recovery but such filial considerations did not normally influence his conduct.) Yet though they were naturally angry at this betrayal—the Earl of Thanet told the Prince to his face it was 'the greatest calamity that had happened to the country since the death of Mr Fox'[70]—the opposition leaders showed little regret for any opportunities lost by their continued exclusion from office. William Elliot thought the Prince's decision a 'happy deliverance', and claimed that for the opposition to accept office at such a period of crisis would have been 'deterimental both to their character and to the publick Interest.'[71]

The division between the Prince Regent and his former allies was soon aggravated by a discussion in the Commons which stemmed directly from the Prince Regent's assumption of royal power. In May 1811, the Duke of York was reinstated as Commander-in-Chief. The decrepit Sir David Dundas, now aged 75, was anxious to lay down the post he had held since the Mary Anne Clarke scandal, and it was actually on the Cabinet's recommendation that the Prince Regent decided to reinstate his brother. The Duke of York *was* the best man for the post, but it is impossible not to believe that the Cabinet realized that their recommendation of him would be as satisfying to the Prince Regent—who was grateful for his brother's loyalty during the Regency Crisis—as it would be infuriating to the opposition. Moreover, the alternative would have been the appointment of one of the Prince Regent's Whiggish friends, the Earl of Moira or the Duke of Northumberland (who were both full generals) who would be neither as popular with the Army nor as easy for the Cabinet to co-operate with.

The announcement of the Duke of York's reinstatement was followed by Viscount Milton's giving notice of a motion objecting to it. Some of the more moderate oppositionists, fearing a revival of the passions of 1809 and reluctant to antagonize the Prince Regent, were disturbed at this. 'Several of our friends are expressing uneasiness to me on the subject of Lord Milton's motion, which is contrary to the wish of every individual connected with us', Auckland told Lord Grenville. 'It is said that Mr. Horner and Mr. Charles Wynn think themselves bound to support it.'[72] The Marquess of Buckingham tried to persuade his younger son, Lord George Grenville, who had only recently entered Parliament, to absent himself from Milton's motion, telling him 'how little he had to do with the end of a question which he had not seen or known in its beginning'.[73] Lord George did not take this advice, though his own brother, Earl Temple, did stay away and wrote afterwards, 'I see I should have been driven to divide, had I attended, almost exclusively with those with whom I have no wish to be seen acting in political union.'[74] In fact, as well as Temple's own brother, his two Wynn cousins and another cousin, the Hon. Richard Neville, were in the minority of 147 to 296. Lord Grenville, who had refused to express an opinion beforehand, afterwards told Thomas Grenville that he wished he had advised Temple to attend, and that he was glad to have had four other nephews in the minority, for 'I consider this as the last blow in public opinion to Parliament & all Parliamentary leaders.'[75]

The most important business of the session however was not such as to give the demoralized opposition much leverage. This was the discussion of the bullion question between 6 and 15 May. The debates included some of the longest—one by Vansittart ran to 74 columns of Hansard—and certainly the most technical speeches of the whole period. The controversy concerning whether Britain should resume cash payments, as Francis Horner argued, or should continue the free circulation of paper currency, as Vansittart advocated, was not one that engaged the opposition leaders to any great extent (apart, possibly, from Lord Grenville) and it was rather a wonder that over 200 MPs stayed to hear the interminable lecturing. One back-bencher finally burst out, 'Mr Speaker, I don't like this business at all. I think it is a humbug.'[76]

The Triumph of Perceval

The session of 1811 which had begun in such desperate circumstances for the ministry ended on 24 July. Though Perceval was still the Prime Minister there was no guarantee of his being continued in that rôle. It was generally assumed that once the period of restricted regency expired, and the Prince Regent assumed the royal powers unfettered, Perceval would at last be dismissed. Whether he would be replaced by Grey and Grenville was now less certain, however. Wellesley had persuaded the Prince Regent that greater exertions had to be made in the Peninsula, and as Grey and Grenville were of the opinion that the whole policy of the Peninsular War was misguided, and as Perceval believed that greater exertions were not feasible, it was Wellesley who appeared the best man to organize an increased war effort. The Dukes of Norfolk, Northumberland and Devonshire, the Marquess of Lansdowne, and Lord Holland were said to favour his leadership.[77]

By promoting Wellesley, the Prince Regent could rid himself of Perceval, whom he had always, till February 1811, professed to abhor, while avoiding surrendering himself to the overbearing Grey and Grenville, yet at the same time bring many of his private friends into office. Wellesley was also favoured by the Prince Regent's brothers (with the exception of the Tory Duke of Cumberland whose influence was, however, increasing), as they expected that Wellesley would help them with patronage.[78] By the beginning of December Wellesley's private court of toadies were confident that he would become premier as soon as the restrictions expired. Even MacMahon, the Prince Regent's secretary, seemed to believe this.

Perceval's natural resentment at Wellesley's preparations for his assumption of power was aggravated by the fact that the two men's conflict of opinions over the war had proceeded to the point of a total breakdown of understanding. 'Wellesley and Perceval are quarrelling like Cat and Dog', it was reported in September:

'The former having previously made his pleasure known to the P.R. and the D. of York, served Perceval with a requisition à la Francaise, for an *additional* Army of 30,000 men and £3,000,000 for Galicia. Perceval made answer that tho' he had succeeded in begetting ten Children, that supply fell very short of the Army which Wellesley wanted and that he saw no other mode, except the efforts of the united vigour of the Cabinet, of creating it, and that as for the money it was out of the question. Upon this Wellesley fell into a rage and vowed he would never act with Perceval again, whereupon the said P . . . told him he might kiss his—!!!'[79]

In preparation for the Prince Regent's assumption of unrestricted power, the Cabinet began in mid-November to discuss the arrangement of the Royal Household. The Prince Regent was to have the same household and Civil List as a king, but this meant that a separate establishment had to be made for George III. The Cabinet favoured seconding part of the household to become a separate establishment for the King, but the Prince Regent wanted his household intact, and a whole new establishment, with new officers, set up at the public expense for his father. He also wanted his accumulated debts of £522,000 to be paid by a parliamentary grant. Perceval considered that expenditure on this scale and for such a purpose would not be popular either in or out of Parliament,[80] but it was not so much the unpopularity as the principle of the thing to which he objected. So, just as in 1810 he had defied the Prince by insisting on proceeding by bill rather than by an address, and by insisting on restrictions, so a year later he had the hardihood to cross the Prince Regent in his financial designs.

This was a perfect opportunity for Wellesley. Nothing was more alien to his nature than public or private parsimony, and the whole issue, on which his sympathies were instinctively with the Prince Regent, was the obvious occasion to mark his separation from his colleagues. He showed his hand at a Cabinet meeting on 18 December 1811, at which the question had been brought down to whether there should be a parliamentary grant supplementary to the Civil List of £150,000 or merely of £100,000. Though Wellesley finally acceded to the unanimous opinion of the other ministers that the grant should be fixed at £100,000, he afterwards insisted that the Prince Regent should be told that he personally favoured the larger sum.[81] He now seemed to be in no doubt that he would be taking over as Prime Minister as soon as the period of restricted regency expired, and it was perhaps further to prepare the way for this that he told Bathurst on 17 January 1812 that he was resigning the Foreign Seals, though he said he was prepared to 'continue in office until his successor was appointed'.[82]

Some time earlier, Yorke, unable 'to bear up against the constant confinement & anxiety' of the Admiralty and 'the wear & tear of Body & Mind which belongs to an unremitting attendance on the House of Commons', had resigned.[83] This meant that Perceval had two vacancies to fill in a Cabinet which was in all probability destined to last only another month. Castlereagh was approached, but he was reluctant to come in without Sidmouth, and Sidmouth was objected to by the Prince Regent.[84] There was also the question of Catholic relief. The personal objections of George III, which had been the major grounds for opposing it, could no longer be regarded once the period of restricted regency expired. In a Cabinet on the Catholic issue on 20 January 1812, in which Perceval, Liverpool, Yorke and Ryder maintained their opposition to relief, Wellesley, supported by Camden, Saunders Dundas (now succeeded as the second Viscount Melville), Mulgrave and Westmorland insisted 'that it was essential to the existence of the country and to the Prince Regent that the first act of his government should be the expression of his intention to *amiliorate the situation of the Catholics'*.[85]

Thus the government was in disarray. The Prince Regent, however, lacked the courage to take the initiative. He could not nerve himself to send for Grey and Grenville. The most he could bring himself to do was to suggest that they should be included in a coalition. Perceval, backed up by Eldon the Lord Chancellor, advised against this. They knew Grey and Grenville would refuse, and then make political capital by accusing the Prince Regent (and the ministers) of insincerity. Perceval actually drafted a letter to the opposition on 11 February explaining that the Prince Regent was reluctant to change his ministers, being 'so well satisfied with the principles upon which [they] have acted, and with the success which has attended their measures', and being afraid that any chance would endanger 'the cause of our allies by shaking their confidence in my determination to support them.' At the same time 'irreconcilable conflict upon certain more important points of foreign & domestic policy' made any coalition impracticable.[86]

Next morning the Prince Regent changed his mind, and Sheridan drafted an invitation to the opposition to 'strengthen his hands and constitute a part of his Administration'. Possibly the phrase Sheridan used on the Prince Regent's behalf, 'some of the early friends of his political life', was meant to exclude Grenville from the offer[87]—not presumably because the Prince Regent held it against Grenville that he would not 'talk bawdy', as one of the Prince Regent's friends suggested,[88] but because of a sense of slight dating back to the 1806 ministry. At any rate, the Duke of York, acting as his brother's emissary, went first to Grey alone. Grey refused to receive the Duke of York except in Grenville's presence and the Duke had to interview the two men together. The letter he delivered was, according to Grenville 'more offensive than I could have believed',[89] added to which the Duke said that the Prince Regent considered if Grenville 'insisted on including Lord Temple and others he would be very unreasonable'.[90] Accordingly, Grey and Grenville rejected this offer of a part share in office, on the grounds that 'they differed with the present Administration upon almost every political subject—many of them of the highest importance and only secondary to the Catholic question'.[91] Even before the offer was made Grenville had told Grey:

'I do not believe we can carry the P. with us in such a system of public measures decidedly announced and *resolutely persevered* in, as can alone save the country. . . . I have therefore so little taste for such an undertaking after 30 years of public life, and in the evening of our days, that I freely confess to you in confidence I do not believe it *can* be presented to me in a shape that will induce me to look at it. My only anxiety is in this difficult situation so to conduct myself as honourably to discharge what I owe so many persons who have acted both honourably and kindly towards me.'[92]

Thus their decision had in effect been made even before they heard the Prince Regent's terms.

The attitude of Grey and Grenville obliged the Prince Regent to continue Perceval in office, much to the rage of Wellesley.[93] The latter made one last bid for the premiership in an audience with the Prince Regent on 17 February. He told the Prince Regent

'that he could not continue if Mr Perceval was first minister: that he could not serve under him: that the administration ought to be formed by the introduction of Lord Castlereagh and Mr Canning: that he was the only person who could induce both to accept: that he did not care what situation he himself was placed in: that he did not indeed care whether he was included in the arrangement: all that he wished was to see an administration formed strong enough to uphold the Prince's Government: and he suggested the idea that Lord Moira would be the fittest man to be at the head of such an administration.'[94]

The Prince Regent repeated this conversation to Eldon. Eldon told Perceval, and the latter summoned a Cabinet to consider this latest instance of Wellesley's disloyalty. Wellesley's last friend in the Cabinet, Bathurst, 'a man of warm heart, but sharp temper', had finally turned against him because of his threats of resignation,[95] and the Cabinet was unanimous in deciding

'that Lord Wellesley's conduct has been such as to make it necessary for Mr Perceval to state to the Prince that Lord Wellelsley's resignation must be immediately accepted; and that it should be further represented to the Prince that not one of the present Cabinet would continue, if Lord Wellesley remained in office.'[96]

Wellesley's resignation was accepted next day.

Wellesley employed the first weeks of his unexpected retirement in writing a lengthy self-justification, of which the fair copy ran to 86 pages. Towards the end of this he referred to the way in which, on a variety of topics, his judgment had been over-ruled and his suggestions 'mutilated', and he claimed that in every instance 'the public interests have suffered in proportion to the degree in which his suggestions had been modified or rejected.'[97] But the greater part of the paper was taken up with a discussion of war aims. He emphasized the need of a direct and decisive blow against France, and virtually adumbrated Clausewitz in his exposition of the view that the degree of exertion in war should be commensurate with its political aims. He wrote:

'The Plunder of a Fishing Town, the Destruction of a Basin, And the Burning of a few Ships upon the Stocks might be sufficient Acts of Aggression in a quarrel about a Sugar Island, and upon a balance of profit and loss between dried fish burnt Ships and Sugar might compel a hostile nation to think of Peace. In Lord Wellesley's Judgement however such operations were wholly inapplicable to the character of the present war.'[98]

It can be said, however, that his notion of what was possible in the way of total mobilization of resources, though it pointed forward to what was done in the twentieth century, ignored the political realities of his own country in his own day. Moreover, he had an exaggerated notion of the strategic benefits to be gained from a total victory in Spain. Yet his statement was so eloquent, so sincere, that it is difficult not to feel sorry for the two years of misunderstandings and frustration he had experienced in the Cabinet. He had been no more able to understand the cautious realism of Perceval than Perceval had been able to see that there was more in Wellesley's ideas than the empty magniloquence of a gigantic vanity. Wellesley's statement included eight sides expatiating on his career as Governor-General in India, during which he had gained 'experience in the immediate direction of Military Enterprizes upon a more extended and comprehensive Scale than had ever perhaps fallen under the sole management of any Statesman in the Country'. It was precisely those 'Indian Enterprizes' which from the beginning of his Cabinet career had puffed Wellesley up with conceit and armed his colleagues with resentment against that conceit, thereby preventing any agreement on the Peninsular War. And from that basic disagreement, most of Wellesley's foolishness and intrigue had stemmed.

As soon as Wellesley had been removed, his post was offered to Castlereagh, who accepted. Sidmouth, Buckinghamshire and Bragge Bathurst were brought into the Cabinet a month later. The recruitment of Sidmouth and his friends was not altogether popular with some of the ministry. The concession of three Cabinet posts was thought 'excessive', and the Duke of Richmond confessed that 'as a steady Pittite I own I feel a little alarmed.'[99] This coalition with Sidmouth cannot be explained in terms of Perceval fishing for extra votes in the Commons, even though one biographer suggests this was the reason.[100] The Sidmouth following had been dwindling steadily since 1804, and could now scarcely be put at 20, rather too few to be worth three places in the Cabinet, if there were no other factors involved. The real reason surely was that Perceval believed Sidmouth and his friends would be on personal grounds an asset to his Cabinet. They were safe, conservative men, in tune with the prejudices of the people whose support Perceval relied on. There was no idea of approaching Canning. Perceval wanted nothing to do with adventurers who favoured new political alignments, approaches to the opposition, and so forth. The reconstructed Cabinet was probably the most united (and the most uniformly adverse to constitutional change) since the reign of George II. And it was utterly under Perceval's control. As Canning remarked, 'the star of P. is predominant—it must be confessed—& why he should not be Minister for 20 years like Sir Robt Walpole I cannot pretend to say.'[101]

8

The Months of Crisis

The Brink of Catastrophe

THE real significance of Perceval's establishment of a united conservative government in March 1812 is to be seen, not in the narrow context of parliamentary politics, but in its relation to the unprecedented national emergency which faced the country was passing in 1811 and 1812. Never before had there been more need of a strong government enjoying widespread public confidence. The country was facing the crisis of the war. Napoleon's closure of European ports to British shipping was beginning to take effect; Britain's international trade was in desperate straits and the government's retaliatory measures were apparently making the situation worse. Relations with the USA were declining into hostility. The continent was united at Napoleon's back against Britain, and at any moment the irresistible weight of Europe might be mobilized against the British Army in Spain.

Largely because of the economic crisis there was widespread discontent, not merely amongst the lower classes, but also in the middle classes whose support of the oligarchy was indispensable at any time of social tension. The fact that so much of the country's wealth was already tied up in trade and industry, and was totally dependent on the stability of credit, made Britain uniquely vulnerable to the risk of economic collapse resulting from a widespread loss of confidence. The fact that since the late 1790s paper currency had replaced specie as the circulating medium meant that the breakdown of commercial credit would result immediately in the existing form of money becoming valueless, which would cause nationwide panic and confusion. Already in 1811, numerous country banks had failed, triggering off whole series of bankruptcies in their neighbourhoods. There was a real risk of the same thing happening all over the country, and the government had no resources to prevent such a catastrophe. At best, it could only refrain from adding to the confusion by its own precipitancy.

Yet the whole framework of government had never been less secure. The illness of George III and the regency of his son meant that the ministers no longer had the confidence of the Crown on which they relied to tide them over their relative weakness in the House of Commons. At any moment, it seemed, the unpredictable Prince Regent might dismiss them from office and the narrowness of their majority in the Commons constantly threatened them with parliamentary defeat. At the same time the opposition, for all its numerical strength,had never been less capable of providing an alternative government. The disputes of January 1811 had made it clear that any ministry Grey and Grenville formed would be dogged by even more bitterness and frustration than the ministry of 1806. Moreover, the events of the previous eight years had altogether discredited both ministers and opposition in the eyes of the public. Each successive crisis, the fall of Addington's ministry, the fall of Grenville's, the Convention of Cintra, the Melville scandal, the Duke of York scandal, the Canning—Castlereagh duel, the Walcheren failure, had strengthened the belief of people outside politics that public men were ineffectual and corrupt, and the activity of borough and county meetings up and down the country showed the voters' increasing anxiety for an alteration of the political system.

In effect the whole structure of oligarchic rule, with its unequal alliance between Crown, upper class and middle class, was on the point of collapse. Though the upper class had surrendered none of its control of the wealth and institutions of the country, it was now too divided by party conflicts to present a united front to the dangers that encompassed it, while the Crown, instead of providing a fixed point of reference, now contributed an additional factor of instability. The middle class, aroused from its customary docility by eight years of oligarchic failure, focussed its discontent on the two issues on which the ministry was most open to criticism—reform and international trade. The revived campaign for reform, and the agitation against the Orders in Council enforcing the blockade of the continent (the measure with which the government had replied to Napoleon's closure of Europe's ports) were nothing less than a middle-class attack on the upper class.

The reform movement had not at first maintained the impetus it had gained from the Duke of York scandal. The breakdown of the reform campaign in Parliament had been mirrored by divisions and confusions out of doors. Analysis of the situation, elaboration of aims, understanding of which social groups would be friendly and which, ultimately, hostile to reform—all these things were still in their infancy (in a sense they had regressed since the 1790s), and the unanimity generated by the Duke of York case turned out to be short-lived. For the first part of 1810 the Walcheren enquiry had absorbed public attention and contributed to further disillusionment with the ministers, but the Burdett riots which developed out of public anger at the Walcheren expedition showed up the divisions within the reform cause. Burdett's arrest inspired petitions for parliamentary reform from Reading, from Liverpool ('signed by 3,000 persons, many of them . . . of the most respectable description and of considerable property and influence.'[1]), from Worcester and Canterbury. A motion by Brand on 21 May 1810 for parliamentary reform was defeated 234 to 115 and led to more petitions. But the Yorkshire reformer Wyvill disapproved of Burdett's conduct in resisting the Speaker's warrant, and withdrew his name from the requisition for a county meeting in Yorkshire.[2] He disapproved too of ideas for a taxpayer franchise and equal electoral districts put forward by his former ally, Walter Fawkes. Early in June, he urged his associates to leave reform where 'the debate on Mr Brands Motion hast left it'. He pointed out:

'the defection of Mr Fawkes, & the rapid growth of Burdettism among the Manufacturers in the West of Yorkshire leave little reason to our Friends to hope, that their temperate Counsels would be adopted by the County of York; & Middlesex also, as I have understood from Mr Byng, is in a state of similar embarrassment.'

He thought the moderates

'should watch, & whenever it may offer, should seize the favourable opportunity to unite themselves as generally as possible to the well disposed & sober-minded part of the Public. I fear the most calamitous consequences can only thus be prevented.'[3]

The Burdett riots had a quite different, but equally cooling effect on Francis Place and the reformers in Westminster. They had planned to mark Burdett's release from the Tower by a tremendous demonstration of support both for him personally and the reform cause. On the day of his release a triumphal procession was organized. Houses were festooned with blue ribbons, and crowds of well-dressed citizens wearing blue favours gathered to see him pass. Burdett however had a patrician distaste for being mobbed. While in the Tower, members of the Foxite opposition had flocked to visit him, and their company seems to have restored him to some sense of what he owed his own class. He decided he did not relish being dictated to by a plebeian caucus. He began to complain of 'what they call my Committee,' and told one Whig, 'I have no Committee'.[4] Consequently, while his supporters waited for his release, he sneaked out down the river. From that point on, the Westminster Committee never really trusted him. It had been a lesson on how far their

dependence on figureheads like Burdett worked against their real
aims.

During 1811 the reformers turned their attention to their greatest
deficiency, the lack of a nationwide organization. In April Wyvill
told Earl Stanhope:

'a plan has been proposed for uniting the two parties of Reformers,
so long & so unfortunately separated, under the auspices of Sir F.
Burdett & Mr Fawkes on the part of the less moderate Class, &
Mr Brand & Mr Tracy on the part of their more moderate
Friends.'[5]

On 10 June 1811, at a large reform dinner attended by Major
Cartwright, Burdett, Cochrane and Wardle, as well as the Whig
MPs Thomas Coke and C. C. Western, an association was established
known as 'The Union For Parliamentary Reform According To The
Constitution'. During the following year, it was rechristened the
Hampden Club, and under that name played a vital role in organizing
support for parliamentary reform in the years after 1812. In the
short-term however 'The Union' made little impact. On the day
following the reform dinner, a reform petition from Kent was presented
to the Commons, and one MP remarked blandly, 'At particular
periods the people appeared to be intent on the measure, but, when
they saw into whose hands it had got, they recovered their usual
good sense.'[6] Despite protests at this from Sir John Newport and
Whitbread, it was not immediately obvious that the sneer was
unjustified.

The progress of the middle-class reform campaign coincided with
the revival of working-class unrest in industrial areas. Apart from
some labour disputes, there had been no major disturbances in the
North since 1802. In February 1811, however, there came reports
from Oldham of night meetings attended by men with fowling
pieces,[7] and on 11 March 1811, 60 stocking frames were broken by
rioters at Arnold in Nottinghamshire. During the following fortnight
there were more frame breakings in Nottinghamshire and at Ilkeston,
Derbyshire. The dislocation of the export trade by the war, the
replacement of properly knitted stockings by stockings made of
'cut outs' sewn together, and the fact that the coming into fashion of
trousers meant there was less domestic demand for men's stockings,
had led to unemployment and wage reductions amongst the
Nottinghamshire stockingers. In Lancashire and Cheshire, too, trade
dislocations had led to unemployment and discontent. There were
petitions to Parliament for help from Bolton and Manchester, but
there were also reports of night meetings near Manchester in October,
and talk of a delegate being sent into the neighbouring counties. A
Chesterfield man claimed:

'the people in general is in one mind and wishes a Change in

government and to shake of this Burdion of the National debt &
if that was done away with the taxes would be small but the
people knows that never can be efected with out the present
government is done away with and that work would cost a deal of
Blood shed if not Rightley gone about But says he the people is
awair it must be done quiet at the impulse of the moment and not
give the Common sort of people time to think but strike at the
Root at once.'8

On 4 November 1811, one of the spies employed by the Bolton JP
Ralph Fletcher informed his master that he had been told of the
existence of 1,000 men at Nantwich who knew the use of arms and
who wanted 'a revulotion so as to shake off the National debt & this
present Royal fameley and to Establish a Common welth and then
the people would be free and not till that End was accomplished.'9

On 10 November there were more framebreaking disturbances in
Nottinghamshire, and after two days the town magistrates of
Nottingham asked for troops to be sent to the area. At the beginning
of December the disturbances spread to Derbyshire and Leicestershire.
Letters signed by or on behalf of 'General Ludd' were received by
the intended victims. From this the term *Luddite* was derived and
applied, not only to the framebreakers, but also subsequently to the
dissidents in Yorkshire and Lancashire. Almost from the beginning
the outrages obviously went beyond mere industrial sabotage.
Haystacks were fired. On Christmas Eve a game preserve belonging
to Lord Middleton was attacked, the keepers beaten up, and a
hundred pheasants destroyed. During the same week two Derbyshire
farmhouses were robbed by armed men, and a third was attacked
but the assailants were driven off. On 28 December a coal wagon
was burnt.10 Even the poor were not spared. "The rioters have adopted
a system by which they levy contributions on the villages and
actually subsist themselves on the produce of their plunder', claimed
the Lord Lieutenant of Nottinghamshire.11

Another disturbing feature was the way in which the outrages
were spreading, and it was not long before information began to
pour into the Home Department indicating that the outbreak was
part of a large-scale conspiracy. Two delegates from Nottingham
were reported at Stockport.12 One of Fletcher's spies heard that at
Leeds, 'they are divided in their opinion tho the Revolutions are the
strongest side the other is for a Reform in parlement they other is
for doing the business compleat.'13 Thousands were said to be ready
in Ireland. There were branches of the conspiracy at Sunderland
and Darlington. According to the men at 'Neasbraw' (Knaresborough?)
who were in contact with the Westmorland dissidents, there were
good men at Kendal and Appleby. At Northallerton 'there is a few
good Citizens but do not hold any Reguler Meetings nor could he

get them to promiss to Correyspond.'[14] Fletcher's spy 'B' was told in February that there were 40,000 committed men in Nottinghamshire, Derbyshire and Leicestershire,[15] while another informant heard that, 'By the last returns the number who carry on the present system of outrage are 1700 committed Men, who are a sort of point de ralliment.'[16]

Both Fletcher at Bolton and the Duke of Newcastle at Nottingham thought arms were being manufactured at Birmingham,[17] but the two London stipendiary magistrates, Nathaniel Conant and Richard Baker, who were sent to Nottinghamshire to assist enquiries were less convinced,[18] and one of their colleagues back in London scotched the report that delegates from Nottingham were at Spitalfields.[19] Nevertheless, though the Nottinghamshire disturbances had died away by April 1812, there was open disaffection in Birmingham, Lancashire and the West Riding. At Birmingham someone chalked up on some walls 'No Orders in Council, No King, No Parliament' and a handbill was found saying:

'Ye Men
of
Birmingham,
how long will ye
hug the chains
of Slavery and
Oppression.'[20]

In Yorkshire, industrial sabotage had begun in January 1812 with the firing of a textile mill near Woodhouse Carr. Whereas in Nottinghamshire Luddism took the form of breaking up old machinery as a protest, in Yorkshire the target was new, labour-saving equipment that threatened jobs. On 11 April 150 men attacked a large new mill at Rawfolds, Liversedge, which was defended by its owner, William Cartwright, some of his hands, and five men of the Cumberland Militia. The attackers were beaten off and two of them—one a former employee made redundant by Cartwright's new machinery, the other the 19-year-old son of the Vicar of Low Moor, himself a former shearman—were fatally wounded. A week later, Cartwright was shot at on the way home from Huddersfield where he had been giving evidence against one of the militiamen who had refused to fire on the attackers.

On 28 April William Horsfall, another mill owner, was shot down by four men and died 38 hours later. Three of the men were later hanged for this crime on the evidence of the fourth. Three days after the Rawfolds battle, there was a food riot in Sheffield during which the mob, 'after breaking a few windows and destroying some potatoes', attacked the arms store of the local militia, seized 222 muskets and, swinging them by the barrels, smashed off the stocks against the

walls.[21] This wanton destruction at least indicated that the rioters
were not plotting an armed insurrection, as they would then have
wished to keep the guns for use, but arms raids occurred elsewhere
in Yorkshire during the subsequent weeks.

In Lancashire it was claimed that there was a general underground
movement centred at Manchester, called 'The Northern National
Army',[22] and that a general insurrection was planned for 1 May
1812:

'Arms—Spikes, Knives, Cutlasses, Bows and arrows. Spike Balls
to Lame the Horses feet in the Streets—its also intended to have
Ropes across the Streets and Lanes to trip up the Horses . . . .
Mode of Attack—Each Sett to Murder the Affluent in their own
Neighbourhoods; also such poor as will not join them in taking
their property and uniting with them in the work:—Its supposed
this will be done in the space of three Hours. Bounty—To each on
swearing in two pounds two shillings.'[23]

There were food riots in several Lancashire towns, and a serious
disturbance in the Manchester Exchange on 8 April arising from
the last minute cancellation of a public meeting called to discuss the
Orders in Council. The requisition for this meeting had been signed
by the headmaster of the free grammar school, the warden of the
collegiate church and six other clerics. The effect of the cancellation
was that the crowd which gathered for the meeting had nothing to
do. For some time they waited impatiently in the news room of the
Exchange. 'Some of the boys, apparently from a want of occupation,
were pulling off each other's hats and throwing them to a distance,
to compel the owners to go for them.' The first window was broken
accidentally by a hat, after which the crowd proceeded to smash all
the furniture in the room.[24]

On 20 April, five men were killed and 18 wounded in an unsuccessful
attack on a steam weaving mill at Middleton, and there were more
fatalities next day when the mob gathered again and were dispersed
by troops. Another steam weaving mill, at West Houghton, was
burnt down on 24 April. Horsfall's assassination, in neighbouring
Yorkshire, was four days later.

It is frequently said that the government committed more troops
to the disturbed northern counties than they had sent to Portugal
under Sir Arthur Wellesley at the beginning of the Peninsular War.[25]
This is true, but then Sir Arthur's original army in 1808 was a
particularly small one, and the troops concentrated in the Luddite
counties were only a fraction of the forces available at the time in the
whole of Great Britain. In fact more of the Home Department's and
the House of Commons' time was taken up by a series of dramatic
murders in the East End of London (the so-called Ratcliffe Highway
murders) than was devoted to the hints of far-flung conspiracy in the

north. Southey, who had fancied himself as an expert on lower-class affairs since denouncing factory conditions in his *Letters from England: by Don Manuel Alvarez Espriella*, published anonymously in 1807, later wrote of the necessity of writing something more on the subject, 'for the purpose, if possible, of making our men in power see the imminent danger in which our throats are at this moment from the Luddites'[26] — as if the government saw no particular danger from them. Yet even the alarmist Southey saw the danger as only partial:

> 'The truth of what Espriella says of a manufacturing populace, and of what he saw in last year's 'Register' upon the *sinking* of Jacobinism from the middle and reasoning classes, down to the mob, is exemplified at this time in the state of the manufacturing countries. It is well for us that we have not a Pitt and Grenville Administration, or, with this system of *United Englishmen,* so undeniably existing, there would soon be an end to all liberty in England. I do not think the country in danger, but it is very certain that the tendency and object of these proceedings is to bring about a second reign of Jack Cade.'[27]

The economic conditions at the root of Luddism however were also the cause of the increasing hostility to the government on the part of industrial employers. Lower-class disaffection of the sort experienced in the 1790s was thus for the first time associated with middle-class disaffection. The middle-class's sense of the growing economic crisis was indicated by the way criticism of the Orders in Council displaced the reform campaign as the main focus of agitation towards the end of 1811. A motion by Whitbread for papers on the Orders in Council on 13 February 1812 was rejected in the Commons by 136 votes to 23, but on 3 March Brougham moved for a select committee on the Orders in Council; Canning, who as Foreign Secretary had inaugurated the policy of full-scale trade war, now spoke against the Orders, and, though he was demolished by Perceval, the opposition mustered 144 votes to 216. Brougham's response to this defeat was to urge his friends in all parts of the country to whip up petitions. Petitions soon came in from the Leicestershire framework knitters, from the Yorkshire woollen manufacturers, from the Staffordshire pottery interest, from Birmingham, Blackburn, Glasgow, Kendal, Liverpool, Sheffield, Shrewsbury and Worcester. From Bolton and Preston came petitions begging not merely for a speedy end to the war, but also for parliamentary reform.

The issue of the Orders in Council actually provoked many fewer petitions than the questions which also came up in the spring of 1812, of the renewal of the East India Company's Charter. Moreover there were counter-petitions in favour of the Orders from Liverpool, Scarborough, Bristol, Glasgow, North Shields and Sunderland.

Nevertheless Perceval was sufficiently impressed to concede a parliamentary committee on the subject. Yet the situation was more serious than even he recognized, for so long as Napoleon maintained his Continental System intact, Britain's economic plight was bound to deteriorate, whether the Orders were rescinded or not. There was therefore every probability of the agitation amongst both employers and employees getting worse. In many ways Perceval's consolidation of his ministry had been achieved just in time.

The parliamentary opposition meanwhile had proceeded one step closer to total demoralization. As in the American War of Independence, general war-weariness, and the economic hardships resulting from the war, had stimulated criticism of the financial abuses of the government, and the series of finance committees established in the Commons in succession to the first committee of enquiry into sinecures set up on 10 February 1807, provided a steady flow of authentic information on abuses. As Wardle's crony Madocks told his Boston constituents in a widely circulated address dated 3 March 1811, there was a need

'to watch with a constitutional jealousy over the application of the vast revenue and resources of the country(the more liable, from their extended scale, to be perverted to the ends of private peculation or public corruption), to lighten the burdens of taxation, by introducing reform and economy into every branch of the public expenditure; to conciliate the affections, by redressing the grievances of the People, and to do no more than common justice to their industry and patience, by suppressing abuses and detecting corruption.'

On 7 February 1812 a bill to prohibit the grant of offices in reversion was defeated in a thinly attended House. In April 1812 Thomas Creevey revived a project of two years earlier, to question the huge incomes which the Tellers of the Exchequer drew from public expenditure. Besides two Tellerships with established salaries, there were two others drawing as fees a fixed percentage of *all* public spending. These were worth in war-time about £24,000 per annum each. One was held by Earl Camden, the other by Lord Grenville's brother the Marquess of Buckingham. Grenville was naturally disturbed by Creevey's scheme. He wrote to Grey and Ponsonby:

'to express my sense of the conduct which Ld B & I have a right to expect on such an occasion from the Party *as a body*. Not weak & hollow support, much less neutrality, or even hostility, as Fremantle seems to anticipate, but warm, cordial, & zealous support, in speeches from the Leaders & in votes from the Body. I have declared unequivocally that if this expectation is disappointed my line is taken—nothing shall persuade me to continue for another hour my connection with a Party capable of such conduct.

> I shall openly & unequivocally disclaim the connection as one
> which I cannot retain without dishonour to myself & treachery to
> my Brother.'[28]

The Marquess's elder son, Earl Temple, seems to have hoped that
the Grenvile and Foxite wings of the opposition would split on the
issue,[29] but Grey did not hesitate to commission Whitbread and
Brougham to beseech Creevey to drop his motion. They failed, but
when Creevey brought forward his motion on 7 May he received
little support, and was defeated by 146 votes to 38. Nevertheless,
the publicity which Buckingham's Tellership received was
embarrassing (later in the year Camden wrote to him and persuaded
him that they should give up a third of their fees as a sop to public
opinion). It was evident that the Grenvilles' position within an
opposition increasingly influenced by reform ideology was becoming
more and more precarious, and what little enthusiasm Lord Grenville
personally had left for his rôle as opposition leader seems to have
dissolved during the late spring. Thus at the very moment when the
whole governing system faced its greatest challenge, the opposition,
a key element within that system, was at its most divided.

The Murder of Perceval

The examination of witnesses by the Commons committee on the
Orders in Council continued for several days. Then, on Monday 11
May, while he was passing through the lobby of the House on his
way to attend the committee, Perceval was shot dead by a psychopath,
John Bellingham.

Perceval's fellow politicians were horrified. The Prince Regent
sent a letter of condolence to the Commons, urging them to make
some provision for Perceval's family, and when Castlereagh moved
an address of thanks to this message, it was Ponsonby who seconded
him. 'In most faces there was an agony of tears', recorded the
Speaker, 'and neither Lord Castlereagh, Ponsonby, Whitbread, nor
Canning could give a dry utterance to their sentiments.'[30]

Bellingham was immediately tried for murder. During Lord Chief
Justice Mansfield's summing up, most of the court, and even Mansfield
himself, wept openly.[31] Even Bellingham was contrite. He had been
vainly seeking redress from the government for business losses
incurred in Russia and had taken the Home Department's suggestion
that he should take whatever measures he thought fit as a hint that
he would best serve his cause by shooting someone. He told the
court:

> 'To government's non-attendance to the dictates of justice is
> solely to be attributed the melancholy catastrophe of the
> unfortunate gentleman, as any malicious intention to his injury
> was the most remote from my heart. Justice, and justice only,
> was my object.'[32]

In the twentieth century there would have been little doubt of Bellingham's insanity, but the jury were impressed by his apparently rational manner. He was sentenced to death, and on 18 May he was publicly hanged at Newgate.

There was at the time a widespread belief not only that Bellingham was sane, but that his crime was politically motivated, and while Perceval's upper-class acquaintances grieved, many of the lower classes openly rejoiced. From Hythe it was reported that local labourers hailed Perceval's assassination 'as an auspicious event'.[33] At Newcastle under Lyme the news was announced by a man who 'came running down the street, leaping in the air, waving his hat round his head, and shouting with frantic joy, "Percival is shot, hurrah! Percival is shot, hurrah!"'[34] At Nottingham the populace paraded with flags and drums in celebration.[35] There was a spate of anonymous threats to the Prince Regent's life, 17 of which, and half a dozen more or less friendly warnings, are preserved in the Home Office papers.[36] One, sent on 23 May to Vansittart, who succeeded Perceval as Chancellor of the Exchequer, came from Nottingham, was signed 'Ned Ludd', and was in the same handwriting as other Ludd letters sent to prospective victims in the northern counties. It threatened him with the same fate as Perceval if there was no change of government policy. Another letter, sent to Ryder, warned,

'Bellingham's glorious Deed will be followed by others still greater and you & the Infernal Regent the great Whore master of England will follow your old partner Percival Surely the Blood of Despard Smith Cundell & poor Bellingham Call for Justice on the Blood hounds that Surround the throne of England.'

These two letters arguably originated with genuinely active conspirators. The same was not true of others. One, threatening, 'there will be upwards of thirty of the Ministerial party put to death in less time than a fortnight, if the Marquis Wellesley is not made prime minister of England', obviously did not represent mainstream Jacobin policy. Two other threatening letters demanded that Burdett should head a new government. Scrawls saying, '5000 For The Heads of the Prince R Lord Castlereagh and Secretary Ryder No Poppery Britons Prepare for Slaughter' and

'Prince Regent
Damd Raskel
We have is life be fore Long.'

seem to have been outbursts of sheer bravado. Another letter, of 27 May, in bad Latin, addressed to 'Turpissimus Virorum', used the phrase 'Sanguis vel Panem', that is, *Bread or Blood,* a slogan frequently chalked up on walls in 1812. But its most interesting feature was the illustrations scrawled below the signature 'XW'—a bloody knife, a chalice, and a pistol being fired. No other of the death threats of 1812 were similarly decorated, but a few years later illustrations of this sort became a regular feature of the threatening letters sent out in industrial disputes in Scotland. Many of the people who wrote in anonymously were evidently almost as much cranks as Bellingham himself. They included a couple of religious enthusiasts, a man who claimed to be the writer of other anonymous threats and offered to surrender himself on condition his starving family were paid £1,000, and the man who sent Colonel MacMahon four pages of doggerel, part of 'Emancipation, a Tragedy in many Acts, as it is to be performed on Englands Stage'. Another correspondent of MacMahon's wittily combined personal insult with a recommendation of a coalition ministry, by suggesting that 'if the Prince Regent presents his *broad bottom* to the Assassins he will sustain no injury.'

When, 12 years earlier, the madman Hadfield had tried to shoot George III at Drury Lane theatre, many people had written letters of congratulation at the King's escape but there had been no threats at all. Nor was it that an unsuccessful attempt on a king was so much less startling than the murder of a minister; after Damiens' abortive attempt on the life of Louis XV in 1757, 'shoals of seditious papers and verses, in print and manuscript', had appeared in France.[37] The number and tone of the anonymous scribbles inspired by Perceval's assassination, as compared to the response to Hatfield's attempt on George III, was a measure of how much more unpopular the ministerial régime had become since 1800.

The New Order

After Perceval had been shot, the first words addressed to Bellingham once his identity had been ascertained were: 'Villain, how could you destroy so good a man, and make a family of twelve children orphans?'[38] But it was not only Perceval's numerous offspring who were left destitute. His Cabinet, the 'miserable remains of the miserable remains of Pitt's Administration'[39] were left without their leader, without the one man who, for all his intellectual deficiencies, had had the courage to grasp power and hang on to it. At first they thought they could carry on. They met on 13 May to discuss whether they could survive without recruits. When the question was put only the oafish Westmorland answered a straight 'yes'. Mulgrave and Harrowby thought it impossible, and the others were doubtful.[40] While Liverpool took over the Treasury, therefore, Vansittart was brought in as Chancellor of the Exchequer, and approaches were also made to Canning and Wellesley. On 21 May 1812, however, an address calling on the Prince Regent to take steps to secure an efficient administration, proposed by the Tory back-bencher Stuart Wortley, was carried by 174 votes to 170, and the Cabinet resigned.

The Prince Regent sent for Wellesley to form a government. The ex-ministers had been shy of Wellesley ever since their experience of him as a colleague, but at this juncture they were outraged by the publication, first of the correspondence he had been having with Liverpool during the previous few days, and secondly of a statement by Benjamin Sydenham based on his own much longer memorandum on the subject of his reasons for resigning in February. Consequently, the ex-ministers refused to serve with him. Wellesley had no choice but recourse to Grey and Grenville. He saw the two men on both 23 and 24 May. The chief topic of discussion was Wellesley's *idée fixe*, the campaign of his brother Arthur (recently created Earl of Wellington) in Spain. Possibly as a result of the fall of Ciudad Rodrigo and Badajoz to Wellington's troops, Grey and Grenville had at last retreated from their total condemnation of the lavish expenditure on Britain's insecure foothold in the Peninsula, and they now conceded that the war there involved 'questions, not of principle, but of policy, to be regulated by circumstances, in their nature temporary and fluctuating, and in many cases known only to persons in official stations'.[41] After a few more days they virtually capitulated to Wellesley's views on the matter.[42]

The Prince Regent, by no means gratified by the readiness of Grey and Grenville to serve with Wellesley, had urged the outgoing Cabinet to unite with Wellesley, but after a meeting on 27 May they refused. Wellesley explained his terms to Grey and Grenville on 1 June. They were to have the nomination of four out of 12, or five out of 13 Cabinet posts. Erskine and Moira had already been nominated by the Prince Regent, and Canning by Wellesley, so as not to narrow their choice.[43] There was thus no suggestion that the opposition were intended to be a minority in the Cabinet, especially not on the Catholic issue. Nevertheless Grey and Grenville refused, explaining:

'It is to the principle of discussion and jealousy that we object; to the supposed balance of contending interests in a Cabinet so measured out by preliminary stipulation. The times imperiously require an Administration united in principle and strong in mutual reliance.'[44]

In view of their own disputes in January 1811, it seems doubtful whether they could have produced a more united Cabinet themselves, and probably their real objection was to the principle of being cut in as junior partners by Wellesley, who was now as much an object of suspicion to them as he was to his own former colleagues. Even the *parvenu* Creevey could complain of Wellesley and Canning as

'two fellows without an acre of land between them, the one an actual beggar, both bankrupts in character, one entirely without

Parliamentary followers, the other with scarce a dozen. . . . in the
abundance of their high honor and character [they] condescend
to offer to Earl Grey of spotless character, followed by the Russells
and the Cavendishes, by all the great property of the Realm and
by an unshaken phalanx of 150 of the best men in Parliament,
these honourable worthies offer Earl Grey so circumstanced four
seats in the Cabinet to him and his friends.'[45]

Following Grey and Grenville's letter of refusal the Prince Regent
commissioned the Earl of Moira to try his hand at mediation. Moira
was the Prince Regent's most loyal and most honest friend, but he
was not the best man for such a task, being stiff and reserved and
notoriously anxious for his own betterment under the Prince Regent's
aegis. On this occasion, moreover, he seems to have judged the issue
in advance, for two days before interviewing Grey and Grenville he
told his own brother:

'The opposition are behaving as ill as possible. An unhandsome
impatience at not having everything at their own disposal makes
them fight off upon petty distractions and little captious forms. I
regard it as impossible to settle anything with them.'[46]

Moira ensured the fulfilment of his own prophecy. He made what
appeared to be an unlimited offer to Grey and Grenville, but when
they asked him whether they would be free to change the officers of
the Household he acknowledged that the Prince Regent had said
nothing about protecting anyone but insisted it would be 'impossible
for him [Lord Moira] to concur in making the exercise of this power
positive and indispensable in the formation of the Administration
because he should deem it on public grounds particularly objectionable.'[47] On this apparently secondary issue the negotiation was
broken off with expressions of regret.

Moira's complaint to his brother may have been disingenuous,
but it had some justification. As in 1809 and 1811 Grey and Grenville
stuck excessively to forms, veiling behind a show of scrupulous
caution their private disinclination to do anything beyond what
was required of them by their position in the public eye. Thus on the
day of the interview with Moira, Grenville wrote to his brother, the
Marquess of Buckingham:

'My apprehension is that the Household officers will resign; though
I rather hope that the Prince or Moira will make a point of
keeping them; for the nearer I look at this, the less hope I can
have of really doing any good. I do not expect that our ground
will be popular with our friends, but I think it is solid.'[48]

But the opposition rank and file were not deceived. One Whig
commentator observed:

'I dare say Lords Grey and Grenville meant extremely well, but
they have bungled the matter so as to put themselves in the

wrong, both with the public and their own troops. The bad faith
of the Court is nothing. If they suspected that bad faith, they
should have put it to the proof, and made it clear to all the world
that the Court did not mean them well: at present they have
made the Court the object of public love and compassion.'[49]

On 8 June 1812, Liverpool became Prime Minister with the same
colleagues as had resigned two and half weeks earlier. 'We are all
much obliged to the Talents for giving you yr situation again, &
strength to maintain it', one supporter told the new premier.[50] But
from Spain Wellington wrote:

'You have undertaken a most gigantic task and I don't know how
you will get through it. When I was in office matters were not
very successfully carried on in the House of Commons when Mr.
Canning, Lord Castlereagh, and Perceval were on the Treasury
Bench, and to all appearances at least acted well together. I
should think that you won't have the assistance of both of the
survivors of poor Perceval; and you will scarcely be able to get on
in the House of Commons with only one of them.'[51]

As it turned out, Liverpool's prime ministership was to be the
longest of the nineteenth century. Trouble still continued in the
North. In Washington the constitutional arrangements for declaring
war on Britain were in progress. Yet in fact the crisis had already
been weathered. On 23 June the Orders in Council were revoked,
and on the same day, on the other side of Europe, Napoleon's armies
crossed the border into Russia, thereby bringing the Continental
System to an end. Though British trade did not pick up immediately
with the collapse of Napoleon's system of economic warfare, the
revocation of the Orders in Council generated a new mood of optimism
in the commercial sector which did much to tide it over the difficult
months ahead. The news of Wellington's great victory at Salamanca
on 27 July 1812 also hoped to revive enthusiasm for the war. By the
end of the year there were strong signs of economic recovery. There
were still dangers to come, but the worst was over. Perceval had
lived just long enough to ensure the survival of his cause and of his
country.

PART THREE: What the Politicians Achieved

1
The Aims and Conduct
of the War

Aims

So far we have discussed the war with France only in terms of its effect on domestic politics. This is not necessarily the best way to understand the war. In some ways it encourages a belief in a kind of reciprocal process, whereby the foreign war which affects internal affairs is itself seen as the natural and inevitable corollary of domestic inequality and repression: oligarchy translated into foreign policy so to speak. In reality, however, the situation was much more ambiguous.

Early in 1795 the British *chargé d'affaires* at Berne wrote to the Foreign Secretary on the subject of the upheavals in France:

'if this Revolution has been attended with misery and wretchedness to nations and millions of individuals . . . it has also been productive of some good in opening the eyes of men on the real character of Frenchmen, and of exhibiting to the world in its true colours that horrid mass of infamy, perfidy, and wickedness of every description, which has been so long concealed under the veil of politeness and urbanity, to the great misfortune, at all ages, of those who mistook the appearance for the reality. . . . They are become like a second race on earth, and it may truly be said that the world is inhabited by two sets of human beings, by men and Frenchmen. And unfortunately these monsters are not confined to their own limits, for those who are expelled are as exceptionable as those who remain in France.'[1]

This was only an extreme instance of the francophobia which had become general in Britain since the era of Louis XIV, and to which dread of the new French political ideals was merely a final addition. Yet the war with France was not a war undertaken out of prejudice or fear. Those who, like Burke, preached the necessity of extirpating the revolutionary ideas which France was attempting to spread throughout Europe, did not have the ear of the British government when the war first broke out in 1793, and when, later in the 1790s, they were established as a distinctive element amongst the government's supporters, their particular views were generally discounted.

It was true that during 1792 the British government viewed with increasing dismay the growing aggression of France towards her neighbours and the growing violence of her government at home, but it was the French who, on 5 February 1793, finally took the initiative of declaring war. Once war had been declared of course the British could justify all proceedings as self-defence. Pitt later said that the aim of the war was 'Security—security against a danger the greatest that ever threatened the world'.[2] This was genuinely believed by many people who actually fought in the war and there even seems to have been systematic attempts made to indoctrinate British troops with this idea. In a questionnaire addressed by the Commander-in-Chief to generals commanding military districts in February 1801, the last of 15 queries asked whether the men had been instructed as to the nature of the expected fighting against:

'a savage and implacable Enemy, who has the Insolence and Barbarity to aim at the Slavery of Our Persons, the extinction of Our Religion and the destruction of Our Navy, Our Commerce and Constitution, so long the Envy and Admiration of the World'.[3]

Even the American diplomat Rufus King saw the war as a struggle 'to save those invaluable rights, for the preservation of which, for others as well as for herself, Great Britain has so nobly contended'.[4]

Yet in its conduct the war in no way assumed the appearance of a war of self-defence, and Wilberforce later wrote:

'The war with France, which lasted so many years and occasioned such an immense expense of blood and treasure, would never have taken place but from Mr Dundas's influence with Mr Pitt and his persuasion that we should be able with ease and promptitude, at a small expense of money or men, to take the French West India islands, and to keep them when peace should be restored.'[5]

There is no real evidence that Pitt was in fact initially motivated by any such desire to take advantage of France's other preoccupations. Nevertheless it was the case that *after* the war had been declared, Dundas persuaded Pitt to manipulate the situation for Britain's own commercial benefit. Dundas considered it obvious that,

'be the causes of the war what they may, the primary object ought to be, by what means we can most effectually increase those resources on which depend our naval superiority, and at the same time diminish or appropriate to ourselves those which might otherwise enable the enemy to contend with us in this respect . . . . I consider offensive operations against the colonial possessions of our enemies as the first object to be attended to in almost every way in which Great Britain can be engaged.'[6]

To Grenville, Dundas justified this policy on the grounds of necessity and expediency, as if the French colonies were to be Britain's wages for crusading against French revolutionary doctrines:

'if we do not manfully make up our minds to some determinate stand for the preservation of *British interests* involved in this contest, we are playing the part of spendthrift bankrupts, who for the sake of a few years' brilliant *éclat*, have made up their minds to terminate their career by a desperate suicide . . . . We are drove from necessity into the war from the best and wisest motives, because if we did not then interpose, the frenzy of the principles which reigned in France would have extended itself to this country, and overturned every chance we had of preserving our own constitution. I likewise feel as much as anybody that if, by the continuance of the war and the great exertions we are making for that purpose, we can contribute to the restoration of the French monarchy it is a most desirable event for the future tranquillity of this country and of Europe'; but —

and here Dundas proclaimed his true creed —

'if the consequence of having successfully contributed to do so is to be an abandonment of all those possessions and all that consequent power upon which our future greatness must rest, I beg to wash my hands of such a system.'[7]

Yet even men as alert to commercial exigences as Lord Auckland and George Rose questioned Dundas' emphasis. Auckland, writing to Grenville in support of the view expressed by the emigré Jarry that 'our first and great object ought to be to destroy the Convention [i.e. the French government]', stated:

'It appears to me that if we are materially diverted from that object by the pursuit of conquests, whether on the continent of Europe or in the East or West Indies, we risk the fate of the whole war and of the existing race of mankind. May it be added, that we do this in pursuit of acquisition which we might have without effort or expense? For it is in Europe only that the successes of the allied armies, and the commanding superiority of our naval force, can enable us to compel the French nation to such conditions and sacrifice as may be thought necessary for our future safety and tranquillity.'[8]

And Rose agreed with Auckland 'in every syllable you say to Lord Grenville'.[9]

Dundas' 'Blue Water' policy, which was virtually a system for maintaining the war indefinitely rather than for bringing it to a

successful conclusion, was also criticized by the Duke of Portland's
followers, especially by Windham who believed that the only way to
end the war was by encouraging a counter-revolution in France
which would overthrow the revolutionary régime in Paris. As late
as 1803, after a decade of disappointments, he wrote 'External
success must I allow come first; but external success, were it much
greater than we have any reason to hope, will never do it alone.'[10]

Windham often appeared to believe that the principal aim of the
war was the restoration of the Bourbons, hence his preoccupation
with the possibility of a royalist counter-revolution. But this apparent
bias was due to his being more cogent in expressing the ideas of the
moment than in working out his theories in full, and on other occasions
he seemed to disagree with Dundas only in detail. In 1796, for
example, he acknowledged the prime importance of securing the
Cape of Good Hope.[11] William Wickham, another of the Portland
group, and, during the 1790s, the principal British agent involved
in fomenting anti-revolutionary feeling on the continent, also accepted
the importance of commercial factors. Discussing the question of
partitioning smaller European states he told Grenville:

'Every partition scheme is so decidedly hostile to our manufactures
and to the sale of our colonial productions, as well as to our free
communication with the Continent and our influence there, that
it is never to be resorted to but as the lesser of two evils; and, in
this case, as the only mode of preventing France from remaining
without a Continental enemy, and perhaps with the means in her
hands of shaking to the foundation our manufactures and colonies
themselves.'[12]

Even George III who above all others might have been expected to
view the war in the light of a royalist crusade, entered into the
commercial spirit. When in 1796 there was a project of ceding Corsica
to Russia, it was George III who instructed that care should be
taken 'to secure the ports being at all times kept open for us, and
that our trade shall be favoured over all other nations as to ease of
port duties.'[13]

It is tempting to see this emphasis on commercial interests
as a response by the government (albeit a government of landed
proprietors) to the increased importance of trade and manufactures
in the period of the Industrial Revolution. By and large, however,
the government's commercial bias represented nothing new. Extension
or security of trade had been a major objective in every war undertaken by Britain since Cromwell's era. What was new was that the
revolutionary war also had an ideological dimension, which suffered
from the preoccupation with trade.

When the war resumed in 1803 there was even less concern for the
ideological aspects. Though universally feared, Napoleon had to a

great extent been accepted into the brotherhood of European monarchs. During the 1790s the war had been seen as total, and justifying any expedient. Thus when the Austrians murdered two French diplomatic envoys in 1799 Thomas Grenville reported:

'It is undoubtedly a dirty piece of business, and I therefore indulge myself in talking of it as being probably the act of the Directory to get rid of two men who have both been named to succeed in the ensuing vacancy; there is very little truth in this suggestion, but it is better than abusing the Austrians, and the Directory are very little entitled to the benefits of truth and candour.'[14]

After 1803, the conduct of the war reverted to the more usual form of eighteenth-century war, as conflict between civilized communities. Though the system of exchanging prisoners virtually broke down, there was a degree of contact between the hostile nations. J. Cleaver Banks was allowed to travel to Paris to examine Sanskrit manuscripts in the Bibliothèque Nationale. A British midshipman who broke parole in France to escape was dismissed the Royal Navy in 1806, and in 1813 a lieutenant who escaped by jumping parole was actually sent back.[15] In the Peninsular War there were many instances of courtesy. When the French in Portugal had been totally cut off from the outside world, Foy their commander constantly sent flags of truce to borrow English newspapers: when Wellington sent to know why he wanted them, 'Foy, with much readiness, replied that he had been speculating in the English Funds, and was very anxious about the price of Consols'.[16] And when Wellington intercepted French couriers to Madrid with letters from Mme Joseph to Joseph Bonaparte, he used to withhold the letters as containing useful information, but had the news they contained of Joseph's two ailing daughters transmitted verbally under flag of truce.[17] Such courtesies would have been inconceivable in the 1790s.

Similarly, the strategic preoccupation of the renewed war were different. Security and trade remained Britain's two principal concerns, but whereas during the 1790s security had been largely a catchphrase, disguising the fact that the build-up of Britain's commerical advantages was the government's main objective, after 1803, with the increasing enlargement of the British manufacturing sector, the increasing economic vulnerability resulting therefrom, and the increasing attempts by Napoleon to isolate and destroy Britain's commerce, it became the case that the security of Britain and the security of her trade became the same thing. But the objections pointed out by Auckland and others during the 1790s remained valid. The pursuit of trade was not the way to inflict a shattering defeat on France, either with a view to overthrowing her government or merely to checking her aggression. All the ministers, with the apparent exception of Dundas, realized that the war was different from all earlier wars, and that whereas in all earlier wars the enemy had had relatively limited objectives, for which he was prepared to make a limited expenditure of effort, and therefore could be deterred by a limited defeat, in the case of the war against Revolutionary and Napoleonic France, there was no limit either to the enemy's objectives nor to the resources which he was prepared to commit, and in consequence only a total overthrow could bring the war to a conclusion. Yet Britain's commercial orientation prevented her from contributing adequately to the overthrow of France.

Conduct

As well as being caught between two conflicting aims, the overthrow of the French on the one hand, and the promotion of trade on the other, British war policy was influenced by the fact that the potential size of her army was limited by social and political considerations. Britain's manpower was still relatively small, of course, but more important than this was the comparative weakness of the Crown, which had prevented military institutions from developing a central position in the state. The large-scale mobilization of human resources which was already practicable on the continent would have been inconceivable in Britain. In addition to the anti-militarist bias of British society there was the fact that the country's economy depended on a free market in labour, which made anything more than partial conscription generally unacceptable. But the very factors which inhibited Britain's military strength contributed to giving her financial resources with which to make up this deficiency. During earlier wars, particularly the Seven Years' War, British ministers had exploited this situation with great success by frustrating France's objects in Europe with subsidies to her own continental allies, and at the same time defeating France at sea, disrupting her commerce, and sending small armies to seize her colonies. Because of the difficulty of evolving any new strategy more appropriate to the new type of war in the 1790s, because of the memories of the Seven Years' War as an epoch of unparalleled military glory, and because of the continuing preoccupation with colonial and commercial factors, the ministers attempted to fight the French Revolution by the methods which had been so successful against Bourbon France. But though the defeat of France and her allies at sea, at the First of June in 1794 at St Vincent and Camperdown in 1797, at the Nile in 1798 and at Trafalgar in 1805, preserved Britain from the threat of invasion, and though commerce-raiding by British cruisers virtually destroyed French maritime trade, British naval activity, could do nothing to weaken France's hold on the continent, and increased rather than reduced French political commitment to the war.

Equally, the policy of subsidizing allies to check the French advance in Europe, though it had been adequate for the limited warfare of Louis XV's era, failed to bring about any overwhelming defeat of France of the sort needed to end the new kind of war. The futility of the British subsidy policy was increased by Britain's poor relations with her allies, resulting from division of aims. These divisions might have been permissible in the conditions of limited warfare, but were fatal in the face of Revolutionary France. Thus, prior to 1801, the Austrian chief minister Thugut used the war against France as an opportunity to extend Austria's borders, and by concentrating on the prospective military position at the end of the war, at the expense of the more immediate need to evolve a workable strategy, caused his armies to be defeated in succession. 'If he were paid to thwart all our measures, and to favour those of France, he could not do it more effectually', complained Grenville, the British Foreign Secretary.[18] Grenville's brother described Austria's objective as

'the open and absolute territorial possession of Piedmont, Savoy, Venice, and the great part of Tuscany . . . in addition to all this, they are to reoccupy their Austrian Netherlands; and . . . our acquiescence in all this enormous plan of plunder is to be purchased, not by their acceding to our plans or measures, but by their substituting others for their own distinct advantage.'[19]

Tsar Paul of Russia pursued no such selfish nationalist policy, but the difficulties of military cooperation with armies ultimated directed by Thugut strained his patience. Nor did he find Britain a congenial ally. The Anglo-Russian expedition to North Holland in 1799 broke up amidst mutual recrimination, and when the British captured Malta and refused to surrender it to Paul, to whom it had been earlier promised, the Russians withdrew from the alliance. The subsidy policy also brought about the near-collapse of British credit at the beginning of 1797. After the European war resumed in 1805 (two years after Britain's own renewal of hostilities with France), there was less problem with divided war aims, but French power had increased to such an extent, and Russia and Austria had so far lost enthusiasm for the struggle, that Napoleon was able by 1807 to achieve the virtual isolation of Britain.

Although during most of the 1790s Britain's major commitment of troops was in the West Indies, there were also sporadic interventions in Europe, either in a role auxiliary to the much larger armies of Britain's allies, as in Flanders in 1793-5, or for limited objectives such as the landings at Toulon in 1793, at the Helder in 1799 and at Ferrol and Cadiz in 1800. Even the most successful feat of British arms on land prior to the 1802 peace, the expulsion of the French from Egypt in 1801, was in fulfilment of limited objectives, being viewed merely as a piece of diplomatic leverage in anticipation of a negotiation for peace. As Dundas told the commander of the expedition:

'All that I have seen or heard confirms to me, that upon the question of Egypt, more or less modified, will turn the whole question of our negotiation, and it is in order to take away from the enemy all advantages they expect from it, or, if they cannot be taken away entirely, to divide or (if I may use the expression) to neutralize them, that we now send you up the Mediterranean.'[20]

And in the event, the news of the British victory in Egypt came too late to influence the peace terms with France.

When the war was renewed in 1803 British policy continued to depend on the major share of land warfare being undertaken by allies, in spite of the earlier failure of such a policy, and in spite of the fact that for the first two years of the war there were no allies forthcoming. It was only when Austria and Russia resumed hostilities with France in the autumn of 1805 that Pitt initiated any large scale military effort, and in accordance with Britain's self-adopted auxiliary function in land warfare, the armies Pitt sent to Hanover and Naples late in 1805 were withdrawn as soon as Napoleon's victory at Austerlitz exposed them to the full weight of French power.

Shortly afterwards, Pitt's death caused a change of government in Britain. The new war minister was Windham, formerly the leading critic of Dundas' policy. But he was unable to evolve any alternative strategy, and for the first few months of the new ministry no new disposition of troops was made. Then, in September, the news arrived that Buenos Aires had been captured by an unathorized expedition from Cape Town. Involvement in South America was fully in keeping with the commercial and colonial orientation of the war previously upheld by Dundas, and in fact Dundas (now Viscount Melville) was later to recommend South America to the attention of Windham's successor.[21] Windham had only the haziest of ideas how the invasion of South America could bring about the defeat of France in Europe:

'with the discontents in France described in Lord Lauderdale's letter, and with the establishment on the continent of South America followed by a hearty support of the war in this country, the period may not be far distant . . . . when the power of Bonaparte may begin to totter, and, if once thrown out of its balance, fall to the ground with very little struggle.'[22]

Viscount Howick, the newly appointed Foreign Secretary, objected to the plan:

'Whilst we are acquiring colonies, the enemy is subjugating the Continent, and though I am by no means disposed to raise doubts of our ability to maintain the contest in this manner, I cannot help fearing the effect of any system which might enable the

French, either completely to subdue the remaining Powers of the Continent, or to engage them in opinion against this country.'[23] The series of expeditions despatched by Windham to the Rio de la Plata ended in ignominous failure. In spite of this, Britain quickly gained a monopoly of South American trade, suggesting that the expeditions would have been an expensive irrelevancy even if they had succeeded. Windham and his colleagues had already left office when the final failure at Buenos Aires occurred. Their successors continued the old policy of expeditions for limited British objectives, or to give token support to allies. The attack on Copenhagen and the seizure of the Danish fleet in September 1807 was of the first category, and the despatch of Sir John Moore to Sweden in 1808 was of the second.

After 1808, as is well-known, the ineffectual opportunist policy of previous years was replaced by a systematic overseas commitment in the Peninsula. Spain and Portugal were in many ways an ideal theatre for a major British expedition, being close enough to France to represent a serious threat, while being sufficiently accessible by sea to utilize Britain's naval superiority. In fact, however, Britain merely stumbled into a Peninsular policy. Initially, as in the Flanders campaign of 1793 or the North German campaign of 1805, British ministers saw the British Army's role as merely auxiliary. The brunt of the effort was to be borne by a subsidized ally. The collapse of Spain's armies and the consequent retreat of the British expeditionary force at the end of 1808 persuaded the British ministers to turn their attention elsewhere, and after the evacuation of Coruña a British presence was only maintained in the Peninsula because the anxious pliability of the Portuguese persuaded Castlereagh to maintain an army in Portugal.

Castlereagh was already turning his chief attention to yet another expedition to Holland to capture a French naval squadron and to distract Napoleon in his campaign against Austria. This scheme culminated in the Walcheren fiasco. Yet when the Spanish resistance to the French continued, and co-operation with the Spanish leaders was resumed, Britain's auxiliary rôle eventually blossomed into a major commitment. Though British troops were never more than a small proportion of the allied forces in the Peninsula, they were responsible for preventing the military collapse of the rest, and their commander, Wellington, eventually became generalissimo of the Spanish armies. Yet in the European context the Peninsular War was a mere side-show. Wellington constantly complained of his government's neglect of the Peninsular theatre. Thus in August 1810 he was able to write, 'I acknowledge that it has appeared to me, till very lately, that the Government themselves felt no confidence in the measure which they were adopting in this country',[24] and 12 months later he was still protesting: 'I begin to suspect the Government of treachery. Nothing can be so fatal to the cause as to distress us for money, and yet all the measures of the Government appear to have that sole object in view.'[25] At the same time, the French never threw their full energies into the contest, and it was Napoleon's failure to reinforce his sorely-pressed armies in Spain because of his wish to concentrate his maximum force against Russia in 1812, which precipitated the collapse of the French military position in the Madrid theatre. It was not till Wellington's victory at Vittoria in northern Spain, on 21 June 1813, that the world awoke to the fact that Britain was inflicting major defeats on the French. By that time the decisive blow had already been struck in Russia, and Napoleon himself was hard pressed by Austria and Russia in the main central European battle zone.

2
Government Economic Policy

The Influence of Adam Smith

THOUGH much less an immediate concern than the war, government economic management during the 1790s and 1800s had crucial effects on society during the war years, particularly with regard to the growth of trade and manufactures.

The publication of Adam Smith's *The Wealth of Nations* in 1776 had marked the beginning of a new era in which the growing sense of the extent to which Britain's prosperity depended on commerce and industry made the problems of economics a major preoccupation of public men. Foremost amongst those who absorbed Smith's ideas were Pitt and Lord Grenville. 'We in truth formed our opinions on the subject together', Grenville reminded Pitt in 1800, when the latter seemed to be departing from orthodoxy, 'and I was not more convinced than you were of the soundness of Adam Smith's principles of political economy till Lord Liverpool lured you from our arms into all the mazes of the old system.'[1] Yet, as Grenville acknowledged, there remained some who had not been converted. The first Earl of Liverpool, who was President of the Board of Trade till 1804 and whose own son became a leading exponent of *laisser faire*, belonged to an earlier generation of thought and was an old-style mercantilist to the last. Sir John Sinclair, the agricultural reformer, who had known Smith personally, developed a new form of interventionist doctrine, recommending amongst other things the use of surplus government revenues to develop new industries. After Pitt's death, financial ministers like Perceval and Vansittart seem to have embraced the government's need to manipulate the money supply for revenue purposes with a readiness that suggests that they, too, may have had some positive anti-Smithian system, but they were widely criticised on theoretical grounds at the time.

It was one of the paradoxes of the period that the war, which might have been expected to encourage governmental intervention in economic affairs, coincided with the triumph of *laisser faire* doctrines so that, in a period when market forces were remarkably distorted by war-time difficulties, their free operation was permitted as never before. And it was of course a paternalist power structure which presided over this *laisser faire*. *Laisser faire* had not yet been identified politically with a distinct social class which posed a threat to the traditional power structure, and thus it was that a paternalist order indulged, for purely doctrinal reasons, in a massive and crucial abdication of its potential role.

Yet politicians' concern for economics was not merely theoretical. Pitt especially maintained close touch with industrialist MPs like Peel and (during his brief parliamentary career) John Horrocks, and with international traders like Baring. Peel said of him that 'no minister ever understood so well the commercial interests of the country'.[2] But there were no permanently organized industrial lobbies in this period. The General Chamber of Manufacturers established in March 1785 collapsed after only two years because of divisions of views on Pitt's commercial treaty with France.[3] A fragmentary General Committee of Merchants met in London in 1796-7 and again in 1801. In Manchester, a Commercial Society established in 1794, which might have acted as a lobbying agency, declined from its very inauguration.[4]

On several occasions, however, support was whipped up on a specific issue, most notably in the case of the mass-petitioning against the Orders in Council in 1812. The government's adherence to theory was such, however, that the only instances of submission to pressure whether parliamentary or extra-parliamentary were in the cases where the original policy was recognised to be weak in theoretical justification. For example, when Pitt proposed an excise on iron in 1796, he was aware of the Smithian objection to excise on necessities and allowed himself to be persuaded to drop the idea by Sir John Sinclair and the Earl of Dundonald, who urged that it would inhibit the iron industry. The scheme was revived by Lord Henry Petty in 1806; a committee was set up to lobby MPs and though the bill passed the Commons by ten votes it was given up.[5] Similarly the giving up of the Orders in Council in 1812 was not so much a capitulation to pressure as an acknowledgment of the theoretical impropriety of interfering with the freedom of trade.

In other instances, the government's defiance of public opinion on issues where it felt the public to be misinformed indicated the rigidity of its convictions. During the dearth of 1800 even widespread food rioting did not suggest to the minister that their policy might be inadequate. In 1808 the refusal to consider wage-fixing in the cotton industry also led to riots. When in 1812, during the height of the Luddite troubles, a bill to protect the Nottinghamshire framework-knitting industry was proposed, MPs, anxious not to incur unpopularity at such a time by expressing their true opinions, avoided the debates on the issue: on one occasion there was not even a quorum for as Gravenor Henson, the framework-knitter's leader complained, 'they ran out of the House when our business came on like wild fire'.[6] In the Lords speakers of all political complexions denounced the bill. Lauderdale thought 'it was founded upon most mischievous principles of legislation'. Liverpool argued that 'the less commerce and manufactures were meddled with by legislation the more they were likely to prosper'. In the same speech he made the first recorded use of the term *laisser faire* in Britain. Sidmouth 'trusted in God, that no such principle would be again attempted to be introduced in any Bill brought up to that house'.[7]

This firmness was characteristic of the period. Government policy often seemed inconsistent, apparently protecting employers but refusing to protect employees, but closer investigation shows that this was not so. Of the two most notorious pieces of alleged class legislation of the period, the Corn Laws were seen as a special case, as is discussed below, and the Combination Acts were regarded as fully in keeping with the *laisser faire* system. Though the idea of prohibiting combinations was denounced by Burdett with references to Adam Smith, the general belief was that combinations whether of workers or masters were interferences with the market forces.

Pitt, whose economic policy dominated this period even after his death, showed his Smithian orthodoxy in two main areas — in his preference for raising revenue by taxation rather than by increases of the Nation Debt, and in his refusal to consider regulation either of wages or of the cost of living. With regard to the former point, revenue by taxation, Pitt did of course raise enormous sums by loans and the number of stockbrokers active in the City rose from about 430 in 1792 to 726 in 1812.[8] But the fact that only 42 per cent of the cost of the war was paid for by loans, as compared to 81 per cent. of the cost of the American War of Independence, indicates that there was a deliberate policy departure, and the new policy was certainly that recommended by Smith.[9] If it had not been for the preference expressed by Smith for taxation instead of loans it is possible that the war-time governments would have engaged in massive loan-raising. Precisely what would have been the effect of this is not clear. It does not appear that the money raised in government loans and the money invested in commerce and industry came from precisely the same source, but it is not clear how much money actually invested in commerce and industry during the war might have been diverted to less productive uses by more extensive government borrowing. Equally it is not clear whether the sources tapped by government loans could have raised substantially more than they did, so that the government's taxation policy might in any case have been inevitable. Nevertheless, a heavier level of government borrowing must certainly have had some adverse effect on industrialization, whereas taxation seems to have operated on the industrial sector relatively favourably.

Economic Regulation

The issue of wage regulation arose during the first major food shortage of the war, in the winter of 1795-6. Whitbread proposed a bill to Regulate the Wages of Labourers in Husbandry which would have renewed the obsolete power of JPs to fix wages. This idea was eloquently denounced by Pitt, who asked the Commons

'to consider the operation of general principles, and rely upon the effect of their unconfined exercise .... trade, industry, and barter would always find their own level, and be impeded by regulations which violated their natural operation, and deranged their proper effect. . . .'

He argued that even such basic legislation as the Poor Law perpetuated poverty:

'The laws of settlement* prevented the workmen from going to that market where he could dispose of his industry to the greatest advantage, and the capitalist from employing the person who was qualified to procure him the best return for his advances ....
He conceived, that to promote the free circulation of labour, to remove the obstacles by which industry is prohibited from availing itself of its resources, would go far to remedy the evils and diminish the necessity of applying for relief to the poor rate.'[10]

Pitt's attitude was not inhumane. For example he suggested making relief for large families 'a matter of right and honour, instead of a ground for opprobrium and contempt':

'this will draw a proper line of distinction between those who are able to provide for themselves by their labour, and those who, after having enriched their country with a number of children, have a claim upon its assistance for their support.'[11]

Nevertheless, he was fixed in his belief that excessive regulation would be fatal to the economy, and certainly worse than the evils it would attempt to remedy. Grenville, who was even more doctrinaire, acknowledged in the similar circumstances of 1800 that his 'steady persuasion' was

'that example, and (at the very utmost) the execution of the subsisting laws, can alone remedy the evil, which laws, and the

*i.e. The Law of Settlement, 13 & 14 Charles II, c. 12 (1662) which enabled J.P.s to return to their parish of origin any person who moved into a parish who could not give security that he would never be a charge on the poor rate.

introduction of an artificial system have created, and which new laws, and a system still more forced can only increase.'[12]

An analogy may be drawn between the conviction that the economic situation would inevitably find its own level, and the contemporary belief that social inequalities effectually balanced out. In both cases it was believed that natural laws were operating for the general welfare of society, with which it would be absurd and dangerous to tamper. There existed, however, considerable popular demand for wage-fixing. In November 1799 the JPs in the hundred of Salford (which included Manchester) were obliged to issue a handbill telling workers:

'It requires little experience to know that at all times, the price of labour ought and must be free and unshackled. It is governed by a greater or less demand, which depends on circumstances beyond the control of masters or servants.'[13]

A year later the JPs of Buckinghamshire, with the countenance of the Lord-Lieutenant, the Marquess of Buckingham, came out in favour of wage-fixing, but the discouraging attitude of Grenville, Buckingham's brother, prevented the question being raised officially.[14] Both Whitbread and the Earl of Warwick, Lord-Lieutenant of Warwickshire, spoke in Parliament in favour of wage-fixing, but received little support.

Whitbread's bill in 1796 had applied only to farm labourers. In 1808 George Rose proposed a bill to fix a minimum wage for Lancashire cotton operatives. 'The measure', he said, 'was proposed with the consent of the masters as well as of the journeymen.'[15] Ralph Fletcher, the Lancashire JP whose inveterate hunting down of working-class reformers is described in an earlier chapter, urged the government to be sympathetic on this issue,[16] and Sir Robert Peel and Samuel Horrocks, the two largest mill-owners in Lancashire, who were also both MPs, subscribed 30 guineas each towards the expenses of the workers' delegation which travelled to London to promote the bill.[17] (Horrocks had however told the delegates that he considered 7s. a week to be a sufficient wage.[18])

The bill met a frigid reception in the Commons. No one spoke in favour. Even Rose, the proposer, whose notions tended more towards the idea of a fixed as distinct from a minimum wage,[19] confessed that he proposed the bill, 'not from a conviction of the propriety of fixing the minimum wages, but in compliance with the wishes of a numerous and respectable class of persons who were now suffering peculiar hardships'.[20] Perceval was not totally unsympathetic. He had earlier urged the cotton manufacturers to meet in Manchester to fix prices, but the manufacturers had preferred a bill.[21] Perceval, however, merely told the Commons how glad he was that the issue had been discussed, even though the wage-fixing bill ought to be rejected as doing more harm than good.[22] Davies Giddy, spokesman of the Cornish commercial interest, argued that previous high wages had caused more men to take to the cotton trade than it could support.[23] Viscount Milton said that the consequence of wage-fixing would be the discharge of workmen, 'by which they would be reduced to complete misery'.[24] Even Peel denounced 'the principle of the measure', cited the shutting up of foreign markets as the cause of the distress, and claimed 'the fact was, that masters were now suffering from this cause still more than the men'.[25] After a brief debate which was concluded by the Hon. Henry Lascelles quoting Adam Smith, the bill was withdrawn. Subsequent petitions from the cotton operatives in 1809 were summarily rejected by a Commons select committee.[26]

Agitation for wage-fixing derived from the war-time rise in food prices. By July 1800 wheat prices had risen to 136s. 4d. a quarter. It was widely believed that the increases were due to grain speculators building up hoards to make extra profits. Lord Chief Justice Kenyon denounced such practices from the bench, and in July 1800 a corn-factor was convicted in his court for selling at 44s. a quarter oats he had purchased the same day for 41s.[27] A general meeting at Kidderminster, and Worcester Common Hall urged Parliament to legislate against speculators.[28] The clergy were circularized to provide information on grain supplies in their parishes, and many of them made circumstantial allegations as to engrossing taking place to their certain knowledge.[29] It is indeed almost certain that in a period of sharp price rises, both farmers and dealers were generally reluctant to sell prematurely on a rising market, and that even without calculated speculative hoarding, the atmosphere of crisis encouraged prices to rise beyond even the levels justified by the shortage. But the economic experts of the day, including the ministers, denied this. Believing as they did in a realtively crude supply and demand theory of price levels, they were unable to see that a period of shortages brought into operation other factors. The widespread belief that the high prices were caused by speculators they attributed to public ignorance, an attitude that was strengthened by their disapprobation of the food riots which occurred in many places. Adam Smith himself had eloquently denounced the widespread folk prejudices about speculators: 'A dearth never has arisen from any combination among the inland dealers in corn, nor from any other cause but a real scarcity', he had written. 'The popular fear of engrossing and forestalling may be compared to the popular terrors and suspicions of witchcraft.'[30] Such prejudices were in fact pinpointed by one Lord-Lieutenant as a major cause of the shortage—the dealers readiness to trade, 'is further damp'd by another more permanent cause: the manner in which Merchants or Jobbers in Corn have been lately treated by those High & rever'd Authorities, who have & ought to have so much influence over the minds of the People. Under one odious name or other [they] have been held up to the ignorant people as the wicked causes of their suffferings. Dealers in corn are withdrawing from the trade, afraid to traffick in an article trafficking in which, has render'd them liable to so much obloquy & calumny, & to be run at by an ignorant populace, without confidence in protection from those who ought to be more enlighten'd.'[31]

The Home Secretary seems to have been impressed by this explanation, for writing to another Lord-Lieutenant two months later he confessed that enlarging the grain supply seemed impossible,

'unless the market is free, and encouragement is given to speculation and competition, and it is in vain to expect that Capitals should be employed with this view, unless the most perfect confidence prevails that the use of them will be uncontrouled and the produce of them enjoyed in perfect security not only to the person, but of the moral and social character of those whose fortunes are so engaged.'[32]

Acting on these principles, the government refused to enact any measures to regulate the trade. Much parliamentary time was taken up by committees which recommended to the public the use of brown bread, fish and other alterations of diet, but which refused even in the face of food riots to tamper in any way with the freedome of the market. The establishment view seemed to be that price-fixing was altogether impolitic. Grenville claimed that, 'if a maximum should ever be adopted, it would have the effect of instantly plunging the people into all the miseries of famine; and of aggravating tenfold the distresses they now laboured under'.[33] Wilberforce went even further, asserting that food prices were beyond human control: 'The power of parliament did not extent to the alteration of the course of things as they appeared in nature; they were under the dispensation of Providence only.'[34] Nor was the measure of government purchase of foreign grain, which had been resorted to unsuccessfully in 1795, again attempted. The Home Secretary later referred to

'the Principles I have professed & the opinion I have explicitly & uniformly avowed with respect to the interference of Government in the supply of any part or district of the Kingdom with provisions, in any other manner than by holding such assistance in readiness as may enable the Magistrates to secure the freedom of the Markets & to protect the persons & property of those who frequent them.'[35]

It was a question not of inhumanity but of principle. This same Home Secretary saw no inconsistency in subscribing £300 in his private capacity for the purchase of foreign corn to sell cheap at Nottingham market, within the sphere of his own personal local influence.[36] Such private intervention was also quite widespread in Devonshire. Lords Fortescue, Rolle and Clifford all organized grain supplies in the immediate neighbourhood of their country seats. Rolle even brought two shiploads of grain from London.[37] Eventually, this intervention was extended to cover the whole county, Fortescue as Lord-Lieutenant organizing the local JPs for this purpose.[38] Parliament itself asked the King to advance money from the Civil List to aid the East End of London, where there was no great magnate to undertake the role of local benefactor. This surely was pushing the principle of no public intervention to its limit, but since the King provided the money from his *quasi*-private income, the principle was preserved nonetheless.

In 1804, following a bumper harvest, the country faced the opposite problem—glut. Ministers who had refused to act in time of dearth saw no inconsistency in legislating in time of plenty. A bill was prepared to raise the import duty on wheat. The chief spokesman for the agricultural interest, C. C. Western (who was later prominent in the debate on the more famous 1815 Corn Law) initially spoke of raised duties being necessary because the increases in agricultural wages, poor rate payments, and a 13½ per cent depreciation in money had rendered the existing tariffs established in 1791 by 31 Geo. III c.30 obsolete.[39] He later elaborated his views into a theory that Britain should be self-sufficient in food production and that in order to achieve this agriculture needed a high tariff wall.

'It was nothing less than a measure to prevent thousands of acres of land throughout the country from being deserted by the plough, to prevent farmers from converting their lands to other purposes besides those of sowing corn. It was a measure to prevent the recurrence of that scarcity which had been felt in so dreadful a manner some years ago; and ultimately, to make the price of corn moderate and cheap. These things could never be done by importation; they must be done by holding out a sufficient inducement to the farmer to cultivate grain.'[40]

Some Lancashire MPs and two of the City of London members were dubious about the bill, but the only substantial opposition came from Earl Stanhope in the Lords, who claimed the bill aimed at raising prices, and in the end became so violent in his denunciations that all the other peers rounded on him in disapproval. The theories of free trade were not mentioned in any of the debates: even Stanhope was so far from embracing *laisser faire* doctrines that he proposed a system of public granaries to tide Britain over periods of dearth. The new legislation (44 Geo. III c.53 and c.109) raised import duties from 24s 3d per quarter when wheat was under 50s a quarter, and 6d if over 54s, to 30s 3¾d if under 63s and 7½d if over 66s. There appear no substantial grounds for believing that there was any large-scale retreat from arable farming, and in spite of Western's plausible exposition of the public utility of the increases, the real motivation seems to have been the desire to preserve profits, which had been extremely high in previous years. (The 1815 Corn Law, which has also generally been regarded as a measure to protect farmers' profits, has recently been reinterpreted as an attempt to prevent renewed peace-time competition from leading to the collapse of smaller farmers and to the discouragement of necessary capital investment.[41] In view of the fact that the directly analogous 1804 legislation was passed in war-time, it seems doubtful whether most MPs' motives in 1815 were so altruistic, whatever the larger views of ministers.)

Though Parliament was essentially a Parliament of landlords who were unlikely to neglect their own interests, the support given by the government to the 1804 Corn Law derived not so much from cynicism or expediency as from the belief that agricultural self-sufficiency was a desirable—and achievable—end in itself, even though it was in conflict with the economics of Britain's growing dependence on the importation of raw materials and the exportation of manu-factured goods. The government regarded itself as having a special obligation to safeguard the bare existence of the populace, though not otherwise entitled to interfere with questions such as clothing and shelter which were apparently still seen to some extent as *luxuries*. Food, in fact, was regarded as a kind of special case, the one essential commodity, somehow separate from the rest of the economy. The government's other invasions of *laisser faire*, directly affecting as they did the commercial and industrial sector, are therefore the more startling.

In 1793 the outbreak of war caused a sharp downswing in trade and various business partnerships found themselves in difficulties. Exchequer bills worth £2m were issued to tide over the worst affected firms.[42] This was done again in 1797, 1807, 1808 and 1811. In the latter year £6m worth of bills were allocated for this purpose, and though rather more than half (119 out of 205) applications for aid were granted, only £1,390,000 was issued.[43] At about the same period, a Commons select committee appointed to consider a petition for relief from weavers suffering from the falling off of trade, advised that:

'Grants of pecuniary aid, to any particular class of persons suffering under temporary distress, would be utterly inefficacious as to every good purpose, and most objectionable in all points of

view; particularly as they could not fail of exciting expectations unbounded in extent, incapable of being realised, and most
likely to destroy the equilibrium of labour and of employment,
in the various branches of Manufacture, of Commerce, and of
Agriculture.'[44]
This report, though it concerned the question of aid to employees
rather than to employers, was nevertheless relevant in its general
principles to the issue of government support of the business
sector during slumps, and really said little beyond reaffirming
stock *laisser faire* doctrines. Yet the government had been willing
to meet the business sector halfway in periods of crisis, possibly
because, though it stalwartly refused to admit that war-time
conditions involved any distortion of the market economy, the
effects of the war at least in terms of short-term trade fluctuations
was so glaringly obvious that the government felt obliged to make
ad hoc payments. This policy prevented a loss of confidence in the
City which might have affected government borrowing adversely,
while at the same time avoided the necessity of establishing the
unprecedented legislative and bureaucratic machinery that would
have been required for economic regulation. Quite apart from the
political and practical impossibility of setting up such machinery,
the doctrinaire insistence that market forces must operate at all
costs meant that no one would have even known in abstract *how* to
regulate the economy. Though Peel said of Pitt, 'no minister ever
understood so well the commercial interests of the country', the
knowledge of Pitt and his immediate circle was limited to theoretical
generalizations. It was only after 1815 that the practical knowledge
of how to apply the theory caught up with the theory itself.

Suspension of Cash Payments
Yet there was one other economic initiative of the war years, extorted
entirely by war-time circumstances in spite of the government's
own objection to the principle of the measure, which was worth a
flood of regulations and was in fact the most significant administrative
act of the period: the suspension of cash payments. The Orders
in Council against enemy trade, equally controversial at the time
and much better known to posterity, were not an initiative—they
were in retaliation against similar French measures—nor were
they particularly significant in that most of the bad effects
attributed to them were in reality due to the French policy that
had provoked tham, and as they involved interference in another
country's trade they cannot be regarded as altogether contrary
to the logic of *laisser faire* as a system of domestic policy. The
suspension of cash payments, on the other hand, was a revolutionary
new departure with tremendous consequences. A basic premise

of classical economics was the fixed value of money, which, by providing a stable point of reference, acted as the main pivot in the operation of market forces. In 1797 the shortage of bullion caused by the exportation of gold in subsidies to Britain's allies obliged Pitt to decide on the measure of prohibiting the Bank of England from honouring its notes with cash. In effect, Britain went off the gold standard with regard to internal trade, and no attempt was made to regulate the issue of banknotes.

This step, undertaken as a measure of war-time necessity, not only contributed to a rate of inflation stimulating to the industrial sector, but actually created the monetary situation which made commercial expansion possible in a period of heavy taxation and commercial dislocation. Market forces were, to put it another way, no longer operating properly because of the war, though the government refused to acknowledge this, and it was only by detaching the distorted market forces from the pivot of gold, that is, by suspending cash payments, that economic paralysis was avoided. Though Sir John Sinclair pointed out that 'an increase of labour or industry, a more extended commerce and an increased revenue, required perpetual additions to the circulating medium of a country',[45] no full theory was ever elaborated to show the benefits of 'the paper system' as it was called.

Its defenders' main argument was that its effects were not harmful, and that the war could not be fought without it.[46] Besides Sinclair these defenders of 'the paper system' included Nicholas Vansittart whose deficit finance policy was widely criticized on orthodox grounds in the post-war years, and who pooh-poohed objections to 'the paper system' by claiming that its critics 'either suspect some latent fallacy in their own doctrines, or think them inapplicable to practical purposes'.[47]

Objections came to a head in 1811. The critics not only had the support of orthodox theory (as early as 1801 the Earl of Suffolk had criticized paper currency with lengthy quotations from Adam Smith[48]) but included amongst their number the most respected economists on both sides of politics, Francis Horner and William Huskisson. David Ricardo made his début as an economic expert on the same side. For once both *The Edinburgh Review* and *The Quarterly Review* agreed on an issue. After four nights of highly technical debates in the Commons 'the paper system' was vindicated by 180 votes to 75, almost certainly because it was realized that the alternative was the giving up of the war. It was certainly not appreciated to what extent this one major transgression of the Adam Smith system made possible all the rest of the government's indulgence in orthodoxy, by providing an element of flexibility in the economy to which the alternatives would have been either massive regulation, or collapse. What this meant in real terms will be discussed in the next chapter.

3

The Economic Consequences
of the War

Introductory

'Our commerce had flourished, our wealth had increased, our
possessions had multiplied. . . . War, the curse of every other
nation, had to Great Britain been a comparative blessing.' So boasted
Viscount Hamilton in 1808.[1] There was great justice in this claim.
Despite the government's policy failures in both the economic and
the military sphere, it was the developments of these years of war
which were to provide the basis for British domination of the world
economy during the next 60 years.

The currently established view of the Revolutionary and Napoleonic
Wars' effects on Britain, as presented for example by E. P. Thompson,
is that they were crucial in reducing what social and economic
status the labouring classes had previously possessed, and thereby
occasioned the emergence of a working-class consciousness.[2] The
effects of the wars in purely economic terms have been largely
neglected. Asa Briggs offers the standard set of assumptions—they
are scarcely more than that—when he suggests that the cotton and
pottery industries would have expanded more without the war, and
the iron industry and farming would have been spared the excessive
growth which led to the post-war recession.[3] The view that the war
might have been generally beneficial, pioneered by J. L. Anderson,
does not appear to have inspired much conviction.[4] Yet it is not too
much to say that Britain's international position in the nineteenth
century was what it was, mainly because of what happened between
1793 and 1815.

At the beginning of the 1790s Britain was already the most
powerful trading nation in the world, and her internal economy was
geared to overseas commerce to a greater extent than in any other
country. Perhaps a third of Britain's total industrial production
was being exported, and the proportion was increasing. Also, much

of the industrial product consumed at home was made from imported raw materials purchased with the balances derived from the export and re-export trade. Britain was at this time a major primary producer in certain sectors, notably tin and copper, but a much larger proportion of her domestic exports were of manufactures than was the case with France, her nearest rival.

Britain's commercial lead was only partly due to superior technology. By the end of the eighteenth century it is true that Britain had several hundreds of steam engines operating in textile mills and mines and foundries. The French by comparison had only a handful of water-powered cotton mills and a few steam engines for mines and furnaces, including five steam engines at the Le Creusot foundry. The first German cotton mill, using the already outmoded water-frame, was built near Düsseldorf as late as 1794. Although the first atmospheric engines for pumping to be set up on the continent were installed near Charleroi as early as 1721. 70 years later there were still only a handful of such engines operating in the mines in that area. Britain did, therefore, have a distinct technological advantage, but for the period prior to the outbreak of European war in 1792 the significance of this can be exaggerated. The real technological breakthrough was yet to come in the iron industry, and with richer local supplies of ore, the Silesian and other continental iron-producing areas fairly rivalled the British. Cotton, the industry which more than any other grew with the extension of steam power, was still only of secondary importance. In 1789 cotton exports had been only a fifth in value of woollen exports. Moreover, steam power could at first only be applied to one part of cotton textile manufacture, spinning, and even by 1808, when yarn was generally power spun, there were still only 28 or 30 power weaving mills in the country.[5] The mill at West Houghton destroyed by rioters in 1812 was the first successful large power loom mill. Britain's advantage came not from technology, but from the superior organization of labour and capital. It was because the British commercial and industrial sectors had more finance and more enterprise than in other countries, and not because they had more labour-saving devices, that Britain flourished.

The Elimination of Foreign Competition

The war years saw not only massive progress—both technological and organizational—in the British iron and cotton industries, but, even more important, the virtual extinction of many of Britain's economic rivals. The 'Atlantic Sector' of the European economy more or less collapsed. There was a shift of industry from coastal areas supplying overseas markets, to inland areas supplying home markets, and in some parts of France and Holland there was even an aggregate shift of capital from trade and industry into agriculture.[6] This was almost entirely the result of British naval activity during the war.

Curiously enough, Britain's naval industry, on which her command of the sea depended, was not only one of the most organizationally inefficient of British industries, but produced an article which by international standards was markedly inferior. French 80-gun ships, for example, were larger than the British 110-gun *Ville de Paris* and were less crank, that is, less prone to heel before the wind. In the British capital ships the lowest tier of guns, comprising the heaviest part of the broadside, was usually within three feet of the water-line, and could not be used when the vessel was heeling excessively under sail in choppy weather, because of the danger of shipping water and capsizing. The French ships on the other hand, with their lowest gun ports seven feet above the water-line, and sailing comparatively upright, could use their heaviest guns with safety. Often the British ships carried too great a weight for their size, which spoilt their handling and weakened their structure. French naval defeats were largely the result of superior British gunnery and of the French policy of trying to disable British vessels by firing into their rigging, instead of into their hulls. The significance of this can be seen in the much higher proportion of fatal casualties on French ships exposed to direct cannon fire from British vessels, as compared to the very high proportion of wounded to dead on British ships where most casualties were inflicted, not by cannon fire direct, but by small-arms fire and by splinters and debris from the rigging overhead. It was by such marginal advantages that Britain won command of the seas, and with the larger enemy warships cleared from the ocean, it was left to naval brigs and privateers to complete the work by suppressing enemy activity at sea.

On 31 December 1793 the Royal Navy had in commission only 42 sloops and no gun brigs; by 30 September 1801 it had 112 sloops and 75 gun brigs as well as 112 line of battleships, 11 fifties and 147 frigates.[7] In addition, no less than 10,605 letters of marque were issued to British privateers between 1793 and 1814,[8] though not all of them to vessels engaged in full-time marauding. In fact the Royal Navy accounted for the bulk of foreign shipping captured and condemned as prizes.[9] The first and principal victim was France, as may be seen from the following figures:

	1787-9 annual average	1819-21 annual average
Imports	548,130,500 francs	427,995,833 francs
Exports	488,193,867 francs	380,142,867 francs

The most important long-term loss to the French was her colonial trade:

	1787-9 annual average	*1819-21 annual average*
Colonial imports	233,704,300 francs	90,982,200 francs[10]

Before France declared war on Britain in 1793, her West Indian colonies were twice as populous as the British. Guadaloupe and Martinique had larger populations than any British island save Jamaica, and Jamaica had only half the population of St Domingo.

	Population	Value of exports
British West Indies	520,889	£5,182,291
French West Indies	963,779	£10,631,326
Dutch West Indies	200,000	£3,000,000[11]

Britain eventually conquered all the French colonies save St Domingo and there the establishment of the negro state removed the enormously rich plantations altogether from the European colonial system.

In European waters, too, British naval intervention added its burden to the disruption of revolution and land war. By 1799 France's external trade had dropped by nearly half.[12] There was an initial revival under Napoleon, but by 1814 French trade was 35 per cent. down on the 1806 figure.[13] There was some recovery after the war, though the Turkey and Levant trade, traditionally one of France's most important assets, suffered a more permanent setback:

	1787-9 annual average	*1819-21 annual average*
Imports	39,961,267 francs	21,291,067 francs
Exports	19,561,033 francs	8,628,233 francs[4]

Perhaps more important than the long-term reduction of trade was the fact that French merchants and industrialists were deprived of the opportunity for capital accumulation by 20 years of war-time hardships, at precisely that stage in their country's economic development when large-scale capital accumulation was vital for future growth. Actual losses were perhaps less crucial than the failure to make the gains possible to British entrepreneurs.

Spain had been enjoying a considerable economic revival during the eighteenth century, especially in Catalonia. In 1772 customs revenues were at 53 million *reales*. By 1792 they had more than tripled, to 182 million *reales*. This prosperity continued after the outbreak of war on the continent, but only so long as Spain was Britain's ally against France. In 1795 Spain made peace with France and during the following year she decalred war on Britain. In 1799 her customs brought in only 59 million *reales*.[15] Not that Britain permitted any serious interference in her vital imports of Spanish wool, even while the two countries were at war. Except in 1798 and 1808 there was no significant falling off of Spanish wool exports to Britain.[16] After Spain itself became a battleground in 1808, the Spanish economy totally collapsed, and her domination of the trade with her own colonies was usurped by Britain.

Portugal, too, suffered by the opening up of Brazil to Britain after 1808. At their peak in 1799, Portuguese manufactures exported to her own colonies were worth 14,080,000 *cruzados* (about £1,750,000). The value of such exports in 1807 were down to 2,936,000 *cruzados* because of British competition and war-time dislocations, and fell to 568,000 *cruzados* in 1808. They remained under 2,000,000 *cruzados* a year (or less than one seventh of their 1799 peak) till 1815.[17] 'Great Britain has ruined Portugal by her·free trade with the Brazils', reported Wellington, 'not only the customs of Portugal, to the amount of a million sterling per annum, are lost, but the fortunes of numerous individuals, who lived by this trade, are ruined.'[18]

Neutral countries benefitted from the war, but only so long as they remained neutral. Save for a brief interlude of defiance quashed by Nelson at the Battle of Copenhagen in 1801, Denmark was neutral till 1807, and gained an important share of the Mediterranean trade. There was also a major, if fluctuating, expansion of Anglo-Danish trade.

	£ British domestic exports to Denmark	£ British exports (real values)
1802	351,371	232,283
1803	1,852,607	770,216
1804	3,809,603	1,722,458
1805	4,217,286	1,867,918
1806	1,420,290	627,181
1807	3,319,014	3,010,967[19]

In September 1807, a British fleet arrived off Copenhagen for the second time in less than 10 years, and Danish neutrality came to an end. In the next seven years, half of Denmark's merchant marine—1,560 vessels valued at £8m—was captured or sunk by the British, customs dues at Copenhagen fell by 90 per cent, and the disruption of communications between Denmark proper and Norway by the British blockade had a major impact on the growth of Norwegian separatism. In 1814 Norway became part of Sweden. By this arrangement Denmark lost her main source of naval supplies and her principal recruiting ground for seamen, so that as a commercial power she never recovered.[20] Britain also conquered the relatively insignificant Danish West Indian islands of Santa Cruz, St Thomas and St John. (By 1814 the only West Indian island controlled by a European state other than Britain or Spain, by that time her ally, was St Barthelémy, an island only eight square miles in area, which had been ruled by the Swedes since being ceded to Sweden by France in 1784.)

The other major neutral maritime nation was the USA. As a neutral, the United States enjoyed a great expansion of her re-export trade and also of her carrying trade, that is, the transporting of cargoes between one foreign country and another without landing at a home port. During the war years, moreover, the United States became a major primary producer of cotton and grain. By 1807, three fifths of the cotton used in Britain was grown in the States,[21] and the settling of the lands west of the Alleghenies enabled the Americans to produce enough cheap wheat to cash in on the disruption of grain supplies in war-torn Europe. Moreover, the British blockade of Spain between 1795 and 1801, and 1805 and 1808 helped the Americans to invade the profitable South American markets. In the period 1788-96, only 26 Boston vessels visited Chilean ports. In the next 12 years the total was 226. Trade with South America increased seven-fold in six years:

	US Exports to South America	US Imports from same
1795	$1,389,219	$1,739,138
1801	$8,437,659	$12,799,888[22]

($1 = 5s British)

Figures for the growth of US trade in this period were distorted by the rise of export prices in the 1790s,[23] but the growth was still spectacular. It might have been even greater had it not been the case that war-time hazards affected even neutrals. Infringement of the contraband regulations promulgated by the belligerents led to an undeclared war between the US and France in the late 1790s, and between the US and Britain after 1807. Between 1807 and 1812 Britain seized 917 American ships, France 741, Denmark 70, and Naples 47.[24] The Americans also suffered from the activities of the Barbary principalities, which for most of the period were Britain's allies. The US together with Sweden, were at war with Tripoli between 1801 and 1805, peace being made only after a prolonged blockade and several attacks on the Tripolitans. The Americans blamed this war on the influence of the British *chargé d'affaires*, Bryan McDonough, who was also physician to the Bey of Tripoli.[25] The outbreak of war between the US and Algiers was prevented or at least delayed by the commencement of full-scale hostilities between Britain and the US in 1812 (Denmark was also at war with Algiers in 1800, and Portugal with both Algiers and Tunis).

The deterioration of Anglo-American relations contributed to a decline in US trade after 1807. In 1812 war broke out between the two countries. The Americans were initially successful in inflicting ignominious defeats on the British frigates *Guerrière, Macedonian* and *Java*, but the Royal Navy soon had nearly all American shipping bottled up in port. The last part of American trade to be extinguished was their grain exports to Spain, on which the British and Spanish armies depended. This was permitted under licence till the restoration of the Baltic trade in 1814 provided an alternative source of supplies.[26] The following figures show the extent of the growth, and of the subsequent collapse:

	$ imports	$ exports	$ re-exports	$ net profits of carrying trade
1791	30,500,000	19,012,000	500,000	6,200,000
1807	144,740,342	108,343,000	59,644,000	42,000,000
1809	61,029,726	52,203,000	20,798,000	26,000,000
1811	57,887,952	61,317,000	16,023,000	40,800,000
1813	22,177,812	27,856,000	2,848,000	10,200,000
1814	12,967,859	6,927,000	145,000	2,600,000[27]

American trade did not return to its 1807 level for *20 years* after 1814. For Britain on the other hand, it was 1814, the final and most strenuous year of the war, that was the record year.

British Trade in War-Time

While ruining her rivals, Britain flourished. The rate at which British trade grew was less rapid than it had been prior to the outbreak of war, nevertheless grow it did, especially in the 1790s, in spite of an evident shrinkage of world trade as a whole.

Average annual official values in £

	Imports	Exports	Re-exports
1788-1792	18,861,600	15,314,000	5,599,600
1798-1802	29,900,800	24,150,800	16,080,800
1808-1812	31,600,000	29,300,000	13,200,000
1814 only	35,400,000	35,800,000	28,900,000[28]

Yet this was not because British trade was not subject to the hazards of war. Though British frigates and sloops could prevent enemy trade, they largely failed to suppress hostile privateers, and though convoys were used on the high seas, audacious French raiders continued active and occasionally even cut out British coasters within sight of English coastal resorts. The rate of loss for round trips to foreign ports was more than one ship in every 20 sailings.[29] Yet the enemy was less of a hazard than the usual gamut of bad weather, accidents and mistakes. Between 1793 and 1800, 2,967 vessels were lost by accident, and 2,861 by enemy action.[30] During the slightly longer period 1793-1802, 8,890 new merchant ships were built, and 2,218 prizes were recommissioned for British use.[31] In September 1793 there were 16,329 British merchant ships with a normal crew of 118,952. By September 1803 there were 21,445 ships with 155,445 crew, and by 1815, 24,860 ships with normal crews totalling 177,309. It was probably in the matter of crews that British merchant shipping was worst affected by the war, because of the constant use of press-gangs to recruit for the Navy, and in 1795 and 1805 the imposition of recruiting quotas on all British ports, enforced by embargoes. Even naval vessels had many foreign seamen. One officer claimed that of 563 seamen on his ship, ten were West Indians, 28 Americans, 11 Germans, eight Swedes, seven Danes, six Portuguese, four Spanish, two Bengali, and one each from the Netherlands, Ragusa and Corsica.[32] Many merchantmen must have had even more exotic complements.

There was also the special difficulty of these years, Napoleon's pioneer attempt to bring Britain to her knees by economic warfare, by his closure of continental ports to British shipping after 1807. An American observer claimed that:

'the Continental system, as they called it, and as they managed it, was promoting to the utmost extent the views of England; was, instead of impairing her commerce, securing to her that of the whole world; and was pouring into her lap the means of continuing the war, just as long as her ministers should think it expedient.'[33]

The only truth in this, however, was that the British blockade imposed in retaliation caused even more immediate hardship on the continent than the Continental System did in Britain. French customs receipts dropped from 51,700,000 livres in 1806 and 60,483,000 livres in 1807 to a mere 18,500,000 livres in 1808 and 11,500,000 livres in 1809.[34] But, as international traders on the continent had a less crucial role in their national economies than did the merchants and entrepreneurs of Britain, their hardships were relatively less significant at the national level. In Britain, the West India merchants soon accumulated a surplus of colonial goods for which they could no longer find markets, and textile producers also found themselves in difficulties by 1808. Taken in conjunction with the political weakness of the Portland and Perceval ministries and the re-emergence of working-class unrest (itself occasioned partly by the trade slump) the increasing dislocations of the British business sector might indeed have brought the country to its knees had not the Continental System collapsed first, in 1812.

That British commerce was able to stave off the worst effects of the Continental System for almost all the five years of its operation was due to British traders' extraordinary flexibility in discovering and exploiting new markets. This was made possible by the fact that British merchant partnerships were by later standards extremely unspecialized. Many houses traded with countries in two or even three continents, both imported and exported, and concentrated on no individual commodity.[35] Consequently, though not especially efficient competitively, they were able to shift the focus of their operations very easily. Even during the 1790s they had rapidly taken over the trade of the captured West Indian islands. The commencement of the Continental System coincided with the opening up of the South American markets. In spite of the bad start made with the Buenos Aires expeditions of 1807-7, Britain soon cornered the Rio de la Plata market. In 1808 the Portuguese monopoly of Brazilian trade was given up, and for a time in 1810 the British enjoyed a preferential rate of customs duties, lower even than that paid by Portuguese nationals.[36] In 1812 four fifths of British exports to South America were to Brazil.[37] The statistics for the expansion of British trade with South America and with the captured (i.e. former French, Dutch and Danish) West Indies are as follows:

	£ imports to Britain	£ exports
1806	1,226,525	1,795,962
1807	1,341,454	1,326,260
1808	2,837,724	4,829,636
1809	5,090,409	6,381,668
1810	6,961,389	5,970,061
1811	3,831,286	3,046,819
1812	2,471,426	4,114,987[38]

British merchants also found new routes into Europe. Exports to Germany fluctuated wildly, hitting rock bottom in 1811, the year in which the blockade was most effectively enforced:

	£ exports to Germany
1806	5,608,424
1807	351,410
1808	1,531,617
1809	5,952,780
1810	2,153,194
1811	60,917
1812	198,509

But there was a steadier growth in the exports to the British military base in the Mediterrcnean, Gibraltar, Malta and, after 1809, the Ionian Islands, whence commodities, often colonial re-exports, were clandestinely transported into Italy and even into southern France:

Trade with Gibraltar, Malta and Ionian Islands

	£ imports	£ exports
1806	113,899	773,002
1807	188,883	1,599,617
1808	396,034	4,286,084
1809	994,969	5,757,423
1810	827,772	4,024,274
1811	407,516	5,364,025
1812	552,470	8,722,525

Sweden, Britain's ally till 1810, was another backdoor into Europe:

	£ imports	£ exports
1791	267,770	74,743
1806	192,139	175,240
1807	218,791	653,193
1808	370,839	2,358,322
1809	430,679	3,523,923
1810	426,560	4,870,584
1811	376,952	522,520
1812	223,210	2,307,977[39]

After Sweden's declaration of war on Britain on 17 November 1810, British ships were convoyed by the Royal Navy through the Great Belt, running the gauntlet of Danish gun-boats, and once in the Baltic, dispersed off the Swedish coast equipped with forged papers and with crews schooled to give question-proof accounts of having sailed from American ports. The Tsar's ukase of 31 December 1810 permitted colonial produce to be imported in colonial bottoms, so that scarcely had Sweden's ports been closed to *bona fida* British merchants ships, than Russia's ports opened to the same vessels sailing under American colours.[40] Danish gun-boats in the Great Belt were for the most part kept at bay by Royal Navy escorts, though five Danish (or rather Norwegian) brigs sailing out of Kristiansand captured an entire returning convoy of 47 merchantmen off The Naze on 19 July 1810.[41] (Of these ships, 17 or 18 were genuinely American.)[42]

Prior to the establishment of the Continental System, Britain's trade with the United States had also been increasing, each country being the other's largest single market. The Anglo-American trade balance was enormously in Britain's favour, export to the USA, mainly of manufactured goods, being worth perhaps three times imports (though these imports included the raw cotton needed for the expanding Lancashire textile industry). The trade balance between the USA and the West Indies was in the American's favour, the Americans supplying the bulk of all provisions, apart from dry fish, to the Caribbean, to the value of about £1.5m annually, and purchasing roughly £1m worth of rum, sugar and coffee anually.[43] This American surplus in the US—West Indian trade was perhaps as little as one tenth of the American deficit in trade with Britain. The difference was made up from America's profits from her successful exploitation of the war-time needs of other European countries. Till 1808, therefore, the USA played a vital part in the British commercial system, even though there were disputes over American infringements of Britain's contraband regulations. When Britain responded to the Continental System by imposing a total blockade of the continent, Anglo-American relations rapidly deteriorated and even before the outbreak of war between the two countries in 1812, trade between them was dwindling.

This, taken together with the increasing effectiveness of the French blockade regulations, and with a recession in the South American trade caused by the flooding of the markets in the previous three years, led to a commercial slump in 1811, with only exports to the Mediterranean bases showing any increase.

	To USA	To South America etc.	To Northern Europe	To Mediterranean Bases
		Exports in £		
1810	7,813,000	5,970,061	11,221,000	4,024,274
1811	1,432,000	3,046,819	2,358,000	5,364,025[44]

The effect of the counter-blockade on relations with the USA was constantly reverted to in parliamentary debates on the subject of the Orders in Council establishing the counter-blockade. On 23 June 1812 these Orders in Council, insofar as they affected American vessels, were revoked. In one sense it was already too late. The United States had declared war during the previous week. But in another sense, the worst of the crisis was already over, for Napoleon's invasion of Russia had ended the network of alliances he depended on to exclude British trade from Europe.

The new trade outlets developed during the war, together with the disruption in Europe and the progress of industrialization in Britain, gave Britain a decisive advantage over the rest of Europe by 1815. This can be seen by comparing the percentage of import and export trade with different parts of the world, in the immediately pre-war and immediately post-war years. The most striking feature of the comparison is the relative decrease of imports from, and increase of exports to, other European countries. Imports are given as a percentage of total British imports, and exports as a percentage of total British exports:

		1789-93	1815-19
N. Europe	Imports	26.4	16.8
	Exports	28.5	35.5
S. Europe	Imports	19.0	10.9
	Exports	18.2	18.9
Asia	Imports	20.0	25.7
	Exports	12.3	15.0
Africa	Imports	0.6	1.0
	Exports	4.4	0.8
British N. America	Imports	1.4	2.0
	Exports	4.8	4.2
USA	Imports	6.6	9.2
	Exports	18.8	15.5
British W. Indies	Imports	24.5	26.8
	Exports	12.5	11.4
Foreign W. Indies and S. America	Imports	1.5	7.5
	Exports	0.3	8.4

Internal Readjustments

The wars which gave Britain such advantages obviously had their cost. Indeed they cost more, much more, both in total cost and taken year by year, than any previous war. Expenditure on the war was 16 per cent of gross national income in 1811, the same percentage as in 1915.[45] There was also a massive diversion of labour: perhaps as many as 600,000 men engaged full-time in the Army and Navy, or for vital parts of the working year in the Militia and Volunteers. Yet trade and industry continued to expand during the war. During the Seven Years' War there had been virtual stagnation; during the American War of Independence, considerable recession; during the two World Wars of the twentieth century (especially the Second World War) crippling retrogression. It is normal for major wars to be fought at serious cost to the national economy. Britain between 1793 and 1815 was unusual in fighting a major war and getting richer at the same time. The total cash expenditure of the war was indeed probably exceeded by the total increment in national wealth during the period of conflict: a unique achievement.

This is not to deny that the war brought in its train fluctuations in trade, stagnation in certain sectors, and an increased frequency of bankruptcy, including the epidemic of bank failures in 1811. The fantastic success of the iron and steel industry which nearly *quadrupled* its productive capacity during the war years, could not of course be rivalled by other industries. And for the working classes there was a decline of real (and sometimes of nominal) earnings which led to food riots and industrial unrest, though it is worth noting that the Luddite troubles, easily the most important popular disturbances of the war years, stemmed, in Yorkshire at least, not from a recession, but from the ready availability of industrial capital which made possible the introduction of the mechanized processes against which the Luddites were protesting.

But these domestic difficulties were in part the symptoms of internal growth, for Britain's enormous advantage relative to other countries was only half the story of these years. There were also crucial developments within Britain itself.

First there was war-time inflation. During the war domestic prices rose by about 3.3 per cent per annum.[46] This was caused by bad harvests and war-time trade fluctuations periodically forcing up prices, and the increased amount of money in circulation preventing them from returning subsequently to former levels. That there was more money in circulation was the result of the general increase of economic activity which acted on the supply of money at a time when the normal limitations on expansion of the money supply had been removed by the Bank of England's suspension of cash payments in 1797. Previously, banknotes had been issued for convenience of handling: £9,643,000 worth were in circulation in July 1795.[47] After 1797, however, they became the normal circulating medium in Britain, though they did not become legal tender till 1811. In that year Lord King requested his tenants to pay an extra quantity of paper currency to make up for its depreciated value compared to gold coin, being probably inspired not so much by his theoretic objection to the 'paper system' as by 'that mercenary disposition which is attributed with very little reserve to his Lordship by all his tenantry',[48] and a bill had to be rushed through Parliament making paper currency legal tender.

There was no attempt to control the amount of paper in circulation. In October-November 1800 the monthly average value of Bank of England notes in circulation was calculated at £15,878,400, and by mid-July 1811 the estimate was £22,558,000.[49] There was also a large increase in the number of country banks, all of them issuing increasing quantities of their own notes. In 1809 the face value of stamped notes issued by country banks was £14,500,000, and there were also some unstamped notes circulating.[50] The face value of the money and money instruments in circulation in Britain may well have more than doubled during the wars. That inflation was not more than 3.3 per cent per annum was an indication that economic expansion absorbed most of the increase in the money supply which it generated. In fact, easy money was probably the crucial factor enabling war-time expansion. There was lavish capital investment in spite of the war. For example, the West India, Brunswick, London, East India, Commercial and Rotherhithe Docks were all opened between 1802 and 1813, transforming London's port facilities, and it was noticed that:

'Amidst the warfare in which we are now engaged for our preservation and existence as a Nation, it is a matter of exultation and self-confidence to reflect, that the most considerable and most important of our public works suffer, comparatively speaking, but little interruption.'[51]

In house-building, too, after a depression in the late 1790s, there was massive expansion between 1800 and 1815.[52] Ready money also encouraged entrepreneurs. The high figure of 2,112 bankruptcies in 1811 (as compared to an annual average of 938 for the previous decade, and 496 for the 1780s) undoubtedly denoted a serious commercial crisis, but the war-time rise in bankruptcy rates generally indicated both an increased level of business and also an increased readiness to take risks.[53] Yet the 3.3 per cent inflation was the most important concomitant of this situation of ready money. It favoured industrial entrepreneurs and farmers at the expense of employees, landlords and rentiers. Inflation, by enabling entrepreneurs to purchase raw materials at last year's prices, operated as a mechanism for taking money from non-productive property owners (i.e. landlords and rentiers) and giving it to the men whose acumen and solvency were contributing dynamically to industrial growth. Wage-earners were also adversely affected, of course, and their loss in terms of real wages was further gain for the industrialist. The larger landlords, including the peerage, to some extent protected themselves by increased efficiency in their estate management, but amongst the lower and middle classes these years saw a substantial accumulation of economic power in the hands of entrepreneurs, at the expense both of bourgeois rentiers and workers.

Taxation, too, favoured the entrepreneur, at least in relative terms. Fifty-eight per cent of the cost of the war was covered by taxes, as compared to 21 per cent of the cost of the War of the Austrian Succession, 20 per cent of the Seven Years' War, and 19 per cent of the American War of Independence.[54] War taxes altogether totalled £542.1m. The greater part of these were taxes on consumption, including duties totalling £230.2m on malt, tea, sugar, spirits, wine, salt, beer and tobacco, which all affected general living standards. Property tax by comparison raised £155.6m (but over a shorter period) and affected only the richer half of the population. Property tax returns consisted of a signed declaration of one's income if it was between £60 (the sum below which one was exempt) and £200 (the sum below which one paid rates according to a sliding scale). People with incomes over £200 per annum (which included most entrepreneurs) merely stated that they were liable to the full rate and set down the sum they proposed to pay. The General Commissioners investigated these statements and could examine tax-payers. It was more usual for industrial entrepreneurs, possessing more complex, multifarious and unpredictable sources of income, to understate their incomes than it was for landowners, farmers and tradesmen.[56] Assessed taxable income under Schedule D (which included industrial and commercial profits) hardly increased in 1803-13 while income under Schedule B (agricultural profits) went up by a half in the same period not because of stagnation in trade and industry and expansion of farming, but because of the relative easiness of getting away with low tax claims in trade and industry.

	1803	1810	1813
	£	£	£
Total property assessed	105,018,456	121,193,777	130,057,746
Total Schedule A (Property)	38,498,136	51,885,879	57,129,047
Total Schedule B (Agricultural profits)	24,275,057	33,376,216	36,864,523

Total Schedule D	£	£	£
(Trade, industry			
and professions)	34,854,674	34,402,223	34,383,632
Of which:			
Yorks	1,813,537	1,840,421	1,762,535
Lancs	2,240,347	1,799,084	1,583,731
Staffs	461,434	495,120	525,048
Warwicks	571,519	601,498	592,375
London	6,813,990	6,534,502	6,697,990.[57]

Moreover, in the export trade—precisely that sector which was most successfully promoted by British military and naval power—goods for export either had large export drawbacks or in some cases, were not subject to excise at all,[58] and, therefore, also contributed little to the expenses of the war by way of indirect taxation.

Farmers were not as well placed as industrial entrepreneurs to evade taxes—a tax collector could sit on a stile and value a field of wheat which was open to any passer-by to see—and they also had to pay higher poor-rates: in Sussex in 1803 they were 23s per head of population, in Buckinghamshire and Oxfordshire over 16s 6d, but in the West Riding 7s, and in Lancashire only 5s. Nevertheless, farmers also benefited from the war because it gave them what was virtually a protected market. Between 1775 and 1786 the average annual grain imports were 564,413 quarters, whereas between 1799 and 1810 the average imports were 1,417,003 quarters, a large increase which, however, was inadequate for Britain's needs and would certainly have been much greater if it had not been for the war. During the 1800 grain shortage, the Earl of Warwick complained of farmers playing guinea whist and mixing brandy with their wine while bothering to cultivate only two thirds of their land,[59] and Henry Hunt afterwards wrote of the period 1801-2:

'If a farm was to be let, scores were riding and driving over each other, ready to break their necks to take it, to rent it at any price. Not only farmers, but tailors, tinkers, grocers, linen-drapers and all sorts of tradesmen and shopkeepers, were running, *helter-skelter*, to be farmers; men connected with the press, and cunning attorneys were joining in the chase; men of all professions, indeed, were now eager to become gentleman farmers.'[60]

In 1810 is was reported from the West Country, 'the whole of the landed Interest are in a state of unexampled & growing prosperity'. Tenants were offering double rent for the renewal of seven year leases:

'It is notorious that the whole mass of the Landed Proprietors & Tenants in this part of the country are comparatively in a much better condition than they were at the Commencement of the

Revolutionary War with France. For the general Expences of Living & Taxes have increased about half since that period but Rents & the value of produce have increased in a much higher proportion. The same observation will apply still more strongly to the North of England ... You may depend upon it therefore that the War is not merely indifferent to these important classes, but is absolutely and unequivocally popular with them.'[61]

The prosperity of farmers was also indicated by the extensive enclosing of common pastures and wastes. This is usually interpreted merely as a measure of demand, but it also demonstrates the existence of readily available money for the legal and fencing and drainage costs. It might even be that farmers were at something of a loss to know what else to do with their profits. Between 1761 and 1792 average acreage of commons and wastes enclosed annually was 14,996 acres; between 1793 and 1801, it was 30,432 acres and between 1802 and 1815, following the General Enclosure Act of 1801, 52,839 acres.[62]

This happy state of affairs for the farmer was not so fortunate for the bulk of the country's population, the labour force, who were already receiving a decreasing share of the nation's increasing prosperity because of inflation. In the quinquennium of 1788-92 wheat prices averaged 49s 1d per quarter; 20 years later the average was 101s 4½d per quarter.[63] When, towards the end of the wars and during the immediate post-war period, the poorer classes sought a violent remedy to starvation economics, the governing class reacted speedily and manifested great reluctance to make concessions, and this, too, was a result of the wars. In the 1790s especially, the conflict was social and ideological as well as nationalistic, and the upheavals all over Europe (not least in Ireland) infected the richer classes with an acute fear of the poorer. The old traditions of paternalism, of the frank intercourse of free Britons, withered as much because of the paronoia of the rich, as because of their hunger for maximized profits. At the same time the war provided the rich with weapons with which to indulge their fears: the Volunteers, and a larger Army, and the universal excuse of *national security*. At the moment of crisis, all the propertied classes rallied to one banner. Apparent exceptions like Earl Stanhope or Sir Francis Burdett were as loathed by the opposition as they were by the government. Opposition JPs and Lords Lieutenant were as active against Luddites as were ministerialist stooges. Thus the war not only fostered the enlargement of the gulf between richer and poorer, but also provided the means of countering the discontents which inevitably accompanied this process.

It may be seen how few of those wartime changes derived from the initiative of the government. Diplomatic endeavours to find new markets never made up for the loss of markets closed by hostilities. The establishment of a virtual monopoly of colonial produce as a result of the policy of Dundas and his successors, though it helped undermine Napoleon's Continental System, was neither permanent nor, while it lasted, unambiguously an advantage. The real benefits of the war derived from the suspension of cash payments and the destruction of rival commerce. The first was the result of an emergency expedient adopted with the utmost reluctance at a moment of crisis. The other was the outcome of a traditional policy, almost an instinctive reflex, since systematic interference with enemy trade had been standard British practice, not merely in previous wars against France, but in every war as far back as Queen Elizabeth's time. The real achievement of the British government was that it merely survived to preside passively over Britain's economic development but even that, under prevailing conditions, was achievement enough.

NOTES TO CHAPTERS

The abbreviations of manuscript sources are listed on pages 377-8.

Introduction
1 CAMPBELL, J. LORD, *The Lives of the Chief Justices of England*, 3 vols., 1857 vol. 3 pp. 169-71
2 Cf. DAVIS, D. BRION, *The Problem of Slavery in the Age of Revolution*, 1975 pp. 373-85
3 BUTTERFIELD, H., *George III Lord North and the People 1779-80* 1949, p. VI

Part One
1 OLIGARCHY
1 LAURENCE, J., 'On the Nobility of the British Gentry', *Pamphleteer* xxiii. (1824) pp. 159-205; p. 160. In 1820, 22,627 persons paid duty on armorial bearings, cf. *Parl. Papers* 1835 XLIX p. 91
2 *H. M. C. Lonsdale*, p. 147 to Lonsdale 21 April 1794
3 THOMAS, 'Marriage Patterns' *P.S.* 26 p. 102
4 GREVILLE, FULKE *The Life of the Renouned Sr Philip Sidney*, 1652, p. 79.
5 NAMIER, L., *England in the Age of the American Revolution* 1930, pp. 6-15
6 *The Spectator*, no. 108, 4 July 1711
7 *Political Register*, vol. 2, p. 57, 17 July 1802
8 LADY HOLLAND, *Journal*, vol. 1, p. 206, 20 Nov. 1798
9 ASPINALL and SMITH, *English Historical Documents*, vol. 11, pp. 204-5, Grosvenor to Pitt 14 May 1804
10 P.RO.N.I. T 2541 IK 17 Abercorn to Hamilton, 3 Jan. 1801
11 WILBERFORCE, *Life*, vol. 1, p. 383
12 LORD HOLLAND, *Memoirs*, vol. 1, p. 191
13 *Parl. Debates* vol. 16, col. 276, 28 March 1810
14 Devon R.O., 152H C1809 OZ, Ellenborough to Sidmouth, 2 February 1809
15 LADY HOLLAND, *Journal*, vol. 1, p. 205, 20 Nov. 1798
16 BUTLER, C., *Reminiscences*, 1822, pp. 181-2
17 LUCAS, C., *The Infernal Quixote*, 4 vols., 1801, vol. 2, pp. 46-52, 67-69
18 N.L.S., Minto Mss, E. L. Dalkeith to G. Elliot, 12 April [1806]

19 LORD HOLLAND, *Memoirs*, vol. 2, p. 43 N
20 MELBOURNE, *Papers*, p. 25, F. Lamb to Lady Melbourne,
    6 March 1800
21 BACON, *Life Of Suffield*, p. 30, E. Harbord to Suffield, 13 March 1807
22 *H. M. C. Dropmore*, vol. 4, p. 96, Grenville to Whitworth, 20 Feb. 1798
23 JOHNSON, W. B. ed., *Memorandoms For... The Diary between 1798
    and 1810 of John Carrington*, 1973, p. 114, 10 May 1805
24 Wentworth-Woodhouse Muniments F33/79, Oddie to Fitzwilliam,
    8 Aug. 1809
25 Bodleian Ms. Top. Oxon. 281, f 67, W. Smith to Marlborough, 16 Dec. 1801
26 Northants, R.O., Milton Mss 69
27 *H. M. C. Dropmore* vol. 6, p. 438, Whitworth to Grenville, 9 Feb. 1801
28 ibid., p. 466, Wickham to Grenville, 7 March 1801
29 B. M. Add. 59,012, 7 June 1804
30 Bodleian Ms Eng. Lett c. 60, f 36, Yorke to Portland, 6 June 1809
31 TWISS, *Life of Eldon*, vol. 2, p. 145, cf. *Parl. Debates* vol. 18, col. 1017,
    25 January 1811
32 B. M. Add. 58986, Reeves to Grenville, 5 June 1806
33 Devon R.O., 152M C 1812 OZ, 6 April 1812
34 *H. M. C. Dropmore*, vol. 3, p. 195, 8 August 1795
35 *Parl. Debates*, vol. 4, cols. 340-1, 10 April 1805
36 GEORGE III, *Correspondence*, vol. 5, pp. 534-5 (n.2 to p. 533),
    Wellesley Pole to Richmond, 7 March 1810
37 N.L.W. 10804D, Wynn to Southey, 29 April 1807
38 WILBERFORCE, *Life*, vol. 2, pp. 454-6
39 *The Fallen Angels! A Brief Review of the Measures of the Late
    Administration. . . .* 1807, p. 5
40 *The Reasoner*, 30 January 1808. Letter from 'One of the People',
    28 January 1808
41 RANBY, *Influence of the Crown*, p. 39. Ranby was actually quoting a
    phrase used by the Foxite Tierney
42 COLCHESTER *Diary*, vol. 1, p. 18
43 SIDNEY, E., *The Life of Sir Richard Hill, Bart.*, 1839, p. 498
44 Bodleian Ms Eng. Lett. c. 60, f 27, 3 March 1806
45 Northants R.O., Milton Mss 67/2, Laurence to Fitzwilliam, 31 Dec. 1805
46 Durham R.O., D/LO/F 996(3) draft H. Vane Tempest to Richmond,
    Dec. 1809
47 N.L.S., 1041, f 77, 24 July 1799
48 Northants R.O., Milton Mss 68/1, Grant to Fitzwilliam, 17 June 1806
49 FRANCIS *Memoirs*, vol. 2, p. 451
50 *State of the Representation of England and Wales, delivered to the
    Society, the Friends of the People, 9 February 1793*, p. 32. OLDFIELD
    Representative History, vol. 6, p. 285 foll. cf. OLDFIELD *History of
    Boroughs.* Figure for influence in 1793 may be an underestimate
51 FONBLANQUE, *Annals of Percy*, vol. 2, p. 565-6, 4 February 1806
52 JUDD, G. P., *Members of Parliament 1734-1832*, New Haven 1955,
    Appendix 6
53 THOMAS, 'Marriage Patterns', *P.S.* 26, p. 101
54 JAMES, *Regimental Companion*, vol. 4, p. 305
55 GLOVER, *Peninsular Preparation*, pp. 145-6
56 JAMES, *Regimental Companion*, vol. 3, p. 472
57 FORTESCUE, *British Army*, vol. 11, p. 31
58 *Parl. Debates*, vol. 7, col. 1134, 14 July 1806
59 LEWIS, M., *Social History of the Navy 1793-1815*, 1960 p. 31. He gives
    131 sons of peers out of a sample of 1,800, but this probably includes *all*

the sons of peers in a complete sample of 3,500 officers commissioned 1793-1815 and surviving till 1823.

60 AUSTEN, JANE, *Persuasion*, chap. 3
61 HARDCASTLE, *Life of Campbell*, vol. 1, p. 48, J. Campbell to G. Campbell, 16 January 1800
62 Cf. THOMPSON, F. M. L., *Landed Society*, p. 32
63 P.R.O., HO, 42/44, Duke of Northumberland's letter of 30 July 1798
64 N.L.W., Glansevern Mss 8431, copy Powis to C. W. W. Wynn, Nov. 1808
65 Wentworth-Woodhouse Muniments, Sheffield, F 51/127
66 Devon R.O., 1262 M/L8 Cholwick to Fortescue, 17 July 1795
67 Wentworth-Woodhouse Muniments, F 51/18, F 51/33, F 51/44
68 Devon R.O., 1262 M/L7
69 B.M. Add. 37,886, f 65, 18 Feb. 1807
70 *A Dialogue between Thomas Telltruth and John Bull* (handbill, 1806, in Northampton Public Library)
71 *To the Freeholders of the County of Northampton* (handbill, 1806, in Northampton Public Library)
72 BACON, *Life of Suffield*, pp. 45-6, Harbord to Suffield, 7 Oct. 1810
73 BOHSTEDT, 'Riots', pp. 238-241
74 N.L.W. 481D, Wynn to Southey, 22 Feb. 1811
75 HEWITSON, A., *History of Preston*, Preston 1883, pp. 79, 130, 166, foll; HARDWICK, C., *History of the Borough of Preston and its Environs*, Preston 1857, pp. 660-1
76 HEWITSON, *Preston*, p. 370 n.
77 Lancs R.O., DDK, 1687, Alty to Derby, 20 Nov. 1796
78 FARINGTON, *Diary*, vol. 4, p. 209
79 B. M. Add. 38,257, f 211, Dundonald to Liverpool, 6 May 1814
80 ibid., f 248, Dundonald to Liverpool, 13 May 1814
81 B. M. Add. 38,258, f 51, Dundonald to Liverpool, 14 June 1814
82 B. M. Add. 29,472, f 176, Dundonald to Lady Liverpool, 25 April 1814
83 B. M. Add. 38,258, f 5, Dundonald to Liverpool, 1 June 1814
84 ibid. f 51, Dundonald to Liverpool, 14 June 1814

85 Northumberland R.O., 2DE. 113/3, Delaval to Allen, 28 Nov.? 1770
86 N.L.S., Minto Mss, JE 9
87 CRAWFORD AND BALCARRES, EARL OF, 'Haigh Cannel', *Transactions Of The Manchester Statistical Society*, 1933-4, pp. 15-16; cf. A. Birch, 'The Haigh Ironworks, 1789-1856: A Nobleman's Enterprise During The Industrial Revolution', *Bulletin Of The John Rylands Library*, 35 (1952-3), pp. 316-333
88 BAILEY, *Agriculture of Durham*
89 FONBLANQUE, *Annals of Percy*, vol. 2, p. 653
90 *Annual Register*, 1794, p. 327
91 RAYBOULD, *Black Country*, pp. 92, 191-3
92 BAILEY, *Agriculture of Durham*, p. 37-8
93 LEWIS, W. J., *Lead Mining in Wales*, Cardiff 1967, p. 164
94 MITCHELL and DEANE, *British Historical Statistics*, pp. 154, 157
95 THOMPSON, F. M. L., *Landed Society*, p. 264
96 RAYBOULD, *Black Country*, pp. 151, 191-3
97 Durham R.O., D/LO/B 33, report on leasing collieries, 27 Oct. 1814, pp. 3-4
98 TAYLOR, A. J., 'The Subcontract System in the British Coal Industry', in PRESSNELL, L. S., ed. *Studies in the Industrial Revolution*, 1960, pp. 215-235
99 Durham, R.O., D/LO/B 33 report on leasing collieries, 27 Oct. 1814, pp. 2-4

100 SPRING, D., 'English Landowners and Nineteenth Century Industrialism', in WARD, J. T., and WILSON, R. G., ed *Land and Industry*, 1971, p. 16-62; p. 33
101 N.L.W., Picton Castle Mss 4115, lease, 12 Feb. 1806
102 FARINGTON, *Diary*, vol. 4, pp. 138-9, 28 May 1807
103 *Gentleman's Magazine*, 1804, vol. 74, p. 1243

2 VOTERS AND PUBLIC OPINION

1 CANNON, J., *Parliamentary Reform 1640-1832*, 1973, pp. 293-8
2 OLDFIELD, *Representative History*, vol. 4, p. 607
3 WARD, T.A., *Peeps into the Past*, ed. A. B. Bell, 1909, p. 192
4 *Parl. Papers*, 1806, XII, p. 359, cf. 1852, IX, p. 462
5 FARINGTON, *Diary*, vol. 4, p. 99, 11 March 1807
6 OLDFIELD, *Representative History*, vol. 4, p. 464
7 Wentworth-Woodhouse Muniments, F 72/19
8 JUPP, P., *British and Irish Elections 1784-1831*, Newton Abbot 1973, pp. 86-8
9 Bodleian Ms Top. Oxon. 281, f 28, foll.
10 Berks R.O., D/EPb 028, f 76b, Radnor to Folkestone, 18 Aug. 1812
11 Lancs R.O., DDK 1687, Alty to Derby, 28 March and 25 April 1796
12 Northants R.O., Milton Mss 72, and *The Northampton Mercury*, 9 and 16 May 1807
13 B. M. Add. 38, 757 f 34
14 HARDCASTLE, *Life of Campbell* vol. 1, p. 290, Campbell to father, Oct. 1812
15 *Nottingham Records*, vol. 8, p. 49
16 Northumberland R.O. ZR1 32/2, Memo Book, 5 May 1807
17 B. M. Add. 38,334, f 29, Beckford in House of Commons, 13 Nov. 1761
18 [SIMOND, L], *Journal of a Tour and Residence in Great Britain during the Years 1810 and 1811*, 2 vols., Edinburgh 1815, vol. 1, p. 37, 17 Feb. 1810
19 Cf. HOLTMAN, R. B., *Napoleonic Propaganda*, Baton Rouge 1950
20 McDOWELL, R. B., ed. *The Correspondence of Edmund Burke*, 9 vols., Cambridge 1958-70, vol. 8, p. 36, Burke to Windham, 16 Oct. 1794
21 *Parl. Hist.* vol. 34, col. 161, 31 Dec. 1798
22 'DIOGENES', *Every Day Characters*, 1806, p. vii
23 *Parl. Papers*, 1826-7, XVII pp. 24-5, and p. 45
34 GRAY, *Perceval*, p. 132
25 Grey Mss, Durham, 47/1/28, Ponsonby to Grey, 23 Oct. 1808
26 WELLINGTON, *Supplementary Despatches*. vol. 6, p. 185, Wellesley to Castlereagh, 14 Nov. 1808
27 ASPINALL, *Politics And The Press*, p. 89
28 ibid., p. 92
29 ASQUITH, 'Perry and *The Morning Chronicle*', pp. 348, 367
30 WINDHAM, *Diary*, p. 322, Burke to Windham, 16 Oct. 1794
   ASPINALL, *Politics And The Press*, pp. 86-7
31 GRAY, *Spencer Perceval*, p. 133
32 Berks R.O. D/DPb 025 f 68a, Althorp to Folkestone, 26 March 1809
33 N. Yorks R.O. ZFW 7/2 141/5, Syvill to Cartwright, 10 April 1805
34 *Political Register*, vol. 15, p. 644, 29 April 1809

3 THE POLITICAL CONSCIOUSNESS OF THE WORKING CLASSES
  1 *Parl. Papers,* 1806, XII, p. 359, cf. 1852, IX, p. 462
    Parl. Papers, Poor Law Returns 1803-4, demy folio 13 (vol. 13 of
    supplement to Parl. Reports, First Series).
  3 FOSTER, J. O., 'Capitalism and Class Consciousness in earlier Nineteenth
    century Oldham', Cambridge Ph.D., 1967, p. 304
  4 WALLAS, *Place,* pp. 37-8
  5 *Parl. Papers,* 1801-2, VII, 1812, XI (Census Returns)
  6 SEAMAN, 'Democratic Societies', pp. 350-1
  7 P.R.O., HO, 42/108, Kinnard to Beckett, 6 July 1810; HO 42/117,
    Story to H. Goulbourn, 19 Sept. 1811; *Annual Register* 1804, p. 409;
    ibid. 1806, p. 450
  8 P.R.O., HO, 42/95, Story et al. to Hawkesbury, 13 May 1808
  9 *Parl. History,* vol. 31, col. 887, Second Report of the Secret Committee
    of the House of Lords, 7 June 1794
 10 SEAMAN, 'Democratic Societies', pp. 30-32
 11 B.M. Add. 27, 808, f 60-61
 12 PLACE, F., *The Autobiography of Francis Place, 1771-1854,* ed. M. Thale,
    Cambridge, 1972, pp. 57, 68-70
 13 HENDERSON, *Adolphus,* p. 80
 14 ibid., p. 86
 15 [SOUTHEY], *Espriella's Letters,* vol. 1, pp. 119-20
 16 N. COHN, *The Pursuit of The Millenium,* 1957, *passim*
 17 SANDERSON, M., 'Literacy and Social Mobility in the Industrial
    Revolution in England', *Past and Present,* 56 (1972), p. 75-105
 18 LAWSON, J., *Letters to the Young on Progress in Pudsey during the
    Last Sixty Years,* Stanningsley 1887, pp. 39-40
 19 *Parl. Papers,* 1843, XXVI, pp. 67-8
 20 THOMPSON, E. P., *Making of the Working Class,* pp. 484
 21 *Parl. Papers,* 1843, XXVI, p. 173
 22 *Parl. Papers,* 1834, X, p. 418
 23 FRENCH, G. J., *Life and Times of Samuel Crompton,* 2nd edit.,
    Manchester 1860, p. 102
 24 *Parl. Papers,* 1816, III, p. 337
 25 *Parl. Papers,* 1808, II, p. 121
 26 *Parl. Papers,* 1803, VIII, p. 901 (p. 13 of the Minutes of Evidence on
    Cotton Weavers)
 27 *Parl. Papers,* 1816, III, p. 205, cf. FAREY, J., *General View of the
    Agriculture and Minerals of Derbyshire,* 3 vols. 1815-17, vol. 3, pp. 503-4
 28 P.R.O., WO, 25/2907
 29 Wentworth-Woodhouse Muniments, F 45/74, copy Read to Pelham,
    9 Aug. 1802
 30 P.R.O., HO, 42/66, Read to Pelham, 10 May 1802
 31 Wentworth-Woodhouse Muniments, F 45/112, Fitzwilliam to Pelham,
    27 Sept. 1802
 32 ibid., F 45/117, Becket to Fitzwilliam, 28 Jan. 1803
 33 P.R.O., HO, 42/66 copies of Wormald, Gott and Wormald handbills at
    Troubridge and Frome
 34 *Parl. Papers,* 1824, V, p. 573
 35 ibid., p. 574
 36 ibid., p. 608
 37 THOMPSON, E. P., *Making of the Working Class,* p. 509
 38 P.R.O., HO, 42/47
 39 BOHSTEDT, 'Riots', p. 396, N 164
 40 ibid., pp. 52-3
 41 ibid., p. 1

42 ibid., p. 27
43 ibid., pp. 8-10
44 STEVENSON, J., 'Disturbance and Public Order in London 1790-1821', Oxford D. Phil., 1973, pp. 243-4, 258
45 PEAKE, R. B., *Memoirs Of The Colman Family*, 2 vols., 1841, vol. 2, p. 309
46 P.R.O., HO, 42/51, Portland to mayors of Banbury and Stafford in 1800
47 BOHSTEDT, 'Riots', pp. 118-23
48 P.R.O., HO, 42/51, f 262, Gepp to Portland, 18 Sept. 1800
49 P.R.O., HO, 102 17/2, f 197, Forbes to Fife, 3 April 1800
50 P.R.O., HO, 42/48, George to Arden, 16 March 1800
51 *Parl. Papers*, 1824, V, pp. 479, 529-32
52 BOHSTEDT, 'Riots', p. 369
53 ibid., pp. 108-9
54 P.R.O., HO, 42/107
55 P.R.O. HO, 42/44, Walford to Portland, 24 Sept. 1800
56 P.R.O., HO, 42/55/487

4 CHURCH AND RELIGION

1 FARINGTON, *Diary* vol. 7, p. 94, 3 Aug. 1812
2 P.R.O., HO, 42/87, Chippindale to Fletcher, 29 Jan. 1806
3 ALGER, J. G., *Englishmen in the French Revolution*, 1889, pp. 95-6
4 Cf. FREND, *Letters*, p. 80, Hammond to Frend, 3 April 1808
5 HALHED, N. B., *A Calculation on the Commencement of the Millenium*, 1795, p. 12
6 HALHED, N. B., *The Whole of the Testimonies to the Authority of the Prophecies and Mission of Richard Brothers, as Prince and Prophet of the Hebrews*, 1795, p. 81
7 BUCKINGHAM, J. S., *Autobiography*, 2 vols., 1855, vol. 1, p. 241
8 KIRBY, *Wonderful And Eccentric Museum*, vol. 4, pp. 260-301
9 WYNDHAM, H. A., *A Family History 1688-1837. The Wyndhams of Somerset, Sussex and Wiltshire*, 1960, p. 310
10 Wentworth-Woodhouse Muniments, F 33/18.
11 COLERIDGE, *Biographia Literaria*, chap. 11
12 B.M. Add. 47, 795, Foley to Morison, 3 April 1802
13 CONYBEARE, W. J., *Essays Ecclesiastical And Social*, 1855 pp. 4-27
14 N.L.W., Coed-y-maen Mss 10 f 779, Elmsley to Wynn, 19 Oct. 1799
15 WARD, W. R., 'The Tithe Question in England in the Early Nineteenth Century', *Journal Of Ecclesiastical History*, 16 (1965), pp. 67-81; espec. pp. 69-73
16 *Parl. Papers*, 1835, XXII
17 BEZODIS, P. A., 'The English Parish Clergy and their Place in Society, 1660-1800' Trinity Coll. Fellowship Dissertation, 1949, p. 60
18 *Edinburgh Review* vol. 13, pp. 28-29, Oct. 1808
19 *A Letter from Montagu Burgoyne, Esq .... Giving a Summary Account of the Prosecution, Conviction, and Deprivation of the Rev. Dr. Edward Drax Free, &c*, 1830
20 B.M. Add. 47, 795, Foley to Marison, 3 April 1802
21 ibid
22 B.M. Add. 47, 795, Foley to wife, 11 Sept. 1806
23 *H.M.C. Dropmore*, vol. 6, p. 87, Scott to Grenville, 27 Dec. 1797
24 ROSE, *Diaries* vol. 2, p. 513, Rose to Melville, 18 Sept. 1814
25 THOMPSON, E. P., 'Patrician Society, Plebian Culture', *Journal Of Social History*, 7 (1974) pp. 382-405; pp. 391-2

26 [SOUTHEY], *Espriella's Letters*, vol. 2, pp. 283-4.
27 NICHOLSON, I., *A Sermon against Witchcraft*, 1808
28 *Annual Register*. 1811, Chronicle, p. 94
29 *Parl. Papers*, 1818, XVIII, p. 93 foll.
30 V. & A. Ms. 86 EE 68, Journal of J. Russell in Yorkshire. 1799, pp. 18-19
31 LAWTON, G., *Collectio Rerum Ecclesiasticarum De Diœcesi Eboracensi*, 2 vols., 1840, vol. 1, pp. 91-2
32 EDWARDS, M. L., *After Wesley*, 1935, pp. 165-172
33 V. & A., Ms. 86 EE 68, Journal of J. Russell in Yorkshire, 1799, p. 13
34 *Parl. Papers*, 1852-3, LXVIII, pp. 127, 152
35 HOBSBAWM, E., *Labouring Men*, 1964, p. 32
36 Northants R.O., Milton Mss X, 1605, Bundle 2, Oastler to Fitzwilliam, 2 July 1807
37 SOUTHEY, *Letters*, vol. 2, p. 249, Southey to Wynn
38 BOGUE and BENNETT, *History Of Dissenters*, vol. 5, p. 329
39 BOLAM, C. G., GORING, J., et. al., *The English Presbyterians*, 1968, pp. 21-5, 172-4, 178-180
40 BOGUE and BENNETT, *History Of Dissenters*, vol. 4, pp. 319-23
41 ibid., vol. 4, pp. 320, 330
42 ibid., vol. 2, pp. 98-9; vol. 3, p. 330
43 ibid., vol. 4, pp. 314-5
44 ibid., p. 315
45 DALE, R. W., *History of English Congregationalism*, 1907, pp. 584-5
46 SHIPLEY, C. E., ed. *The Baptists of Yorkshire*, 1912, p. 98
47 DITCHFIELD, G. M., 'The Parliamentary Struggle over the Repeal of the Test and Corporation Acts, 1787-1790', *English Historical Review*, 1974 (89) pp. 551-477; espec. p. 562
48 JAY, W., *The Autobiography and Reminiscences of the Revd William Jay*. 1854, pp. 302, 332
49 CANTON, W., *A History of the British and Foreign Bible Society*, 5 vols., 1904-10, vol. 1, pp. 471-8
50 CLARKE, W. K. L., *A History of the S.P.C.K.*, 1959, p. 150
51 ibid., pp. 141, 148
52 BROWN, F. K., *Fathers of the Victorians*, 1961, *passim*
53 ibid., pp. 285-316

5 LOWER-CLASS UNREST BEFORE 1803

1 McGRIGOR, J., *Autobiography and Services*, 1861, p. 41
2 DINMORE, R., *An Exposition of the Principles of the English Jacobins*, Norwich 1796
3 STANHOPE, G., and GOOCH, G. P., *Life of Charles Third Earl Stanhope*, 1914, p. 148
4 HARDY, T., *Memoir of Thomas Hardy*, 1832, pp. 59-60
5 SEAMAN, 'Democratic Societies', pp. 82, 277
6 *Account of the Proceedings of a Meeting of the London Corresponding Society . . . . 26 October 1795*
7 N.L.W., Harpton Court Mss C/334, Frankland to sister, 16 Nov. 1795
8 *Proceedings and Speeches at the Meeting The Seventeenth November, 1795, at St. Andrew's Hall, Norwich*, Norwich (1795), p. 24
9 WALLAS, *Place*, p. 25 N., Place to Harrison, 15 Feb. 1842
10 PLACE, *Autobiography*, pp. 151, 154
11 P.R.O., HO. 42/61 f 311, Coke to Portland. 24 March 1801
12 ibid., HO. 42/43, Roberts to Portland, 21 April 1798; HO 42/70, Goldson to Pelham, 23 March 1803; N.L.S. 1041 f 45, 'EM' to Dundas, 10 April 1798

13 Wentworth-Woodhouse Muniments, F 45/100, Sept. 1802
14 P.R.O., HO, 42/125, Lawson to Chamberlain, 25/26 July 1812
15 ibid., HO, 42/127 and 128, information 15 Sept., 7 and 8 Oct. 1812
16 B.M. Add. 27, 808 f 124-7
17 P.R.O., HO 42/73, memo, 27 Sept. 1803, enclosed in Dalrymple to Home
     Dept., 22 Sept. 1803
18 ibid., HO 42/124, Honeywood to Sidmouth, 26 June 1812
19 SEAMEN 'Democratic Societies', p. 287
20 PLUMER WARD, *Memoirs,* vol. 2, pp. 16-17, 27 Oct. 1819
21 P.R.O., HO, 42/46, anon. copy 27 Jan. 1798
22 ibid., HO, 42/46
23 B.M. Add. 27, 808 f 91
24 P.R.O., HO, 42/42
25 *Parl. Reports First Series,* vol. 10, p. 813
26 B.M. Add. 27, 808 f 88-95
27 *Parl. Reports First Series,* vol. 10, pp. 796-7
28 P.R.O., HO, 42/46, Lawson to Portland, 27 March 1799; HO, 42/47,
     Senhouse to Portland, 28 April 1799
29 B.M. Add. 27, 808 f 90
30 P.R.O., HO, 42/48, 31 March 1800
31 ibid., HO, 42/51, f 199, 16 Sept. 1800
32 ibid., HO, 42/51, f 301-2, Upton to Hatton Garden J.P.s 20 Sept. 1800
33 ibid., HO, 42/52, f 211
34 ibid., HO, 42/62, f 140
35 N.L.S., 1041 f 87, Earl of Coventry to Dundas, 7 Oct. 1800
36 P.R.O., HO, 42/55, f 226, Graham to J. King, 26 Dec. 1800
37 Wentworth-Woodhouse Muniments, F 44/59, information of Lowe,
     1 Dec. 1800
38 ibid., F 44/62, information of Warren, 2 Dec. 1800
39 P.R.O. HO, 42/61, f 292, copy information of AB, 22 March 1801
40 ibid., HO, 42/61, f 617, Fitzwilliam to Portland, 18 April 1801
41 Wentworth-Woodhouse Muniments, F 45/22, Dawson to Fitzwilliam,
     31 July 1801
42 ibid., F 45, 10 April 1801
43 P.R.O., HO, 42/62, f 315, Fitzwilliam to Portland, 30 July 1801
44 ibid., HO, 42/62 f 199, Bancroft to Portland, 23 June 1801
45 ibid., HO, 42/62, f 441, Fletcher to Pelham, 31 Aug. 1801
46 Wentworth-Woodhouse Muniments, F 45/26, Beckett to Fitzwilliam,
     22 Aug. 1801
47 P.R.O., HO, 42/62, f 1, Bancroft to Portland, 2 May 1801
48 ibid., HO, 42/62, f 73, Gore to J. King, 3 May 1801; f 11, Hay to Portland,
     4 May 1801
49 ibid., HO, 42/62, f 110, Bancroft to Portland, 27 May 1801
50 ibid., HO, 42/62, f 76, Hay to Portland, 18 May 1801; f 195, ? to J. King
     23 June 1801
51 ibid., HO, 42/62, f 304 ·
52 ibid., HO, 42/65, Fletcher to Pelham, 7 Jan. 1802
53 ibid., HO, 42/65, same to same, 3 April 1802
54 ibid., HO, 42/65
55 ibid., HO, 42/65, Fletcher to King, 7 July 1802
56 ibid., HO, 42/65, Fitzwilliam to Pelham, 7 June 1802
57 ibid., HO, 42/65, same to same, 1 July 1802
58 Wentworth-Woodhouse Muniments, F 45/58, 15 July 1802, cf. P.R.O.,
     HO, 42/65, Fitzwilliam to Pelham, 20 July 1802
59 P.R.O., HO, 42/66, Fitzwilliam to Pelham, 25 Sept. 1802

60 ibid., HO, 42/66, same to same, 27 Sept. 1802
61 ibid., HO, 42/65, Jones to Pelham, 18 July 1802
62 ibid., HO, 42/65, Bruges et al. to Pelham, 26 July 1802
63 ibid., HO, 42/66, Read to Pelham, 9 Aug.; Read to J. King, 13 Sept. 1802
64 ibid., HO, 42/70, Fletcher to Pelham, 3 Feb. 1803
65 ibid., HO, 42/66, depositions, 23 Nov. 1802
66 ibid., HO, 42/66, Parket to Pelham, 1 Dec. 1802
67 ibid., HO, 42/70, Hey to Pelham, 10 March 1803
68 ibid., HO, 42/70, Haden to Pelham, 5 March 1803
69 ibid., TS, 11/639
70 Cf. BENNETT, R., 'French Prisoners of War or Parole in Britain 1803-
    1814', London Ph.D., 1964, pp. 138, 197, 245
71 Wentworth-Woodhouse Muniments, F 45/15, Cooke to Fitzwilliam,
    21 April 1801
72 cf. ELLIOTT, M., 'The "Despard Conspiracy" Reconsidered' *Past and
    Present*, 75 (1977) pp. 46-61

6 THE IDEAS OF THE JACOBINS

 1 THELWALL, J., *The Tribune*, vol. 3, pp. 107-8; speech 28 Oct. 1795
 2 CARTWRIGHT, J., *A Constitutional Defence Of England, 1796, passim*
 3 GERRALD, *A Convention &c.*, p. 49
 4 ibid., p. 4
 5 STEPHENS, *John Horne Tooke*, vol. 2, p. 86
 6 GALE JONES, J., *Speech Delivered at the Ciceronian School on the
    Following Question: At this Awful Moment of Difficulty and Danger,
    which best Deserves the Public Confidence, Mr. Pitt or Mr. Fox?* 1795, p. 15
 7 B.M. Add. 27, 808 f 113
 8 PAINE, T., *The Rights Of Man*, Part Two, chap. 3 (p. 22 of 1st edit.) and
    chap. 4 (p. 35 of 1st edit.)
 9 STEPHENS, *John Horne Tooke*, vol. 2, p. 172, speech 28 May 1796
10 ibid., vol. 2, p. 173
11 THELWALL, J., *Sober Reflections on the Seditious and Inflammatory
    Letter of the Right Hon. Edmund Burke to a Noble Lord*, 1796, p. 24
12 P.R.O., HO, 42/45, Bancroft to Portland, 24 April 1799; and deposition of
    Mulhollan, 11 April 1799
13 ibid., HO, 42/45, Kinnard to Wickham 2 Feb. 1799
14 ibid., HO, 42/55, f 499
15 ibid., HO, 42/61, f 112-4; HO 42/62, f 644
16 ibid., HO, 42/47, R. J. Pitt to Wickham, 22 April 1799, enclosure
17 JONES, D. J. V., *Before Rebecca*, 1973, p. 214
18 PAINE, T., *The Rights Of Man*, Part Two, chap. 5 (p. 152 of 1st edit.)
19 *Parl. History*, vol. 31, col. 873, resolution of Edinburgh Convention,
    12 Dec. 1792
20 THELWALL, *Peaceful Discussion and not Tumultuary Violence*,
    pp. 19-21
21 THOMPSON, E. P., *The Making of the English Working Class*,
    pp. 157-160
22 WATERS, A. W., prefatory life in edition of *The Trial of Thomas Spence
    in 1801*, Leamington Spa, 1917
23 SPENCE, T., *The End of Oppression*, 1795, p. 1
24 SPENCE, T., *The Restorer of Society to its Natural State*, 1801, p. 26
25 ibid.,
26 B.M. Add. 27,808, f 284, Spence to Hall, 27 June 1807
27 ibid., Add. 27,808, f 152
28 *Parl. History*, vol. 35, col. 1512, Jekyll, 5 June 1801
29 GERRALD, *A Convention &c*, p. 87

30 ibid., p. 119
31 THELWALL, *Peaceful Discussion and not Tumultuary Violence*, pp. 1-2
32 GODWIN, W., *Enquiry Concerning Political Justice*, 1797 ed., vol. 2, p. 2
33 ibid., vol. 1, p. 238
34 ibid., vol. 1, pp. 221-2; vol. 2, p. 3
35 ibid., vol. 2, p. 474
36 B.M. Add. 27,808, f 114
37 HILL, C., 'The Norman Yoke' in SAVILE, J., ed., *Democracy and the Labour Movement*, 1954, pp. 11-66
38 GERRALD, *A Convention &c* pp. 90-91
39 LORD SEMPILL, *A Short Address to the Public on the Practice of Cashiering Military Officers without a Trial, and a Vindication of the Conduct and Political Opinions of the Author*, 1793, p. 20
40 BAXTER, J., *New And Impartial History Of England* (1796), pp. vii and ix
41 Cf. especially his later writings, *England's Aegis*, 1804, and his letter to Viscount Materosa, 15 June 1808, *Cartwright Life And Correspondence* vol. 1, pp. 359-66
42 See note 37
43 B.M. Add. 27, 808 f 115-6
44 *Parl. Papers*, 1801, III, p. 183
45 PRESTON, T., *The Life and Opinions of Thomas Preston Patriot and Shoemaker*, 1817, p. 36
46 *Parl. Reports First Series*, vol. 10, p. 832
47 *Annual Register*, 1800, Chronicle p. 34

7 ANTI-REFORM PROPAGANDA IN THE 1790s

1 WINDHAM, *Papers*, vol. 2, p. 213, Portland to Windham, 11 Jan. 1794
2 MORE, H. *Thoughts on the Importance of the Manners of the Great to General Society*, 1788, p. 95
3 HOWELL, T. B., *State Trials*, 34 vols., 1809-28, vol. 22, col. 826
4 BOWLES, J., *The Retrospect*, 1798, pp. 242-7
5 ibid., pp. 311-12
6 DAUBENEY, C., *Anti-Radicalism*, 1821, p. vii
7 RANDOLPH, J., *A Charge . . . . to the Clergy of Oxford*, Oxford 1802, p.15
8 ibid
9 (More), *Village Politics*, p. 11
10 BOWLES, *Protest against T. Paine*, p. 5
11 ibid., p. 4
12 *A Dialogue between a Gentleman and a Mechanic* (?1800), pp. 5-6
13 BOWLES, J., *Dialogues on the Rights of Britons*, 1792, 2nd Dialogue, pp. 8-9
14 PALEY, *Reasons for Contentment*, p. 12
15 [BOWDLER], *Reform or Ruin*, pp. 27-8
16 PALEY, *Reasons for Contentment*, pp. 4-5
17 [REEVES. J.], *Thoughts on the English Government addressed to the Quiet Good Sense of the People of England. Letter The First*, 1795, pp. 5-6. (Copy in U.L. Cambridge marked, 'By John Reeves, the prince of spies')
18 PALEY, *Reasons For Contentment*, pp. 5-6
19 JONES, W., *One Pennyworth of Truth, from Thomas Bull to his Brother John*, (1792)
20 *Anti-Jacobin Review and Magazine*, Prospectus, July 1798
21 BOWLES, *Protest against T. Paine*, pp. vii-viii of 2nd and 3rd editions (not in 1st)

22 [MORE], *Village Politics*, p. 5
23 JONES, W., *John Bull's Answer to his Brother Thomas, Second Letter* (1792), p. 5
24 JONES, W., *John Bull, In Answer to his Brother Thomas* (1792)
25 [BOWDLER], *Reform Or Ruin*, pp. 14-15
26 WILBERFORCE, W., *A Practical View of the Prevailing Religious System of Professed Christians . . . . contrasted with Real Christianity*, 1797, pp. 404-5
27 [MORE], *Mendip Annals*, p. 151
28 *The Apprentice Turned Master*
29 *The Hampshire Tragedy*
30 [BOWDLER], *Reform or Ruin*, p. 15
31 ibid., pp. 18-19
32 [MORE], *Mendip Annala*, pp. 243-4
33 [BOWDLER], *Reform or Ruin* p. 28
34 Cf. WATSON, R., *Miscellaneous Tracts on Religious, Political, and Agricultural Subjects*, 2 vols., 1815, vol. 1, pp. 448-493
35 WALSH, P. G., *Livy. His Historical Aims and Methods*, Cambridge, 1961, pp. 48, 66. MASON, S. M., 'Livy And Montesquieu' in DOREY, T. A., ed. *Livy*, 1971, pp. 118-158, espec. pp. 146-8

Part Two

1 THE ADDINGTON MINISTRY

1 FRANCIS, *Memoirs*, vol. 2, p. 309, Duchess of Devonshire to Francis, 29 Nov. 1798
2 WILLIS, 'Pitt's Resignation', *B.I.H.R.* 44, p. 256
3 FARINGTON, *Diary*, vol. 3, p. 14, 7 Nov. 1804, acc. Lawrence
4 SCARLETT, P.C., *A Memoir of the Right Honourable James, First Lord Abinger*, 1877, p. 57
5 FRANCIS, *Memoirs*, vol. 2, p. 470
6 FAY, C. R., *Huskisson And His Age*, 1951, p. 71, Huskisson to wife, 3 April 1803
7 ASPINALL, A., 'The Cabinet Council 1783-1835', *Proceedings Of The British Academy* 1952, pp. 145-252
8 ADAIR, *Duke of Devonshire*, p. 13
9 FARINGTON, *Diary*, vol. 1, p. 139, 27 Jan. 1796
10 BUCKINGHAM, *Court and Cabinets*, vol. 3, p. 128, Grenville to Buckingham, 2 Feb. 1801
11 ibid., p. 129
12 WILLIS, 'Pitt's Resignation', *B.I.H.R.* 44, p. 250
13 STANHOPE, *Pitt*, vol. 3, p. 267
14 WILLIS, 'Pitt's Resignation', *B.I.H.R.* 44, p. 252
15 ibid., p. 253
16 ibid., p. 254
17 STANHOPE, *Pitt*, vol. 3, p. xxvii
18 BUCKINGHAM, *Court And Cabinets*, vol. 3, pp. 128-131
19 HOLLAND, *Memoirs*, Vol. 2, pp. 181, 212
20 BUCKINGHAM, *Court And Cabinets*, vol. 3, p. 131
21 *H.M.C. Dropmore*, vol. 6, p. 473, Grenville to Carysfort, 16 March 1801
22 *Parl. History*, vol. 35, col. 946, 10 Feb. 1801
23 ibid., col. 1187, 1190-94
24 *H.M.C. Dropmore*, vol. 6, p. 443, 11 Feb. 1801
25 Devon R.O., 152M/C1801 OZ 26, Gower to Addington, 19 Feb. 1801
26 N.L.W. Coed-y-maen Mss 20, Temple to Wynn, 31 March and 12 April 1801

27 Bucks. R.O., Grenville Mss 30/63, Buckingham to T. Grenville, 12 April 1801
28 STANHOPE, *Pitt*, vol. 3, p. 280, 7 Feb. 1801
29 B.M. Add. 33,139, f 203 and f 205-6, T. Pelham to Ld. Pelham, 9 Feb. and [? 11 Feb.] 1801
30 B.M. Add. 33,107, f 39, Elliot to Pelham, 18 April 1801
31 HARDCASTLE, *Life of Campbell*, vol. 1, p. 66, 28 March 1801
32 FARINGTON, *Diary*, vol. 2, p. 231, 22 April 1804
33 STANHOPE, *Pitt*, vol. 3, p. 303
34 LEWIS, *Administrations Of Britain*, p. 275, Milman to Lewis, 27 Jan. 1858
35 ROSE, *Pitt and Napoleon*, pp. 326-7, Canning to Pitt, 28 Aug. 1801; MARSHALL, *Rise of Canning*, pp. 224 foll.
36 WINDHAM, *Papers*, vol. 2, p. 174, Cobbett to Windham, 7 Oct. 1801
37 *Parl. History*, vol. 36, cols. 55, 3 Nov. 1801; also AUCKLAND, *Journal and Correspondence*, vol. 4, pp. 137-9, various letters
38 WILLIAM COBBETT, *Autobiography*, pp. 89-90
39 GEORGE III, *Correspondence*, vol. 3, p. 613, George III to Hawkesbury, 30 Sept. 1801
40 *The Morning Chronicle*, 5 Oct. 1801
41 PLUMER WARD, *Memoirs*, vol. 1, pp. 50-51. Pitt to Mulgrave; *H.M.C. Dropmore* vol. 7, pp. 56-8, Dundas to Grenville, 10 Oct. 1801; *Castlereagh Correspondence* vol. 5, pp. 29-38, memo by Castlereagh; *H.M.C. Dropmore*, vol. 7, p. 54, Canning to Grenville, 7 Oct. 1801; *Minto Life And Letters*, vol. 3, p. 227, Minto to wife, 27 Nov. 1801
42 B.M. Add. 33,109, f 158-168; MINTO, *Life and Letters*, vol. 3, p. 239, Minto to wife, 15 Feb. 1802
43 *H.M.C. Dropmore*, vol. 7, pp. 30-33, Grenville to Hawkesbury, 15 July 1801
44 GEORGE III, *Correspondence*, vol. 3, p. 616, 19 Oct. 1801
45 *H.M.C. Dropmore*, vol. 7, pp. 50, 55, 67, Pitt to Grenville, 5, 9 and 26 Oct. 1801
46 ibid., p. 54, Canning to Grenville, 7 Oct. 1801
47 WINDHAM, *Papers*, vol. 2, p. 173, Windham to Addington, 1 Oct. 1801
48 Northants R.O., Milton Mss 58, Carnarven to Fitzwilliam, 25 Oct. 1801
49 ibid., 59, Laurence to Fitzwilliam, 15 Oct. 1801
50 MELVILLE, *Cobbett*, vol. 1, p. 137, Folkestone to Cobbett, 20 Oct. 1801
51 *Morning Post*, 29 Oct. 1801
52 *H.M.C. Bathurst*, p. 26-7, Pembroke to Bathurst, 25 Oct. 1801
53 B.M., Add. 48,222, f 141, Granville Leveson to Boringdon, 4 Nov. 1801
54 Berks R.O., Braybrooke/Glastonbury Corresp. D/E, 26 Nov. 1801
55 *H.M.C. Dropmore*, vol. 7, pp. 57-8, Dundas to Grenville, 10 Oct. 1801
56 *H.M.C. Bathurst*, p. 28, Camden to Bathurst, 2 Nov. 1801
57 *Times*, 6 Nov. 1801
58 LEVESON GOWER, *Correspondence*, vol. 1, p. 306, Lady Bessborough to Granville Leveson, 10 Nov. 1801, cf. GLENBERVIE, *Diaries* vol. 1, p. 272, 31 Oct. 1801
59 GLENBERVIE, *Diaries*, vol. 1, p. 273, 31 Oct. 1801
60 *H.M.C. Dropmore*, vol. 7, pp. 66-7, T. Grenville to Grenville, 23 to 31 Oct. 1801
61 Bodleian Ms Eng. Lett. d. 80, f 28-9, Grenville to Newport, 12 Nov. 1801
62 MINTO, *Life And Letters*, vol. 3, p. 229, Minto to wife, 17 Dec. 1801
63 B.M. Add. 47,569, f 112, Fox to W. Smith, 15 Nov. 1801
64 Grey Mss, Tierney to Grey, Oct. 1801
65 ibid., endorsement by Grey on a letter from Tierney, 21 Dec. 1801

66 ibid., Tierney to Grey, Feb. 1802
67 ROSE, *Diaries*, vol. 1, p. 442, Bishop of Lincoln to Rose, 23 Dec. 1801
68 *H.M.C. Dropmore*, vol. 7, p. 80, T. Grenville to Grenville, 24 Feb. 1801
69 BUCKINGHAM, *Court and Cabinets*, vol. 3, p. 190, T. Grenville to Buckingham, 27 Feb. 1801
70 B.M. Add. 41,852 f 99 and f 102, Grenville to T. Grenville, 25 Feb. and 1 March 1802
71 BUCKINGHAM, *Court and Cabinets*, vol. 3, p. 200, Grenville to Buckingham, 12 March 1802
72 B.M. Add. 37,846 f 188, Grenville to Windham
73 *Courier*, 14 May 1802
74 *Morning Post*, 18 May 1802
75 AUCKLAND, *Journal and Correspondence*, vol. 4, pp. 154-5, 7 May 1802
76 *Parl. History*, vol. 36, col. 854-5, 27 May 1802
77 STIRLING, *Coke Of Norfolk*, vol. 2, pp. 5-6, Coke to Windham, 6 July 1802
78 LADY HOLLAND, *Journal*, vol. 1, p. 217, 18 Dec. 1798
79 BRENTON, *St Vincent*, vol. 2, pp. 159-161
80 ST VINCENT, *Letters*, vol. 2, pp. 447, 479 n.
81 BRENTON, *St Vincent*, vol. 2, pp. 174-5
82 ST VINCENT, *Letters*, vol. 2, p. 557
83 BENTHAM, *Life Of Samuel Bentham*, p. 138
84 ibid., p. 205, and BRENTON, *St Vincent, passim*
85 ST VINCENT, *Letters*, vol. 2, p. 191, St Vincent to Grey, 6 Aug. 1802
86 BARROW, *Memoir*, p. 257
87 *Parl. Papers*, 1805, VIII, pp. 209-15
88 MARKHAM, *Correspondence*, pp. 16-17, St Vincent to Markham, 23 and 24 Dec. 1802
89 ST VINCENT, *Letters*, vol. 2, pp. 19-20
90 MARSDEN, W., *A Brief Memoir of the Life and Writings of the Late William Marsden*, 1838, p. 103 N
91 TUCKER, *St Vincent Memoirs*, vol. 2, p. 235
92 MARKHAM, *Correspondence* pp. 26-7 n.
93 *Concise Statement of Facts, relative to the Treatment experienced by Sir Home Popham since his return from the Red Sea*, 1805, p. 2
94 ibid
95 *A Few Brief Remarks on a Pamphlet entitled 'Observations on the Concise Statement of Facts, privately circulated by Sir Home Popham'* 1805, p. 11
96 *Parl. Papers*, 1805, IV, pp. 273-4, 679-80
97 MALMESBURY, *Diaries*, vol. 4, p. 78, Canning to Malmesbury, 20 Oct. 1802
98 BUCKINGHAM, *Court And Cabinets*, vol. 3, p. 212, Grenville to Buckingham, 20 Oct. 1802
99 *H.M.C. Dropmore*, vol. 7, p. 118, Buckingham to Grenville, 1 Nov. 1802
100 B.M. Add. 41,852, f 135, Grenville to T. Grenville, 2 Nov. 1802
101 *H.M.C. Dropmore*, vol. 7, p. 124
102 ibid., vol. 7, p. 126, Pitt to Grenville, 15 Nov. 1802
103 MALMESBURY, *Diaries*, vol. 4, pp. 91-2, Canning to Malmesbury, 9 Nov. 1802
104 ibid., pp. 111-117 Diary, Nov. 1802
105 Northants R.O., Milton Mss 61, Laurence to Fitzwilliam, 15 Nov. 1802
106 *H.M.C. Dropmore*, vol. 7, p. 131, Pitt to Grenville, 3 Dec. 1802
107 BUCKINGHAM, *Court And Cabinets*, vol. 3, p. 249, Grenville to Buckingham, 1 Feb. 1803

108 *H.M.C. Dropmore*, vol. 7, p. 141, T. Grenville to Grenville, 1 Feb. 1803
109 ROSE, *Diaries*, vol. 2, p. 157, 30 Sept. 1804
110 Grey Mss, Fitzwilliam to Howick, 7 April 1807
111 ROSE, *Pitt and the Great War*, p. 479, Rose to Bishop of Lincoln, 21 Nov. 1802
112 ROSE, *Diaries*, vol. 2, pp. 27-8, Diary, 21 Feb. 1803
113 BUCKINGHAM, *Court and Cabinets*, vol. 2, p. 283, Grenville's narrative
114 ibid., pp. 288-9
115 *H.M.C. Dropmore*, vol. 7, p. 158, Addington to Pitt, 12 April 1803
116 MARSHALL, *Rise of Canning*, p. 243
117 B.M. Add. 33,111, f 162, draft Pelham to Addington, 14 April 1803
118 *H.M.C. Dropmore*, vol. 7, p. 159, Addington to Pitt, 14 April 1803
119 ibid., pp. 159-161, Pitt to Addington, 15 April 1803
120 STANHOPE, *Pitt*, vol. 4, pp. 36-7
121 FARINGTON, *Diary*, vol. 2, p. 100, 19 May 1803
122 BUCKINGHAM, *Court and Cabinets*, vol. 3, p. 293, Grenville to Buckingham, 18 April 1803
123 FOX, *Memorials and Correspondence*, vol. 3, p. 406, Fox to Grey, March 1803
124 Northants R.O., Milton Mss 62, Fox to Fitzwilliam, 25 April 1803
125 Devon R.O. 152M/C 1803 OZ 234, Miss Gore to Addington, 2 May 1803, and endorsement
126 WARD, R., *A View of the Relative Situations of Mr Pitt and Mr Addington*, 1804 p. 39
127 *H.M.C. Dropmore*, vol. 7, p. 169, T. Grenville to Grenville, 28 May 1803
128 MARSHALL, *Rise Of Canning*, p. 241
129 Devon R.O., 152 M/1803 OZ 243, 4 June 1803
130 N.L.S., Minto Mss M 45/5, Minto to Elliot, 8 June 1803
131 *Political Register*, vol. 3, col. 393, 19 March 1803
132 ibid., vol. 4, col. 41-9, 9 July 1803
133 Devon R.O., 152 M/C 1803 OZ 43, Yorke to Addington, Oct. 1803; PLUMER WARD. *Memoirs*, vol. 2, p. 20
134 MACDONAGH, *Viceroy's Postbag*, p. 304, 2 Aug. 1803
135 PELLEW, *Sidmouth*, vol. 2, p. 230, Addington to J. H. Addington
136 N.L.W., Coed-y-maen Mss 1, T. Grenville to Wynn, 14 Nov. 1803
137 B.M. Add. 48,222, f 163, Granville Leveson to Boningdon, 7 Oct. 1803
138 FOX, *Memorials and Correspondence*, vol. 4 p. 9, Fox to O'Brien, 26 June 1803
139 ibid., vol. 3, pp. 429-30, Fox to Grey, 19 Oct. 1803
140 LEVESON GOWER, *Correspondence*, vol. 1, p. 431, Lady Bessborough to Granville Leveson, 11 Sept. 1803
141 FOX, *Memorials and Correspondence*, vol. 3, pp. 434-5, 27 Nov. 1803
142 ibid., pp. 441-3, Fox to Fitzpatrick and to Grey, 6 Dec. 1803; B.M. Add. 41,856 f 122, Fox to T. Grenville 20, Dec. 1803
143 ibid., p. 443, 17 Dec. 1803
144 *H.M.C. Dropmore*, vol. 7, p. 203, Grenville to Pitt, 31 Dec. 1803
145 BUCKINGHAM, *Court And Cabinets*, vol. 3, p. 342, 10 Jan. 1804 (misdated 30 Jan.)
147 *A Letter To Robert Ward, Esq., M.P.*, 1804, p. 79
147 B.M. Add. 41, 851, f 220, Buckingham to T. Grenville, 13 Jan. 1804
148 FOX, *Memorials and Correspondence*, vol. 4, p. 16, Fox to Fitzpatrick, 27 Jan. 1804
149 ibid., p. 22, same to same, 24 Feb. 1804
150 ibid., p. 16, 27 Jan. 1804
151 Northants R.O., Milton Mss 64, T. Grenville to Fitzwilliam, 28 Jan. 1804

152 ibid., Carnarvon to Fitzwilliam, 8 Feb. 1804
153 MINTO, *Life And Letters*, vol. 3, p. 303, Minto to wife, 24 Feb. 1804
154 *H.M.C. Dropmore*, vol. 7, p. 212, Carysfort to Grenville, 2 Feb. 1804
155 STANHOPE, *Pitt*, vol. 4, p. 117
156 *Letter to Robert Ward, Esq. M.P.*, 1804, p. 85
157 *H.M.C. Dropmore*, vol. 7, p. 213, Pitt to Grenville, 4 Feb. 1804
158 MALMESBURY, *Diaries*, vol. 4, p. 289, 19 Feb. 1804
159 GREY, *Life and Opinions*, p. 80
160 PRICE, C., ed. *Letters of R. B. Sheridan*, 3 vols., Oxford 1966, vol. 2,
     p. 216, Sheridan to wife, 27 Feb. 1804
161 MOORE, T., *Memoirs of the Life of the Rt. Hon. R. B. Sheridan*, 1825,
     p. 325
162 GLENBERVIE, *Diaries*, vol. 1, p. 372, 15 March 1804
163 N.L.W., Coed-y-Maen Mss 8, f 1, account of politics at this period
164 Northants R.O., Milton Mss 64, Carnarvon to Fitzwilliam, 8 Feb. 1804
165 N.L.W., 4814D, 4 April 1804
166 LEWIS, *Administrations of Britain*, p. 275, Milman to Lewis, 27 Jan.
     1858
167 Devon R.O., 152M/C 1812 OZ, Buchan to Sidmouth, 16 April 1812
168 *Times*, 29 Feb. 1804
169 ibid., 5 March 1804
170 PELLEW, *Sidmouth*, vol. 2, p. 276
171 *H.M.C. Dropmore*, vol. 7, p. 217, T. Grenville to Grenville, 31 March
     1804
172 FOX, *Memorials and Correspondence*, vol. 3, p. 455, Fox to Grey,
     March 1804; vol. 4, p. 40, Fox to Lauderdale, 9 April 1804
173 *H.M.C. Bathurst*, p. 41, Bathurst's narrative
174 *Political Register*, vol. 5, col. 621, 28 April 1804, letter by 'Sylva'
175 N.L.W., 4814D, Wynn to Southey, 4 April 1804
176 BUCKINGHAM, *Court And Cabinets*, vol. 3, pp. 348-9, Grenville to
     Buckingham 19 April 1804; *H.M.C. Bathurst*, p. 34, Bathurst's
     narrative
177 STANHOPE, *Pitt*, vol. 4, pp. 154-6, Pitt to Eldon and reply, 22 April
     1804; vol. 4, pp. i-iii, Pitt to King, 21 April 1804
178 N.L.W., Coed-y-maen Mss 8, f 1, account of politics of this period
179 Devon R.O., 152 M/C 1803 OZ, 231 and 232, Eliot to Addington, 20 and
     31 December 1803
180 STANHOPE, *Pitt*, vol. 4, p. 132
181 COLCHESTER, *Diary*, vol. 1, p. 501, 1 May 1804
182 N.L.W., 4814D, Wynn to Southey, 30 April 1804
183 STANHOPE, *Pitt*, vol. 4, p. 162
184 ibid., pp. iv-viii, Pitt to Eldon, 2 May 1804
185 ibid., p. x, George III to Pitt, 5 May 1804
186 ibid., p. 166, George III to Eldon, 5 May 1804
187 ROSE, *Diaries*, vol. 2, pp. 122-3, 7 May 1804
188 B.M. Add. 41, 856, f 169, 6 May 1804
189 *H.M.C. Bathurst*, p. 39, narrative
190 Kenyon Mss 27, Wynn to Kenyon, 22 May 1804
191 FARINGTON, *Diary*, vol. 2, p. 250, 9 June 1804
192 *H.M.C. Bathurst*, p. 40, narrative
193 MALMESBURY, *Diaries*, vol. 4, p. 322, 30 May 1804
194 ibid., p. 303, 7 May 1804
195 N.L.S., Minto Mss 45/5, Minto to Elliot, 9 May 1804
196 *H.M.C. Carlisle*, p. 734 Pitt to Carlisle, 15 May 1804, cf. Canning Mss 19,
     Canning to wife, 16 May 1804

197 C.U.L. Add 6958, Euston to Pitt, 5 and 12 May 1804
198 *H.M.C. Bathurst,* p. 39, narrative
199 LEVESON GOWER, *Correspondence,* vol. 2, p. 90, Granville Leveson to Canning, 1 June 1805
200 MALMESBURY, *Diaries,* vol. 4, p. 302, 7 May 1804
201 TWISS, *Life of Eldon* vol. 1, p. 449, Eldon to Perceval, in 1810 or 1811
202 Devon R.O., 152M/C 1804 OZ, Bond to Addington, 23 May 1804

2 THE SECOND MINISTRY OF PITT

1 MARSHALL, *Rise of Canning,* p. 272; Canning Mss 19, Canning to wife, 13 and 16 May
2 BAMFORD, F. and DUKE OF WELLINGTON, ed., *The Journal of Harriet Arbuthnot* 2 vols., 1950, vol. 1, p. 13, 13 March 1820
3 *H. M. C. Bathurst,* p. 41
4 STANHOPE, *Pitt,* vol. 4, p. 231, Auckland to Pitt, 18 Dec. 1804
5 FOX, *Memorials And Correspondence,* vol. 4, p. 57, Fox to Holland, 24 July 1804
6 ibid., vol. 4, p. 7, Fox to Grey, 17 Dec. 1804
7 MINTO, *Life And Letters,* vol. 3, p. 335, Minto to wife, 15 May 1804
8 B.M. Add. 38, 736, f 76, Carlisle to Huskisson, 27 Dec. 1804
9 B.M. Add. 35, 715, f 76, Nepean to Hardwicke, 10 June 1804; B.M. Add. 35, 750 f 76, Sligo to Hardwicke, 13 June 1804
10 MINTO, *Life And Letters,* vol. 3, p. 342, Minto to wife, 30 May 1804
11 GLENBERVIE, *Diaries,* vol. 1, pp. 382-3, 27 June 1804
12 GEORGE, PRINCE OF WALES, *Correspondence,* vol. 5, p. 15, Moira to Macinahon, 12 May 1804
13 ROSE, *Diaries,* vol. 2, p. 181-2
14 GEORGE III, *Correspondence,* vol. 4, p. xxiii
15 Devon R.O., 152M/C 1804 OZ, Addington to Yorke copy, 24 Dec. 1804
16 Canning Mss, 29D Diary, 1 Jan. 1805
17 LEVESON GOWER, *Correspondence,* vol. 2, p. 24, Lady Stafford to Granville Leveson, 7 March 1805; ibid. p. 53, same to same, 17 April 1805
18 P.R.O., Chatham Mss 30/70/4, f 246
19 GEORGE III, *Correspondence,* vol. 4, p. 274 n. 1, Canning to Granville Leveson 6 Jan. 1805; cf. ROSE *Diaries,* vol. 2, p. 175, 30 Oct. 1804
20 LEVESON GOWER, *Correspondence,* vol. 2, pp. 11, 25, 30-31, 54, 60
21 *H.M.C. Bathurst,* p. 44, 31 Jan. 1805
22 LEVESON GOWER, *Correspondence,* vol. 2, pp. 2-3, Lady Bessborough to Granville Leveson, 1 Jan. 1805
23 Devon R.O., 152M/C 1805 OZ, Rous to Addington, 8 Jan. 1805
24 WINDHAM, *Diary,* p. 448, 13 Feb. 1805
25 LEVESON-GOWER, *Correspondence,* vol. 2, p. 43, Lady Bessborough to Granville Leveson, 29 March 1805
26 N.L.S., Minto Mss 1E 17, 22 Feb. 1805; cf. Minto Mss 45, f 5, Minto to Elliot, 13 June 1803 for Trotter's obligation to Minto
27 ROMILLY, *Diary,* vol. 3, p. 44, 19 June 1812; cf. vol. 2 pp. 336-7, 14 June 1810
28 *H.M.C. Dropmore,* vol. 7, p. 225, T. Grenville to Grenville, 1-7 April 1805
29 LEVESON GOWER, *Correspondence,* vol. 2, p. 52, Lady Bessborough to Granville Leveson, 7 April 1805
30 WILBERFORCE, *Life,* vol. 3, p. 223, Legard to Wilberforce 1806
31 HARDCASTLE, *Life of Campbell,* vol. 1, p. 150, Campbell to G. Campbell, 17 May 1804
32 WILBERFORCE, *Life,* vol. 3, pp. 219-20
33 AUCKLAND, *Journal and Correspondence,* vol. 4, p. 237 n.

34 WILBERFORCE, *Life,* vol. 3, p. 220
35 LEVESON GOWER, *Correspondence,* vol. 2, p. 54; *H.M.C. Bathurst.*
    p. 46, Harrowby to Bathurst, 21 April 1805
36 PELLEW, *Sidmouth,* vol. 2, p. 357, Sidmouth to J. H. Addington
    20 April 1805; cf. *H. M. C. Bathurst,* p. 45, Harrowby to Bathurst,
    21 April, and p. 47, Camden to Bathurst, 22 April 1805
37 GEORGE III, *Correspondence,* vol. 4, p. 315 NZ
38 B.M. Add. 35, 706, f 210, Yorke to Hardwicke, 26 April 1805
39 STANHOPE, *Pitt,* vol. 4, p. xxiii, George III to Pitt, 22 April 1805
40 LAUGHTON, J. K., ed. *Letters and Papers of Charles, Lord Barham,*
    3 vols., 1906-10, vol. 3 p. 73, Middleton to Melville, 16 April 1805, and
    p. 74, Middleton to Thomson, 17 April 1805
41 BARROW, *Memoir,* pp. 277-8
42 WILBERFORCE, *Life,* vol. 3, pp. 229-30
43 PLUMER WARD, *Memoirs,* vol. 1, p. 254, 19 Oct. 1809
44 PELLEW, *Life of Sidmouth,* vol. 2, p. 360, Sidmouth to J. H. Addington,
    22 April 1805
45 Devon R.O., 152 M 1805 OZ, 16 April 1805
46 PELLEW, *Sidmouth,* vol. 2, p. 358
47 ibid., pp. 363-4, 28 April 1805
48 ibid., p. 325, Addington to Bond, 8 Nov. 1804
49 *Political Register,* vol. 7, col. 696, 11 May 1805
50 HUNT, *Memoirs,* vol. 2, pp. 160-1
51 DINWIDDY, J. R., 'Parliamentary Reform as an Issue in English
    Politics, 1800-1810', London Ph.D., 1971, p. 76
52 *H.M.C. Dropmore,* vol. 7, p. 194, Carysfort to Grenville, 30 Oct. 1803
53 ibid., p. 268, T. Grenville to Grenville, 1-5 May 1805
54 Northants R.O., Milton Mss 66, f 3, C.L. Dundas to Fitzwilliam,
    11 March 1805
55 BUCKINGHAM, *Court and Cabinets,* vol. 3 p. 418-9, Grenville to
    Buckingham, 22 May 1805
56 ibid. pp. 421-2, 27 May 1805
57 YONGE, *Liverpool,* vol. 1, p. 195 n, 5 July 1805
58 *H.M.C. Dropmore,* vol. 7, p. 279, Grenville to T. Grenville, 24 June 1805
59 ibid., p. 282, Buckingham to Grenville, 27 June 1805
60 PELLEW, *Sidmouth,* vol. 2, p. 372, Sidmouth to Bragge, 5 July 1805
61 ibid., p. 375, Buckinghamshire to Disbrowe, 5 July 1805; cf. YONGE,
    Liverpool, vol. 1, p. 195 N, Hawkesbury to Liverpool, 5 July 1805
62 Devon R.O., 152M/C 1805 OZ, Sidmouth to Bragge, 10 July 1805
63 MALMESBURY, *Diaries,* vol. 4, p. 339.
64 AUCKLAND, *Journal And Correspondence,* vol. 4, p. 242, Henley to
    Auckland, 11 July 1805
65 Devon R.O., 152 M/C 1805 OZ, Sidmouth to Bragge, 10 July 1805
66 ibid., Sidmouth to J. H. Addington, 11 July 1805
67 B.M., Add., 47,569, f 230-236, letters, 8-16 July
68 PELLEW, *Sidmouth,* vol. 2, pp. 392-3
69 FOX, *Memorials and Correspondence,* vol. 4, p. 87, Fox to O'Brien,
    7 July 1805
70 ibid., vol. 4, p. 96, Fox to Grey, 12 July 1805
71 ibid., vol. 4, pp. 83-4, same to same, 6 July 1805
72 ibid., vol. 4, p. 96, same to same, 12 July 1805
73 ibid., vol 4, p. 85, Fox to Adair, July 1805
74 *H.M.C. Dropmore,* vol. 7, p. 294, Buckingham to Grenville, 12 July 1805
75 *H.M.C. Bathurst,* p. 48, Pitt to Bathurst, 15 July 1805
76 FOX, *Memorials and Correspondence,* vol. 4, p. 105, Fox to Adair,

28 August 1805
77 ibid., vol. 4, p. 89, O'Brien to Fox, 7 July 1805
78 *H.M.C. Bathurst*, p. 49, Camden to Bathurst, 30 August 1805
79 N.L.S., Minto Mss, *passim*, especially in 1806
80 MINTO, *Life and Letters*, vol. 3, p. 368, Minto to wife, 2 Sept. 1805
81 ROSE, *Diaries*, vol. 2, pp. 201-2, 22 Sept. 1805
82 ibid., p. 199
83 *H.M.C. Dropmore*, vol. 7, pp. 306-7, T. Grenville to Grenville, 4 Oct. 1805
84 MARSHALL, *Rise of Canning*, p. 293
85 BUCKINGHAM, *Court And Cabinets*, vol. 4, pp. 9-10, Grenville to Buckingham, 6 Jan. 1806
86 ibid., vol. 3, p. 450, same to same, 11 Nov. 1805; p. 458, Grenville to Buckingham, 1 Dec. 1805; vol. 4, pp. 5-6, T. Grenville to Buckingham, 6 Jan. 1806
87 GREY, *Life and Opinions*, p. 104
88 BUCKINGHAM, *Court and Cabinets*, vol. 4, pp. 9-10, Grenville to Buckingham, 7 Jan. 1806
89 B.M., Add., 41,851, f 246, Buckingham to T. Grenville, 9 Jan. 1806
90 BUCKINGHAM, *Court and Cabinets*, vol. 4, p. 5, T. Grenville to Buckingham, 6 Jan. 1806
91 FOX, *Memorials and Correspondence*, vol. 4, pp. 127-8, Fox to Holland, 1 Jan. 1806
92 BUCKINGHAM, *Court and Cabinets*, vol. 4, p. 11, T. Grenville to Buckingham, 12 Jan. 1806
93 AUCKLAND, *Journal and Correspondence*, vol. 4, p. 247, Henley to Auckland, 1 Oct. 1805; LEVESON GOWER, *Correspondence*, vol. 2, p. 159, Lady Bessborough to Granville Leveson, 15 Jan. 1806
94 *Quarterly Review*, vol. 57 (1836), p. 491, Wellesley to Croker, 22 Nov. 1836
95 *H.M.C. Dropmore*, vol. 7, p. 328, Wellesley to Grenville, 20 Jan. 1806, and Auckland to Grenville, same date; p. 329 Fox to Grenville, 21 Jan. 1806; WINDHAM, *Diary*, p. 455, 20 Jan. 1806
96 B.M., Add., 43, 337, f 2 Notes, c. 25 Jan. 1806
97 ibid.
98 *H.M.C. Lonsdale*, p. 158, Essex to Lowther, 23 Jan. 1806
99 LEVESON-GOWER, *Correspondence*, vol. 2, pp. 162-4, Lady Bessborough to Granville Leveson, 23 Jan. 1806
100 MARSHALL, *Rise of Canning*, p. 290

3 THE MINISTRY OF ALL THE TALENTS
1 *H.M.C. Lonsdale*, p. 164, Canning to Lowther, 9 Feb. 1806
2 GEORGE, PRINCE OF WALES, *Correspondence*, vol. 4, p. 327, Northumberland to MacMahon, 6 Feb. 1806
3 J. C. HOBHOUSE, *Authentic Narrative of the Westminster Election of 1819*, 1819, p. 340; *Political Register* 1806 passim; PATTERSON, *Burdett*, pp 175, 185-6
4 PELLEW, *Sidmouth*, vol. 2, p. 412, Sheridan to Sidmouth, 23 Jan. 1806
5 N.L.W., Coed-y-Maen 5, f 7, Grenville to Wynn, 6 Sept. 1805
6 WINDHAM, *Diary*, p. 456, 28 Jan. 1806; Northants R.O., Milton Mss 68 f 3, Elliot to Fitzwilliam, 5 Feb. 1806; Althorp Mss, T. Grenville to Spencer, 7 Feb. 1806
7 PELLEW, *Sidmouth*, vol. 2, p. 417, Rous to Sidmouth
8 COLCHESTER, *Diary*, vol. 2, p. 80, Redesdale to Abbot, 18 Sept. 1806

 9 LORD HOLLAND, *Memoirs,* vol. 1, p. 209
10 *H.M.C. Dropmore,* vol. 8, p. 24, Spencer to Grenville, 10 Feb. 1806
11 *H.M.C. Bathurst,* p. 57, Bathurst to Grenville, 28 Jan. 1806
12 B.M. Add. 42,774, f 207, Eldon to Rose, n.d. 1807
13 B.M. Add. 48,219, f 145, Bovington to Canning, 23 Feb. 1806
14 PELLEW, *Sidmouth,* vol. 2, p. 413, Sidmouth to Bragge, 31 Jan. 1806
15 *H.M.C. Dropmore,* vol. 8, p. 22, Buckingham to Grenville, 10 Feb. 1806
16 B.M. Add. 41,856, f 196-8, 28 Jan. 1806
17 ibid., f 202, 29 Jan. 1806
18 ibid., f 205, 4 Feb. 1806
19 Northants R.O., Milton Mss 66/5, 4 Feb. 1806
20 *H.M.C. Dropmore,* vol. 8, p. 42, T. Grenville to Grenville, 27 Feb. 1806;
    LORD HOLLAND, *Memoirs,* vol. 1, p. 219 N.
21 *H.M.C. Dropmore,* vol. 8, p. 33, T. Grenville to Grenville, 17 Feb. 1806
22 Northants R.O., Milton Mss 68, Dundas to Fitzwilliam, 30 Jan. 1806
23 *H.M.C. Dropmore,* vol. 7, p. 346, Windham to Grenville, 28 Jan. 1806
24 N.L.S., Minto Mss I.E 19, Minto to wife, 31 Jan. 1806
25 B.M., Add., 37,883, f 56, Laurence to Windham, 4 Feb. 1806
26 Grey Mss 59, Whitbread to Grey, 7 Feb. 1806, and reply
27 Northants R.O. Milton Mss 68/2, Dundas to Fitzwilliam, 5 Feb. 1806
28 B.M. Add. 37,883, f 149, Francis to Windham, 9 March 1806
29 Northants R.O., Milton Mss 68/5, Fox to Fitzwilliam, 2 and 4 Feb. 1806
30 ROMILLY, *Diary,* vol. 2, p. 128, 8 Feb. 1806
31 BUCKINGHAM, R. DUKE OF, *Memoirs of the Court of George IV,*
    2 vols., 1859, vol. 1, pp. 338-9, Wynn to Buckingham n.d. 1822
32 Bodleian Ms Eng. Lett. c 60, f 22, Yorke to Earl of Bristol, 26 Feb. 1806
33 HORNER, *Memoirs and Correspondence,* vol. 1, p. 340, Horner to
    Murray, 4 Feb. 1806
34 *Parl. Debates,* vol. 6, col. 335
35 FRANCIS, *Memoirs,* vol. 2, p. 457
36 *Independent Whig,* 30 March 1806
37 N.L.W., 4814D, Wynn to Southey, 8 Nov. 1810
38 B.M., Add., 51, 469, f 33, Lauderdale to Fox, 19 March 1806
39 B.M., Add., 51, 471, A.
40 CARTWRIGHT, *Life and Letters,* vol. 1, p. 321, Wyvill to Cartwright,
    23 March 1806
41 ibid., p. 338, same to same, 6 Feb. 1806
42 HARVEY, 'Ministry of all the Talents', *H.J.* 15, pp. 633-4
43 BUCKINGHAM, *Court and Cabinets,* vol. 4, p. 10, Grenville to
    Buckingham, 7 Jan. 1806
44 *H.M.C. Dropmore,* vol. 8, p. 321, Windham to Grenville, 11 Sept. 1806
45 B.M. Add. 51,468, f 107, Vansittart to Fox, 5 Feb. 1806
46 B.M. Add. 34,457, f 38, Gwydir to Auckland, 21 Sept. 1806
47 LORD HOLLAND, *Memoirs,* vol. 2, p. 112.
48 *H.M.C. Dropmore,* vol. 8, p. 367, Grenville to Howick, 29 Sept. 1806;
    B.M. Add. 51,530, Grenville to Holland, 14 Sept. 1806
49 *Parl. Debates,* vol. 3, col. 554, 18 Feb. 1805
50 ibid., col. 558
51 ibid., vol. 6, col. 570, 28 March 1806
52 COLCHESTER, *Diary,* vol. 2, p. 77, 15 July 1806; cf. *H.M.C. Dropmore,*
    vol. 8, p. 113, Grenville to Windham, 23 April 1806; p. 118, Windham to
    Grenville, 24 April 1806
53 Canning Mss 214, f 29, Canning to wife, 31 Jan. 1806
54 ROSE, *Diaries,* vol. 2, pp. 246 foll., 9 Feb. 1806
55 Welbeck Mss, Canning to Titchfield, 20 April 1806, quoted in HINTON,

'General Elections of 1806 and 1807', p. 36

56 Lonsdale Mss, Ward to Lowther, 20 Feb. 1806, quoted HINTON, 'General Elections of 1806 and 1807', p. 36
57 Bodleian Ms Eng. Lett. c. 60, f 26, Yorke to J. Yorke, 3 March 1806
58 *H.M.C. Lonsdale*, p. 174, Essex to Lowther, 10 March 1806
59 B.M. Add. 38,736, f 123-4, Melville to Huskisson, 28 Jan. 1806
60 Canning Mss 21, f 70, Canning to wife, 10 March 1806
61 ROSE, *Diaries*, vol. 2, p. 263, 22 Feb. 1806
62 COLCHESTER, *Diary*, vol. 2, p. 31, 27 Jan. 1806; *H.M.C. Dropmore*, vol. 7, p. 345, Windham to Grenville, 28 Jan. 1806
63 *H.M.C. Dropmore*, vol. 8, p. 44, Grenville to Fox, 28 Feb. 1806
64 ibid., p. 46, Fox to Grenville, 1 March 1806
65 ibid., p. 106, Fox to Grenville, 18 April 1806
66 ibid., vol. 7, p. 341, Wellesley to Grenville, 26 Jan. 1806
67 PAULL, J., *Letter to The Right Honble. C. J. Fox on the Subject of his Conduct upon the Charges Made by Mr. Paull against the Marquis Wellesley by a Lover of Consistency*, 1806, p. 2
68 *H.M.C. Dropmore*, vol. 8, p. 171, Windham to Grenville, 2 June 1806
69 ibid., pp. 175 and 179-80, Grenville to Windham and reply, 4 June; same to same, 5 June
70 *H.M.C. Lonsdale*, p. 182, Canning to Lowther, 8 April 1806
71 Canning Mss 21, f 196, Canning to wife, 5 June 1806
72 ibid., f 201, same to same, 10 June 1806
73 *H.M.C. Lonsdale*, p. 191, Bathurst to Lowther, 11 June 1806
74 Canning Mss 21, f 224-7, Canning to wife, 16 June 1806
75 ibid., f 242, same to same, 20 June 1806
76 ibid., f 274-7, 1 July 1806
77 ibid., f 280, 2 July 1806; and Canning Mss 63, Canning to Grenville copy, 1 July 1806
78 ibid., 21 f 288, Canning to wife, 5 July 1806
79 B.M. Add. 42,773, f 117, Canning to Rose, 7 July 1806
80 Canning Mss 21, f 290, Canning to wife, 5 July 1806
81 *H.M.C. Dropmore*, vol. 8, p. 441, Carysfort to Grenville, 27 July 1806
82 B.M. Add. 41,952, f 265, Grenville to T. Grenville, 1 Aug. 1806
83 Canning Mss 21, f 309-10, Canning to wife, 23 July 1806
84 B.M. Add. 42,773, f 119, Canning to Rose, 9 Aug. 1806
85 *H.M.C. Lonsdale*, p. 200, Canning to Lowther, 26 Sept. 1806
86 B.M. Add. 42,773, f 127, Canning to Rose, 14 Aug. 1806; *H.M.C. Dropmore*, vol. 8, p. 283, Canning to Wellesley, 14 Aug. 1806
87 Canning Mss 21, f 334, Canning to wife, c. 10 Aug. 1806
88 STAPLETON, *Canning and his Times*, p. 97, Canning to Boringdon, 29 Aug. 1806
89 B.M., Add., 42,773, f 159-160, Canning to Rose, 2 Sept. 1806
90 ibid., f 178, 12 Sept. 1806
91 LEVESON GOWER, *Correspondence*, vol. 2, p. 222, Lady Bessborough to Granville Leveson, 28 Oct. 1806
92 *H.M.C. Lonsdale*, p. 200, Canning to Lowther, 26 Sept. 1806
93 STAPLETON, *Canning and his Times*, p. 104, Canning to Boringdon, 24 Sept. 1806
94 *H.M.C. Lonsdale*, p. 214, Long to Lowther, 24 Oct. 1806
95 ibid., p. 226, Mulgrave to Lowther, 20 Nov. 1806
96 ibid., p. 223, Canning to Lowther, 23 Nov. 1806
97 B.M. Add. 48,219, f 179, Canning to Norington, 25 Nov. 1806
98 *H.M.C. Lonsdale*, p. 222 Ward to Lowther 23 Nov. 1806
99 B.M. Add. 48,219, f 157, Canning to Boringdon, 23 Aug. 1806

100 B.M. Add. 35,395, f 156, Yorke to Hardwicke, 12 Sept. 1806
101 B.M. Add. 37,415, f 19 and 23, A. Wellesley to Wellesley, 3 and
     22 Oct. 1806
102 BUCKINGHAM, *Court and Cabinets*, vol. 4, pp. 29-31, Grenville to
     Buckingham, 9 May 1806
103 B.M. Add. 41,854, f 24-5, Temple to T. Grenville, 10 May 1806
104 BUCKINGHAM, *Court and Cabinets*, vol. 4, p. 52-3, T. Grenville to
     Buckingham, 21 July 1806
105 *H.M.C. Dropmore*, vol. 8, p. 320, Windham to Grenville, 11 Sept. 1806
106 ibid., p. 340, Howick to Grenville, 19 Sept. 1806
107 B.M. Add. 41,851, f 270, Buckingham to T. Grenville, 21 Sept. 1806
108 HINTON, 'General Elections of 1806 and 1807', p. 218
109 *Kentish Chronicle*, 28 Nov. 1806, quoted Hinton p. 92
110 B.M. Add. 38,737, f 184, 12 Jan. 1807
111 Harrowby Mss (at Sandon Park) 4, f 46 foll., Ryder to Harrowby 3 Jan.
     1807, quoted by ASPINALL, A., 'The Canningite Party', *Transactions of the
     Royal Historical Society* 4th ser. 17 (1934), pp. 177-226
112 ROSE, *Diaries*, vol. 2, pp. 311-17, Canning to Rose, 7 Feb. 1807
113 Canning Mss 22, f 4, 7 Feb. 1807
114 ibid., f 3
115 *H.M.C. Dropmore*, vol. 9, p. T. Grenville to Grenville, 23 Feb. 1807; ibid.,
     p. 67, Holland to Howick, 6 March 1807; LADY HOLLAND, *Journal*,
     vol. 2, p. 208, 2 March 1807; ibid., p. 211, 8 March 1807
116 Canning Mss 22, f 47-8, Canning to wife, 27 Feb. 1807
117 ibid., f 74, 10 March 1807
118 *Parl. Debates*, vol. 9, col. 279, 26 March 1807
119 ANSTEY, R., 'A Reinterpretation of the Abolition of the British Slave
     Trade, 1806-1807' *English Historical Review* 1972 (87), pp. 304-332;
     espec. pp. 327-9
120 HARVEY, 'Ministry of all the Talents', *H.J.* 15, pp. 642-3
121 *Parl. Debates*, vol. 8, col. 706, 708
122 BUCKINGHAM, *Court and Cabinets*, vol. 4, p. 133, Grenville to
     Buckingham, 7 March 1807
123 *Parl. Debates*, vol. 9, col. 693
124 N.L.I., Ms. 8023 (6), 4 Feb. 1806
125 LORD HOLLAND, *Memoirs*, pp. 162-8
126 CHART, D. A., ed. *The Drennan Letters*, Belfast 1931, pp. 371-2,
     Drennan to Mrs McTier, 14 Jan. 1807
127 Grey Mss 6/17, f 8, Bedford to Howick, 5 Jan. 1807
128 ibid., 47/1, f 6A, Howick to Ponsonby, 31 Dec. 1806
129 LORD HOLLAND, *Memoirs*, vol. 2, p. 184
130 *Times*, 19 March 1807
131 BUCKINGHAM, *Court and Cabinets*, vol. 4, p. 140, 16 March 1807
132 B.M. Add. 34,457, f 248, Grenville to Auckland, 17 March 1807
133 N. Yorks. R.O. ZFW 7/2 196/8, Duncombe to Wyvill, 25 March 1807
134 PLUMER WARD, *Memoirs*, vol. 1, p. 342, Diary, 19 Jan. 1811

4 THE PORTLAND MINISTRY

  1 Devon R.O., 152M/C 1807 OZ, Sidmouth to Bishop of Gloucester,
     3 April 1807
  2 N.L.W., 10804D, Wynn to Strachey, 8 April 1807
  3 SOUTHEY, R., *History of the Peninsular War*, 3 vols., 1823-32, vol. 1,
     p. 53

4 B.M. Add. 37,309, f 170, Portland to Wellesley, 24 March 1807
5 WALPOLE, *Perceval,* vol. 2, p. 16 n. Perceval to Huskisson, 21 Aug. 1809
6 MALMESBURY, *Diaries,* vol. 4, p. 386, Summer 1807
7 FARINGTON, *Diary,* vol. 4, p. 36, 12 March 1808
8 GREY, *Perceval,* p. 319
9 WALPOLE, *Perceval,* vol. 1, p. 242, 20 March 1807
10 COLCHESTER, *Diary,* vol. 2, p. 381, 15 May 1812
11 ibid., loc. cit
12 FARINGTON, *Diary,* vol. 5, p. 196, 20 June 1809
13 PLUMER WARD, *Memoirs,* vol. 1, p. 408, 20 March 1811
14 *Parl. Debates,* vol. 22, col. 309
15 GLENBERVIE, *Diaries,* vol. 2, p. 11, 23 Jan. 1808
16 ROMILLY, *Memoirs,* vol. 1, p. 91
17 B.M. Add. 35,395 f 181, Yorke to Hardwicke, 7 June 1807
18 BUCKINGHAM, *Court and Cabinets,* vol. 3, p. 130, Grenville to Buckingham, 2 Feb. 1801
19 ibid. vol. 4, p. 289, Grenville to Temple, 15 Dec. 1808
20 *Edinburgh Review* 30 (1818), p. 196
21 B.M. Add. 34,457, f 273, Cooke to Auckland, 1 April 1807
22 BUCKINGHAM, *Court and Cabinets,* vol. 4, p. 166, Fremantle to Buckingham, 15 April 1807
23 ibid., p. 167, same letter
24 ibid., pp. 172-3, Grenville to Buckingham, 27 April 1807
25 HINTON, 'General Elections of 1806 and 1807', pp. 330-1
26 ibid., pp. 338, 343-6
27 ibid., p. 349; and BUCKINGHAM, *Court and Cabinets,* vol. 4, p. 173, Grenville to Buckingham, 27 April 1807
28 MELBOURNE, *Papers,* p. 44, Diary 13 May 1807
29 HINTON, 'General Elections of 1806 and 1807', pp. 357, 360
30 ibid., pp. 379, 664-5
31 ibid., p. 416
32 ibid., p. 410
33 Kenyon Mss 27, Dowager Lady Kenyon to Alice Kenyon, 22 March 1804
34 *Political Register,* vol. 10, p. 161, 2 Aug. 1806
35 BUCKINGHAM, *Court and Cabinets,* vol. 4, p. 189, 25 June 1807
36 N.L.W., 10804D, Wynn to Saxton, 21 July 1807
37 BUCKINGHAM, *Court and Cabinets,* vol. 4, p. 118, Grenville to Buckingham, 10 Feb. 1807
38 ibid., p. 148, same to same, 26 March 1807
39 ibid., p. 182, 17 June 1807
40 ROBERTS, *Whig Party,* pp. 328-9
41 Cf. B.M. 41,853, f 243, Grenville to T. Grenville, 22 April 1812; *Parl. Debates,* vol. 14, col. 149; Earl Grey Mss, Holland to Grey, 2 Dec. 1816; HARVEY, 'Grenville Party', pp. 263-6
42 B.M. Add. 51,571, f 13, Holland to Thanet, 1811 or 1812
43 Grey Mss, Holland to Grey, 2 Dec. 1816
44 *H.M.C. Dropmore,* vol. 9, p. 149, T. Grenville to Grenville, 22 Nov. 1807
45 LADY HOLLAND, *Journal,* vol. 2, p. 285, 20 Jan. 1811
46 Grey Mss, Grey to Holland, 6 Dec. 1807
47 ibid., Grey to Whitbread, 29 May 1808
48 ibid., Grey to Holland, 6 Dec. 1807
49 *H.M.C. Dropmore,* vol. 8, pp. 346-7, Howick to Grenville, 20 Sept. 1806
50 Grey Mss, Ponsonby to Grey, 23 Nov. 1807
51 ibid., Tierney to Grey, 7 Dec. 1807

52 BUCKINGHAM, *Court and Cabinets,* vol. 4, p. 209, Grenville to Buckingham, 23 Nov. 1807; B.M. Add. 42,852, f 324, Grenville to T. Grenville, 22 Nov. 1807
53 B.M. Add. 51,544, Holland to Grey, 30 Nov. 1807
54 B.M. Add. 41,857, f 69, Ponsonby to T. Grenville, 25 Nov. 1807
55 BUCKINGHAM, *Court and Cabinets,* vol. 4, p. 222, T. Grenville to Buckingham, 25 Dec. 1807
56 N.L.W., Coed-y-maen Mss 20, Temple to Wynn, 24 Dec. 1807
57 BEATTIE, W., *Life and Letters of Thomas Campbell,* 3 vols., 1849, vol. 2, p. 149, Campbell to Mayow, 14-15 July 1808
58 COLERIDGE, *Biographia Literaria,* chap. 10
59 BUCKINGHAM, *Court and Cabinets,* vol. 4, p. 240, Grenville to Buckingham, 10 Aug. 1808
60 MOORE, *Diary,* vol. 2, pp. 242-3, 23 July 1808
61 STAPLETON, *Canning and his Times,* p. 159
62 MOORE, *Diary,* vol. 2, p. 261, 8 Sept. 1808, p. 271, 2 Oct. 1808
63 BUCKINGHAM, *Court and Cabinets,* vol. 4, p. 264, Wellesley to Temple, 14 Oct. 1808
64 CASTLEREAGH, *Correspondence,* vol. 4, p. 42
65 BUCKINGHAM, *Court and Cabinets,* vol. 4, p. 250, anon. to Buckingham, 17 Sept. 1808
66 FARINGTON, *Diary,* vol. 4, p. 100, 19 Sept. 1808
67 DELAVOYE, A. M., *Life of Thomas Graham Lord Lynedoch,* 1880, p. 269
68 WORDSWORTH, W., *Concerning the Relations of Great Britain, Spain, and Portugal, to each other, and to the Common Enemy, at this Crisis; and Specifically as Affected by the Convention of Cintra,* 1809, p. 3
69 CASTLEREAGH, *Correspondence,* vol. 6, p. 453
70 *H.M.C. Bathurst,* p. 75, Canning to Bathurst, 16 Sept. 1808
71 WELLINGTON, *Supplementary Despatches,* vol. 6, p. 402, Wellesley to Castlereagh, 14 Oct. 1809
72 GRAY, *Perceval,* p. 184, 18 Sept. 1808
73 CASTLEREAGH, *Correspondence,* vol. 6, p. 454, 26 Sept. 1808
74 BUCKINGHAM, *Court and Cabinets,* vol. 4, p. 277, Temple to Buckingham, 7 Nov. 1808
75 NEALE, A., *Letters from Portugal and Spain,* 1809, pp. 247-8
76 NAPIER, *War in the Peninsula,* vol. 1, p. 480
77 BUCKINGHAM, *Court and Cabinets,* vol. 4, p. 283, T. Grenville to Buckingham, 5 Dec. 1808
78 Canning Mss 32, Canning to Castlereagh, 31 Dec. 1808
79 ibid., Canning to Portland, 30 Dec. 1808
80 NAPIER, *War in the Peninsula,* vol. 1, p. 500
81 WOLFE, C., 'The Burial of Sir John Moore at Corunna', first published 1817
82 BUCKINGHAM, *Court and Cabinets,* vol. 4, p. 313, Temple to Buckingham, 3 Feb. 1809
83 STAPLETON, *Canning and his Times,* pp. 163-4
84 B.M. Add. 34,457, f 491, Grenville to Auckland, n.d. 1808
85 Grey Mss 55, Tierney to Whitbread copy, 29 Dec. 1808
86 CREEVEY, *Papers,* vol. 1, p. 92, Whitbread to Creevey, 20 Dec. 1808
87 Grey Mss, Grenville to Grey, 20 Dec. 1808
88 *H.M.C. Dropmore,* vol. 9, p. 253, T. Grenville to Grenville, 31 Dec. 1808
89 Grey Mss, Grey to Ponsonby, 23 Dec. 1808
90 *H.M.C. Dropmore,* vol. 9, p. 254, T. Grenville 31 Dec. 1808
91 ibid., p. 266, same to same, 10 Jan. 1809

5 THE REVIVAL OF REFORM

1 *Quarterly Review*, vol. 8, pp. 345-6, (Dec. 1812)
2 *Political Register* vol. 13 col. 226, 13 Feb. 1808
3 ibid., vol. 9, col. 366-8, 15 March 1806
4 BAMFORD, *Life of a Radical*, vol. 1, p. 21
5 LE MARCHANT, *Memoir of Althorp*, pp. 121-2
6 GALBRAITH, G., ed., *The Journal of the Rev. William Bagshaw Stevens*, Oxford 1965, p. 374, Stevens to Burdett, 3 June 1796
7 Bodleian Ms. Eng. Let. c 64, f 78 foll., 22 Jan. 1799
8 *Life of the Late Thomas Coutts, Esq.* anon. c. 1822 ; *The Earl of Dundonald's Answer to the Mis-statements contained in the Life of the Late T. Coutts, Esq.*, 1822, p. 6
9 BROUGHTON, *Recollections of a Long Life*, vol. 2, p. 96, 27 March 1818
10 BAMFORD, *Life of a Radical*, vol. 1, p. 20
11 ibid.
12 *Parl. Debates*, vol. 22, col. 171
13 Bodleian Ms. Eng. Hist. b. 197, f 78-80, Childs to Russell copy, c. 1820
14 Cf. FORTESCUE, J. W., *Dondonald*, 1895, pp. 98-9; LLOYD, C., *Lord Cochrane*, 1947, pp. 114-129
15 Cf. ATLAY, J.B., *The Trial of Lord Cochrane before Lord Ellenborough*, 1897, and ELLENBOROUGH, E. LORD, *The Guilt of Lord Cochrane in 1814*, 1914
16 B.M. Add. 38,257, f 250 1, Dundonald to Cochrane, 13 May 1814
17 B.M. Add. 38,258, f 51, Dundonald to Liverpool, 14 June 1814 Cf. also GEDDES, D. 'How "Habeas Corpus" came to Canada: The Bills on Credit Scandal—Quebec 1783' *Three Banks Review*, 112 (Dec. 1976) pp. 50-65, for some details of the career of the Hon. John Cochrane
18 *Parl. Debates*, vol. 35, col. 92, 29 Jan. 1817
19 BROWN, J., *Thoughts on Civil Liberty*, 1765, p. 121
20 DUNDONALD, *Autobiography of a Seaman*, vol. 2, p. 263
21 *Fallen Angels!* anon. 1807, p. 3
22 *Courier*, 23 June 1807
23 *Political Register*, vol. 12, col. 33-4, 11 July 1807
24 ibid., 11 Aug. 1812
25 BARNES, T., *Parliamentary Portraits*, 1815, p. 25
26 EVANS, T., *Christian Policy the Salvation of Empire*, 2nd edit., 1816, pp. 22-3
27 ADAIR, *Duke of Devonshire*, p. 13
28 N. Yorks. R.O., ZFW 7/2, 208/4, Cartwright to Wyvill, 5 Dec. 1808
29 GEORGE III, *Correspondence*, vol. 5, p. 489, George III to Ryder, 20 Jan. 1810
30 BURGOYNE, M., *A Letter from Montagu Burgoyne, Esq....on the Present State of Public Affairs; and the Representation of the County of Essex*, 1808, p. 47
31 Bodleian Ms Eng. His. d. 216 (M. W. Patterson's draft of *Burdett and his Times*), p. 319
32 LORD HOLLAND, *Further Memoirs*, p. 56
33 FLOWER, B., and CLIFFORD, H., *Proceedings of the House of Lords in the Case of Benjamin Flower*, Cambridge 1800, pp. 54-5
34 ibid., pp. 67-8
35 See above pp. 8
36 STEPHENS, *Horne Tooke*, vol. 2, p. 89
37 BOWLES, J., *A Postscript to Thoughts on the Late General Election, as Demonstrative of the Progress of Jacobinism*, 1803, pp. 103-4 and fn.
38 WALLAS, *Francis Place*, p. 42

39 PATTERSON, *Burdett and his Times*, p. 184
40 SAXTON, 'Westminster Committee', Section 2, p. 29 and n. 2
41 ibid., p. 21
42 WALLAS, *Francis Place*, p. 45
43 SAXTON, 'Westminster Committee', Section 2, p. 29 and N 2
44 *Political Register*, vol. 9, p. 885, 14 June 1806
45 B.M. Add. 41,857, f 31, Markham to T. Grenville, 27 May 1807
46 *Times*, 21 May 1807
47 ibid., 22 May 1807
48 GEORGE, PRINCE OF WALES, *Correspondence*, vol. 6, p. 116, Kent to Dodd, 8 Jan. 1807
49 FARINGTON, *Diary*, vol. 3, p. 112, 25 Sept. 1805
50 P.R.O., CO 71/33, Cochrane Johnstone to Hobart, 30 Nov. 1801
51 Bodleian Ms Eng. Hist. b. 197 f 64 and f 66, Burdett to Pomeroy, 23 Feb. 1807, and reply 28 Oct. sic 1807
52 GEORGE, PRINCE OF WALES, *Correspondence*, vol. 5, p. 375, Cochrane Johnstone, to Gordon, 2 May 1806, and reply 3 May 1806
53 ALEXANDER, B., ed., *Life at Fonthill 1807-1822*, 1957 p. 119, Beckford to Franchi, 28 Jan. 1812
54 N.L.S., 2572 f 172-4, copies A. F. Cochrane to B. Cochrane, 18 Oct. and 2 Nov. 1808
55 HERON, R., *Notes*, 1850, p. 40
56 WILLIAMS, O., *Life and Letters of John Rickman*, 1912, p. 137, Rickman to Poole, 31 Jan. 1806
57 *Political Register*, vol. 10, pp. 274, 345, 367-9, 439-41, 23 and 30 Aug. and 13 Sept. 1806
58 *Mentoriana*, p. 13
59 ibid., p. 9
60 ibid., p. 10
61 ibid., p. 17
62 ibid., p. 19
63 *A Letter to His Royal Highness*, p. 12
64 ibid., p. 32
65 *The Agent, and His Natural Son*, p. 108 n.
66 ibid., pp. 103-4
67 *A Letter to His Royal Highness*, p. 24 n.
68 *Mentoriana*, pp. 7, 8
69 Bodleian Ms Eng. His. b. 196 f 9-10
70 HAGUE, *Letter to the Duke of York*, p. 25
71 ibid., pp. 13, 20
72 ibid., pp. 27, 33
73 McCALLUM, *Rival Queens*, p. 33
74 McCALLUM, *Observations on the Duke of Kent*, pp. 17, 18-19, 32
75 ibid., pp. 19, 53-4
76 ibid., p. 1
77 ibid., p. 65
78 McCALLUM, *Rival Queens*, p. 86
79 McCALLUM, *Observations on the Duke of Kent*, p. 26
80 HOGAN, D., *An Appeal to the Public and a Farewell Address to the Army*, 1808, p. 51
81 *Political Register*, vol. 14, col. 936-40, 17 Dec. 1808
82 THOUMINE, R. H., *Scientific Soldier*, 1968, pp. 128-137
83 McCALLUM, *Rival Queens*, pp. 89-90
84 B.M. Add. 38,243, f 1 and 50, Gibbs to Hawkesbury, 1 Sept. and 20 Oct. 1808
85 Irish State Papers 620/35/119a, anon. to Wardle, 7 Feb. 1798

86 ibid., 620/18/9/5, Cornwallis to Portland, 13 March 1799
87 APPERLEY, C. J., *My Life and Times by 'Nimrod'*, ed. E. D. Cuming, Edinburgh 1927, p. 96
88 *Parl. Debates*, vol. 11, col. 1002 foll., 23 June 1808
89 DODD, A. H., *The Industrial Revolution in North Wales*, Cardiff 1933, p. 25(
90 ODDY, J. J., *An Address to the Worshipful the Mayor and Alderman, and to the Capital Burgesses, and Gentlemen Electors of the Antient Town and Borough of Stamford*, 1809, p. 49 n.
91 McCALLUM, *Rival Queens*, pp. 34, 40-41; cf. CLARKE, *Rival Princes*, vol. 2, p. 26
92 McCALLUM, *Rival Queens*, pp. 36-7
93 CLARKE, *Rival Princes*, vol. 1, p. 72
94 McCALLUM, *Rival Queens*, p. 51
95 CREEVEY, *Papers*, vol. 1, p. 115
96 N.L.W., 4814D, Wynn to Southey, 30 Aug. 1810
97 GEORGE PRINCE OF WALES, *Correspondence*, vol. 6, p. 498, Kent to Fitzherbert, 18 Dec. 1809
98 Grey Mss., Rosslyn to Grey, 9 Feb. 1809
99 BUCKINGHAM, *Court and Cabinets*, vol. 4, pp. 319-20, Fremantle to Buckingham, 16 Feb. 1809
100 LORD HOLLAND, *Further Memoirs*, p. 29
101 Grey Mss., Rosslyn to Grey, 9 Feb. 1809
102 ibid., Auckland to Grey, 6 March 1809
103 HORNER, *Memoirs and Correspondence*, vol. 1, pp. 454-5
104 Berks. R.O., D/Epb 025 73C, 17 March 1809
105 B.M. Add. 41,854, f 245, Spencer to T. Grenville, 4 April 1809
106 BUCKINGHAM, *Court and Cabinets*, vol. 4, p. 319, Fremantle to Buckingham, 16 Feb. 1809
107 N.L.W., 4814D, Wynn to Southey, 8 Nov. 1810
108 N. Yorks. R.O., ZFW 7/2/208/37, Duncombe to Wyvill, 2 April 1809
109 REID, *Colonel Wardle*, pp. 176-7
110 *Northampton Mercury*, 8 April 1809
111 ibid., 15 and 17 April 1809
112 N.L.W., Glansevern Mss 2203, E. Jones to R. Jones, 14 April 1809; and 8780, copy E. Jones to Cobbett, 12 April 1809
113 *Political Register*, vol. 15, col. 644, 29 April 1809
114 CURRY, K., ed., *New Letters of Robert Southey*, 2 vols., 1965, vol. 1, p. 505, Southey to Danvers, 20 March 1809
115 REID, *Colonel Wardle*, p. 63
116 Berks. R.O., D/EPb 025 f 30
117 ibid.
118 ibid., f 3, Radnor to Folkestone, 19 Dec. 1809; f 6, Ellis to Folkestone, 6 Jan. 1810; f 15, Wardle to Folkestone, 18 Sept. 1809
119 ibid., f 65, East to Folkestone, 7 April 1809
120 ibid., f 67, Radnor to Folkestone, 30 March 1809; and f 68, Althorp to Folkestone, 26 March 1809
121 ibid., f 68
122 *Parl. Debates*, vol. 14, col. 510-11
123 *H.M.C. Dropmore*, vol. 9, p. 292, T. Grenville to Grenville, 7 April 1809
124 *Parl. Debates*, vol. 14, col. 149
125 Northants. R.O., Milton Mss. X1605, Folkestone to Milton, 30 March 1809
126 ibid.
127 Berks. R.O. D/EPb 025 f 64, Milton to Folkestone, 1 April 1809
128 ibid., 028 f 187, copy Folkestone to Waithman, 20 April 1809

129 *Parl. Debates*, vol. 14, col. 354
130 ibid., col. 361-2
131 HORNER, *Memoirs and Correspondence*, vol. 1, p. 493, Horner to Ward, 24 May 1809
132 *Parl. Debates*, vol. 14, col. 936
6 THE COLLAPSE OF THE PORTLAND MINISTRY
 1 ROBERTS, *Whig Party*, p. 314
 2 *H.M.C. Dropmore*, vol. 9, p. 282, T. Grenville to Grenville, 25 March 1809
 3 ibid., p. 284, same to same, 28 March 1809
 4 ibid., p. 286, same to same, 30 March 1809
 5 Grey Mss., Fitzwilliam to Grey, 10 Jan. 1810
 6 PLUMER WARD, *Memoirs*, vol. 1, pp. 242-3, Canning to Portland, 24 March 1809
 7 WALPOLE, *Perceval*, vol. 1, p. 353, Canning to Perceval, June 1809
 8 WELLINGTON, *Supplementary Despatches*, vol. 5, p. 131, A. Wellesley to Richmond, 27 July 1807
 9 RUSSELL, J., *Recollections and Suggestions 1813-1873*, 1875, pp. 26-7
10 FESTING, G., *John Hookham Frere and his Friends*, 1899, p. 83, Canning to Frere
11 Canning Mss., 19, Canning to wife, 9 Jan. 1804
12 ibid., 24, f 91, same to same, 22 March 1809
13 GRAY, *Perceval*, pp. 215-6
14 Canning Mss 33, Canning to Portland, 5 May 1809
15 GRAY, *Perceval*, p. 217
16 Grey Mss, Tierney to Grey, 27 May 1809
17 B.M. Add. 48,222 f 188, Granville Leveson to Boringdon, 10 April 1809
18 Canning Mss 34, Canning to Castlereagh, 21 March 1809
19 *H.M.C. Bathurst*, p. 112
20 STANHOPE, *Conversations with Wellington*, p. 289, 29 Oct. 1842; cf. ELLESMERE, *Personal Reminiscences of Wellington*, p. 130, 14 Sept. 1826; B.M. Add. 48,222 f 188, Granville Leveson to Boringdon, 10 April 1809
21 GRAY, *Perceval*, p. 217
22 Canning Mss 33, Canning to Portland, 13 June 1809
23 WALPOLE, *Perceval*, vol. 1, p. 352, Perceval to Canning, 25 June 1809
24 Grey Mss, Tierney to Grey, 7 July 1809
25 ibid., same to same, 24 Sept. 1809
26 GEORGE III, *Correspondence*, vol. 5, p. 311, Liverpool to George III, 11 July 1809
27 BUCKINGHAM, *Court and Cabinets*, vol. 4, pp. 349-50, Fremantle to Buckingham, 13 Aug. 1809
28 ibid., p. 349
29 STANHOPE, *Conversations with Wellington*, p. 157, 22 Sept. 1839
30 Canning Mss 34, Mulgrave to Canning, 9 Sept. 1809
31 WALPOLE, *Perceval*, vol. 1, p. 362, Canning to Perceval, 31 Aug. 1809
32 *H.M.C. Bathurst*, pp. 115-6
33 WALPOLE, *Perceval*, vol. 1, p. 365, Perceval to Canning, 4 or 5 Sept. 1809
34 ibid., p. 365 n, Perceval to Arden, 3 Sept. 1809
35 *H.M.C. Bathurst*, pp. 117-8
36 ibid., p. 119
37 FARINGTON, *Diary*, vol. 5, pp. 224-5, 8 Sept. 1809
38 BUCKINGHAM, *Court and Cabinets*, vol. 4, p. 363, Fremantle to Buckingham, 12 Sept. 1809

39 GEORGE III, *Correspondence*, vol. 5, pp. 340-1, Canning to Portland, 12 Sept. 1809

40 Canning Mss 23, f 56, Canning to wife, 19 Sept. 1809

41 ROSE, *Diaries*, vol. 2, pp. 350-1, Sturges Bourne to Rose, 17 Sept. 1809

42 Canning Mss 23, f 52, Canning to wife, 15 Sept. 1809

43 GEORGE III, *Correspondence*, vol. 5, p. 368 n.1, Ellis to Banning, 2 Oct. 1809

44 LONDONDERRY, *Castlereagh*, p. 43, Castlereagh to Stewart, 22 Sept. 1809

45 LORD HOLLAND, *Further Memoirs*, p. 35

46 WILBERFORCE, *Life*, vol. 3, p. 431, Wilberforce to Babington, Nov. 1809

47 ORMOND, G. W. T., *The Arniston Memoirs*, Edinburgh 1887, p. 266, J. Canning to Dundas, 27 Sept. 1809 [Prints '27 April']

48 As 46

49 WELLESLEY, F. A., ed., *The Diary and Correspondence of Henry Wellesley First Lord Cowley 1790-1846* [1930], p. 49

50 Canning Mss 33, memo by Ellis

51 KIRBY, *Wonderful and Eccentric Museum*, vol. 3, p. 156

52 GEORGE III, *Correspondence*, vol. 5, p. 368 n.1, Ellis to Binning, 2 Oct. 1809

53 KNIGHT, C., *Autobiography of Miss Cornelia Knight*, 2 vols., 1861, vol. 2, p. 264, Diary 23 Sept. 1809

54 PLUMER WARD, *Memoirs*, vol 1, p. 360, 24 Jan. 1811

55 LONDONDERRY, *Castlereagh*, pp. 41-2, Castlereagh to Stewart, 22 Sept. 1809

56 ibid., p. 40, Castlereagh to Londonderry, 3 Oct. 1809

57 B.M. Add. 41,853, f 41, Grenville to T. Grenville, 20 Sept. 1809

58 BUCKINGHAM, *Court and Cabinets*, vol. 4, p. 376, Grenville to Perceval, 29 Sept. 1809

59 Grey Mss, T. Grenville to Grey, 2 Oct. 1809

60 WINDHAM, *Papers*, vol. 2, pp. 356-7, Windham to Grey, 29 Sept. 1809

61 Devon R.O., 152M/C 1809 OZ, Sidmouth to J. H. Addington, 22 Oct 1809

62 ibid., copy Sidmouth to Chatham, 6 Oct. 1809

63 ROSE, *Diaries*, vol. 2, pp. 413-4, 23 Oct. 1809

64 GEORGE III, *Correspondence*, vol. 5, pp. 423, 448, 459, Perceval to George III, 26 Oct., 13 and 25 Nov. 1809

65 Devon R.O., 152M/C 1810 OZ, Sidmouth to Bathurst, 7 Jan. 1810

66 B.M. Add. 45,036, f 143, Robinson to Yorke, 5 Oct. 1809

67 WELLESLEY, *Papers*, vol. 1, p. 249, Sydenham to Wellesley, 16 Sept. 1809

68 ibid., p. 264, Wellesley to Wellesley Pole, 8 Oct. 1809

69 ROSE, *Diaries*, vol. 2, p. 401, 3 Oct. 1809

70 PLUMER WARD, *Memoirs*, vol. 1, pp. 255-62, Perceval to Melville, 5 Oct. 1809

71 B.M. Add. 45,036, f 63, Perceval to Yorke, 24 Oct. 1809

72 B.M. Add. 45,042, f 87, Yorke to J. S. Yorke, 5 Oct. 1809

73 N.L.W., 4814D, Wynn to Southey, 21 July 1809

74 ibid., same to same, 22 Feb. 1811

75 COLCHESTER, *Diaries*, vol. 2, p. 216, 3 Nov. 1809

76 MALMESBURY, EARL OF, *Letters of the First Earl of Malmesbury his Family and Friends*, 2 vols., 1870, vol. 2, p. 191, Fitzharris to Malmesbury, 20 Nov. 1809

77 PLUMER WARD, *Memoirs*, vol. 1, p. 259, Perceval to Melville, 5 Oct. 1809

7 THE PERCEVAL MINISTRY

1 B.M. Add. 37,295, f 176, Wellesley to Anstruther, 30 Oct. 1809
2 FARINGTON, *Diary,* vol. 6, p. 258, 8 April 1811
3 ROSE, *Diaries,* vol. 2, p. 165, 30 Sept. 1804
4 Cf. *H.M.C. Dropmore,* vol. 5, p. 49, Wellesley to Grenville, 12 May 1799
5 ELLESMERE, *Reminiscences of Wellington,* p. 86
6 BUCKINGHAM, *Court and Cabinets,* vol. 4, p. 397, anon. to Buckingham, 4 Dec. 1809
7 WELLINGTON, *Supplementary Despatches,* vol. 7, p. 258, memo by Meyrick Shawe
8 ibid., pp. 258-9
9 ibid., p. 258
10 BUCKINGHAM, *Court and Cabinets,* vol. 4, p. 435, anon. to Buckingham, 4 Dec. 1809
11 WELLINGTON, *Supplementary Despatches,* vol. 7, p. 265, memo by Meyrick Shawe
12 *H.M.C. Dropmore,* vol. 10, p. 245, T. Grenville to Grenville, 10 Sept. 1812
13 WELLINGTON, *Supplementary Despatches,* vol. 7, p. 266, memo by Meyrick Shawe
14 *Camden Society,* Series 3, vol. 79, p. 31, Wellington to Wellesley Pole, 6 April 1810
15 POOLE, *Stratford Canning,* vol. 1, pp. 91, 128
16 GRAY, *Perceval,* p. 275
17 ibid., p. 275 n. 3
18 ibid., p. 435, Ryder to Harrowby, 22 Oct. 1811
19 WALPOLE, *Perceval,* vol. 2, p. 125, Wellesley to Perceval, 22 July 1810
20 PLUMER WARD, *Memoirs,* vol. 1, p. 429, 23 Feb. 1812
21 *H.M.C. Bathurst,* p. 160, memo
22 GEORGE III, *Correspondence,* vol. 5, p. 485, Perceval to George III, 15 Jan. 1810
23 Canning Mss 24, f 67, Canning to wife, 12 March 1810
24 WELLINGTON, *Supplementary Despatches,* vol. 7, p. 260, memo by Meyrick Shawe
25 B.M. Add. 51,544, f 230-31, Holland to Grey, 3 Jan. 1810
26 Grey Mss, Grey to Holland, 5 Jan. 1810
27 ibid.
28 P.R.O., HO 42/107
29 FREND, *Letters,* p. 87, Hammond to Frend, 24 April 1810
30 P.R.O., HO 33/1 Gottwalty to Freeling, 29 May 1810
31 Grey Mss, copy Grenville to Whitbread, 23 April 1810
32 Bucks R.O., D/Fr 55, Temple to Fremantle, 27 May 1810
33 N.L.W. 10804D, Wynn to Strachey, 29 May 1810
34 *H.M.C. Dropmore,* vol. 10, pp. 29-30, Grey to Grenville, 1 May 1810
35 GREY, *Life and Opinions,* p. 240, Grey to Grenville, n.d.
36 B.M. Add. 37,295, f 244 foll., Wellesley to Perceval, 13 March 1810
37 WALPOLE, *Perceval,* vol. 2, p. 80, Perceval to Richmond, 30 April 1810
38 HARVEY, 'Grenville Party' pp. 381-2
39 BUCKINGHAM, *Court and Cabinets,* vol. 4, p. 431, anon. to Buckingham, 2 April 1810
40 WALPOLE, *Perceval,* vol. 2, p. 80, Perceval to Richmond, 30 April 1810
41 PELLEW, *Sidmouth,* vol. 3, pp. 26-7, Sidmouth to Bathurst, 27 April 1810
42 WALPOLE, *Perceval,* vol. 2, p. 81, Perceval to Richmond, 30 April 1810
43 BUCKINGHAM, *Court and Cabinets,* vol. 4, p. 455, anon. to Buckingham, 1 Oct. 1810

44 B.M. Add. 37,295, f 272, Perceval to Wellesley, 28 April 1810
45 ibid., f 282, Wellesley to Perceval, 3 May 1810
46 WALPOLE, *Perceval*, vol. 2, p. 140, Wellesley to Perceval, 14 June 1810
47 ibid., pp. 150-1, Perceval to Castlereagh, 22 Aug. 1810
48 *H.M.C. Dropmore*, vol. 10, p. 55, Buckingham to Grenville, 17 Oct. 1810
49 WALPOLE, *Perceval*, vol. 2, p. 155, Canning to Perceval, 25 Sept. 1810; GRAY, *Perceval*, p. 399
50 BUCKINGHAM, *Court and Cabinets*, vol. 4, p. 455, anon. to Buckingham, 1 Oct. 1810
51 WELLINGTON, *Supplementary Despatches*, vol. 7, p. 5, Wellington to Wellesley-Pole, 15 Dec. 1810
52 PLUMER WARD, *Memoirs*, vol. 1, p. 335, 15 Jan. 1811
53 AUCKLAND, *Journals and Correspondence*, vol. 4, p. 359, Grenville to Auckland Nov.[1810]
54 BROUGHAM, *Memoirs*, vol. 1, p. 512, Brougham to Grey, 18 Dec. 1810
55 WALPOLE, *Perceval*, vol. 2, p. 170 n.
56 PLUMER WARD, *Memoirs*, vol. 1, p. 305, 2 Jan. 1811
57 ibid., p. 300, 1 Jan. 1811
58 ibid., p. 336, 17 Jan. 1811
59 ibid., p. 340, 19 Jan. 1811, quoting Manners Sutton
60 HORNER, *Memoirs and Correspondence*, vol. 2, p. 56, Horner to Murray, 30 Jan. 1811
61 CREEVEY, *Papers*, vol. 1, p. 138, Creevey to wife, 19 Jan. 1811
62 *H.M.C. Dropmore*, vol. 10, pp. 98-9, Buckingham to Grenville, 9 Jan. 1811
63 ibid., vol. 10, p. 104, T. Grenville to Grenville, 11 Jan. 1811
64 LADY HOLLAND, *Journal*, vol. 2, pp. 285-6, 20 Jan. 1811; cf. PLUMER WARD, *Memoirs*, vol. 1, pp. 347-8, 21 Jan. 1811
65 GREY, *Life and Opinions*, pp. 271-2, Grey to wife, 18 Jan. 1811
66 LADY HOLLAND, *Journal*, vol. 2, p. 286, 20 Jan. 1811
67 *H.M.C. Dropmore*, vol. 10, pp. 103-4, Grey and Grenville, memo, 11 Jan. 1811
68 ibid., vol. 10, p. 101, Grey to Grenville, 10 Jan. 1811
69 PLUMER WARD, *Memoirs*, vol. 1, p. 383, 9 Feb. 1811
70 STIRLING, *Coke of Norfolk*, vol. 2, p. 97, Wilbraham to Coke, 4 Feb. 1811
71 Northants R.O., Milton Mss 79, Elliot to Fitzwilliam, 2 Feb. 1811
72 *H.M.C. Dropmore*, vol. 10, p. 142, Auckland to Grenville, 1 June 1811
73 ibid., p. 149, T. Grenville to Grenville, 8 June 1811
74 ibid., p. 148, Temple to Grenville, 7 June 1811
75 B.M. Add. 41,853, f 227, Grenville to T. Grenville
76 *Parl. Debates*, vol. 20, col. 139
77 BUCKINGHAM, *Court during the Regency*, vol. 1, p. 127, anon. to Buckingham, 17 Sept. 1811
78 ibid., pp. 156-7, same to same, 2 Dec. 1811
79 N.L.W., Coed-y-maen Mss, Temple to Wynn, 15 Sept. 1811
80 GRAY, *Perceval*, p. 438
81 WALPOLE, *Perceval*, vol. 2, p. 230, Wellesley to Perceval, 18 Dec. 1811
82 *H.M.C. Bathurst*, p. 164, memo by Bathurst, 17 Feb. 1812
83 Bodleian Ms Eng. Lett. c. 60, f 82, Yorke to Perceval, 15 Dec. 1811
84 *H.M.C. Bathurst*, p. 164, memo by Bathurst, 17 Feb. 1812
85 *H.M.C. Dropmore*, vol. 10, p. 192, Buckingham to Grenville, 23 Jan. 1812
86 GEORGE IV, *Letters*, vol. 1, pp. 2-4, Feb. 1812
87 *H.M.C. Bathurst*, p. 165, memo
88 AUCKLAND, *Journal and Correspondence*, vol. 4, p. 379, Bulkeley to

Auckland, 28 Dec. 1811
89 BUCKINGHAM, *Court during the Regency,* vol. 1, p. 230, Grenville to Buckingham
90 *H.M.C. Dropmore,* vol. 10, p. 205, memo
91 ibid., vol. 10, pp. 214-5, Grey and Grenville to York, 15 Feb. 1812
92 ibid., vol. 10, p. 197, 28 Jan. 1812
93 BUCKINGHAM, *Court during the Regency,* vol. 1, pp. 259-60, anon. to Buckingham, n.d.
94 *H.M.C. Bathurst,* p. 166, memo.
95 WELLINGTON, *Supplementary Despatches,* vol. 7, pp. 285-6, memo by Meyrick Shawe
96 *H.M.C. Bathurst,* p. 166, memo
97 B.M. Add. 37, 295, f 287
98 ibid., f 269; cf. VON CLAUSEWITZ, C., *On War* trans. J.J.Graham, ed. F.N. Maude, 3 vols., 1908, vol. 1, pp. 11-13
99 GRAY, *Perceval,* p. 450
100 ibid.
101 Canning Mss 25, f 80, Canning to wife, 5 March 1812

8 THE MONTHS OF CRISIS
1 *Parl. Debates,* vol. 17, col. 114
2 N. Yorks. R.O., ZFW 7/2, 219/19, Wyvill to Fawkes, 11 May 1810
3 ibid., 219/30, Wyvill to Strickland, Wrightson, Doyle and Duncombe, 4 June 1810
4 C.U.L. Add. 7621, Burdett to Smith, 29 June 1810
5 N. Yorks R.O., ZFW 7/2 227/3, 22 April 1811
6 *Parl Debates,* vol. 20, col. 568
7 P.R.O., HO 42/114, Chippindale to Fletcher, 21 Feb. 1811
8 P.R.O., HO 42/117, Fletcher to Beckett, 12 Oct. 1811
9 ibid., same to same, 21 Nov. 1811
10 P.R.O., HO 42/119, paper docketed 'Statement of Outrages &c from Nottingham'
11 P.R.O., HO 42/117, Newcastle to Ryder, 2 Dec. 1811
12 P.R.O., HO 42/118, Buckley to Ryder, 26 Dec. 1811; copy Newton to Bulkeley, 28 Dec. 1811; HO 42/119, Lloyd to Bulkeley, 1 Jan 1812
13 P.R.O., HO 42/119
14 ibid., Fletcher's spy's information, 6 and 14 Jan. 1812
15 P.R.O., HO 42/120, information, 17 Feb. 1812
16 P.R.O., HO 42/121, Haines to Tempest, 23 March 1812
17 P.R.O., HO 42/119, Fletcher to Beckett, 21 Jan. 1812; HO 42/120, Newcastle to Ryder, 29 Feb. 1812
18 P.R.O., HO 42/120, Conant to Beckett, 5 Feb. 1812
19 ibid., Mozer to Beckett, 12 Feb. 1812
20 P.R.O., HO 42/122, Villiers to Ryder, 10 April 1812
21 ibid., Fenton to Grey, 16 April 1812; Cochrane to Cholmley, 17 April 1812
22 ibid., Silvester to Ryder, 27 April 1812
23 ibid., anon. to Hay, 27 April 1812
24 PRENTICE, *Recollection of Manchester,* pp. 50-51
25 DARVALL, F.O., *Popular Disturbances and Public Order in Regency England,* 1934, p. 1
26 SOUTHEY, *Letters,* vol. 2, p. 282, Southey to T. Southey, 17 June 1812
27 ibid., p. 269, Southey to Danvers, 9 May 1812
28 N.L.W., Coed-y-maen Mss 5, f 289, Grenville to Wynn, 14 April 1812
29 Bucks R.O., Fremantle Mss D/FR 55, Temple to Fremantle, 14 and 15 April 1812

30 COLCHESTER, *Diary*, vol. 2, p. 380, 12 May 1812
31 *A Full Report of the Trial of John Bellingham, for the Murder of the Right Hon. Spencer Perceval*, Hull 1812, p. 37
32 ibid., p. 32
33 MILES, *Correspondence*, vol. 2, p. 375, Miles to Popham, 13 May 1812
34 PRENTICE, *Recollection of Manchester*, p. 46
35 PEEL, F., *The Rising of the Luddites Chartists and Plug Drawers*, Brighouse 1895, pp. 156-7
36 P.R.O., HO 42/123
37 *A Particular and Authentic Narrative of the Life, Examination, Tortures and Execution of Robert Francis Damien*, 1757, p. 15
38 JERDAN, W., *The Autobiography of William Jerdan*, 4 vols., 1852-3, vol. 1, p. 136
39 HUGHES, E., ed., *The Diaries and Correspondence of James Losh*, 2 vols., Durham 1962-3, vol. 1, p. 12, 23 May 1812
40 TWISS, *Life of Eldon*, vol. 2, p. 210
41 *H.M.C. Dropmore*, vol. 10, p. 272, memo by Grey and Grenville to Wellesley, 24 May 1812
42 *Authentic Correspondence and Documents, explaining the Proceedings of the Marquess Wellesley, and The Earl of Moira*, 1812, p. 50, Grey to Wellesley, 29 May 1812
43 ibid., p. 54, communication, 1 June; pp. 62-3, Moira to Grey, 3 June; p. 72, Wellesley to Grey, 4 June 1812
44 *H.M.C. Dropmore*, vol. 10, pp. 279-80, Grey and Grenville to Wellesley, 3 June 1812
45 GORE, J., ed., *Creevey's Life and Times*, 1934, p. 55, Creevey to wife, 3 June 1812
46 *H.M.C. Hastings*, vol. 3, p. 295, Moira to Hastings, 4 June 1812
47 *H.M.C. Dropmore*, vol. 10, p. 287, memo 6 June 1812
48 BUCKINGHAM, *Court of the Regency*, vol. 1, p. 353, 6 June 1812
49 HOLLAND, S. LADY, *A Memoir of the Rev. Sydney Smith*, 2 vols., 1855, vol. 2, p. 94, Smith to Jeffrey, June 1812
50 P.R.O.N.I., T.2541 IK 20, Abercorn to Liverpool, 23 June 1812
51 WELLINGTON, *Supplementary Despatches*, vol. 7, p. 343, 9 June 1812. [Wellington wrote in ignorance of Liverpool's temporary resignation, and of Wellesley's and Moira's attempts to form an alternative government; but his words were still relevant to the situation as it finally emerged.]

Part Three
1 THE AIMS AND CONDUCT OF THE WAR

1 *H.M.C. Dropmore*, vol. 3, p. 7 Fitzgerald to Grenville, 13 Jan. 1795
2 *Parl. History*, vol. 34, col. 1442, 17 Feb. 1800
3 Devon R.O., 152M/C1801 OM 14
4 *H.M.C. Dropmore*, vol. 6, p. 445, R. King to Grenville, 12 Feb. 1800
5 WILBERFORCE, *Life*, vol. 2, p. 391, memo 1828
6 *Parl. History*, vol. 35, col. 1072-3, 25 March 1801
7 *H.M.C. Dropmore*, vol. 6, p. 38, Dundas to Grenville, 24 Nov. 1799
8 AUCKLAND, *Journal and Correspondence*, vol. 3, pp. 137-8, Auckland to Grenville, 7 Nov. 1793
9 ibid., p. 140, Rose to Auckland, n.d.
10 HUSKISSON, *Papers*, p. 59, Windham to Huskisson, 29 Dec. 1803
11 WINDHAM, *Papers*, vol. 2, p. 8 Windham to Dundas, 1 May 1796
12 *H.M.C. Dropmore*, vol. 6, p. 298, Wickham to Grenville, 15 Aug. 1800

13 ibid., vol. 3, pp. 261-2, George III to Grenville, 20 Oct. 1796
14 ibid., vol. 5, p. 46, T. Grenville to Grenville, 9 May 1799
15 LEWIS, M., *Napoleon and his British Captives*, 1962, pp. 46-7
16 ELLESMERE, *Personal Reminiscences of Wellington*, p. 128, 14 Sept. 1826
17 STANHOPE, *Conversations with Wellington*, pp. 224-5, 17 April 1840
18 *H. M.C. Dropmore*, vol. 5, p. 147, Grenville to T. Grenville, 16 July 1799
19 ibid., vol. 5, pp. 281-2, T. Grenville to Grenville, 15 Aug. 1799
20 DUNFERMLINE, J. LORD, *Lieutenant General Sir Ralph Abercromby, K.B.*, 1861, pp. 247-8
21 CASTLEREAGH, *Correspondence*, vol. 7, p. 444, Melville to Castlereagh, 3 June 1808
22 *H.M.C. Dropmore*, vol. 8, p. 321, Windham to Grenville, 11 Sept. 1806
23 GREY, *Life and Opinions*, p. 135, memo.
24 WELLINGTON, *Despatches*, vol. 6, p. 347, Wellington to Liverpool, 19 Aug. 1810
25 ibid., vol. 8, p. 191, Wellington to Stuart, 15 Aug. 1811

2 GOVERNMENT ECONOMIC POLICY

1 STANHOPE, *Pitt*, vol. 3, p. 248, 24 Oct. 1800
2 *Parl. History*, vol. 35, col. 622, 7 May 1802
3 READ, D., *The English Provinces*, 1964, pp. 27-33
4 REDFORD, A., ed., *Manchester Merchants and Foreign Trade 1794-1858* Manchester 1934, p. 51
5 O'BRIEN, 'Government Revenue', p. 389
6 *Nottingham Records*, vol. 8, p. 157, Henson to Roper, 2 July 1812
7 *Parl. Debates*, vol. 23, col. 1248-50, 24 July 1812
8 O'BRIEN, 'Government Revenue', p. 57
9 SMITH, A., *The Wealth of Nations*, Book 5, chap. 3
10 *Parl. History*, vol. 32, col. 708, 12 Feb. 1796
11 ibid., col. 710
12 BUCKINGHAM, *Court and Cabinets*, vol. 3, p. 100, Grenville to Buckingham, 24 Nov. 1800
13 ASPINALL, A., ed., *Early English Trade Unions*, 1949, p. 31
14 BUCKINGHAM, *Court and Cabinets*, vol. 3, p. 100, Grenville to Buckingham, 24 Nov. 1800
15 *Parl. Debates*, vol. 11, col. 425
16 P.R.O., HO 42/95, Fletcher to Hawkesbury, Feb. 1808
17 HAMMOND, B. and J., *The Skilled Labourer, 1919*, p. 75
18 HINTON, 'General Elections of 1806 and 1807', p. 391
19 *Parl. Papers*, 1834 X, p. 442
20 *Parl. Debates*, vol. 11, col. 425
21 *Parl. Papers*, 1834 X, p. 425
22 *Parl. Debates*, vol. 11, col. 427-8
23 ibid., col. 426
24 ibid., col. 426
25 ibid., col. 427
26 *Parl. Papers*, 1809, III, p. 311
27 *Annual Register*, 1800, Chronicle, p. 23
28 P.R.O., HO 42/52, f 102 and 144
29 ibid., HO 42/55, f 110, f 230, f 335, f 339
30 SMITH, A., *The Wrath Of Nations*, Book 4, chap. 5. Digression Concerning the Corn Trade and Corn Laws
31 P.R.O., HO 42/51, f 34-5, Fitzwilliam to Portland, 3 Sept. 1800
32 ibid. HO 42/55, f 469, draft Portland to Gower, 29 Nov. 1800

33 *Parl. History,* vol. 35, col. 839-40, 5 Dec. 1800
34 ibid., col. 795, 24 Nov. 1800
35 Devon R.O., 1262 M/L 72, Portland to Fortescue, 17 April 1801
36 P.R.O., HO 42/52, f 17 Portland to Wakefield, 7 Oct. 1800
37 BOHSTEDT, 'Riots', p. 428
38 ibid., p. 440
39 *Parl. Debates,* vol. 2, col. 781, 20 June 1804
40 ibid., col. 1087, 20 July 1804 .
41 HILTON, B., *Corn, Cash, Commerce; the Economic Policies of the Tory Governments 1815-1830,* Oxford 1977
42 O'BRIEN, 'Government Revenue', p. 210
43 DUFFY, 'Bankruptcy and Insolvency in London', p. 190
44 *Parl. Papers,* 1810-11, II, p. 390 (13 June 1811)
45 SINCLAIR, J., *Thoughts on Circulation and Paper Currency,* 1810, p. 15
46 *Parl. Debates,* vol. 19, col. 960 foll
47 ibid., col. 920
48 *Parl. History,* vol. 35, col. 1265-6

3 THE ECONOMIC CONSEQUENCES OF THE WAR

1 *Parl. Debates,* vol. 10, col. 38, 21 Jan. 1808
2 THOMPSON, *Making of The Working Class,* pp. 147-9
3 BRIGGS, A., *The Age Of Improvement 1783-1867,* 1959, pp. 171-2
4 ANDERSON, J. L., 'Aspects of the Effect on the British Economy of the Wars against France 1793-1815', *Australian Economic History Review,* 12 (1972) pp. 1-20
5 *Parl. Papers,* 1808, II, p. 143
6 CROUZET, F., 'Wars, Blockade, and Economic Change in Europe, 1792-1815', *Journal Of Economic History* 24 (1964), pp. 567-88
7 *Parl. Papers,* 1803-4, VII, p. 228-9
8 ibid. 1842, XXVII, p. 379
9 ibid. 1808, IX, p. 151 foll.
10 MOREAU, *Tableau Comparitif*
11 COBBETT, W., *Letters to the Right Honourable Henry Addington,* 1802, Tables 1 and 2
12 LEVASSEUR, E., *Histoire du Commerce de la France,* 2 vols., Paris 1912, vol. 2 p. 19
13 ibid. pp. 97-8
14 MOREAU, *Tableau Comparitif*
15 VICENS VIVES, *Economic History of Spain,* p. 603
16 *Parl. Papers,* 1806, XII, p. 199, and 1812, X, p. 55
17 BOXER, C. R., *The Portuguese Seaborne Empire 1415-1825,* 1969, p. 385
18 WELLINGTON, *Despatches,* vol. 6, p. 329, Wellington to Wellesley, 10 Aug. 1810
19 *Parl. Papers,* 1808, XI, pp. 252-3
20 *New Cambridge Modern History,* vol. 9, p. 488; cf. VIBAEK, M., *Den Danske Handels Historie,* Copenhagen 1932-8, p. 300
21 NORTH, *Economic Growth Of The U.S.,* pp. 26-7
22 VICENS VIVES, *Economic History Of Spain,* p. 580; PITKIN, T., *A Statistical View,* p. 191
23 NORTH, *Economic Growth Of The US,* pp. 26-7
24 JOHNSON, E.R., ed., *History of the Domestic and Foreign Commerce of the United States,* 2 vols., Washington 1915, vol. 2, pp. 29-30
25 P.R.O., HO 42/58, f 294-7, R. King to Pelham, 28 Nov. 1801
26 NORTH, *Economic Growth Of The U.S.,* p. 56; cf. Sir Charles Vaughan Mss, K Journal 1813 mentions several licences to American vessels carrying

cargoes of salt, wine, fruit, etc., from Spain; presumably they had just landed grain.

27 NORTH, *Economic Growth Of The U.S.*, pp. 221, 228, 249
28 MITCHELL and DEANE, *British Historical Statistics*, pp. 281-2. The figures for 1808-12 and 1814 are given in Mitchell and Deane's tables for total UK trade: the earlier figures, from a different series, are for British trade only. The 1808-12 and 1814 figures for British trade given here have been rectified by comparing figures for both British and UK trade in the years 1800-1804, for which years both British and UK figures are available. These 'official values', originally derived from obsolete valuation tables, understate imports by nearly 50 per cent. and exports by roughly 25 per cent. but since they do not reflect price inflation they are a reliable index of growth.
29 WRIGHT, C., and FAYLE, C. E., *A History of Lloyds*, 1928, pp. 186, 452-5
30 ibid., pp. 183, 451
31 ibid., p. 451
32 HAMILTON, R. V., ed. *Letters And Papers of Admiral of The Fleet Sir Thos. Byam Martin*, 2 vols., 1898-1903, vol. 2, p. 70, T. B. Martin to H. Martin, 5 May 1808
33 ADAMS, *Memoirs*, vol. 2, p. 145, 8 Aug. 1810
34 *Parl. Debates*, vol. 21, col. 1157
35 DUFFY, *'Bankruptcy and Insolvency in London'*, pp. 303-4
36 MANCHESTER, A. K., *British Pre-eminence in Brazil its Rise and Decline*, Chapel Hill 1933, p. 89 n. 80
37 ibid., p. 97 and N 111
38 MOREAU, *State of The Trade of Great Britain*
39 ibid
40 RYAN, A. N., 'The Defence of British Trade with the Baltic, 1808-1813', *English Historical Review* 74 (1959), pp. 443-466
41 ibid., p. 453
42 ADAMS, *Memoirs*, vol. 2, p. 169
43 PITKIN, *A Statistical View*, pp. 168, 180; *Parl. Papers* 1806, XII, p. 427, 1808, XI, pp. 226-37
44 MITCHELL and DEANE, *British Historical Statistics*, p. 311; MOREAU, *State of the Trade of Great Britain*
45 MITCHELL and DEANE, *British Historical Statistics*, pp. 368, 399 n.
46 O'BRIEN, 'Government Revenue', p. 242
47 *Parl. Debates*, vol. 19, col. 838
48 MILES, *Correspondence*, vol. 2, p. 364, Miles to Moira, 12 July 1811
49 *Parl. Papers* 1801, V, p. 3, and 1810-11, X, p. 333
50 PRESSNELL, L. S., *Country Banking in the Industrial Revolution*, Oxford 1956, p. 145
51 *Annual Register*, 1804, p. 353
52 CHALKLIN, C. W., *The Provincial Towns of Georgian England*, 1974, pp. 285-292; cf. GOEDE, C.A.G., *The Stranger in England*, 3 vols., 1807, chap. 1
53 DUFFY, 'Bankruptcy and Insolvency in London', pp. 307-8; cf. table 2-2 and p. 165
54 O'BRIEN, 'Government Revenue' p. 19
55 ibid., p. 9
56 O'BRIEN, P. K., 'British Incomes and Property in the Early Nineteenth Century', *Economic History Review*, 2nd ser. 12 (1959-60), pp. 255-67; HOPE JONES, A., *Income Tax in the Napoleonic Wars*, Cambridge 1939, pp. 117-8.

57 *Parl. Papers,* 1812-13, XII, p. 305; and 1814-15, p. 91
58 O'BRIEN, 'Government Revenue', p. 357
59 *Parl. History,* vol. 35, col. 833, 834, 835, 14 and 17 Nov. 1800
60 HUNT, *Memoirs,* vol. 2, p. 38
61 B.M. Add. 45,038, f 13, East to Yorke, 31 Aug. 1810
62 SLATER, G., *The English Peasantry and the Enclosure of Common Fields,* 1907, p. 267
63 MITCHELL and DEANE, *British Historical Statistics,* p. 488

Bibliographical Guide

The following list is in three sections: (A) manuscripts, (B) printed books, (C) articles and unpublished dissertations. Though including the most important primary sources, this list is in no sense intended as a comprehensive and systematic bibliography, but merely as a guide to the abbreviated titles given in the notes. Works which have been cited only once have been cited with their full titles in the notes and do not appear again in the following guide; nor do periodical publications. In section (B) secondary works are distinguished by a †, and pamphlets by a *. All books were published in London unless specifically stated otherwise.

(A)

The following abbreviations have been used in citations of manuscript sources.

Berks. R.O.	Berkshire Record Office, Reading
B.M.	British Library, Department of Manuscripts, London
Bodleian	Bodleian Library, Oxford
Bucks R.O.	Buckinghamshire Record Office, Aylesbury
C.U.L.	Cambridge University Library, Cambridge
Devon R.O.	Devon Record Office, Exeter
Durham R.O.	Durham Record Office, Durham
Lancs. R.O.	Lancashire Record Office, Preston
N.L.I.	National Library of Ireland, Dublin
N.L.S.	National Library of Scotland, Edinburgh
N.L.W.	National Library of Wales, Aberystwyth
Northants	Northamptonshire Record Office, Northampton
Northumberland R.O.	Northumberland Record Office, Newcastle upon Tyne
N. Yorks R.O.	North Yorkshire Record Office, Northallerton
P.R.O.	Public Record Office, London

P.R.O.N.I.   Public Record Office of Northern Ireland, Belfast
S.R.O.   Scottish Record Office, Edinburgh
V & A   Victoria and Albert Museum, London

As well as manuscripts in the above locations, the following collections have been cited:
Canning Mss, in Leeds Public Library, Archives Department, Leeds
Grey Mss, in Department of Palaeography and Diplomatic, Durham University, Durham
Kenyon Mss, in possession of Lord Kenyon, at Gredington, Flintshire
Sir Charles Vaughan Mss, in Codrington Library, All Souls College, Oxford
Wentworth-We odhouse Muniments, in Sheffield Central Library, Sheffield

(B)

ADAIR, R., *Sketch of the Character of the Late Duke of Devonshire* 1811

ADAMS, J. Q., *Memoirs of John Quincy Adams*, ed. C. F. Adams, 12 vols. Philadelphia 1874-7

* *The Agent and his Natural Son*, 1808

†ASPINALL, A., *Politics and the Press* 1780-1850, 1949

ASPINALL, A., and SMITH, E. A., ed. *English Historical Documents*, vol. II, 1959

AUCKLAND, W. LORD, *The Journal and Correspondence of William, Lord Auckland*, ed., G. Hogge, 4 vols., 1861-2

BACON, R. M., *A Memoir of the Life of Edward, Third Baron Suffield*, printed for private circulation, Norwich 1838

BAILEY, J., *General View of the Agriculture of the County of Durham*, 1810

BAMFORD, S., *Passages in the Life of a Radical*, 2nd ed., 2 vols., Heywood 1842

BARROW, J., *An Auto-biographical Memoir*, 1847

BENTHAM, S. M., *The Life of Brigadier-General Sir Samuel Bentham K.S.G.*, 1862

BOGUE, D., and BENNETT, J., *History of Dissenters, from the Revolution in 1688 to the Year 1808*, 4 vols., 1808-12

[BOWDLER, J.], *Reform or Ruin: Take your Choice*, 1797

* BOWLES, J., *A Protest against T. Paine's 'Rights of Man'*, 1792

BRENTON, E. P., *Life and Correspondence of John, Earl of St Vincent*, 2 vols., 1838

BROUGHAM, H. LORD, *Life and Times of Henry Lord Brougham*, 3 vols., Edinburgh 1871

BROUGHTON, J. LORD, *Recollections of a Long Life*, ed. Lady Dorchester, 6 vols. 1909-11

BUCKINGHAM, R. DUKE OF, *Memoirs of the Court and Cabinets of George III* 4 vols., 1853-5

BUCKINGHAM, R. DUKE OF, *Memoirs of the Court of England, during the Regency*, 2 vols., 1856

CARTWRIGHT, J., *The Life and Correspondence of Major Cartwright*,
ed. F. D. Cartwright, 2 vols., 1826

CASTLEREAGH, R. LORD, *Memoir and Correspondence of Viscount
Castlereagh, Second Marquess of
Londonderry*, ed. Charles, Marquess of
Londonderry, 12 vols., 1848-53 (later vols.
entitled *Correspondence, Despatches and
other Papers)*

CLARKE, M. A., *The Rival Princes*, 2nd ed., 2 vols., 1810

COBBETT, W., *Autobiography*, ed. W. Reitzel, 1947

COLCHESTER, C. LORD, *The Diary and Correspondence of Charles
Abbot, Lord Colchester*, ed. by second Lord
Colchester, 3 vols., 1861

COLERIDGE, S. T., *Biographia Literaria*, 2 vols., 1817 (Numerous
subsequent editions)

CREEVEY, T., *The Creevey Papers*, ed. H. Maxwell, 2 vols., 1903

DUNDONALD, T. EARL OF, *The Autobiography of a Seaman*, 2 vols.,
1860 ·

ELLESMERE, F. EARL OF, *Personal Reminiscences of the Duke of
Wellington*, ed. Countess of Strafford, 1903

FARINGTON, J., *Diary*, ed., J. Greig, 8 vols., 1922-8

FONBLANQUE, E. B. de, *Annals of the House of Percy*, 2 vols., printed
for private circulation, 1887

FORTESCUE, J. W., *A History of the British Army*, 13 vols., 1899-1930

FOX, C. J., *Memorials and Correspondence of Charles James Fox*, ed.
J. Russel, 4 vols., 1853-7

FRANCIS, P., *Memoirs of Sir Philip Francis, K.C.B.*, ed. J. Parkes and
H. Merivale, 2 vols., 1867

FREND, W., *Letters to William Frend from the Reynolds Family of
Little Paxton and John Hammond of Fenstanton, 1793-1814*,
ed., F. Knight, Cambridge, 1974

GEORGE III, *The Later Correspondence of George III*, ed., A. Aspinall,
5 vols., Cambridge, 1962-70

GEORGE IV, *The Correspondence of George, Prince of Wales 1770-1812*,
ed. A. Aspinall, 8 vols., 1963-71

GEORGE IV, *The Letters of King George IV, 1812-30*, ed. A. Aspinall,
3 vols., Cambridge 1938

*GERRALD, J., *A Convention the only Means of Saving us from Ruin*,
1794

GLENBERVIE, S. LORD, *The Diaries Of Sylvester Douglas, Lord
Glenbervie*, ed. F. Bickley, 2 vols., 1928

†GLOVER, R., *Peninsular Preparation*, Cambridge 1963

†GRAY, D., *Spencer Perceval, The Evangelical Prime Minister,
1762-1812*, Manchester 1963

GREY, C., *Some Account of the Life and Opinions of Charles Second
Earl Grey*, 1861

*HAGUE, T., *A Letter to His Royal Highness the Duke of York, or an
Exposition of the Circumstances which Led to the Late
Appointment of Sir Hew Dalrymple*, 1808

HARDCASTLE, M. S., *Life of John, Lord Campbell*, 2 vols., 1881
HENDERSON, E., *Recollections of the Public Career and Private Life
    of the Late John Adolphus*, 1871
*Historic Manuscripts Commision Report on the Manuscripts of Earl
Bathurst preserved at Cirencester Park*, 1923
*Historic Manuscripts Commision Report on the Manuscripts of the Earl
of Carlisle preserved at Castle Howard* 1897
*Historic Manuscripts Commission Reports on the Manuscripts of
J. B. Fortescue, Esq., preserved at Dropmore*, 10 vols., 1892-1927, cited
as *H. M. C. Dropmore*
*Historic Manuscripts Commission Reports on the Manuscripts of the
Late Reginald Rawdon Hastings, Esq. of the Manor House, Ashby de la
Zouche*, 4 vols., 1928-47
*Historic Manuscripts Commission Report on the Manuscripts of the Earl
of Lonsdale*, 1893
HOLLAND, E. LADY, *Journal Of Elizabeth, Lady Holland (1791-1811)*,
                    ed. Earl of Ilchester, 2 vols., 1908
HOLLAND, H. R. LORD, *Memoirs of the Whig Party during my Time*,
                    ed. fourth Lord Holland, 2 vols., 1852-4
HOLLAND, H. R. LORD, *Further Memoirs of the Whig Party, 1807-
                    1821*, ed. Lord Stavordale, 1905
HORNER, F., *Memoirs and Correspondence of Francis Horner*, ed.
                    L. Horner, 2 vols., 1843
HUNT, H., *Memoirs*, 3 vols., 1820
JAMES, C., *The Regimental Companion*, 7th ed., 4 vols., 1811-13
KIRBY, R. S., *Wonderful and Eccentric Museum*, 6 vols., 1803-20
                    (Also published as *Wonderful and Scientific Museum*)
LE MARCHANT, D., *Memoir of John Charles Viscount Althorp, Third
                    Earl Spencer*, 1876
*A Letter to His Royal Highness, or, a Delicate Enquiry whether he be
more Favoured by Mars or Venus*
LEVESON-GOWER, LORD G., *Lord Granville Leveson-Gower, Private
                    Correspondence 1781 to 1821*, ed.
                    Countess Granville, 2 vols., 1916
LEWIS, G. C., *Essays on the Administration of Great Britain from 1783
                    to 1830*, ed. E. Head, 1864
LONDONDERRY, T. MARCHIONESS OF, *Robert Stewart Viscount
                    Castlereagh*, 1904
*McCALLUM, P. F., *Observations on H.R.H. the Duke Of Kent's
                    Shameful Persecution since his Recall from
                    Gibraltar, together with an Enquiry into the
                    Abuses of the Royal Military College*, 1808
*McCALLUM, P. F., *The Rival Queens, or which is the Darling*, 1810
MacDONAGH, M., *The Viceroy's Postbag*, 1904
MALMESBURY, J. EARL OF, *Diaries and Correspondence of James
                    Harris, Earl of Malmesbury*, ed. third
                    Earl of Malmesbury, 4 vols., 1845
MARKHAM, J., *Selections from the Correspondence of Admiral John
                    Markham during the Years 1801-4 and 1806-7*, ed.
                    C. Markham, 1904

†MARSHALL, D., *The Rise of George Canning*, 1938
MELBOURNE, W. EARL OF, *Lord Melbourne's Papers*, ed.
L. C. Sanders, 1889
MELVILLE, L., *Life and Letters of William Cobbett*, 2 vols., 1913
Mentoriana, 1807
MILES, W. A., *The Correspondence of William Augustus Miles on the French Revolution 1789-1817*, ed. C. P. Miles, 2 vols.,
1890
MINTO, E. COUNTESS OF, *Life and Letters of Gilbert Elliot, First Earl of Minto from 1751 To 1806*, 3 vols. 1874
MITCHELL, B. R., and DEANE, P., *Abstract of British Historical Statistics*, Cambridge 1962
MOORE, J., *The Diary of Sir John Moore*, ed. J. F. Maurice, 2 vols.,
1904
*[MORE, H.], *Village Politics addressed to all the Mechanics, Journeymen, and Day Labourers, in Great Britain*,
MORE, M., *Mendip Annals: The Journal of Martha More*, ed.
A. Roberts, 2nd ed., 1859
MOREAU, C., *State of the Trade of Great Britain with all Parts of the World*, 1822
MOREAU, C., *Tableau Comparitif du Commerce de France avec toutes les Parties du Monde avant la Revolution et depuis la Restauration*, 1827
NAPIER, W. F. P., *History of the War in the Peninsula and in the South of France*, 6 vols., 1828-40
†NORTH, D. C., *The Economic Growth of the United States 1790-1860*,
Englewood Cliffs 1961
Records of the Borough of Nottingham, 9 vols., Nottingham 1882-1956
OLDFIELD, T. H. B., *An Entire and Complete History, Political and Personal, of the Boroughs of Great Britain*,
3 vols., 1792
OLDFIELD, T. H. B., *The Representative History of Great Britain and Ireland*, 6 vols., 1816
*PALEY, W., *Reasons for Contentment, addressed to the Labouring Part of the British Public*, 2nd ed., 1793
The Parliamentary Debates from the Year 1803 to the Present Time,
41 vols., 1812-20
The Parliamentary History of England, from the Earliest Period to the Year 1803, 36 vols., 1806-20
Parliamentary Papers, i.e., *Accounts and Papers, Reports of Commissioners, Estimates, &c, &c, printed by Order of the House Of Commons*
Parliamentary Reports First Series, 15 vols., 1773-1803
PATTERSON, M. W., *Sir Francis Burdett and his Times 1770-1844*,
2 vols., 1931
PELLEW, G., *Life and Correspondence of the Right Hon. Henry Addington, First Viscount Sidmouth*, 3 vols., 1847
PITKIN, T., *A Statistical View of the Commerce of the United States of America*, Harford 1816

PLUMER WARD, R., *Memoirs of the Political and Literary Life of Rober Plumer Ward*, ed., E. Phipps, 2 vols., 1850

POOLE, S. L., *The Life of the Right Hon. Stratford Canning, Viscount Stratford de Redcliffe*, 2 vols., 1888

PRENTICE, A., *Historical Sketches and Personal Recollections of Manchester*, 1851

*RANBY, J., *An Inquiry into the Supposed Increase of the Influence of the Crown, the Present State of that Influence and the Expediency of a Parliamentary Reform*, 1811

†RAYBOULD, T. J., *The Economic Emergence of the Black Country*, Newton Abbot 1973

REID, W. H., *Memoirs of the Life of Colonel Wardle*, 1809

†ROBERTS, M., *The Whig Party 1807-1812*, 1939

ROMILLY, S., *Memoirs of the Life of Sir Samuel Romilly*, 3 vols., 1840

ROSE, G., *The Diaries and Correspondence of the Right Hon. George Rose*, ed. L. V. Harcourt, 2 vols., 1860

†ROSE, J. H., *Pitt and the Great War*, 1911

†ROSE, J. H., *Pitt and Napoleon*, 1912

ST VINCENT, J. EARL OF, *Letters of Admiral of the Fleet the Earl of St Vincent whilst First Lord of the Admiralty 1801-1804*, ed. D. B., Smith, 2 vols., 1922-7 (including as appendix pp. 450-559 *Memoirs of the Administration of the Board of Admiralty under the Presidency of the Earl of St Vincent*

[SOUTHEY, R.], *Letters from England, by Don Manuel Alvarez Espriella*, 2nd ed., 3 vols., 1808

[SOUTHEY, R.], *Selections from the Letters of Robert Southey*, ed., J. W. Warter, 4 vols., 1856

STANHOPE, P. EARL OF, *Life of the Right Honourable William Pitt*, 4 vols., 1862

STANHOPE, P. EARL OF, *Notes of Conversations with the Duke of Wellington, 1831-1851*, 1888

STAPLETON, A. G., *George Canning and his Times*, 1859

STEPHENS, A., *Memoirs of John Horne Tooke*, 2 vols., 1813

STIRLING, A. M. D. W., *Coke of Norfolk and his Friends*, 2 vols., 1908

*THELWALL, J., *Peaceful Discussion and not Tumultuary Violence the means of redressing National Grievances*, 1795

†THOMPSON, E. P., *The Making of the English Working Class*, 1963

†THOMPSON, F. M. L., *English Landed Society in the Nineteenth Century*, 1963

TUCKER, J. S., *Memoir of Admiral the Right Hon. The Earl of St Vincent*, 2 vols., 1844

TWISS, H., *The Public and Private Life of Lord Chancellor Eldon*, 3 vols., 1844

†VICENS VIVES, J., *An Economic History of Spain*, Princeton 1969

WALLAS, G., *The Life of Francis Place, 1771-1854*, 1898

WALPOLE, S., *The Life of the Right Hon. S. Perceval*, 2 vols., 1874

WELLINGTON, A. DUKE OF, *The Despatches of Field-Marshal the*

Duke of Wellington, ed. J. Gurwood,
13 vols., 1834-9

WELLINGTON, A. DUKE OF, *Supplementary Despatches,
Correspondence and Memoranda of
Field Marshal Arthur Duke of
Wellington,* ed., second Duke of
Wellington, 15 vols., 1858-72

WILBERFORCE, R. I., and S., *The Life of William Wilberforce,* 5 vols.,
1838

WINDHAM, W., *The Diary of the Right Hon. William Windham, 1784
to 1810,* ed. H. Baring, 1866

WINDHAM, W., *Windham Papers,* ed., L. Melville, 2 vols., 1913

YONGE, C. D., *Life and Administration of Robert Banks Jenkinson,
Second Earl of Liverpool,* 3 vols., 1868

(C)

ASQUITH, I. S., 'James Perry and *The Morning Chronicle,* 1790-1821',
London Ph.D., 1973

ASQUITH, I. S., 'Advertising and the Press', *Historical Journal,* 18 (1975),
pp. 703-24

BOHSTEDT, J. H., 'Riots in England 1790-1810, with Special Reference
to Devonshire', Harvard Ph.D., 1972 (copy in Devon
R.O.)

DUFFY, I. P. H., 'Bankruptcy and Insolvency in London in the Late
Eighteenth and Early Nineteenth Centuries', Oxford
D.Phil., 1973

HARVEY, A. D., 'The Grenville Party, 1801-1826', Cambridge Ph.D.,
1972

HARVEY, A. D., 'The Ministry of all the Talents: the Whigs in Office,
February 1806 to March 1807', *Historical Journals,* 15
(1972), pp. 619-48

HINTON, M. G., 'The General Elections of 1806 and 1807', Reading
Ph.D., 1959

O'BRIEN, P. K., 'Government Revenue 1793-1815', Oxford D.Phil.,
1967

SAXTON, W. E., 'The Political Importance of the 'Westminster
Committee' of the Early Nineteenth Century',
Edinburgh Ph.D., 1957

SEAMAN, W. A. L., 'British Democratic Societies in the Period of the
French Revolution', London Ph.D., 1954

THOMAS, D., 'The Social Origins of Marriage Partners of the British
Peerage in the Eighteenth and Nineteenth Centuries',
Population Studies, 26 (1972), pp. 99-111

WILLIS, R., 'William Pitt's Resignation in 1801: Re-examination and
Document', *Bulletin of the Institute of Historical Research,*
44 (1971), pp. 239-57

Index

Persons whose years of birth and death are given in parenthesis are included in *The Dictionary of National Biography*.

Entries for twentieth-century historians whose views are discussed are distinguished by †.